THE GREAT
SIEGE
OF MALTA

Bruce Ware Allen

＋·＋·＋·＋

The Great Siege of Malta

＋·＋·＋·＋

THE EPIC

BATTLE

between the

OTTOMAN

EMPIRE

and the

KNIGHTS

OF ST. JOHN

＋·＋·＋·＋

ForeEdge

ForeEdge

An imprint of University Press of New England

www.upne.com

Manufactured in the United States of America

Designed by Mindy Basinger Hill

Typeset in Adobe Jenson Pro

First ForeEdge paperback edition 2017

Paperback ISBN 978-5126-0116-9

The Library of Congress cataloged the hardcover edition as:

Allen, Bruce Ware.

The Great Siege of Malta: the epic battle between the Ottoman Empire
and the Knights of St. John / Bruce Ware Allen.

pages   cm

Includes bibliographical references and index.

ISBN 978-1-61168-765-1 (cloth: alk. paper)—

ISBN 978-1-61168-843-6 (ebook)

1. Malta—History—Siege, 1565.   2. Knights of Malta.   I. Title.

DG992.2.A55 2015

945.8'502—dc23   20150150025

5   4   3   2   1

To

CAPTAIN HERMANN A. ALLEN

(*1919–2010*)

and

CAPTAIN JOHANNES MÜLLER

(*1883–1943*),

who loved all things maritime,

except war

+·+·+·+

Contents

+·+·+·+

Illustrations follow p. 166

+·+·+·+

Illustrations

+·+·+·+

Nay, could their numbers countervail the stars,

Or ever-drizzling drops of April showers,

Or wither'd leaves that autumn shaketh down,

Yet would the SOLDAN by his conquering power

So scatter and consume them in his rage,

That not a man should live to rue their fall.

Christopher Marlowe, Tamburlaine

THE GREAT

SIEGE

OF MALTA

Introduction

Selim I was dying.

It was not expected; the sultan of the Ottoman Empire was only in his fifties and to all appearances perfectly fit. A man with his record would have to be. Called by Europeans Selim the Grim, he had ruled the empire by the sharp edge of his sword for nearly eight years, during which time he managed to depose his father, murder his brothers (and their offspring), conquer the Abbasid Empire, seize Mamluk Egypt, and double the size of his territory. His violence and temper were notorious — to be named one of his viziers was considered as good as a death sentence. Tens of thousands of Shiite heretics were slaughtered on his watch, and all of Anatolia's Orthodox Christians would have followed had not the head of the College of Islamic Law convinced Selim that such an act would displease Allah.

Acknowledged caliph of the Sunni Muslim world in 1517, Selim was ready to turn his full attention toward Christian Europe. It was a disturbing prospect for the West. If Selim's armies could maintain their previous rate of expansion, the Ottoman Empire would engulf all of Italy, Germany, and France and reach the shores of the English Channel and the northern reaches of Scandinavia in less than twenty years. In the early months of 1520, he was gathering his troops along the western coast of Anatolia and readying ships to strike at the offshore islands not already part of his empire.

Fate granted Europe a reprieve. Neither war nor intrigue had put a stop to this phenomenon of a man, but now, as he planned yet another campaign against yet another enemy, a pustule on Selim's leg turned septic and was proving more determined than any army. The doctors could do nothing, and for the dying man, there was nothing left but to pass his unmet ambitions on to his only son and sole heir. Selim's final words to the next sultan, a challenge, really, were that "you will be a great and powerful monarch provided you capture Belgrade and drive the knights from Rhodes."[1]

+·+·+·+

He was referring to the Order of the Knights of St. John and Jerusalem.

These men were among the last of the Roman Catholic military orders. Their origins lay, paradoxically, in a small fraternity of Benedictines who, funded by Italian merchants and sanctioned by the caliph of Egypt, had cared for indigent Christian pilgrims to the Holy Land since 1023. Their medical skills were put to a hard test in 1099 when European soldiers of the First Crusade captured the holy city, producing a mass of wounded soldiers who quickly overflowed the Order's infirmaries. Moved by the Benedictines' work, some patients under their care petitioned to join the Order. On the logic that care for pilgrims could include keeping the pilgrim routes safe, the Order's mandate soon included a martial function. They also adopted the Augustinian Order, it being more aggressive and more open to expelling Islam from the Holy Land.

Despite the pan-European nature of the Crusades, the knights were organized by their countries of origin, or rather their native languages, the so-called *langues* of Provence, Auvergne, France, Aragon, Italy, England, and Germany. Members were drawn exclusively from the elites, which limited their total numbers. What they lost in quantity, however, they more than made up for in quality. As warriors, the knights were formidable — first into battle, last to leave, and inspirational to those who placed religion above secular politics.

As the years passed and the crusades rolled on, the Order grew rich on plunder and donations, established chapters throughout Europe (the quarter of St. John's Wood in London was theirs before Henry VIII decided his needs were greater), and plowed money into castles and fortresses across the Holy Land. Their masterwork, the fortress of *Krak des Chevaliers* in modern-day Syria, has served its intended purpose as recently as 2014. Expelled with the rest of the Crusaders from the Holy Land after the fall of Acre (1191 AD), the Order settled on the island of Rhodes, a green place with countless inlets and bays suitable for sea raiding. They transformed the eastern port city, also called Rhodes, into a formidable fortress city, with strong defensive walls, each section of which was assigned to a separate *langue*.

Nor was Rhodes the only European colony in the eastern Mediterranean. By the end of the fifteen century the Knights of St. John also held the islands of Kos and Leros and the coastal city of Bodrum, while Venice could boast her own holdings on Crete and Cyprus, and Genoa her islands of Chios and Samos. For Genoa and Venice, traditional enemies with a long history of armed conflict, trade had replaced warfare; and like good merchants everywhere, both republics wanted a quiet life at all costs. The knights were a more complex proposition. They accepted the necessity of trade, and even occasional alliances with the enemy, but always maintained that dream of retaking the Holy Land at the back of their minds. A Jerusalem for Christendom, after all, had been the very reason they had come into being.

Until the rest of Europe came on board, however, the dream would have to wait. In the meantime, life was pleasant in Rhodes. The island flowered with rich orchards of figs and dates, busy markets carried all good things from the East: spices and sandalwood, slaves and silk, some of it honestly traded, some stolen at sea. The richer merchants lived in splendid houses, and the Order took a cut of all transactions. On the water, the Order ran protective convoys for Christian merchants, transported Christian cargo and Christian pilgrims, and prowled in search of Muslim and Jewish merchants, and Muslim pilgrims. The chronicler Mustafa Gelal-Zade describes the knights as the "worst of those who live in error, sent by the devil and famous for cunning and artifice, outcasts, accursed workers of iniquity, expert seamen and outstanding navigators."[2]

The Nemesis for the knights was coming on the Anatolian landmass in the form of the Ottoman Turks. The Ottomans, descendants of the minor tribal leader Osman Bey, founded their principality in 1299 in eastern Anatolia. Their power grew steadily over the ensuing years, in time enveloping all of what had been the Byzantine Empire, entitling the sultans to call themselves, not without cause, heirs to the Roman Empire. They had setbacks, to be sure, in men such as Vlad III, *voivode* (warlord) of Transylvania, inspiration for Dracula, who filled a two-mile stretch of road with the impaled bodies of Ottoman invaders, and George Castrioti, aka Skanderbeg of Albania, *athleti Christi*, champion of Christ, *antemurale Christianitatis*, bulwark of Christendom, who for twenty-five years led armies to keep his land, and by extension all of Christian Europe, free of Islam. But for the most part, the Ottomans were able to subdue the unwilling and cajole the undecided in these mountain regions; there were, after all, decided advantages for the newly conquered to profess Islam, not least among them a lower tax rate. Skanderbeg would die in 1468 and Vlad in 1477, and the Ottoman empire continued to engulf the Balkans, though never so far as Belgrade, where Selim's grandfather Mehmed II had been halted in 1456. At sea, the emerging Ottoman navy would take its first tentative steps on the unfamiliar and unstable element, but with little success.

Mehmed II had also made the first serious attempt to expel the knights from Rhodes, in 1480, and failed miserably. He settled for a peace treaty that stipulated an end to piracy, at least for the remainder of his reign — piracy, that is, that affected Ottoman trade. The agreement worked more or less well until 1517, when Selim conquered Egypt. As soon as he had brought that nation into the Ottoman Empire, the knights were no longer of any use to him; indeed, they were a hindrance. With the entire corridor between Constantinople and Alexandria in Ottoman hands, the piratical side of the knights far outweighed any small good they might provide as traders. An adviser to Selim laid the matter out in plain words: "My Sultan, you are resident in a city whose bene-factor is the sea. When the sea is not secure, no ship can come and when no ship comes, Constantinople cannot flourish."[3] It was time for the knights to go, and it was this campaign that Selim was planning when he fell ill. His death set in motion the whirring clockwork of bureaucratic gears that transferred control of the empire to his sole heir, Suleiman.

Suleiman, a quiet, scholarly man, a skilled goldsmith (for all potential sultans were expected to master a useful craft as insurance against personal disaster) was governor of the Crimea at the time. Eight days later, he was in Constanti-nople, where he doled out alms to the poor, death to the wicked, and a promise of continuity to everyone. An anxious Europe sighed in relief. A Venetian am-bassador reported that he had a pleasant expression and that "his reputation is that of a wise lord, he is said to be studious, and everybody hopes that his rule will be good."[4] Other observers spoke of the lamb following the lion.[5] A few heads of state thought the accession an opportunity to pursue their own ambitions at the expense of the empire. The governor of Damascus was one such. He tried, and failed, to set himself up as ruler of Syria. In a matter of weeks, his head arrived in Constantinople inside a casket of vinegar.[6] The lamb, it appeared, had teeth.

Suleiman next turned to Belgrade, where the fifteen-year-old King Louis of Hungary, a young man with a wild streak, had insulted and mutilated a crew of Ottoman diplomats, who had come to discuss the new order in Constantinople. As the Ottoman military machine advanced to take revenge, reports filtered to the rest of Europe, stories of burning villages and Christian heads mounted on spears. Belgrade became a critical Ottoman military base, its inhabitants exiled or enslaved, the land given over to citizens of the Ottoman Empire.[7] The pious of Europe were stunned and turned to God; the impious, like Machiavelli, to black humor. The pragmatic (Venice, Ragusa, and Russia) hastened to congratulate the new sultan on this great victory, and to update their trade agreements.

The defiant, among them the Knights of St. John of Rhodes, prepared for war.

◆·◆·◆·◆

The knights and their unrealistic hopes might have remained a minor nuisance to Islam, but times were changing and the Mediterranean was becoming subject to an arms race in what historian Andrew Hess calls "the sixteenth century world war." The conflict began quietly enough, in the Mediterranean theater at least. At the outset of their reigns, the twin superpowers of the day, Charles V's Habsburg Spain on one end of the sea and Suleiman's Ottoman Empire at the other, paid relatively little attention to the waters between them. It was a highway where both empires endured the regular loss of trade to Christian and Muslim raiders; raiders of both faiths were an unfortunate fact of life, but each ruler could take comfort in knowing that his own pain was no less than that of his counterpart.

For the Muslim corsairs at least, the business proved an increasingly profitable way of making a living in the first decades of the sixteenth century; and as their strength and numbers grew, so too did their ambitions. The Barbarossa brothers, the most successful of the Barbary corsairs, began as small-time bandits on one modest boat, which grew into a fleet that terrorized the entire western Mediterranean. Eventually the elder brother, Aroudj, seized the port of Algiers, then swore fealty to the Ottoman Empire in exchange for both brothers' political legitimacy. On the Christian side, Charles V eventually was able, more or less, to counter the likes of the Barbarossas with his own self-financing raiders in the persons of the Knights of St. John.

War has a tendency to metastasize. The proxy warriors, whether Barbary corsairs or Christian knights, were brilliant in terrorizing the coasts of the Mediterranean, but wayward, not wholly reliable. Rather than agreeing to quash the corsairs once and for all, both Charles and Suleiman chose to augment them with professional navies beholden more strictly to the respective empires. The cost of building and maintaining a fleet is never trivial, but advisers in Madrid and Constantinople (and the corsairs themselves) assured their rulers that the respective empires could well afford it — Charles had the gold and silver of the New World to draw on; Suleiman, a healthy portion of all trade with the Far East. With God and such ferocious men on his side, Charles began to talk openly, if only rhetorically, of retaking Constantinople. Suleiman, for his part, was beguiled by the likes of Khairedihn Barbarossa into believing that a reconquest of Spain was well within his grasp, if he would only trust to Allah, the Barbary corsairs, and the seas.

And so both monarchs succumbed to temptation, and both dispatched motley naval forces to lands not their own, sometimes successfully, sometimes catastrophically, calling for truces when money ran short or when wars elsewhere demanded their attention, never quite getting to the point of total victory, but refusing to call it quits. The long-term goal, simply put, was domination, a restoration of the old Roman Empire, the title to which both Charles, as Holy Roman emperor, and Suleiman, as ruler of Constantinople, the New Rome, felt themselves entitled to. Both felt certain that God would deliver the prize to them and so pave the way for a world sharing the true faith.

It was a long, drawn-out, and costly struggle that would eventually, and critically, come down to the geographical center of the Mediterranean on the tiny sun-blasted outpost of Malta. It began, however, six hundred miles to the east, on the lush green island of Rhodes.

PART ONE

······

*Corsairs
and
Rulers*

1

+·+·+·+

THE SIEGE
OF RHODES, 1521

+·+·+·+

I command you, therefore,
instantly to surrender the island
and fortress of Rhodes.

Letter from Suleiman to L'Isle-Adam

On a summer day in 1521, a desperate hunt was in progress along the northern coastline of Crete. The quarry was riding a horse not his own, on a mission not strictly his either, and being pursued by horsemen who were determined not to let him escape. Both parties had been at it the better part of the day, alternating periods of riding and resting, and keeping a weather eye out for the other. As the sun began to fall, they were coming to the end of the chase, and despite the dangers of the breakneck pursuit after dark and over the sometimes rocky outcroppings that cover the beaches and roads east of Heraklion, neither the pursuers nor the pursued dared to rein in their mounts. At stake was the fate of one of the last Christian fortresses in the eastern Mediterranean.

So the wild ride continued over the scrubby undergrowth, skirting the few gnarled trees that edged the road, and in the increasingly uncertain light, the fugitive and his several companions peered out over the water, straining to see the lanterns of a boat sent to carry him away.

The subject of this chase, Gabriele Tadini de Martinengo, was a military engineer of unusual skill —"few or none his equal at that time."[1] He was not fleeing impatient creditors or outraged husbands; he was running out on his Venetian employers and an extremely lucrative contract for improving their defensive works on the Venetian colony of Crete, an island then at peace with all the world. He was heading to the island of Rhodes, some 250 miles away, where the ancient crusading Order of the Knights of St. John was already under siege by the Ottoman sultan, Suleiman I.

Earlier that year the knights had sent an envoy to Martinengo's employer, the governor of Crete, and requested that he be temporarily seconded to Rhodes, where his expertise would be invaluable. The governor had equivocated. Venice, and by extension all of Venice's colonies, of which Crete was the largest, were currently at peace with the world. To allow such a thing might appear to be unfriendly to Venice's Ottoman trading partners in Constantinople. A decision of this magnitude was too important for him to make alone; he would have to defer to the Venetian senate, some twelve hundred nautical miles away. This would entail a regrettable delay of some weeks, but what could one do? Diplomacy and politics were both slow-growing plants.

The envoy did not take it well. He became, the governor wrote, "very angry, and employed the most extraordinary language, claiming that any failure to turn over that man would spell the end of Rhodes."[2] The envoy left, and the governor put their guest under close observation — though in the event, clearly not close enough. In a matter of days, Martinengo, contacted surreptitiously by the knights, followed his conscience, slipped past his custodians, and took flight.

Only after sunset did Martinengo and his companions come over the heights overlooking the Bay of Mirabella and see the light of a waning July moon sparkle on the water. Offshore was a brigantine, a small swift galley, awaiting his arrival; on the beach was a longboat with strong-armed men ready to row him out to sea. He and his companions, all fustian and leather, stumbled down to the water, dismounted, and climbed aboard, the first leg of the journey completed.[3] Martinengo's Venetian minders were just in time to see the ship raise anchor, drop sails, and head into the darkness. As the moon rose, they cantered back to Heraklion, followed by a half dozen riderless horses.

+·+·+·+

A year earlier, senior knights of the Order had gathered in the stone council chamber at Rhodes to elect Philippe de Villiers de L'Isle-Adam, then grand prior of France and serving the king, Francis I, at Bourgogne, as their new grand master.

It was a respectable choice. L'Isle-Adam's family had provided many knights over the centuries, most famously Jean de Villiers, who had been grand master when Al-Ashraf Khalil in 1291 expelled the Order from Acre, its last stronghold in the Holy Land. Philippe, who had entered the brotherhood at age eighteen, rose steadily through the ranks. He was fifty-eight at the time of his election, and his portraits, presumably somewhat idealized, show him as a white-haired, round-faced, tough, dignified, noble creature — the very model of a Christian knight.

L'Isle-Adam set sail from France to Rhodes in September of 1521. The small flotilla endured a sequence of disasters: fire broke out on an accompanying ship. Lightning hit L'Isle-Adam's own vessel, killing nine and, ominously, destroying the new grand master's sword. As they made their repairs in Sicily, they could see the Barbary corsair and Ottoman admiral Kurtoğlu Muslihiddin Reis loitering just outside the harbor in anticipation, forcing L'Isle-Adam to a prudent escape by night. Despite this formidable string of misfortunes, the grand master elect made landfall at Rhodes before the month was out, and after going through the obligatory ceremonies, settled into his office.

It was not long before he heard from his neighbors. Suleiman I, sultan of the vast and powerful Ottoman Empire, Caliph of Islam, Leader of the Faithful, Custodian of the Two Holy Mosques, and soon to be called the Lawgiver by Islam and the Magnificent by Christendom, sent a diplomatic note of congratulations, proffering friendship and inviting L'Isle-Adam to rejoice in Suleiman's own recent triumphs over Christian Belgrade as well as other "fine and beautiful cities," where he had "reduced the better part of their citizenry by sword or fire and put the rest to slavery." There was little L'Isle-Adam could say in reply, though he did keep up the pretense of diplomacy: "Your propositions for a peace between us are as pleasing to me as they will be obnoxious to Kurtoğlu."[4] The epistolary aggression escalated on both sides, increasingly uncivil, until on June 10, 1522, Suleiman came to the point. Rhodes, he declared, must submit to Ottoman rule. As a man of religion and honor, the sultan would guarantee freedom from excess taxation, from forced conversion, and freedom of passage for all who chose to leave Rhodes, along with their goods and chattels.

L'Isle-Adam did not even bother to answer. Instead, he stepped up preparations for an attack on Rhodes. As early as April, he ordered his men to harvest the crops and bring the yield inside the city walls. What could not be harvested was torched. He dispatched ships to buy oil and wine from Greece. He stepped up production of gunpowder in the mills near the harbor. He instructed the local priests to preach the nobility of armed struggle against the Ottomans. And finally, he sent emissaries across Europe to plead for support: anyone, knight, soldier, or layman, who believed, like Martinengo, in the brotherhood of Christendom should set sail for Rhodes as quickly as possible.

It was a badly timed request. The crusading spirit still flickered fitfully in Europe, but the Holy Land was far away and other problems seemed closer to home. A twenty-one-year-old Charles V, Holy Roman emperor, was at war with Francis I of France (as Suleiman well knew); Venice, never much for war against Constantinople, had just renewed the peace treaty of 1503 with the Ottomans. The Genoese, hoping to curry favor with the new sultan, chose to send military intelligence to Constantinople. Pope Hadrian VI was concerned, but had few military resources outside the Knights of St. John themselves, and he preferred to send those he had against France. Francis I of France gathered a few soldiers, but failed to send them off in time. Rhodes found itself isolated in a sea without allies.

Suleiman, by contrast, was master of his sprawling empire, and with a single command, he was able to conjure up an army of many thousands and a navy of over three hundred sails, galleys and galleasses, barges and brigantines to carry them across the water.[5] On June 25, 1522, the first Ottoman troops made the seven-mile crossing from Marmarice in Anatolia to Rhodes. The Ottoman fleet under Kurtoğlu passed by the fortress city, also called Rhodes, their bands playing on shipboard in case the inhabitants might have overlooked their arrival. The Christians answered the music with a volley of cannon fire. The Ottomans continued on some six miles away to Kalitheas Bay, where they began the long process of unloading men and matériel for what promised to be a long summer. For the next month, within sight of the city and just outside cannon range, they erected a multicolored canvas metropolis over the barren ground; new banners and pennons of various hues and markings sprouted above circular pointed tents and flapped in the offshore breezes, gradually encircling the looming walls of the port city as ever more troops landed on the island. It was a show intended to overawe and discomfort the people of Rhodes, to undermine the confidence that had supported them for the past three hundred years, and the cast of this show just kept growing. By the end of July, the total number of men reached one hundred thousand, including the sultan himself.[6]

Opposing them inside the tawny stone fortress of Rhodes was a core force of six hundred knights of St. John. Now that war had arrived, each knight exchanged the black robes and white cross significant of the Order's service to the sick for the red cloaks and white cross of men prepared for battle. Other Christian soldiers numbered one thousand mercenaries and five hundred native militia, plus 250 Jewish volunteers.[7] An Ottoman chronicler came up with a total even higher, at five to six thousand.[8] The disparity of numbers alone should have given the invading troops confidence. Many were veterans of the sacking of Belgrade, and their chief concern was how many hands would demand a share of the plunder — Rhodes was, after all, a city grown rich on generations of trade and raiding. True, the city was known to the Muslims as a "strong fortress with high walls, one third of it washed by the sea, for over a thousand years a state for the infidel."[9] True also that Mehmed II's attack of 1480 had failed, just as the Mamluk siege of 1444 had come to nothing. But that was all ancient history, and an army as skilled and well equipped as Suleiman's could not fail to succeed where those lesser men had failed.

The Order, however, had not been idle. Rhodes in 1522 was encased in the best defensive works that Italian military engineers since 1480 could contrive. Any attackers would initially have to run across a counterscarp, a wide flat upward incline every inch of which was vulnerable to gunfire from the fort. There followed a vertical drop of anywhere from forty to sixty feet into a ditch itself marked by loopholes at ground level and above that turned the space into a killing ground. Also spotted about the ditch was a system of ravelins, high diamond-shaped bulwarks detached from the fortress itself that commanded the space below. Anyone who overcame these obstacles would then have to contend with heavy firepower from ramparts and five bastions that permitted crossfire against every angle of approach. Finally, thirteen towers framed the walls themselves two and even three layers deep, which could withstand weeks and even months of the heaviest cannon fire before collapsing to a usable breach. Small wonder that the Muslim soldiers' first reaction on first seeing the city they were expected to defeat was just short of mutiny.[10]

Suleiman, however, saw beyond the stone and science that disquieted his troops. He was confident. His own mother had appeared to him in a dream and promised him victory. The season was late, and given the distance of Rhodes from a distracted Europe, and the small likelihood of aid for the knights, his army could proceed without worrying about their backs. After four weeks of hauling innumerable carts full of grain and dried meats, picks and shovels, tents, guns, powder, shot, and all other materials for war, his men were ready, his siege guns in place. These were monstrous bronze cylinders, the fruit of European invention cast largely by European renegades in the armories of Constantinople. The largest, colloquially referred to as basilisks, could take the better part of a day to prepare and load, but once fired, were capable of hurling stone balls six and eight palms in diameter and a thousand pounds in weight. Exactly how many guns of how many sizes in which different positions varies depending on different sources. One account records between sixty and eighty Muslim cannon and mortars arrayed against Rhodes, fully half of which the Christians managed to target and destroy within the first month. There is also a brief mention of brass shells filled with Greek fire, a kind of primitive napalm, the first mention of hollow shells of any kind in the history of artillery. The greatest effect, however, would come from the wall-shattering basilisks, four of which were directed against the bastions of England and Aragon, two against that of Italy.

On July 28, a full month after his arrival, the sultan nodded and the artillerymen lowered smoldering matches to the touchholes of their guns. From the parapets of Rhodes, the defenders could see the sudden wink of muzzle flashes in the distance, followed by the puff of white smoke, then feel the deep boom of shaking air and finally the shuddering of the wall itself as the mammoth cannonballs struck and began the slow work of fracturing and cracking the masonry open. By the end of August, some 1,316 of the largest cannons had been fired, with little to show for it; between this and uncounted mortar fired directly into the city, only twenty-five people were killed.

Simultaneously, Ottoman sappers, or combat engineers armed with picks and shovels, began to etch the stony ground before the walls with a series of deep zigzag trenches, which would enable the troops to approach the city in apparent safety. The defenders of Rhodes, however, had their own artillery, and through careful practice over the years, knew the ranges of the guns to the inch. Ottoman sappers found themselves under a storm of cannonballs that appeared to anticipate their very movements.

There was, however, a second corps of sappers busy digging underground in multipronged attempts to undermine the walls. Day and night these men sat cross-legged in cramped, fetid holes, working by flickering oil lamps, carving out the dirt and stone before them, shoring up the low ceiling with beams and planks, and hauling the detritus to the entrance in baskets. It was a standard tactic of siege warfare at the time. The goal was to create a void beneath the walls, stuff it with gunpowder and light a fuse. (Alternatively, besiegers could dispense with powder and just set the tunnels' wooden supports on fire.) With luck, the wall would collapse and combat soldiers could scramble over the rubble. It was hazardous duty and earned them extra pay; it did not necessarily keep them safe from the enemy.

In siege warfare, it was engineers who made the difference, which is why L'Isle-Adam had been so keen on getting Martinengo.[11] To track the Ottoman miners, the Brescian crafted a number of large tambourines and attached small bells to them. The wooden frames were pressed into the bare earth beneath the walls. The distant shock of a miner's pick would travel through the soil, causing the nearest diaphragm to quiver and the bells to sound, and so direct Christian sappers where to dig countermines. When the opposing tunnels met, Christians drove out the enemy with incendiaries, then blocked off the tunnel. Even where the Ottomans did manage to lay and detonate charges, defense technology again often triumphed. In building a second line of interior walls, Martinengo incorporated a series of narrow vents into the masonry, allowing the gunpowder's "fury to drain through the rock" and dissipate harmlessly into the air.[12] Rhodes was not an easy nut to crack.

Even hard nuts must give in eventually. On September 4, well over a month after the first shots were fired, subterranean Ottoman gunpowder opened a thirty-foot section of wall defended by the English *langue*. Concealed by the rising dust, Suleiman's Janissaries, elite troops, climbed over the unstable pile of stone, planting green banners of Islam in triumph and preparing to rush the city itself. They never made it. Spanish knights on the right, French knights on the left, lay down a withering crossfire into the Ottoman troops. At the center, Martinengo and a crew of English knights and volunteers rushed forward with pikes to defend the breach. They were soon joined by L'Isle-Adam himself, fresh from celebrating Mass and brandishing a short pike. The fighting was vigorous and said to be costly, but when the encounter broke off, the cross of St. John still flew over Rhodes.

More breaches followed in the coming weeks, and each time the knights fought the enemy to a standstill. And although the Ottomans could not gain entrance, Christian ships were clearly able to weave through Kurtoğlu's naval blockade, taking messages out and the odd company of volunteers in. Christian sources claim that Suleiman marked his displeasure by having Kurtoğlu publically whipped on the deck of the corsair's own ship.

The season was getting late and Suleiman was getting impatient. It was time for a general attack. In the late morning of September 24, fires were lit all around the city walls of Rhodes to create a curtain of black smoke, hiding the Ottoman troops from the defenders, who were anxious to know where the blow might fall. At noon, the sound of trumpets, kettledrums, and pipes spangled the air. Seconds later, tens of thousands of Ottomans let loose a high-pitched yell and burst through the black gloom at every point around the city. Walls with breaches were rushed, walls without breaches were scaled. Within minutes, dozens of Ottoman banners were planted on the walls and cries of victory filled the air.

The defenders were quick to regroup and close with the enemy. Crossfire again poured into Muslim ranks. A flood of determined knights and mercenaries crashed against the onslaught of invaders. Dust and smoke rose and men fell, and shouting was answered by the ringing of steel striking steel. Christians skilled at the deadly balletic movements of pikes and halberds gored their enemy, or severed the odd hand or foot or pound of flesh. Men on scaling ladders were drenched in a blistering rain of hot oil and bubbling pitch poured on them by defenders on the wall. Suleiman watched the spectacle from a high platform well out of harm's way; L'Isle-Adam was in the thick of it, directing his men to hold firm and push back, rushing from one trouble spot to the next, inspiring fresh courage wherever he appeared.

Hours passed, and once more and against all odds, the defenders were succeeding. They toppled scaling ladders, cast down the intruders, and closed up the breaches with enemy dead. As the sun fell onto the horizon, Ottoman troops trudged back to the safety of their own lines. Again the normally impassive Suleiman lost his temper, and not content with a simple whipping, he ordered that his top generals be executed, an order he rescinded the next day after he had a chance to reconsider.

What to do? Sixteenth-century warfare was a warm-weather enterprise, and military campaigns were supposed to wind down by autumn. The days were growing shorter. Autumn rain turned the soil to mud, difficult to tunnel. Disease had entered the invaders' camp and escorted more soldiers off the island and into paradise.

The defenders, also badly mauled in this latest fight, hoped that the Ottomans would follow custom and abandon the island for the winter, giving them at least some time to rest. Spirits rose when, on October 4, a knight arrived from Naples with the announcement that a relief force was assembling at Messina. The Mediterranean sailing season, however, effectively ends by October, and the promised soldiers never arrived. A few volunteers made the trip across the relatively short distance from Heraklion, Crete, to Rhodes, but in nowhere near the numbers needed. The defenders of Rhodes could count on nothing from Europe before spring. Powder and shot and arrows were so limited that L'Isle-Adam forbade any firing without orders from a superior officer. Their final hope was that Suleiman would follow custom and depart before winter. And indeed, on October 31, the Ottoman fleet did depart.

The army, however, stayed behind. Suleiman, whether from stubbornness, or faith in his stars, or because he thought his still-young reputation could not withstand a loss, called up yet more reinforcements from the mainland, and his guns continued to pound the walls, slowly tearing the breaches wider.

November passed. By now, half of the original defenders were either dead and buried, or maimed and useless. Cool weather turned cold, and snow fell on the distant mountains. Despair infected the survivors much as typhus had the Ottomans. Food other than bread and water had all but disappeared. Spies and fifth columnists were found sending messages to the enemy wrapped around arrows; to discourage such behaviors, those caught (including, possibly unfairly, Andreas d'Amaral, grand prior of Castile, L'Isle-Adam's chief rival for power) were quickly tortured and executed.[13]

On December 1, Suleiman sent his first call for surrender. L'Isle-Adam rejected it out of hand. An eyewitness, Sir Nicholas Roberts, wrote that the knights were "determyned to dye upon them in the feld rather than be put upon the stakese; for we doubted [Suleiman] would give us our lyves, considering ther wer slain so many of his men."[14] Others, notably the civilians and clerics who had family in Rhodes, took a longer view and were willing to gamble on Suleiman's good faith. No longer shy in their opinion, they insisted on being heard. Whatever the knights might decide, they, the citizens of Rhodes, were prepared to make a separate peace.

The terms had changed little from Suleiman's original offer before the siege: "You can stay or leave, as you will."[15] Those who chose to leave might do so unmolested, and with their possessions. Those who chose to stay might keep their faith for a full five years without penalty, after which time they could convert to Islam or pay the customary tax owed by the infidel. No property would be taken, no churches would be seized, and new ones might even be built. There was a further condition. The Knights of St. John would have to leave. They might take their relics and other goods, even their weapons, but they were no longer welcome on Rhodes, nor must they trouble Muslims again. It was a bitter cup that L'Isle-Adam had no choice but to accept.

A few days of equivocating, of trying to put off the inevitable, served only to anger the sultan. According to the French chronicler Bourbon, the sultan had his guards take two Christian soldiers and cut off "their noses, their fingers and their ears and gave them a letter to carry to the Grand Master," warning him what lay in store if he delayed any longer.[16] The compact was made; bureaucrats had composed, translated, and copied the official texts of surrender, a dry legal record of the bloody defeat. Now, for form's sake, there had to be a ritual humiliation. L'Isle-Adam was invited to present himself to the Great Sultan, then made to stand outside in the cold for some hours — time enough to appreciate his reduced condition, time enough to ponder the shattered wreck of a stone city behind him, time to reflect on the fact that this defeat would be his legacy.

The flap to the red tent was raised and L'Isle-Adam entered the close, muffled space, lit by brass lamps. Before him, alone, was the man heretofore separated from him by two armies and the walls of Rhodes: Suleiman, tall, wiry, with a delicate complexion, seated on a low-lying octagonal throne of gold.[17] L'Isle-Adam approached the victorious monarch, kneeled, and kissed the soft extended hand of his enemy. According to the Ottoman historian Hafiz, the two men gazed at each other in silence for a time, after which Suleiman praised the grand master for his intrepidity and invited him to convert to Islam. The sultan offered high offices and comforts suitable to a man of L'Isle-Adam's worth. The grand master thanked him but declined, noting that to accept would necessarily degrade his own integrity, the very thing Suleiman professed to prize in him.[18] They went on to discuss the practical matters of the knights' coming departure.

+·+·+·+

Organizing the knights' departure from Rhodes would take a few days, and there was to be no disturbing the emigrants at this time. A few overly ebullient Ottoman soldiers did try to filch civilian property; they were reported, tried in front of the sultan, and executed. The same discipline did not extend to the trappings of religion. The Ottoman chronicler Mustapha Gelal-Zade wrote that, despite Suleiman's promises regarding freedom of conscience, "The victorious soldiers entering the city filled the town with cries of 'Allah, Allah,' struck down idols and removed signs of error in all the churches and filthy temples."[19] He makes no mention of any punishment for such behavior. Martinengo was bundled up and smuggled out of Rhodes on December 20 — Suleiman was always on the lookout for talent, and L'Isle-Adam thought it prudent to remove any temptation.

On December 31, the knights' last full day on Rhodes, Suleiman mounted a white horse and, without benefit of personal aides or the protection of bodyguards, rode through the city gates, past the shattered defense work and half-starved locals, to visit the grand master one last time. The sultan presented him with a richly embroidered robe, and the two commanders again spent some hours together in talk, the record of which, unfortunately, is lost to history.

Meanwhile, the surviving knights had buried their dead, bundled their wounded, and collected their belongings. On the first day of 1523, the remaining members of the Order boarded their galleys, lifted their oars, and slowly headed out of the choppy winter seas south to the island of Crete on the first leg of a journey into an unknowable future. Some of the native Rhodians, whether from fear of uncertainty, or devotion to the order, or distrust of the Ottomans, followed suit. As the grand master returned to his own people, Suleiman watched the departing graybeard and remarked to an underling, "It saddens me to see such an old man driven from his home."[20]

Suleiman would spend the next forty years pressing his enemies in Persia and in Europe, reforming the laws inside his empire, and presiding over the greatest flowering of Ottoman civilization. He would be referred to in Western records as *Gran Signore*, *Gran Turco*, or even, almost affectionately, *Signor Turco*.

For the moment, however, he had established his military reputation and fulfilled his father's hopes. He had defeated the last of the crusading knights and had sent them off, honorably, to trouble Islam no more.

He was twenty-eight years old.

He would live to regret the decision.

2

+·+·+·+

THE ROAD TO MALTA,
1522–1530

+·+·+·+

We have been fighting among ourselves without
end in what are worse than civil wars over trivia, while the Empire
of the Turks, or, more aptly, their land grab, has expanded immensely.

Erasmus, Utilissimam Consultatio de Bello Turcis Inferendo

Releasing the surviving knights into the Mediterranean in January was not as kindly a gesture as it might appear. Anything could happen on a winter sea. The Muslim slaves who normally rowed for the Order had been freed by the victorious Ottomans, leaving the five thousand or so knights and a smaller number of Rhodiot exiles to somehow get the Order's vessels across gray, choppy water to Crete. The long ships twisted and pitched on the water, rose up and crashed down, and the terrified passengers tossed worldly goods overboard to placate the storm. The gesture may have saved their lives, but left them destitute.

A few days later the fleet staggered into Heraklion. Whatever their private feelings — and some had been cheered by stories of Martinengo's exploits — the Venetians had been serenely dispassionate during the siege, and although the locals now clucked sympathetically, their masters were already drafting a letter of congratulations to the sultan on this latest victory.[1] It was an awkward situation all around, and L'Isle-Adam stayed just long enough to refit the fleet and head west, plagued by rough weather and wearied with melancholy. Some of the civilian refugees chose to remain here, some to head to Cyprus, some to accompany the Order wherever it might go.

The ships made a brief stop at Messina, where, as if there were nothing else that could go wrong, plague now broke out in the fleet. The governor of Messina ordered them to remove to the remote bay of Baiae until further notice. It was there, a month later, that they were instructed to come to Rome, just in time to find that Pope Hadrian was dying.[2] The knights' first official task back in Rome was to stand guard while the conclave of cardinals elected a successor. By good fortune, the new pope, Clement VII, had once been a member of the Order himself. While he was full of sympathy and praise, he had no immediate use for them. He did arrange lodging in a convent at Viterbo, just outside Rome, a considerable comedown from the fortress of Rhodes. What might be a suitable substitute? The island of Elba was suggested, as was Cythera, just off the Peloponnese peninsula, and Crete. The first was the possession of the Lord of Piombino, who was unlikely to sell, the latter two the possessions of Venice, who certainly would not sell, not as long as they wanted good relations with the Ottomans. Eventually, someone suggested the island of Malta.

Malta was in the gift of Charles V, Holy Roman emperor and a strong believer in the knights and their mission. L'Isle-Adam, still shaken by their experience at Rhodes, somewhat impulsively offered Charles one hundred thousand ducats for the privilege of settling in Malta, or failing that, Brindisi.[3] Charles wrote back that he was more than happy to have the knights take charge of Malta, so long as they took Tripoli as well and rendered fealty to him rather than to the pope. As a pan-European Christian force, they could not accept the terms. They could, however, at least take a look at the place, pending a more equitable deal.

L'Isle-Adam sent eight men to inspect Malta and see if it might be suitable. However anxious he may have been for a stable home, L'Isle-Adam was not going to grab the first offer that came his way. His commissioners arrived at Malta in August of 1524. Malta in high summer is an inferno and does not set off the island's best features. No surprise then that the opinion of the eight men about the island was not good. The island's defenses, they said, were weak, the soil poor, resources few, well water scarce and brackish, and the people targets of frequent sea raids.

A gloomy assessment, and fair enough, but the knights' contingent was comparing the place to green and pleasant Rhodes. This simply may have been the technique of a sharp buyer denigrating the product before settling on a price. A more balanced report is found in Jean Quintin d'Autun's 1536 book, *A*

Description of the Island of Malta. D'Autun described Malta as a rocky island home to some twelve thousand impoverished natives he considered more or less Sicilians with an admixture of North African: short, stocky, with speech that was more Arab than Latin. He acknowledged the brutal African heat in summer, but wrote that the climate in general is healthy.[4] He praises the quality of what the natives, mostly peasant farmers, could coax from the thin soil — barley, olives, vines, figs, cumin, and cotton, the last two being the island's chief exports — but regrets the quantity, and notes that Malta is fortunate to be situated so close to "most fertile" Sicily, without whose grains they would die of hunger.[5] As a proper Frenchman, he also notes that the women are "not at all bad looking" (*feminae non ignobili forma*).[6]

To anyone lucky enough to hold it, Malta has been, like Guam or Midway or Diego Garcia, a vital military base at the center of contested waters, bang center between Sicily and North Africa, halfway again between Gibraltar and Constantinople. It has been held over the centuries by neolithic people, Phoenicians, Romans, Arabs, Normans, and most recently by Spain as an adjunct to her holdings in Sicily. The natives at that time were divided between the aristocracy, generally off-islanders from Sicily who huddled in the capital city, Mdina, located at the center of the island, and men of humbler station — fishermen, traders, dilettante pirates — who lived a hardscrabble life by the magnificent, sheltered, deepwater harbor facing the east. Less populated is the island's west coast, a place of high cliffs, difficult to scale. The island has been a staging point since antiquity for invasions into Sicily or North Africa, while itself being, as a French visitor in 1550 described it, "by artifice and by nature all but unconquerable."[7]

The emperor was happy enough to lease Malta, but he also wanted the Order to defend Tripoli. This city, another of Charles's possessions, was some 190 miles south of Malta, and the two were coupled in his mind. Since 1510 Tripoli was the easternmost of the several small Spanish holdings that impertinently dotted North Africa's Barbary Coast, the lands between Egypt and Morocco that since their coming into Islam had divided into three dynastic holdings: the Hafsid, the Zayanid, and the Wattasid. Tripoli was strategically important in defending the western Mediterranean. On the plus side, its air was "very salubrious and not subject to any of the bad contagions."[8] The harbor could accommodate carrack-sized merchant ships — useful since the locals, Muslim and at times hostile, could not be counted on for supplies.

On the down side was just about everything else. As on Malta, well water was scarce and brackish. Reliable — that is to say, Christian — food supplies were no closer than Sicily — fifty nautical miles away by sea. Houses and other buildings were ramshackle at best. The city walls, many unstable, would need to be rebuilt from their foundations. Bringing the place up to standard would take the kind of time and money the Order did not have. It was not an enticing offer, and L'Isle-Adam unsurprisingly put it on the back burner. In the meantime, however, the pope did have a job for L'Isle-Adam. The grand master was to put aside his war uniform and become a diplomat. The charge was not rapprochement with the enemies of Christendom, that is to say, Islam, but between the two most powerful Catholic kings of Europe, Charles V of Spain and Francis I of France.

+·+·+·+

Charles V, son of Philip the Fair and Joanna the Mad, was born with the century in Ghent, and royal titles dropped into his wagon like overripe fruit in an October orchard. At six he was duke of Burgundy, at sixteen, king of Spain; in the fullness of time, he would also be king of Sicily, Naples, Jerusalem, the Balearics, the Canaries, and the Indies; archduke of Austria; duke of Brabant, Styria, Carinthia, Carniola, Luxembourg, Limberg, Athens, and Patras; count of Habsburg, Flanders, and Tyrol; count palatine of Burgundy, Hainaut, Pfirt, and Roussillon; landgrave of Alsace; count of Swabia; lord of Asia and Africa, Holland, and the Holy Roman Empire. His holdings in the Americas and the Philippines, as well as the various strongholds on the North African coast, were almost superfluous.

Late portraits of Charles — Titian did several — show a face that was long, ugly, intelligent, self-aware, and intermittently amused. These older pictures stand in stark contrast to an earlier woodcut of the younger man, beardless, even foolish looking, with his gaping mouth and unnaturally protuberant jaw. The impression was magnified in person as he stuttered, spraying spittle on captive audiences, calling to mind descriptions of the Roman Emperor Claudius. As with Claudius, the appearance of simplemindedness was misleading, but one he seems to have been in no great hurry to dispel. He knew his capabilities, and in time so did others. His virtues were a very public loyalty, dedication, and piety.

The same could not be said of the king of France. While Charles wore plain black, Francis I flaunted highly colored brocades. A charming, vain, and fundamentally shallow man, Francis poured out fabulous sums on art and artists (Leonardo da Vinci died while working in his court), on books, and on some of the finest châteaux in France. It was unfortunate that he should live in such turbulent times.

When Charles came to the Spanish throne in 1514, the twenty-year-old Francis had been king of France for a year. Charles was cordial at their first meeting, and Francis could well have imagined that the drooling, slack-jawed Charles might look up to the dashing king of France. Certainly Charles, whose first language was French, acted with a cheerful respect and listened to everything the older king had to say. They might have strolled or ambled along side by side in harmony except for one thing — both men wanted to be Holy Roman emperor.

The title was in the gift of seven electors, all German, and they did not confer it lightly. From the year 800, when Charlemagne was crowned, until 1806, the Holy Roman emperor was secular head of the church, defender of the faith, and the pope's *generalissimo*. There was no money in the title, but it carried significant moral authority. The Holy Roman emperor was, in a sense, the first among equals of Europe's kings, though in practice he was only as strong as his army and his alliances. Francis wanted the title and felt he deserved it. Certainly he had paid enough for it. Honoring custom, Francis handed out four hundred thousand gold pieces to seal the deal.[9] Charles, whose grandfather Maximilian I had held the position, handed out more. In 1519 the title went to Charles.

Francis sought consolation in 1524 by invading Italy and enforcing a dubious claim to Milan. It was an act of vanity that played to his taste for war and intrigue, and it was only the most fleeting of victories. He succeeded in taking the city but was himself captured by Spanish forces while laying siege to the imperial stronghold in Pavia. The French king was settled into a soft captivity in Madrid, while Charles pondered what to do with him. Charles, whatever his faults, was not by nature vindictive. He told the Venetian ambassador, a stickler for details like all Venetian ambassadors, that he hoped the victory would pave the way for a unified Christendom that could battle Islam.[10] Italian and Vatican officials, skeptics by nature, didn't believe this for a minute.[11] Pope Clement was increasingly fretful that Charles, ruler of Naples and Sicily, was already too much at home in Italy, an opinion shared in Venice, Florence, and other city republics farther north.

Pope Clement saw this impasse as an opportunity for L'Isle-Adam. The grand master was, after all, technically a subject of Francis, and it had been to Francis that L'Isle-Adam had sent his earliest requests for aid before the fall of Rhodes. Clement encouraged the grand master to head to Madrid to work out a deal between Charles and Francis, to persuade them to turn their attention against their common enemy of Islam. L'Isle-Adam should also press for a permanent home, Malta by preference.[12]

How much good L'Isle-Adam accomplished for the cause of Christian unity is unknowable. The only point he is said to have resolved was one of protocol: who, when the emperor and monarch were together, should have precedence in entering a room? Charles had deferred to Francis; Francis to Charles. Charles asked L'Isle-Adam his opinion, and L'Isle-Adam turned to Francis: "No one, sire, can dispute that the emperor is the mightiest prince in Christendom; but as you are not only in his dominions but within his palace, it becomes you to accept the courtesy by which he acknowledges you as the first of European kings."[13] Such niceties kept negotiations alive and Francis imprisoned for the better part of a year. L'Isle-Adam meanwhile had other things on his mind, and they must have proved a tantalizing distraction from the ongoing impasse between jailor and prisoner.

He had a chance to take back Rhodes.

+·+·+·+

Even at this late date, there were still men who thought they could get the better of Suleiman. One of them was Ahmed Pasha, Suleiman's general-in-chief during the siege of Rhodes and the face of rough justice to Suleiman's magnanimity. After the knights' surrender, he kept various sacred relics, notably the mummified arm of St. John, for a ransom of thirty thousand ducats.[14]

Now, two years later, he needed them. In 1524, passed over in his ambitions to become chief vizier in Istanbul, Ahmed Pasha had been sent to quell a revolt in Egypt. He did so, and in the doing began to imagine some outsized ambitions for himself. He was officially the governor of Egypt, but according to a Muslim chronicler, "He allowed himself to be led astray by the devil and plotted for the Sultanate."[15] His plan was to resurrect the Mamluk state, with himself as leader, to which end he had succeeded in expelling all troops faithful to Suleiman. Coins were to bear his name, the *khutba* (Friday sermon) to be said in his name.[16]

For this project to work, he would need as much help as he could get, and he did not much care where he got it. If the Knights of St. John could act as a buffer for him on Rhodes, he would be happy to help them get there. There was precedence. The knights had allied with Egyptian Mamluks against the Ottomans in the fifteenth century.[17] Discrete inquiries were made, nods and whispers exchanged, and L'Isle-Adam was convinced that their old enemy was sincere. Was the plan feasible? L'Isle-Adam sent Antonio Bosio (uncle of Giovanni Bosio, who would write the chronicles of the Order), disguised as a merchant, to investigate. What he saw was encouraging. Ottoman rule at Rhodes had been remarkably negligent. The broken walls were unrepaired, the people unhappy, the officials open to discussion. (Of course, the Ottomans might have considered that broken walls were a symbol of strength — what did any city under the sultan have to fear from foreign invaders?) Further trips followed, and Antonio Bosio met with senior Orthodox Christian clerics and Ahmed Pasha's ally, the aga of Janissaries, at Rhodes.

Even after Ahmed Pasha had been assassinated and his pickled head sent to Constantinople (March 27, 1524), the knights pressed on. The island's recapture would galvanize Christian fellowship among European rulers — it was theoretically one subject on which all sides could agree — and L'Isle-Adam wanted to know to what extent those present would be willing to help.

Charles offered twenty-five thousand ducats. The king of Portugal put up another fifteen thousand. Henry VIII of England would eventually pledge twenty thousand ducats, but only after two more years of pouting and a personal visit from L'Isle-Adam.[18] Francis alone was unable to rise to the occasion. His immediate need was the paying of his ransom, which sum required special imposts within his kingdom. Honoring the general sense of collegiality at Madrid, L'Isle-Adam agreed to earmark the Order's French revenues, normally exempt from taxation, for the ransom fund, and even donated money from his own pocket. Terms were agreed, signatures twirled, seals affixed, hands shaken.

It all went to the bad, however. L'Isle-Adam's dream of returning to Rhodes died on the vine, and Francis would double-cross all who believed in him. The king, it turned out, had not been idle during his captivity. In his spare moments, he (and his mother Queen Dowager Louise of Savoy) scribbled letters abusing Charles and pleading for help. The emperor, they said, was a brute, an ambitious tyrant, a danger to peace-loving peoples everywhere. Both mother and son complained about Francis's cruel treatment and requested that the recipient "demonstrate your great munificence and ransom my son."[19] The letters were addressed not to the pope or other European crowned heads, but to Suleiman, and to Ibrahim Pasha, grand vizier of the Ottoman Empire. No record exists of how Suleiman reacted — in general, the sultan cultivated impassivity like a prized tulip. Nevertheless, the letters were a huge advance in Renaissance *realpolitik*, a remarkable proof of Suleiman's reputation and Francis's desperation. When the republics of Venice or Genoa sent ambassadors to the sultan, it demonstrated once again that merchants care only for money; but when a powerful European king, and his mother, trudged to the Grand Porte, "refuge of the world," for aid — that revealed an entirely new realm of possibility.[20]

Suleiman dictated a friendly, if noncommittal, response: "It is not shocking that an emperor should suffer defeat and be taken prisoner. Take courage and do not allow yourself to be cast down."[21] The sultan also gave verbal promises to Francis's envoy of more tangible help and mooted a joint effort at squeezing their common enemy Charles between their own two armies.[22]

The collusion between Francis and Suleiman, like most secrets, did not stay secret for long, though perhaps unfortunately it did not come to light until Charles had released Francis on the promise, unfulfilled, that the French king would not raise arms against the empire. One courier went through a region of Italy under imperial control and, as will happen, was detained, searched, and the letter discovered in his boots. Charles himself would not believe it until he was presented with a copy of the sultan's letter. He was outraged. A Christian might trade with Muslims (Charles himself had extended a treaty of peace and commerce with Suleiman's father). He might even enter alliances with a petty sheik on the North African coast, though only against another Muslim. But for a Christian to solicit a Muslim power against fellow Christians was unimaginable. Charles, in a gesture that seemed quixotic even at the time, challenged Francis to single combat, a challenge idly accepted but never actually fought (though interesting to contemplate).[23]

Others in Europe were less outraged at Francis's intrigues. Indeed, the various powers of Italy — the republics of Venice, Genoa, and Florence, the Duchy of Milan, and even the Pope — now seemed to fear Charles more than Islam, and cobbled together the so-called League of Cognac to preserve their interests against a presumably rapacious Charles. Francis, now freed from prison on the solemn promise that he would renounce his war aims, immediately accepted the invitation to join the league. His envoys suggested that French armies now embark on a full-scale invasion of his own, "without which Charles will inevitably become *signor dil mondo*, king of the world."[24]

In the event, the League of Cognac never fully coalesced, and Charles's troops, unpaid for months, grew restless. With nothing to restrain it and with the natural instincts of a predator, the army, more a mob than a disciplined military force, roused from its fitful sleep and embarked on the very invasion that the league had been formed to prevent. Their target was Rome. German Lutherans, men who despised the Catholic Church, had religious zeal to help motivate them. Others, nominally good Catholics, considered only the city's wealth. The troops trudged down the spine of Italy, their numbers swollen by adventurers and bandits and opportunists until, when they arrived at Rome, they were some forty thousand strong.[25]

The sack of Rome, on May 6, 1527, was straight out of Dante's inferno: civilians were attacked, robbed, and murdered; churches ransacked; priests killed; nuns raped; buildings burned. It was a scandal across Christendom, and Charles was mortified to learn what his men had done.[26] In the following weeks there was some residual fighting in Naples, Savoia; there were some changes of allegiance — Admiral Andrea Doria of Genoa now chose to switch sides from Francis to Charles — but at the end of the day, a general peace was settled and Pope Clement finally crowned Charles Holy Roman emperor in Bologna.

As for the Knights of St. John, they had maintained their neutrality and sat out the conflict. In August of 1526, they disarmed their galleys to demonstrate their indifference to political arguments between Christian rulers. They lost some tapestries in the looting at Rome, but were otherwise little affected materially. Spiritually, however, the more devout members were devastated. These men had put their lives on the line, had lost companions, good Christians, while defending the continent at the edge of Christendom, and all for a people who saw fit to squabble among themselves when their common enemy was still eyeing the landmass of Europe. They had voluntarily contributed to the ransom that freed Francis from Madrid only to find that he had been consorting with the enemy. After five long years with no central location to call their own, utter dissolution of the Order now seemed a distinct possibility, and one that haunted the grand master. On January 21, 1527, L'Isle-Adam gathered an audience of knights to their quarters in Viterbo and announced that he feared he might "prove to be the last Grand Master" and then broke down in tears.[27]

✦·✦·✦·✦

L'Isle-Adam was nothing if not resilient, and with the return of peace in Italy, he returned to the problem of a permanent home. It took another three years, but once all other options were exhausted, L'Isle-Adam capitulated. Charles, unwavering in his loyalty to Christendom, contracted an official donation of Malta and Tripoli to the Order for as long as they remained on the island, to revert to the Emperor should they leave. It was fully accepted on April 25, 1530. The knights now inhabited a fiefdom of Spain, for which they would give him every year on All Saints Day a single falcon — far less than the one hundred thousand gold pieces that L'Isle-Adam had desperately offered just seven years earlier.[28] It wasn't Rhodes, but it was better than nothing. All that remained was for the Order to recover their purpose.

3

+·+·+·+

IN SERVICE
TO THE EMPIRE,
1531–1540

+·+·+·+

Indeed, we must praise the glory of Prince Andrea Doria for
having been one of the great captains of the sea, if it is possible,
in living memory or even to be found in our written history.

Brantôme on Doria

Not even among the Romans or the Greeks,
great conquerors of kingdoms and nations,
has there ever been such a one as he.

Brantôme on Khairedihn Barbarossa

On September 2, 1531, two brigantines, their holds carrying wine and lumber, sailed into the harbor at Modon, modern Methoni in the south of Greece not far from Rhodes, with its sister city Coron one of the Twin Eyes of the Republic of Venice until seized by the Ottomans in 1498. The vessels were piloted by relatives of the port master. Once the ships were tied up safely at dockside, the port master invited the ships' crew and the Ottoman port security to a small celebration in honor of their safe return in these dangerous times. The gathering was enhanced by the free use of wine, which in due course put the guards into a drunken sleep. It was a plan as old as the Aegean. Just before dawn, two hundred armed knights of St. John shifted the lumber concealing them in the ship's hold, crept out, and made their way along the quay, past the tower of Christian bones erected by the Ottomans when they conquered the city.[1] The knights murdered the sleeping guards, seized the main gate, and fired a cannon to signal a squadron of galleys anchored out of sight three miles down the coast. The plan was for this larger force to speed their way to the port and then for the combined troops to take the city.

Nature apparently had other ideas. The wind was capricious that morning. The governor and the townspeople heard the shot — the knights and their mercenary allies waiting down the coast did not. With admirable presence of mind, the governor rallied what soldiers he had along with the more robust natives (who clearly had no interest in freedom from Ottoman rule) against the small force of knights. He also managed to send a messenger to run farther down the coast, where some six thousand Ottoman troops were encamped.

Hours passed. The fighting in town continued with the knights initially getting the worst of it. The tide turned as the second wave of Christians, alerted by a swift boat, now arrived and rushed into battle. Once more on the defensive, the governor ordered the population of Modon to take refuge in the citadel overlooking their homes. The knights and their mercenary allies had the town to themselves, and they made the most of it. As the refugees in the citadel watched, helpless, the invaders sacked and burned their houses and shops. The end came only when the Ottoman troops arrived and sent the knights packing. These men were not able to stop them from taking eight hundred (some claimed sixteen hundred) prisoners ("chiefly women and children") and hauling off booty worth a hundred thousand ducats.[2]

The message, however, was clear. The knights were back in business.

+·+·+·+

The knights' botched attack on Modon had been an unapproved, freelance effort intended as a stepping-stone back to Rhodes, and their failure to take the city did little to boost their reputation. The pope was said to be very disturbed by the incident, both because they had failed to regain some lost borders of Christendom and because the fight had been a triumph for the Ottomans. The fear was that the raid could only goad Suleiman.[3]

Instead, it inspired Charles to follow suit. If this was what a mere half-dozen ships of the Order could accomplish, imagine what a proper armada could do. In the fall of 1532, as Suleiman was engaged in a massive invasion of Hungary (ultimately fruitless), the emperor took the opportunity to retake the ancient ports of the Peloponnese now in the hands of the Ottomans. To this end, he gathered a fleet of thirty-five ships and forty-eight galleys comprising ships of his own, some belonging to the pope, some to the Knights of St. John, and some to the Genoese admiral Andrea Doria, who commanded the expedition.

This tall, long-nosed man was one of the titans of his age. Born in Genoa in 1468, he served as a condottiere, literally a contract man, a mercenary who would fight for the highest bidder in various land campaigns throughout Italy. For the early years of his career, this meant France; as time passed, however, he found that connection less and less attractive. In 1503 Genoa's civic leaders offered him the position of admiral of their fleet, a post he refused on the grounds that he knew nothing of naval combat. They countered that, for a man of his achievements, nothing was too difficult. So it proved to be. In the years that followed, Doria came to be regarded as the finest sailor that Christian Europe could muster. His activities were confined to the shifting winds of Genoese politics, first as allied to the French, independent of the French, allied again, and finally, after the sack of Rome (and slow payment from Francis I) he allied firmly with Charles V, who made certain to pay the annual stipend on time.[4] The expense was worth it to Charles, if only to have access to the considerable balance sheets of Genoese bankers.

The planning took into consideration current realities. Modon was rejected as a target since the knights had left nothing to steal. Coron, sister city to Modon, would do. The city fell on September 23, to be followed by Patras farther east, as far as the two towers guarding the Gulf of Corinth, and the cruise might have gone on even longer had not the weather turned and reports reached them that Suleiman was coming back from Hungary. Doria ordered the fleet home, his own hold richer by a load of cannon worth sixty thousand ducats, the cities of Coron and Patras (unlike Modon) firmly in imperial control.

The expedition marked a significant turning point. It was one thing for corsairs such as the Knights of St. John to raid Suleiman's territory; it was quite another for the Holy Roman emperor to expand the Christian commonwealth into Ottoman territory. Then there were the rumors that Charles intended to place the knights in Coron, far too close to Constantinople for comfort.[5]

The sultan tried to make the best of the situation. He was hampered by the cost of the Hungarian campaign and the rumblings of trouble on his border with Shiite Persia. Throughout 1533, he made several suggestions for a comprehensive peace covering Charles and the pope and other Christian powers.

The overtures came to nothing.[6] There was little choice for Suleiman but to respond with force and in kind. He lacked, however, the means.

It was not that he lacked a navy. Heretofore, the Ottomans had gotten by with small squadrons based in Alexandria, Suez, the Danube, and the Red Sea. They had proven sufficient so long as the remaining Christian stronghold in the eastern Mediterranean behaved, as they generally did. Now that Charles, pushed by the ambitions of the knights, was heading full bore into the eastern Mediterranean, Suleiman had to raise the ante. The Mediterranean east of the Aegean was effectively Ottoman territory that suffered Christian provinces such as Crete, Cyprus, and Chios only so far as they behaved well. Now that an engorged Habsburg fleet was pecking at the eastern Mediterranean, Suleiman needed to expand his navy, and quickly. Beyond that, he would require someone with considerable seafaring experience, another Doria if possible, to command it. That summer, the sultan requested Khairedihn, known to the West as Barbarossa, a legend among the Barbary corsairs, to present himself in Constantinople.

✦·✦·✦·✦

It was the highpoint in a career that had begun decades earlier on the island of Mytilene (Lesbos), where Khairedihn and his elder brother Aroudj had been born to a retired Janissary and his Christian wife. Aroudj, or Oruc, the elder, started out his adult life as a merchant mariner and sometime navy man (and briefly a prisoner of the Knights of St. John), who headed west to try his hand at piracy. He was soon followed by Khairedihn.

Their timing was perfect. In 1492 Ferdinand and Isabella had completed the *reconquista* of Spain, defeating Boabdil, the last Muslim sultan of Granada, and undoing seven hundred years of Muslim rule. Jews were expelled entirely, Muslims allow to remain for the time being under ever stricter rules, culminating in 1505 with the total prohibition of Islam. Many Spanish Muslims, dedicated to their faith, abandoned their native land and washed up on the North African shores. There, combining their need for income with the knowledge of the Spanish coast, they would go on to raid Christian shipping, becoming the nucleus of the Barbary corsairs. Profits were large enough to attract others from the eastern Mediterranean, including the brothers Aroudj and Khairedihn, known to Europe as the Barbarossa (Redbeard) brothers.

In 1505 they settled in Tunis. This prosperous if somewhat rough trading city was Islam's answer to Venice, an essentially neutral port that served the material needs of all comers. The twin forts of Goletta flanked the wide harbor and permitted no more than a handful of ships in at one time. In exchange for the safety of the harbor, men such as Aroudj and Khairedihn paid a share of their takings to the sultan.

Through diligence and hard work, the brothers went from three eighteen-oared vessels to a fleet numbering in the dozens. Tired of sharing the fruits of their labor, they set up independently on the island of Djerba, just off Tripoli and close to the shipping lanes of Sicily. From here they swept the coasts of Italy and Spain, hauling away goods and people and leaving ashes behind.

In 1516 the rulers of Algiers, impressed by their reputation for violence, invited the brothers to help out in a spot of trouble. The entrance to the Algiers harbor was commanded by a Spanish-held *peñon*, or offshore fortress. Aroudj, they felt, would be perfect for getting the Spanish to leave. He did succeed in kicking out the Spanish, but also drowned the rightful monarch in his bath, took the crown for himself, and then offered fealty to Suleiman's father Selim.[7] A bemused Selim, for whom Algiers was just another title to add to a growing list, dispatched a handful of troops to help put the Ottoman stamp on the place and essentially gave Aroudj a free hand to do as he liked.

Aroudj then began to target Spanish holdings in North Africa, albeit with less success. His attempt to take them saw him lose an arm to a Spanish cannonball. He took a year off to recuperate, and when he returned to fighting, he did so with a prosthetic replacement said to have been made of silver. But Aroudj had overreached himself, and perhaps counted too much on fellow Muslims supporting him simply on the basis of their shared religion. In 1519 a young Charles V, allied with the sheik of Oran and some Bedouins, marched on the city of Tlemcen in northwest Algiers. Aroudj fled to the desert. The soldiers followed. Aroudj cast a small cloud of gold coins behind him to distract his pursuers. The tactic failed. He was overtaken, outnumbered, and unwilling to surrender. With a sword in his one good hand, he cut and parried to the end, suffering repeated small wounds until finally he was brought down, fighting "to the very last gasp, like a lion."[8] A Spanish *alverez*, lieutenant, administered the coup de grace, and forever after his family emblazoned the dead man's head on their coat of arms. The body itself was carried back to Iberia, a grisly trophy that spent some time on display, presumably to reassure Spanish Catholics and intimidate Spain's remaining closet Muslims.

Younger brother Khairedihn may have grieved, but he also knew he must consolidate his position. He did so by threatening to leave Algiers: "Hitherto I have given you every assistance and I have fortified your castle by placing in it four hundred pieces of cannon; now appoint whom you please as your governor, and I will proceed by sea to some other place."[9] Tone is everything in political speech. The Algerians, frightened of Spain and of anarchy, begged him to stay, and he allowed himself to be persuaded, but only if he could arrange a stronger connection with the Ottomans. Within weeks, ships arrived from Constantinople with two thousand Janissaries, four thousand militia, and a declaration that Khairedihn was now beylerbey, governor, of Algiers.[10]

For Selim and later Suleiman, the corsairs were a means of hectoring Spain at little cost to themselves. Beyond that, both sultans were happy to leave the western Mediterranean to itself. Or at least, they had been up until now.

✦·✦·✦·✦

That Suleiman needed a world-class fleet and a commander for it was not in dispute, but as to whom that admiral should be among the sultan's courtiers, there were doubts. Barbarossa was still no better than a peasant, a self-made man who had not attended the same palace school (the *Enderûn*) that proper courtiers had done.[11] And he was late.

This peasant, however, knew just how long a delay was enough, and when he did arrive, on November 21, 1533, it was with forty vessels of his own fleet, rich in decoration, powerfully armed, and weighed down with gold and silver, slaves from Europe, beautiful women, exotic animals from inland Africa — all of this not so much tribute but as the trifling gifts of one powerful leader to another. Endorsed by Suleiman's most trusted confidant and grand vizier, Ibrahim Pasha, Khairedihn was appointed as Kapudan-ı Derya, Admiral of the Sea.[12] He immediately headed to the shipyards at Galata, the navy yard of Constantinople, and began the process of creating the sultan's fleet. By the spring of 1534, sixty-one new galleys quietly bobbed in the waters of the Golden Horn, impatient as a line of young schoolboys waiting to be let out to play. He did not keep them waiting long.

The West had endured small-scale sea raids for years, often part-time merchants or fishermen doing a sideline in high-seas robbery or landing near isolated coastal villages to do a bit of robbery or kidnapping for the slave trade. The frequency and extent of these practices had grown significantly in the years after 1492, but the arrival in the West of men such as Khairedihn brought the threat to a whole new level. Backed by the full weight of the Ottoman Empire, Khairedihn sailed up the Italian coast as far as Sardinia, targeting simple villages too small to defend themselves, but also cities as large as Reggio and even Naples, where the Spanish viceroy, Don Pedro de Toledo, scrambled to fortify what he could and evacuate what he could not. The dramatic high point was Khairedihn's nocturnal arrival at Fondi, a town of small importance except that Giulia Gonzaga, the most beautiful woman in Italy and a fine gift for the sultan, was there at the time. Dressed only in a nightshirt, she fled on horseback, disappearing into the mountains just minutes before the admiral's men reached the house. Khairedihn consoled himself by sacking the town.

The raiding, however, was merely an overture to the admiral's real objective, the taking of his old stomping ground of Tunis.

Muley Hassan, the current ruler, had come to the throne by patricide and fratricide, and passed his days with "pleasures so vicious that they cannot be described."[13] His people did not love him, and many longed for a return of the rightful heir whom Muley Hassan had usurped. Hassan was therefore an uneasy man who daily examined the horizon, searching for enemies. When Khairedihn's ships appeared, Hassan's nerve broke. He fled, and Tunis was in Khairedihn's iron hands.

No matter; the ex-ruler was less important than the city itself. As Khairedihn observed to Suleiman, "If the harbor of Goletta were taken and protected by the Ottoman sovereign, the imperial fleet could be stationed in it most of the time. In that case, with the help of God the Sublime, it would become feasible to conquer and subdue Spain from there."[14]

Eventually, perhaps. In the meantime, Khairedihn busied himself with local mischief. He sent agents provocateurs into Tripoli to keep the Knights of St. John stationed there busy. These interlopers fomented riots, which the knights were able to quell, but the expedition rattled the new Grand Master Piero del Ponte wrote to Charles asking for help in taking on Khairedihn. The exiled Muley Hassan also had written the emperor and received a favorable reply — Charles addresses him as a fellow king and refers to Khairedihn as the "enemy of all nations and peoples."[15]

Charles was generally slow to expand his empire — he had a hard enough time with what he already had — but this was something special. Tunis was a relatively small thorn for Charles, but a Tunis under the Ottoman rule was unacceptable. Charles's first thought was to send an envoy either to engage Barbarossa in a separate alliance (as he had Doria) or, failing that, to assassinate him. The envoy was unpersuasive and the assassin was discovered (and executed), leaving Charles with no choice but to gear up his military and try to seize Tunis back by force.

✦·✦·✦·✦

He was well placed to do so. That year had seen a particularly rich windfall of Peruvian gold, enough to pay off old debts and finance a new fleet .[16] On June 13, 1535, Charles's armada of seventy-four galleys and three hundred other vessels sailed from Sardinia with Doria in command. The Knights of St. John sent five galleys, one of them commanded by the thirty-six-year-old veteran of Rhodes, Jean de Valette. Also present was Don Garcia de Toledo, son of the viceroy of Naples and veteran of Doria's service. Four days later, the two hundred knights and the imperial forces landed near the ruins of ancient Carthage, some two miles from La Goletta, twelve miles from Tunis proper. Siege guns — "large, very beautiful, and in great number" — were carted down the coast and aimed at the northernmost of La Goletta's twin strongholds, which guarded the narrow entrance to the port.[17] A few weeks of slow demolition created two serious breaches, one on the landward side, one facing the bay. On July 14, Charles was master of the twin forts and prepared to head inland for Tunis itself.

Khairedihn's lieutenants advised him to leave immediately and head back to sea. He refused, dismissing the Spanish as cowards: "If the infidels see my turban on a hilltop, they'll run for a month."[18]

They didn't. Despite the fact that the trek to the city was long, the sun high, and water scarce, Charles's men kept on coming. Khairedihn was outnumbered, but counted on the fact that his men were well rested. He would defeat the enemy while they were on the march — tired, hot, thirsty, and relatively disorganized. Confident in his position, he roused the soldiers and the citizens, and ordered Moorish cavalry and foot to attack the invaders. He was out of his league. During the Italian campaign, and especially the battle of Pavia in 1525, the Spanish had perfected the military formation of the *tercios*.

The foundation of the *tercio* was a throwback to ancient military structures, updated to take advantage of modern firearms. At its simplest, the *tercio* was a formation of rank-and-file squares comprising up to three thousand specialists, armed either with pikes, swords, or guns. Seen from above, the square units were arrayed like a three-by-three checkerboard, four outer units (*mangas*) of arquebusiers and musketeers meeting at the corners of a central block. Musketeers and arquebusiers manned the outer edges of these blocks; pikemen, their tall, thin weapons pointed upright like so many steel-tipped, unbranched trees, filled up the center. Each block could march in any direction required and re-form in short order to answer the changing needs of the battlefield.

The formation succeeded in large part because the individuals who made up the whole were not short-term volunteer mercenaries, but full-time, professional soldiers with the cohesion and pride that come from months of drilling and marching and fighting under familiar and trusted officers. Amateurs and romantics had no place inside this modern army, and individual dash and bravery were useless against it. Should infantry approach the formation, a musketeer in the outermost rank of gunmen could fire at the enemy, then step back and relinquish his place for the next gunner while he himself reloaded. Should cavalry threaten it, musketeers could count on pikemen to lower their poles, creating what amounted to a metal bramble hedge that no horse would dare to charge.

Between them, the men of the *tercios* could effectively counter any force both up close and at a distance. They were equally good on offense. The sight of these highly disciplined units marching forward in machinelike unison would unnerve the looser formations of any less well-organized or trained soldiers. The arrangement was so successful that it would remain more or less intact (and widely copied in Europe) for the next one hundred years.

Berber horsemen and Khairedihn's corsairs had never experienced anything like the disciplined volley that Spanish *tercios* could lay down. In a letter to his sister Mary, queen consort of Hungary and Bohemia, Charles described what happened next: "They fired their artillery. We responded in kind. They fired their arquebuses. We fired back in equal measure. They charged and we did as well. They fell back. We did not stop going until we had reached their guns and taken them for ourselves."[19]

The key to victory, however, came from a single Italian knight of St. John named Paolo Simeoni. He, along with hundreds of other Christians, was being held prisoner in the dungeons of Tunis. Once the battle outside had gotten underway, these men, either by force or with help from a sympathetic local, managed to break out of their captivity and into the city's armory. With

Simeoni in command, they took up positions on the city wall. Khairedihn, caught between two armies, had no choice but to flee into the desert.

The soldiers thought their duty done and turned to pillage. "They looted shops and mosques, from which they tore apart and ruined many beautiful books ... decorated and written in Arabic script, in gold and azure. They prized gray jasper and other precious stones from the pillars in mosques, though they did not touch a small Christian church."[20] Charles dined that night with the knights on the deck of the *Santa Anna*.[21] There might, he suggested, be time to head up the coast and take the port city of Mahdia on the return voyage. It could be a new home for the Order, he suggested; the knights could have free access to whatever provisions Sicily had to offer, and tax free. Next year, possibly a new crusade.

Muley Hassan, said to have approved the destruction of his city, was put back in charge, but as a vassal to Spain. Charles demanded that privateers should never again trouble Christian shipping, imperial subjects should not be enslaved, and a thousand Spaniards would garrison Goletta, at Muley Hassan's expense. The sheik agreed. What choice did he have? Other than Charles, he lacked any influential friends.

Charles's reasoning for restoring such an unpleasant man to power was less obvious. Perhaps he was bound by his own sense of loyalty to Muley Hassan. Perhaps he thought a Muslim figurehead would demonstrate Spanish goodwill toward the local population. It scarcely mattered; after what his men had done, there was little chance that Tunis would ever love Spain.

As to Khairedihn, he managed to lead his men across the desert to the coast and retake the galleys that one of Doria's underlings was charged with guarding. The guard blamed his own cowardice, but there were rumors of collusion, never confirmed. Regardless, Khairedihn knew that he had to offset the loss of Tunis. While Charles was still in the full flush of victory, Khairedihn gathered his men at Algiers and set sail north to the island of Minorca, where Spanish subjects were celebrating with music and dancing and a pantomime involving the killing of a Moor, for which part a condemned prisoner played the all-too-realistic lead role. The locals cheered as they saw ships with Italian and Spanish flags enter the harbor. Only after the ships spewed forth a stream of cutlass-welding corsairs did they realize their mistake. Khairedihn "fired unexpectedly at the Spanish fortress at Minorca ... , conquered it, made all young men and girls prisoners and took property and provisions."[22] It was enough that, despite losing Tunis, Khairedihn was able to sail into Constantinople with eighteen galleys and still be received as a hero.

+·+·+·+

Seasons change, and in time the events of Tunis faded. In 1538 Charles managed to cobble together a pan-Christian alliance against the Ottomans, even succeeding in seducing the always reluctant Venetians (whose Balkan territories Suleiman was now attacking) with a promise to restore their holdings throughout the Aegean, and even the taking of Constantinople itself. The enterprise was a mare's nest of bad planning, bad communication, and bad seamanship. Charles did not tell Venice that he was negotiating once more with Khairedihn to abandon Suleiman (the hope came to nothing). Doria as naval commander failed to support the Venetian fleet at the naval battle of Prevesa, thus alienating the Venetians from any Christian coalition for the next thirty years. The few pieces of real estate that Doria managed to take were trivial and lost again in the following year, and Khairedihn and his followers continued to launch devastating raids against Spain, Italy, and Sicily. As the decade drew to a close, Charles decided that it would be better to pacify his own part of the Mediterranean, in particular Algiers. The campaign would, he thought, be another Tunis, quick and painless and glory for all.

+·+·+·+

In the summer of 1541, forty ships from Charles's armada dropped anchor at Sardinia for supplies. The locals, desperate to impress these important guests, scrounged the countryside for a suitably remarkable gift. What they came up with was a two-headed calf. Some took this as a bad omen.

Indeed, the entire Algiers expedition was plagued by difficulties from the outset, endless delay not the least of them. A campaign that normally would have begun in early spring was delayed as Charles attended to the empire's other business. His lieutenants were becoming progressively more nervous; but Charles, perhaps recalling Suleiman's success at Rhodes, declared September, despite its unpredictable weather, as "the best time of year" for a naval invasion.[23] This might have been wishful thinking. Charles had considerable sunk costs — the perishable foodstuffs, the soldiers and sailors and bankers who were expecting to be paid. By this point, he needed to invade and more important loot Algiers simply to straighten out the empire's account books. The men were ready now, delay was risky, and God was on their side. (Then too, it was always possible that Charles might convince the governor of Algiers, Hassan Agha, who had been born a Christian, to switch his alliance to the empire.)[24]

Despite serious misgivings, Doria agreed to command the fleet. His doubts were immediately justified by sudden storms. Heavy seas barely allowed the men, among them Tunis veteran Don Garcia de Toledo and rising Spanish commander Don Álvaro de Sande, ashore; the siege guns could not be landed and had to remain uselessly at sea. Charles, still convinced that he had God's favor, called on Hassan to surrender Algiers, but Hassan only laughed. Years earlier, he said, an old enchantress had predicted devastation by land and by sea for any Christian emperor who would attack the city "out of season."[25]

Which is exactly what happened. A fresh storm at sea caused much of the fleet to sink with stores and hands on board. Christian soldiers who made it ashore were forced to spend the night without tents, in deep mud under cold rain, shivering and unable to rest. By morning, Muslim troops exited the city and attacked with the benefit of cannon and dry powder. "We were," wrote the French knight Nicolas Durand de Villegaignon drily, "greater in number and equal in spirit, but they were superior by far in placement and type of arms."[26]

Doria managed to get word to shore that he could anchor some miles up the coast and evacuate the Christian forces. Charles ordered a retreat. The long column, its rear guard defended by the Knights of St. John, was dogged by Berber horsemen who picked off stragglers and retreated at the sign of any serious resistance. At the rendezvous it was clear that there would not be enough space for everyone. Those left behind would soon glut the slave markets of Algiers. (Arab sources claim that thirteen hundred women and children were left behind—"not one escaped"—which, if true, leaves open the question of why they were there in the first place.)[27]

The cost of reclaiming the lands of Christendom, which had seemed so modest ten years before, was proving high indeed. If there was any comfort for Charles at all, it was in the fact that Suleiman, beguiled by his own roving mariners, was paying at least as stiff a price as well. From here on out, the cost would only rise.

4

·+·+·+·

WAR AT SEA,
1541–1550

·+·+·+·

Turgut, who was worth an army.

Selaniki

It is only good sense to kick an enemy while he is down. Just one year after Charles's catastrophic failure in Algiers, war broke out between Spain and France, which lead Francis to send envoys to Suleiman proposing (again) a joint Franco-Ottoman invasion of Italy. He suggested that in spring of 1543, the French armies would cross the Alps into Italy while Suleiman's men invaded Hungary from the south, and Khairedihn with French help attacked Italy by sea. A bold plan, and it might have worked had it not involved Francis.

The Ottomans certainly did their part. On land, Suleiman drove his forces up the Danube and (with French help) captured large chunks of Hungary. At sea, Khairedihn, accompanied by France's ambassador to Constantinople, sacked Reggio, ravaged the coast of Naples, and even laid anchor at the mouth of the Tiber, appearing to threaten Rome itself. In fact, he left the city alone, since the pope was at the time an ally of France. He also scrupulously avoided raiding other port cities friendly to France, and made sure to pay for any provisions he might require of them.[1] He had, moreover, no need to snatch slaves to man the oars; Italian volunteers (*buonevoglie*) all along the western coast readily signed on to be Barbary corsairs, which can only have further unnerved the peninsula's Christian rulers.[2] Doria, hopelessly outnumbered by the 148 Muslim vessels, remained holed up in Genoa.

The fleet arrived on July 20, 1543, at Marseilles, where the Duc d'Enghien, the twenty-four-year-old governor and army commander, was surprisingly unprepared for their Ottoman guests. Perhaps he never imagined that the corsair actually would show up. The duke did what he could, however, showing them every honor, neglecting not "even so much as a hair."[3] Here as elsewhere, all enemies of Charles seemed fascinated by Khairedihn. François Rabelais possessed an oil portrait of him, later the basis for a widely distributed etching; the Venetian poet, pornographer, and blackmailer Pietro Aretino sent him admiring letters. Khairedihn's decades of raiding the Christian coast and seizing Christian shipping served to raise his stature and were balanced at least in part by his respect for (and failure to sack) the odd Christian cloister.

None of which answered the question of what d'Enghien was supposed to do with this powerful resource. Only after prodding by the duke and some weeks of vacillating did Francis, busy elsewhere in his kingdom, declare that the combined Ottoman and French forces should attack Nice, a city under Charles's ally the Duke of Savoy. Together, Christians and Muslims prised open the lower town, which the French sacked; the Ottomans restrained themselves.[4] The upper city held out, and by early September, all forces withdrew on rumors that Charles was heading their way. So ended the Ottoman participation in Francis's latest war, which would continue for four more years, bankrupt France, and achieve none of the king's territorial ambitions in northern Italy. Suleiman would cut his losses, staying well out of things while the Christian powers of Europe continued to fight one another.

In the meantime, the autumn of 1543 was closing in and Khairedihn, concerned for the safety of his ships, wanted to overwinter in the area. This was fine with France. Officials evacuated a good deal of Toulon and allowed the Ottoman fleet to stay there at France's expense. (Francis gave the locals immunity from taxes for ten years to vacate the city.)[5] City houses, suburban houses, and tents sheltered the thirty thousand Muslim soldiers and sailors who "were installed as in a *faubourg* of Constantinople, where they lived according to their customs."[6] They also paid for their food. The locals rejoiced with this large and unexpected windfall, and even Charles's Habsburg ally Genoa shipped off superfluous grain, rationalizing this with the observation that the admiral could easily just steal the foodstuff. Certainly the official view from Toulon was that the fleet's presence was something of a godsend. After the sack of Rome, all Europe knew what Charles's army was capable of. As late as 1789, the town hall at Toulon held a mural of Khairedihn's fleet in Toulon harbor with the quatrain:

This fleet of fraternal oarsmen
Whom tail winds favor so sweetly
It's Barbarossa and his army
Who come to succor us all.[7]

Any affection was not reciprocated. Khairedihn sailed off the following spring, plundering the Italian coast, disgusted that he and Suleiman's French allies had managed to accomplish nothing more than the single abortive raid on Nice; worse, they now reneged on a promised joint attack on Tunis and would not help him to take on Genoa.[8] Still, even if he could not take the city, his fleet could intimidate the citizens, and he made a point of stopping by for a bit of unfinished business. Three years earlier, Andrea Doria's nephew Giannettino had captured Khairedihn's finest lieutenant, Turgut Reis, in Corsica's Girolata bay. Khairedihn wanted him back. In the end, it cost Khairedihn thirty-five hundred ducats — money well spent, as it would later turn out.[9]

This voyage was to prove the old corsair's last. He retired to his house overlooking the Golden Horn, honored for his piety and his achievements. For over forty years he had been a thorn in the side of Spanish ambitions and a terror to Christian inhabitants of the western Mediterranean. Rumors of his presence could move entire armies.[10] The records of his annual voyages in search of ships to seize or towns to sack make for repetitive and depressing reading. These and the greater highlights of his (and his brother's) successes over the years — taking Algiers, taking Tunis, besting the combined Christian fleet at Preveza, seizing papal galleys and treasure ships — all inspired an entire generation of adventurers who followed him and formed the solid foundation of the Barbary corsairs, who would trouble the Mediterranean and beyond for the next three hundred years. In 1546 Turkish chronicles recorded, "The king of the sea is dead," after a bout of digestive troubles (he was a large man) and a quick fever.[11]

It was stunning news for the empire, and as befits such a man as Khairedihn, rumors spread that he had not really died, that four or five hours after his entombment, he was seen wandering about the neighboring streets. His rest was assured by a Greek magus who instructed that a dead black dog be laid at his side within the tomb. Whatever the truth of the matter, he remains to this day in Galata on the shores of the Bosphorus. For sailors, men naturally given to talismans and traditions, his tomb became a necessary place to visit prior to any voyage away from the Grand Porte. As Christians would invoke the Blessed Virgin before setting out on the waters, Ottoman captains would pay respects to the King of the Sea.

+·+·+·+

In the twelve years since 1531, the Order's post at Tripoli, unwanted from day one, had deteriorated. The castle keep was a square Byzantine relic dating from before 645, when the Arabs took over the city, marginally improved by the Spanish after they took the city in 1510. Even then the city walls were only two-and-half meters high and by no means thick. Bringing the defense works up to modern standards would cost, the knights calculated, twenty-five thousand scudi, far beyond their means.[12] Charles was asked for help but was unable to provide it, leaving the Order to make do as best as possible. With little attention from Madrid or from Malta, the string of governors at Tripoli allowed the place to go downhill. The hired soldiers and even the knights gave in to indolence. Bored, idle, and interested only in the next relief ship, they sold or gambled away their weapons, and even their horses, to anyone who would pay. Professionally, Tripoli had become a place for a knight to mark time, endure, and get out of as soon as possible.

That all changed in 1546 when the Order gave command of Tripoli to Jean Parisot de Valette.

It is worth examining this man in some detail. He would in time become the hero of the great siege of Malta, yet his career until that point was marked at every turn by failures, some catastrophic, and sheer bad luck, none of which seem to have retarded his professional rise.

Valette was born in 1494, a son of an old and noble Gascon family, and like his fictional Gascon counterpart d'Artagnan, imbued with both deep sentiment and a sudden temper. His ancestors had fought with St. Louis in the Holy Lands, and at home against the Albigensian heretics. Several had been members of the Order before him, and Jean, at age twenty, joined the *langue* of Provence. He was never to return home again. The soldier and historian Brantôme, who knew him personally, said of Valette: "Over and above his bravery and ability he was a most handsome person — tall and well-built, of a goodly appearance and fine manners."[13] Others say he was more melancholic than cheerful.[14] He was dedicated, intense, hard, and with a clear instinct for command, respected more than liked — a man useful in war. In times of peace, some of his attributes proved more a liability. He had a temper, and losing it had twice landed him in prison — the first time for beating a slave nearly to death in a burst of what Giacomo Bosio, the Italian chronicler of the Order, called "youthful excess" (*giovenile eccesso*). He was forty-three at the time.[15] The second time, again for assault, he served six months and apparently was shriven. A year later, in 1557, he would be elected grand master of the Order.

He served at Rhodes, after which his name is absent from the records until 1534, when he is listed as one of four knights ordered to sail with Andrea Doria. A few years later he helped capture an enemy galley that was then given to him to command. Again, youthful excess got the better of him. Having spotted the double masts and sixteen-oar banks of a Muslim galliot and eager to prove himself, he ordered the helmsman to bring the Order's galley forward. Under the eyes of the rest of the squadron, his oarsmen pulled through a heavy swell toward the enemy. Valette stood at the bow, upright, steady, determined. When the vessels came close, the enemy let loose a volley of arquebus fire. Valette's response should have been to fire his own volley, grapple the ship, and then board her. Instead, his ship's metal-covered beak, a standard-issue ramming device below the waterline on all galleys dating back to ancient Greece, gored the enemy galliot below the waterline. His oarsmen backrowed, and as the beak withdrew from the enemy's hull, water gushed in. Within minutes the Muslim ship had sunk.

Had Valette been reckless, or had he been the victim of an unlucky swell? Whatever his bravery and dash, he had lost a potential prize — worse, he had lost the oarsmen, probably Christian slaves, shackled to the sinking hulk. Seventeen of the wreck's crew were hauled out of the sea and informed Valette that that ship had belonged to the corsair Cacciadiablo, a longtime enemy of the knights. Losing this notable prize seems not to have dampened Valette's career. After serving at Tunis, he was named General of the Galleys in 1537.

He did not get off so easily the next time. While patrolling off the North African coast in 1541, he spotted two galliots and headed forward to engage them. A mistake. His ship was edged into shallow water; he was himself badly wounded and fell unconscious. He awoke to find himself a prisoner of the corsair Kust Ali Abdul Rahman, and for the next two years he languished in the slave quarters at Djerba. (More dramatic chroniclers suggest he was put to the rowing bench.) It was then that he learned the Turkish and Arabic which supplemented his already fluent French, Greek, Italian, Spanish, and

Latin. Oddly, Kust Ali made no attempt to ransom his prisoner, though he would have received a good price. The Order believed that Valette was dead. Whatever the reasoning, the corsair did get fair value in the end. In 1543 he exchanged Valette for his own father.[16]

Valette was taken to Tripoli for recuperation and was appalled at what he saw. He and some like-minded comrades wrote to Charles and the council. The fort, he said, could not be expected to survive any serious attack. If Charles, or Grand Master D'Homedes, was not willing to do something about the place and soon, then the post should be abandoned, to eliminate the cost of maintaining it, and destroyed, to deny any remaining utility to corsairs. Charles made polite noise, but did nothing. In 1546 Valette, whether as reward or punishment or as a test, or possibly as a combination of all three, was ordered to turn Tripoli around.

And so he did. Immediately on taking office, he expelled the city's indigent and demanded loyalty oaths from established citizens. He began to rebuild the defense works, making them capable of absorbing the impact of modern cannon.[17] He cultivated friendships with local sheiks who had no love for the Ottomans. He reorganized the military structure, bringing in new weapons for the garrison and destroying the old. Of the foot soldiers who could not account for their missing weapons, he punished the worst offenders, pardoned the less guilty, and then announced a training regimen worthy of Christian soldiers. As his men began to regain their spirit, Valette went further — he planned a raid.

The target was the ships in the port city of Tagiura, nine miles down the coast and a haven for followers of Khairedihn. Valette's plan required coordinated action by land and sea, at night. Cavalry under the knight Marsile were to approach the city walls and make a display of shouts and gunshots. While the city was distracted on its landward side, two of the Order's vessels would enter the harbor and torch every ship they could reach. Once the cavalry was alerted by the glow of burning ships, they would know that the raid was successful and head home immediately.

The horsemen and sailors set off into the darkness. The night passed. The ships, their mission accomplished, returned just before daylight. The cavalry did not. Dawn broke, the sun glanced over the horizon, then began its morning ascent.

Some four hours later, dust clouds appeared in the direction of Tagiura, followed by the sounds of charging horses, gunfire, and eventually Arab battle cries. Marsiles's men were returning with enemy cavalry in hot pursuit. Valette ordered the artillery to prepare scattershot, then deployed his remaining men outside the gates to form a line against the oncoming charge. Once his own men were out of harm's way, he ordered the guns fired. Between the volley of arquebus fire and cannon shot, they were able to send the enemy cavalry off, but not before Marsile had wheeled about to face his pursuers. His horse was shot from under him, and enemy cavalry captured him and took him back to Tagiura.

The story emerged from the tired and dusty survivors. Marsile had gotten ambitious. They had created their diversion and were preparing to leave when Marsile decided to take the enemy's livestock. It was a bold decision, but it slowed down their retreat enough for the men of Tagiura to chase them down.

A few days later, a herald appeared. The aga of Tagiura sent his regards and offered to return Marsile in exchange for a sum greater than the treasury was able to pay. Valette was forced to take up a collection from his fellow knights, and so brought home his cavalry commander.

Despite this inauspicious beginning, Valette had hopes for Tripoli. In 1547 the knights' ruling council, the Chapter General, gathered in Malta to consider the state of the Order. Valette rose to speak. He contended that despite all his work in Tripoli, much still remained to be done, and quickly, as his local enemies were now petitioning for help from Suleiman. He could point to numerous drawbacks in locating the Order's headquarters in Malta — the distance from their enemies, the weak state of Malta's forts, the sheer number of Malta's forts, the uncertain water supply, and the dependence on Sicily and its Spanish masters for food. Tripoli, by contrast, had several advantages. The city, he noted, was surrounded on three sides by water and could be cut off from land entirely by a digging a moat. The soil around Tripoli was fertile and fed by springwater, capable of producing grain, fruit, wine, and oil. He pointed to his alliances with local sheiks, men who were hostile to Ottoman control. He suggested that the Order could more efficiently expand its influence throughout the region in ways impossible on the island of Malta. It might even, he suggested, be best that the Order abandon Malta and move operations to Tripoli entirely.

This last suggestion was a bit much, but Valette was persuasive and his superiors, who had never quite settled in to Malta or done much to bolster its defense works, did agree to invest more in the city.[18] Fifty more knights would be stationed in Tripoli; the governor's rank would be raised to that of a grand cross, just below that of grand master. Grand Master D'Homedes allotted seven thousand scudi, donated by various European powers, for capital improvements. The money and the troops to guard it came from Marseilles on the *Catarinetta*, a galley famous for speed.

Not enough speed on this occasion. Just off the Bay of Naples, the vessel and its treasure chest was seized, its crew held for ransom (three hundred *scudi* a head), and at a stroke Valette's hopes for an independent stronghold in North Africa were at an end.

The man leading the attack was Turgut Reis, without question the greatest disciple of Khairedihn.

+·+·+·+

There is a story, possibly true, that Valette and Turgut met face-to-face while the corsair was a captive of the Genoese. The knight greeted the prisoner with the hardheaded observation that captivity was merely *usanca da guerra*, the "custom of war"; to which the old corsair replied, *Y mudanca de fortuna*, "and change of fortune."[19]

Turgut, sometimes called Dragut, was born of Muslim peasants in 1485 near Bodrum, then as now a port city in southwestern Turkey (then held, ironically, by the Knights of St. John), and while still a boy, joined some itinerant pirates. He grew into a man of "less than average stature but extremely able-bodied"; he showed a talent for gunnery and was soon recruited to the army, in which capacity he took part in Selim the Grim's 1517 siege of Alexandria.[20] He preferred a life at sea and along with other ambitious young men headed west, where he fell in with Khairedihn, who quickly took Turgut as his protégé. They served together at Preveza, and soon he was outshining the master in daring, cruelty, and sheer encyclopedic knowledge of the Mediterranean's innumerable nooks and crannies. What Turgut's raids lacked in individual drama they more than made up for in number. He was dubbed the Drawn Sword of Islam, a title first given to Mohammed's finest general Khalid ibn al-Walid, and in his own way, Turgut was as troublesome to his enemies as al-Walid was to his. Small wonder Khairedihn paid his ransom to the Genoese.

The Knights of St. John held no terror for him — Malta and its sister island Gozo were sheep to be shorn like any other, and his many trips there each yielded intelligence that would be useful in the coming showdown. Nor was he much intimidated by the power of the Ottoman Empire. His relationship with Constantinople was at times fraught; he did not take orders well and resented Suleiman's tendency to favor men connected at court.

Nevertheless, he had Suleiman's blessing when in 1550 he gathered a small force of corsairs and with them seized three Spanish-held subsidiaries of Tunis: Susa, Monestir, and Sfax. None was much to speak of; they could be taken, they also could be retaken. What Turgut really wanted was a strong, centrally located port city, and he found one in Mahdia, halfway between Tunis and Tripoli. Mahdia's walls were high and thick, her guns clean and functional, the harbor large and sheltered. It was, like Tripoli, surrounded on three sides by water — hard to take, even for Turgut. And so he took the easy route: he suborned a greedy man in a position of power. A dark night, a purse of gold, an unlocked gate, a small spot of quick violence, and by morning Turgut was master of the town. More to the point, he had kept the defensive walls intact.

This was too much for Charles, who just a few years before had thought to take the city for the Knights of St. John. He called for men and munitions — Andrea Doria for starters; Don Garcia de Toledo, with twenty-four galleys and many men; the viceroy of Sicily; and the Knights of St. John. Whether by chance or by design, they arrived while Turgut was raiding the coasts of Italy. His absence did not make the work any easier. Over the course of some days, their cannon chipped away Mahdia's outer defenses and in due course brought a section down. It was long, slow work, however, against determined opponents, and possibly more than could be done in a season. Worse, Turgut returned in August and attacked their rear.[21] He retreated, but no doubt he would return, soon and in force. The Christian commanders met in conference that evening to discuss their next steps. Besides the renewed threat of Turgut and possibly others, autumn was coming and the expedition was ill-placed for a winter siege. It would be the better part of wisdom to cut their losses and withdraw.

And so they might have done, had not Don Garcia risen to speak. Doria might be in overall command, but as a son of the viceroy of Naples and veteran of numerous fights, Don Garcia commanded respect. He had, he said, learned from a deserter from the city that the seaward part of the wall was weaker than other parts, and that the original architects had counted on a sandbar to keep any large vessel from getting near enough to exploit this fact. He suggested that two stout galleys, each drawing very little water, might be bound together, with a platform fixed between them and a heavy battery mounted on top. The work of the cannon would be brief, the attack unexpected, and victory a strong possibility.

A few nights later, the makeshift destroyer was towed to the sandbank and stabilized with four anchors.[22] Dawn broke, the cannons fired, the wall crumbled. The knights boarded skiffs and headed toward the breach, and soon the French knight Giou reached the shattered wall and planted the flag of the Order. An arquebus bullet struck him down. Coppier, another Frenchman, took his place and the knights scrambled up beside him, targets for the Muslim cannon and arquebus fire that now clustered the breach. Guimeran, the third commander, glanced about and noticed a path to a gallery connected to a stone bridge that in turn connected to the city itself. He shouted for his men to follow, and together they opened a new phase in the attack. The knights now passed into Mahdia and advanced street by street and building by building. The untrained locals soon broke off any general defenses and ran to their homes, wives, and children, or out of the city altogether, shifting the bulk of the work on Turgut's men. The corsairs fought bravely, but the pressure was too great. Within hours the Christians had taken the city and with it all that Turgut had stored there.

✦·✦·✦·✦

It is a testimony to Turgut's reputation that this victory occasioned "a public demonstration of joy . . . throughout the city [of Rome]."[23] For Suleiman, the attack was an excuse to quash the truce with the emperor and formally demand the return of Susa, Sfax, Monastir, and Mahdia. Charles replied that they were dependencies of Tunis, an ally of the empire, and that besides, Turgut was a pirate and therefore outside the protection of law. Suleiman changed that soon enough by commissioning this pirate as an admiral of the Ottoman navy and sanjak of Santa Maura (Leucadia, Greece). Charles refused to back down. He ordered Doria to seek out and take down the new admiral once and for all.

What followed was farce. Doria was able to track down and bottle up Turgut's small fleet inside a well-defended bay at Djerba. Cannon kept him at a distance, but Doria was content to wait, confident that supply ships would keep him supplied as long as it took. Meanwhile, all Europe was captivated and eagerly read updates on the situation. An English envoy wrote home that "Dragut must either break through by force, or else escape by land, losing his galleys."[24]

Turgut had other ideas. The guns at the head of the bay kept Doria at a distance while the corsair, unseen, had his men to dig a narrow channel across the sandy soil of the island to a small river giving out on the far side of the island.[25] Within days he and his fleet had slipped away eastward. To add to the insult, the corsair's squadron ran into and captured two vessels carrying provisions to Doria, who was still waiting patiently on the far side of the island.

News of the incident spread quickly, and Spain provided ready excuses to anyone who would listen: "[Members of the imperial court] say that a great storm arose, and that Doria, seeking shelter for his navy, did harbor where hope appointed him, and in the mean season Turgut stole away."[26] Later chroniclers say nothing of a storm, only how Turgut had made Doria a laughingstock.

Turgut eventually arrived back in Constantinople to confer with Suleiman. Of course Monastir and Mahdia should be taken back, they could agree on that. But Turgut wanted more. He suggested that a better target would be the Knights of St. John, famously arguing that "unless you are rid of this nest of vipers you can accomplish nothing."[27] Turgut's motives were at once commercial — the knights interfered with his work — and personal. His brother had been killed and dragged off by the people of Gozo after a 1544 raid, then deliberately burned in Turgut's sight. If the island was to be punished, he wanted to be there.[28]

The sultan, however, preferred to reclaim Mahdia. It had, after all, been lost on Turgut's watch, and Suleiman wanted to retake his old holdings before seeking out new ones. Turgut would accompany the new Kapudan-ı Derya, Sinan Pasha, and see about taking the city back. Sinan's brother, as it happened, was Grand Vizier Rüstem Pasha, and his sister-in-law was Mihrimah, Suleiman's favorite daughter, and so his position was assured.[29] Unfortunately for Turgut, Sinan Pasha was a man with no sailing experience, no army experience, and some bad attributes. The Venetian envoy described him as "ill-mannered and quick to shoot his mouth off, irascible, or rather, vicious," and Muslim accounts call him "viciously contentious, impetuous with words, dreadful and tyrannical." At the end of this expedition, his own men elected to abandon him in North Africa and follow Turgut instead; they were dissuaded by Turgut.

For all his bad qualities, Sinan Pasha did seem shrewd enough to defer to the expert, though he was quick to shift blame if things went badly: "Letters from Malta mention that some of the Turkish prisoners have confessed that their

General had orders to attack Corfu, but perceiving how well it was fortified, he durst not meddle therewith. *He blames Torgut, upon whose representation that it was easy to be had, he attacked Malta*."[30] Unnerved by the high walls at Mahdia, and taking the order to do nothing without consulting Turgut as an excuse, he allowed himself to be talked into Malta instead.

Certainly their timing was fortunate. As of 1536 the knights had a new grand master, and a controversial one. Portraits of D'Homedes show a cadaverous-looking Spaniard with a triangular head ending in a pointed white beard and marked by hooded eyes, one blinded at Rhodes, which fact he often worked into conversation. He was now in his late seventies, and if he had possessed martial ardor in the past, it was gone by the time he reached his new office. Generally placid, but truculent when defied, he might have been a saint had he served a more gentle order. He was free with alms for the poor, and his remaining eye appreciated beauty. Beginning in 1546, he took charge of Birgu's twin peninsula in Grand Harbor, called l'Isola because of the narrow moat that separated it from the mainland, and rather than building fortresses, he created a personal garden paradise. Here the grand master housed exotic animals and cultivated a wide assortment of excellent fruits — "Paradise" apples, dates, apples, pears, plums, peaches, figs. He could stroll over mosaic-tiled pavings, pass by freshwater fountains, and gaze on a stone equestrian statue "colored green, much larger than *le Rustique* in Rome."[31]

As the garden flourished, the defenses of Malta and Gozo and Tripoli were allowed to decay. D'Homedes treated any suggestion in the spring of 1551 that there was a threat from Constantinople with "an admirable calm and firmness of spirit."[32] The arrival in July that year of Sinan Pasha and Turgut with 137 galleys was his comeuppance.[33]

They did not arrive without warning. Official dispatches and general rumor reported the presence of the armada forming in the eastern Mediterranean in May. Wrote Roger Ascham from Charles' court: "The Turks navy is come so big, that they and the French rule all *mare Mediterraneum*. This great navy brought such terror with it that the Venetians were fain afresh to double man and victual Corcyra. Sicily was afraid, Naples was afraid, Rome was afraid, Genoa was afraid, all *mare Mediterraneum* did tremble whither this great navy would go."[34] D'Homedes dismissed the reports, claiming that any Muslim galleys would be headed to Provence, since it was Spain and France that were at war, not the trifling island of Malta. Only the July 18 arrival of one hundred and fifteen ships, ten thousand men, and various siege guns in St. Paul's Bay north of Grand Harbor changed his mind.

If D'Homedes was not the best defender of Malta, Sinan Pasha was not the man best suited to take it. Much to Turgut's disgust, the pasha's considered opinion was that Fort St. Angelo was too difficult a target, and after a few of Sinan's men died of heat exhaustion, Sinan ordered his men to set off to surround the old capital city of Mdina. A contemporary described it as "distant six miles from [Fort St. Angelo], situated upon the top of a mountain, environed on three parts with great valleys full of gravel and large stones very painful to walk on."[35] That city too seemed daunting, though in fact its defenses were largely a matter of local citizens lined up on the ramparts dressed as soldiers. This Potemkin village, all fraudulent make-believe disguising genuine weakness, combined with the lateness of the season and new rumors that Doria was headed toward Malta, was enough to convince Sinan to pack up and leave.

Perhaps to assuage Turgut and his corsairs, perhaps uneasy that he had failed in taking Mahdia, or Fort St. Angelo, or Mdina, Sinan Pasha did agree to one last gesture. Gozo, sister island to Malta, was ripe for the taking. What followed was tragedy.

When the invasion fleet was first sighted, Governor Galatian de Sesse requested that Gozo's women, children, aged, and infirm be sent to Malta proper, thinking it the safer place. D'Homedes refused, saying that their presence would stiffen the resolve of Gozo's men. He was mistaken. The walled castle of Gozo into which all had taken refuge resisted for three days of furious bombardment; some civilians took to sliding down ropes to escape, which was sign enough for Sesse to open the gates. The Ottomans ransacked the town. Six thousand islanders, mostly women and children, including Sesse, were carried off into slavery, save forty whose safety he had negotiated — people too old to be worth much on the rowing bench or slave block. It wasn't all that Turgut had wanted, but it was a victory, and in any event, the campaign was not over. The next stop, and the last chance for Sinan Pasha to show his mettle, was Tripoli.

Here he was in luck. Physical structures had again been allowed to deteriorate, and Gaspard de Vallier, the commander who succeeded Valette at Tripoli, had been allotted only three hundred knights and two hundred soldiers, mostly peasants and criminals from Calabria with little to no military experience.[36] The armada had been expected and the noncombatants of Tripoli evacuated, with unfortunate results: "His navy has summoned Tripoli to surrender; letters say the inhabitants have prayed a respite till they may send to the Grand Master of Malta, and have sent out two ships laden with women, children, and old folks, which are reported to have fallen into the Turk's hands."[37] The guns could be heard back in Malta, which must have unnerved D'Homedes.

Meanwhile, Gabriel de Luetz, Baron et Seigneur d'Aramon, the French ambassador to Constantinople, and his secretary, Nicholas de Nicolay, chanced to stop at Malta on their way home. D'Homedes, desperate for help, asked them to head south and try to persuade Sinan to bargain. D'Aramon made no promises, but agreed to make a detour and do what he could.

What he could do was very little. As a Frenchman and therefore an ally, he was politely received by Sinan. Gifts were exchanged: twenty-five sheep for the ambassador, fine cloth and a small clock for the pasha. D'Aramon nevertheless was unable to dissuade Sinan from his purpose in taking Tripoli. Until the knights surrendered, the game was on. D'Aramon was, of course, welcome to remain as an honored guest to see the outcome.

The outcome was a foregone conclusion. The Calabrians, who had not been told that they were going to Tripoli in the first place, demanded that Vallier surrender in the touching hope that, once having surrendered, they could go home. Even the Spanish knights concurred. Vallier put the matter to a vote, the motion carried, and on August 13, two Spanish knights went to negotiate terms.

The terms were diabolical. All allied Muslim soldiers were killed outright. All Christian mercenaries and volunteers (a good number of them Maltese) were to be enslaved. All the surviving knights were free to return to Malta. The terms were accepted, and, according to reports, rapidly broken; two hundred of the strongest soldiers were put to galleys, and the remaining men, women, and children killed without mercy.[38] True or not, Sinan Pasha had, at a stroke, both humiliated the Order and ruined its future credibility.

His action also threw the Order itself into turmoil. D'Homedes, faced with the twin failures of Gozo and Tripoli, needed a scapegoat. Once D'Aramon had, out of courtesy, escorted the knights back to Malta, the grand master not only had Vallier and two Spanish knights arrested, unfrocked, and charged with cowardice and treason, but also jailed the diplomat himself on a charge of inciting the Turks and, illogically, favoring the French. It was both a contravention of diplomatic immunity and a slap in the face of a man who had gone out of his way to help. Dubious witnesses were hauled in — a convicted forger, a Muslim convert who had sold his children into slavery, and a gunner who had been caught (and been forgiven for) trying to surrender at Tripoli. D'Homedes also arranged for a tame secular judge who had the power to decree a death penalty. It eventually would take the combined intervention of the kings of France and Spain to get D'Aramon released (neither monarch wanted a fight over such trivia as this); Vallier and the two Spaniards were not so lucky and were imprisoned for some years, and bitter feelings between the *langues* remained.

The whole affair was a scandal, and Pope Julius III clearly was concerned with the state of the Order. Although it had been trouble for the knights from the outset and its loss a great weight off them, nevertheless, "Tripoli, from whence the Turk may easily and suddenly, whensoever he list, set upon Siciliy, Naples, or any coast of Italy or Spain, so that the gain of Tunis is thought nothing comparable with the loss of Tripoli."[39] The pope suggested to D'Homedes that the knights might feel safer in Syracuse or Messina, that perhaps Malta was too great a burden for the knights and might be defended better by Spanish troops. The offer was declined, but the sting of it was considerable. If even the pope had lost faith in the knights, what purpose could they possibly serve?

5

+·+·+·+

DJERBA,
1551–1560

+·+·+·+

Los Gelves, madre, malos son de ganar.
(Djerba! Ah, mother, a misfortune to conquer.)

The Order made one brief attempt to restore the honor lost at Tripoli. Valette, now general of the land force, and Leone Strozzi, prior of Capua and general of the galleys, set out on August 6, 1552, with three hundred knights and twelve hundred foot for the fortress of Zoara, west of Tripoli. The locals drove them back into the sea. D'Homedes saw the expedition as a chance to brush Gozo and Tripoli aside, or at least lay new blame on his French and Italian brethren. "This," he claimed piously, "is the greatest defeat that the Order has suffered after that of Rhodes."[1]

To his credit, he did belatedly recognize the need to establish better defense works on Malta, and a year after the disaster at Tripoli did lay the foundation stones for what would become Fort St. Michael on the area then known simply as l'Isola. He also looked into improvements for Fort St. Elmo, the small fort that first greeted all ships entering Grand Harbor. D'Homedes finally died on September 6, 1553, aged eighty-three. D'Homedes's will, written three days earlier, left the bulk of his fortune not, as was customary, to the Order, but to his nephews. The knights were outraged, but powerless. It was left to the poor of Malta to weep at his death and honor him for his habits of charity.

+·+·+·+

Back on the continent, Charles was still struggling to consolidate Italy into, if not part of the empire, then at the very least a passive client. The Italian wars, a series of fifteenth-century conflicts for power and land, largely between France and the Habsburg Empire and including most of the city-states of Italy, make for depressing reading, but were a valuable training ground for such military luminaries as the one-eyed Ascanio Della Corgna, who commanded the five thousand papal troops recruited from the papal dominions against French and native forces at the 1555 siege of Siena. It is likely that this is where he first met Don Garcia de Toledo, then commanding some of Charles's twelve thousand Spanish, Italian, and German soldiers. Here too was Chiappino Vitelli, first of Tuscany's Knights of St. Stephen and frequent soldier of Don Garcia's brother-in-law, Cosimo I de' Medici, then Duke of Florence and later Grand Duke of Tuscany.

Suleiman was, however, sidetracked by war with Persia, which forced him to take three hundred thousand men east. He needed someone to keep Charles occupied, just as Khairedihn had done in the old days. Turgut, described as "some time a pirate and now the Turk's chief doer in all the affairs of Africa and the *mare Mediterraneo*" was the obvious choice.[2]

There was a snag. Two years before, Turgut had attacked a Venetian vessel whose commander he thought insufficiently respectful (no presents, no dipping of sails — the captain had wanted to get home quickly and perhaps was not aware that the other ship belonged to Turgut). To soothe his wounded honor, Turgut killed the crew and burned the barge. Word of this reached Venice, and her ambassadors lodged a protest with Grand Vizier Rüstem Pasha.[3] As Suleiman was courting Venice at the time, the odds were good that some kind of justice would be done. Turgut did not wait to find out. He packed up and headed to Morocco, beyond the influence of the Grand Porte, and remained there for the next two years, happily raiding the coast of Spain.

He was, however, too valuable a resource for Suleiman to dispense with altogether. Sinan Pasha had not really been up to the job; even as he had taken Tripoli in 1551, his own men revolted and tried to sail off with Turgut. What to do? Sinan Pasha had not really been up to the job of senior naval commander, but he had connections. Sadly, Ottoman meritocracy did not always extend to the highly self-willed Barbary corsairs, no matter how talented. Turgut would, when Sinan Pasha died in 1553, also lose out on the title of Kapudan Pasha, which went to a rising young mariner named Piali Pasha. But he was named beylerbey of Tripoli, an honor he had expected back when he helped Sinan Pasha take the place, but which Sinan then gave to another subordinate. Reconciled with Suleiman, Turgut accepted the sultan's request that he take sixty ships and join France in attacking Genoese-held Elba and Corsica. By 1558 the corsair was willing to join the Ottoman fleet, commanded by the young Piali Pasha, as second-in-command, and happily savaged the coasts of Naples, going as far west as Minorca. (For his part, Turgut is known to have fought Vitelli near Maremma during the Siena war.)

✦·✦··✦·✦

Back on Malta, the knights had elected Claude de la Sengle to succeed D'Homedes. The new grand master committed the Order to the task of fortifying the island, bringing in military architects from Italy to make estimates for what could be done. On August 18, 1557, Grand Master Sengle died and left sixty thousand crowns to the Order and his name to l'Isola, the peninsula that holds Fort St. Michael, to be called ever after Senglea. The council took only one day to choose Valette as his successor.

Money was his first concern. Priories belonging to the Order throughout Europe, some of which had not paid their obligations in years, were now enjoined to disgorge accordingly. Malta itself was squeezed. Ancient rights and privileges of her inhabitants over such matters as the appointment of Malta's bishop, respected under the previous four grand masters, were suddenly ignored, taxes increased, sumptuary laws instituted (a civilian in overly garish pants might expect a turn at the galley oars). When Mattew (aka Giuseppe) Callus, a leading Maltese citizen, attempted to protest these new excesses, he was summarily arrested and executed.[4]

The number and extent of the Order's raids in the eastern Mediterranean were increased. The defenses of Birgu and St. Michael were improved, as was Fort St. Elmo. Valette solicited Venetian merchants in Constantinople to report any and all information useful to the Order and paid them to do so. By whatever means necessary, the new grand master was preparing himself, the island, and the Order for whatever chance might bring.

Time, meanwhile, had been delivering its inexorable changes. In 1556 Charles abdicated his Spanish throne to his son Philip II and his archdukedom to his brother Ferdinand I. Charles retired to a quiet life in a monastery, surrounded by walls mounted with clocks. Five years later Philip signed the treaty of Cateau-Cambrésis, which brought peace between Spain and France, and put thousands of European mercenaries out of work. Human nature and politics being what they are, they would not be unemployed for long. Valette saw a good use for such men, as did Juan de La Cerda, courtier to Philip, fourth duke of Medinaceli, and newly appointed viceroy of Sicily.

This was a significant post, dripping with real power that La Cerda seemed eager to use. The timing was good; Sunni Ottomans were once again fighting Shiite Persians for political and religious dominance in the Muslim world. Philip, an armchair general unlike his father, had sent off imperial troops to a serious defeat in 1558 at Mostaganem in Algeria, and could use an easy conquest to boost his own standing. Valette sent an envoy to Philip pointing out that Tripoli under Turgut was turning into another Algiers, only closer to Sicily and Italy, and in need of a good trouncing. La Cerda was preparing a second letter to the same effect when word came back that, as of June 15, 1559, Philip was entirely in agreement. Turgut Reis must be destroyed.

Valette immediately ordered up four hundred knights under Fra Carlo Urre de Tessières, captain general of the Order's galleys, along with fifteen hundred soldiers and support personnel; he himself would remain in Malta. Genoa's Andrea Doria, now aged ninety-three, provided eleven galleys, and to command them, his great-nephew Giovanni Andrea (aka Gianandrea), aged twenty-one and son of Giannettino, captor of Turgut.

Gianandrea Doria lost his father at age six, and was taken under the wings of his elder relative. An early teacher reported his charge as "agreeable, of a lively intelligence. He has already read Caesar's commentaries."[5] In his memoirs, the younger Doria reports that he had accompanied the elder Doria to sea at age eight, had commanded "many galleys" at age fourteen, and at fifteen, commanded all his granduncle's generals.[6] At sixteen he outfitted eight ships, which he would lend to the Spanish. In 1558 he effectively chased the Ottoman fleet under Piali Pasha away from the Italian peninsula. People grew up fast in those days.

For the Djerba expedition, in addition to Doria's fleet came another five galleys from Genoa, five from Naples, four from Sicily, three from the pope, four each from Malta and Florence, and eleven others from various unaffiliated adventurers. La Cerda was not so efficient. He was limited to the Spanish squadron in Sicily, and slow to gather mercenaries from Florence, Genoa, Savoy, Naples, and the Papal States.

La Cerda might be in command, but Philip wanted an experienced captain in charge of the actual troops. He appointed Don Álvaro de Sande, a sort of Spanish Falstaff, a tough, energetic, veteran of nearly thirty years' service, stout from an energetic fondness for food, who gyrated between self-pity and high-flying exuberance and jokes.[7] Sande had been intended by hopeful parents for the priesthood but found his natural medium in war. He served Charles in most of his battles — Mühlberg, Algiers, and notably at the siege of St. Dizier, where he and a colleague had been badly injured, "faces, hands and legs burnt to the bones."[8] The following day, his troops saw him being carried to the front on a chair, on which he swore he would remain until the siege was over. Now forty-eight, he was the watchful eye over the more junior and ebullient commanders, among them Don Sancho de Leyva in command of the Italians, and Tessières in command of the knights.

After a wasted summer and fall, and a grueling voyage from Messina to Malta in early winter, La Cerda arrived at Malta in December, sufficiently undone that he called for a temporary rest. December flowed into January, during which time Valette, anxious for spring and good sailing weather, struggled to provide hospitality for La Cerda and his men. Cramped quarters precipitated disease; the Order's infirmary soon filled with sick men, of whom nearly two thousand died in bed. Not until February 14 were upward of fifty-four warships and thirty-six support vessels from various Christian powers finally able to weigh anchor for Tripoli. It took some fortitude to be out in such weather, and Leyva's crew was surprised to see two Muslim merchantmen off the coast of Kantara. In easier weather, the Italians might have given chase, and as things turned out, it was unfortunate that they did not.

The delays had cost them any hope of surprise. Had the expedition arrived six months earlier, it might well have taken the city. By the time they landed, however, Turgut had been able to bolster Tripoli's defenses to the point that La Cerda's bravado had turned to caution. Better, he said, to take Djerba than Tripoli. It would be an admirable base of operations against Turgut's fortified city as well as against the Barbary corsairs. (Kâtip Çelebi makes the curious observation that Tripoli had Arabs "known for their disloyalty/cowardice," which suggests another missed opportunity for La Cerda.[9])

The knights, wanting only to get back Tripoli, accused La Cerda of bad faith. Others, sick and tired and motivated chiefly by greed, just wanted to abandon the operation as so much bad luck. They might have had a point. Djerba was flat and its waters shallow, poor for navigation; fresh water was scarce, and the natives uncertain. Catalans had landed in 1284 under Roger de Lauria, but abandoned it as more trouble than it was worth. Pedro de Navarro tried to regain it in 1510 and failed, a rare failure in that general's long run of North African conquests. Ten years later, Hugo de Moncada, viceroy of Sicily, had purely nominal control of the place — local sheiks still entertained Muslim pirates operating from their shores. Then there was the humiliation of Turgut's escape from Doria in 1551, still fresh in the minds of all those present. Djerba truly was an island of bad fortune for Spain.

Nevertheless, La Cerda's will prevailed. On March 1, the entire force embarked once more and returned to Djerba, anchoring in heavy seas, waiting for enough calm to beach the ships. It would be another five days and nights, five days exposed to the cold and wet on rolling galleys, before they could disembark and get on with the task of conquering the island.

Someone — exactly who is a mystery — arranged for the first official account of the expedition, an unsigned letter to the king, to be published in Bologna.[10] It's a brief narrative, highlighting the uncooperative weather, the slogging on the island, the hostile reception, Don Álvaro's slight leg wound, Turgut's humiliating retreat, Spain's ultimate victory. Tripoli is not mentioned at all, nor is the threat of the Ottoman fleet, nor the fierce arguments between La Cerda's partisans (Sande), who wanted to stay, and Doria's (the Knights of St. John), who wanted to leave. Again, La Cerda prevailed.

For the optimists, there remained only the task of rebuilding the fort on the far north side of the island. If the Ottomans were to come, it would not be before June, plenty of time to consolidate the Spanish hold on the island and return in triumph to Sicily and Spain.

Tessières sent Romegas back to Malta to inform Valette of the situation. The grand master was not pleased, but there was little he could do other than withdrawing the greater part of his own men. That Tripoli had been sidelined was only part of the problem. The proposed fort was problematic at best, described by a near-contemporary historian as "absent of all man-made and natural advantages, in a remote site without fresh water and without a harbor, which made it impossible to send for any outside aid."[11]

The footsoldiers expected to defend the place apparently had their own doubts about the place. One carved a sonnet over the entrance. It takes the form of a dialogue between author and fort and ends:

Quien te defendera? Non se por cierto.
Que socorro ternas? Solo del cielo.

Who will defend you? I cannot say for certain.
What help will you have? Only that of heaven.[12]

Soldiers who dared were beginning to slink away. They had signed up for combat, of which they had seen little, and for the possible sacking of Tripoli, of which they had seen nothing. Their enlistment terms were nearly up; they had business to attend to. There were locals to rob.

As if this were not enough, the invaders began to fall ill again. Even the Knights of St. John, sticklers for cleanliness, were not spared, and in a few weeks, Fra Urre de Tessières was forced to return to Malta, which put Valette in an awkward position. Would he be within his rights to withdraw his knights entirely? Would it be more politic to support the viceroy, and in consequence the new king, by pushing on? In the end, he ordered replacements for the knights.

Despite disease and wayward soldiers, La Cerda did manage to get an outer wall erected around the central keep. By May 6, the viceroy could announce that he had secured what needed securing and Djerba was now a Spanish protectorate, its days as a clearinghouse for Christian slaves over. What he did not know was that the two merchantmen seen earlier had in fact belonged to Uludj Ali, a Calabrian renegade and lieutenant of Turgut, who had brought news of the armada to Constantinople. Suleiman had dispatched an armada of his own. Four days after La Cerda's announcement of victory, word came from Malta that eighty-six Ottoman galleys had landed at Gozo, robbed it, torched it, and interrogated prisoners. The historian Zekeriyyāzādé (one of Piali's lieutenants on this expedition) claims that the message stated: "The Turks' ships have come, leave the fortress, otherwise they will cut your worthless heads, or they will take you into abject captivity."[13] The message further stated that the armada was heading south, though it could not confirm the target, or indeed whether Piali knew La Cerda's location. (He did.)[14]

Squabbling among the Christians began all over again. The fort was secure, the fort was at risk; the men were firm, the men were unreliable. Gianandrea Doria, ill and confined to bed, argued that it was time to cut and run, but La Cerda would not budge. The Turks might be sailing west, he agreed, but their destination was Tripoli, not Djerba. In any event, storms at sea these past two days must have caused considerable damage to the armada. Besides, as long as Spain held the fort, how dangerous could the Ottomans be?

The answer came the next morning when the Ottoman fleet under the newly promoted grand admiral, Piali Pasha, appeared on the horizon.

Piali Pasha, a "lion tall as a mountain, a crocodile of the sea," so the story went, had been found abandoned as an infant after the siege of Belgrade in 1521, scooped up and brought back to Constantinople, where he was put through the imperial system, eventually graduating from the *Enderûn* school.[15] Described by a Venetian envoy as slightly below average in height, with black hair and pallid skin, he was appointed fleet commander in 1555, in which capacity he supported the French siege of Calvi in that year, captured Oran the following year, Bizerta the year after that, and raided Minorca the year after that.[16] Much of his maritime service was alongside Turgut, nominally as his superior, more realistically as his student. (Oddly, the Venetian envoy to Constantinople in 1562 considered him amiable and humane, but not very bright.)[17]

By now the Ottomans had heard about the Spanish *tercios* and did not, according to Ogier Ghiselin de Busbecq (ambassador to Constantinople for Holy Roman Emperor Ferdinand I), imagine that facing such men would be easy. "So great was their apprehension that many of them, thinking that they were bound on a desperate adventure from which they might never return to Constantinople, made their last will and testament before setting out. The whole city was full of alarm and everyone, whether he embarked or stayed at home, was harassed by grave doubt as to how the expedition might end."[18] Busbecq was, of course, writing for a European audience and well after the fact.

Kâtip Çelebi, writing for the Ottomans, says nothing about any alleged Ottoman fears. He notes only that Piali Pasha approached, anchored twelve miles off Djerba the night before, and lay in wait for whatever the next day would bring.[19] (Zekeriyyāzādé says that the Christians went out seven or eight miles and dropped anchor in the darkness of night. When the sun rose, they were astonished to see the "masts of the imperial fleet, thick as a forest.")[20]

If Piali was worried, he needn't have been. Gianandrea Doria was physically unwell and clearly unable to have the ships line up in battle formation and defy the enemy. And so the Christian captains panicked. Left to their own devices and desperate to flee, the various ships jostled and crashed into one another, creating a gridlock that only a lucky few at the edges could break free of. Worse, the wind changed direction and favored the Ottomans.

Piali Pasha saw all this, but was momentarily constrained by the need to finish morning prayers. Once he was finished, he didn't hesitate. Piali ordered the sails unfurled. He judged the risk of Christian artillery bringing down the yards on his men to be negligible, the advantage of extra running speed against the disordered enemy enormous. So eager were some captains for battle that they ordered the cables to be cut rather than take time to weigh anchor.[21]

The sea battle was short and furious. A crescent of eighty-five Ottoman ships bore down on a confusion of forty-eight Christian vessels.[22] Nineteen Spanish galleys and a dozen other Christian ships were destroyed.[23] Five thousand Christian prisoners were taken, among them, La Cerda's son, Gaston.[24] Those not captured, including much of the army, were beaten back to the fort. A few Christian vessels had managed to get out, but Piali Pasha, "who slays lions and dispatches dragons," ordered twenty-six galleys to chase them down, seizing, among other prizes, the commander of the papal forces.[25] "In sum," reports Çelebi, "on that day the infidel fleet suffered total destruction — never before had there been a defeat of this magnitude."[26]

Night fell. Inside the fort, La Cerda recognized at last his own limits as a military man and turned the responsibility for evacuating the surviving soldiers over to Doria, who replied that, as fleet commander, he was responsible only for getting word back to Sicily. The young admiral planned to sail a small boat through the Ottoman fleet to "rally the sad remnants of our defeat."[27] La Cerda included himself among those who would sneak out that night in one of the five vessels, first for Malta, then to Sicily.[28] They left behind the sounds of riotous Ottomans savoring victory, and the silence of those men ordered to remain within the fort that the viceroy had hoped would make him a great man.

Piali's victory over the Christian fleet, spectacular as it was, would not necessarily translate into victory over the army. Turgut arrived some days later, as did some mainland Arab horsemen.[29] Because the waters were shallow near that part of the island, his ships lay a good way offshore, while his cannons and men were on land. Should the Spanish send a relief force — and Valette had gotten a letter to Sande suggesting that help was coming — those ships would be at risk, the Ottoman forces stranded. Djerba was far from Constantinople, and not all of Piali's coreligionists on the island could be relied upon.

Sande would have come to the same conclusion. The sailing season was still young. Much of the Spanish fleet was intact, and Malta and its knights were not so very far away. Moreover, the fort was by now reasonably strong. Contemporary pictures show the fort as a rectangular affair surrounded by a sea-fed moat, and an irregular four-pointed star also surrounded by a moat, and with good cross-fire capabilities. There were some seventy guns of varying sizes, a good supply of ammunition, and food enough for four months, food being grain and biscuits, salted meat, and a few living horses.[30] Of water, there was less.

With a weather eye on the horizon, Piali ordered his guns drawn up outside the fort and had them pour a steady hail of stone and iron ball. It was slow work, as the guns were relatively small bore, not the large bombards or mortars that a proper siege would have demanded. Nevertheless, with each strike, another piece of stone and mortar chipped, cracked, or shattered and tumbled down into the moat. The defenders did what they could to repair the damage, and each side tried to calculate who would come to the end of his resources first.

By now, the grim news had reached Europe, and Philip's initial instinct was to order Don Garcia de Toledo to mount a rescue operation. The urgency abated somewhat when both La Cerda and Andrea Doria were back in Sicily, and Philip began to take a more measured view. The men in the fort, he noted, were professionals. De Sande, after all, had endured the 1554 siege of Valsenieres by eating "cats, dogs, rats, and anything else he could get his hands on."[31] The enemy would have to abandon the siege eventually. If Sande could hold out for the summer — and there was no reason to suppose he could not — then time would have done the Christians' work for them. Come September, bad weather would force Piali Pasha home. Senseless to send good ships after bad. Let time and God's favor sort these problems out.

Spring shimmered into summer and with it arose the appalling heat of the southern Mediterranean. The Ottomans kept at their labors and managed to create a small breach in the outer wall. This was disconcerting, but it was not enough to allow an army through, not as long as Sande was in charge. Sande did what he could to keep up morale. He ordered a few sorties from behind the walls from time to time, but although one came close to taking Turgut himself, these expeditions accomplished little more than adding to the death toll. ("Their heads were struck off and stuck on the ends of halberds, then planted in the trenches under their very eyes.")[32] On the plus side, fewer men meant more provisions for those who remained.

In late June, Piali Pasha reported to Constantinople that the siege would probably have to be cut short, as they could not storm the fort and could not starve the defenders out. In truth, the problem was not food, but water. The fort's two large cisterns normally were filled by seasonal rains. Rain was slight that season. Worse, one of the containers was located between the fort's central keep and its outer walls. On July 21, the Turks broke through the outer wall, and at a stroke slashed the Christians' water supply.[33] Sande immediately put the men on half-rations.

Nothing will concentrate the mind like thirst. Busbecq, who became closely acquainted with Sande, described the scene as it was told to him:

"Many of them were to be seen stretched on the ground on the point of death, with their mouths agape and continually repeating the single word, 'water.' If anyone took pity on them and poured a little water into their mouths, they revived and sat up and remained in that posture until the effect of the water wore off, when they fell back again and eventually expired from thirst. Many died in this manner every day in addition to those who perished fighting or from disease and the complete lack of medical stores in that desolate spot."[34]

Soon men were slipping out of the fort and surrendering just to get a drink. Even slavery was preferable to this sort of death. Sande, alarmed, called for a solution, and a Sicilian engineer was able to oblige. From the material at hand, he managed to jury-rig an alembic, and through boiling and distilling was able to turn salt water into a limited amount of fresh. Imitators with a view toward quick money soon followed. Extra water could be had for a piastre a cup. The price doubled, then fell to nothing once Sande caught on.

By July 27, wood to fire the alembics gave out. Only three days' worth of water remained. That night Sande rallied the remaining force for one last battle. Under a thin sliver of a moon, the Christian men rushed the Ottoman trenches and fought for two hours with considerable cost to both sides. At the end of that time, the Christians split into two parts, one falling back to the fort, the other, headed by Sande, heading for the shore, hoping to grab a boat and escape the island. He didn't make it. In the garbled version of the English ambassador from Messina, "Don Alvaro de Sandi, the General, after making a sally to obtain water, was taken in the said fort, after having fought bravely for two days."[35]

The Ottoman account was less generous: "[Sande] threw himself into the water apparently either to drown or, if taken prisoner, to pass unrecognized.

Some warriors from among those who themselves had been prisoners recognized that accursed one, saying 'This is the one who was the leader of the troublemakers, and the source of stubbornness and mischief!'"[36] Senior Ottoman officers prevented his being lynched.

Soon after, the final holdouts still inside the fort finally surrendered, though quickly regretted doing so. Piali's own report states that "the champions of the faith, without compassion or pity, raised the Muslim war cry, penetrated the fort, and put all its wicked infidels to the sword."[37]

The half-broken fort on which La Cerda had pinned his hopes had lasted less than three months. Djerba was back in Muslim hands, and by August the Ottoman fleet could sail home in victory. In a deliberate snub at their enemies, the fleet breezed past Malta and stopped for water at the neighboring island of Gozo. Unable to take Piali Pasha on in battle, Valette apparently tried to ransom some prisoners, and failing that, to provide Sande with some biscuit, wine, cloth, and other provisions.[38] (The king of France was also informed that, despite the excellent relations between the Ottomans and his country, it would not be possible to release French captives who had "fought with the enemy.")[39]

The shame of his nephew's defeat was said to have killed Andrea Doria. He was ninety-three. Whether blame attaches more to Gianandrea Doria or La Cerda can be argued. Doria lost the battle; La Cerda made the battle inevitable. Whatever the result, it was Doria's name that continued into history in years to come, generally as less than heroic or effective. They each wrote their accounts and made their excuses; and some years after this affair, La Cerda was made viceroy of Navarre, then later served in the Lowlands, where he resigned after less than a year of ineffective work. His position as viceroy of Sicily was taken by Don Garcia de Toledo, hero of Mahdia. Gianandrea Doria would get a second, and even a third chance to prove himself worthy of his great-uncle.

This was in the future. For now, Piali Pasha was in his glory. Early word of his initial victory reached Constantinople in June. The man himself returned in triumph that September, his galleys filled, if not with treasure at least with some interesting captives, many of them suitable for ransom. Busbecq, who was present at the time, describes the scene — the exuberant crowd, the local Christians being cheerfully abused on the streets, the prisoners marching in chains through the ancient streets of Constantinople. Suleiman watched it all, betraying no emotion of any kind. Busbecq would soon find himself as the de facto intermediary for these men, supplementing their diet of black bread and water with lamb broth and their sleeping quarters with blankets; many died regardless. The high ranking among them appear to have largely recovered from their ordeal. Men who weeks before were parched for water now expected comfort and deference, and ordered the long-suffering Busbecq to find them decent clothing, food, and wine.[40]

Suleiman, who always had an eye for talent, took a personal interest in Sande. Never one to gloat over a defeated rival, the sultan tried to bring the Spaniard to the side of the faithful. Perhaps he could lead troops against the Persians? Would he like to be bey of Egypt? Sande refused and was put in a single room overlooking the Black Sea in the Tower of the Dog, tantamount to a death sentence. Two years later, Emperor Ferdinand bought his freedom for eighty thousand escudos and the return of twenty-five Turkish prisoners.[41] Sande and Busbecq, who arranged the matter, traveled together overland to Vienna, Sande in high spirits, Busbecq paying his meals and lodging.

Back on Djerba, the Christian dead had one more role to play. With the battle won, the bones of the dead of the garrison were gathered and placed in a pyramidal structure twenty-five feet high and sixty feet in circumference, plastered over and known thereafter as the *Burj er Roos*, the Tower of Skulls. This grisly rebuke remained in place, slowly deteriorating and revealing its contents, for nearly three hundred years until 1848, when local Christians had it dismantled and the bones interred in the Catholic cemetery.

6

+·+·+·+

AN ALMOST-PEACEFUL
INTERIM, 1561–1564

+·+·+·+

May God see fit, for the good of Christendom,
to appease the heart of this lord, and divert his forces elsewhere,
for it is impossible that this great naked fury will fall on any place
without leaving a pitiful spectacle and testimony of cruelty.

French ambassador to Catherine de' Medici,
January 20, 1565, Constantinople,

Djerba may have been a pyrrhic victory. Soon after the fleet returned home,
plague broke out in Constantinople: "On his death bed [Grand Vizier Rüstem
Pasha] besought the Turk to deliver such prisoners as were taken at Gerbes;
for he thought the pestilence at Constantinople was caused through their
detention, and he left forty thousand ducats to buy slaves with, in their stead."[1]

Djerba was a blow to the West, and a personal disappointment to Gianandrea Doria — the island seemed determined to embarrass members of the
Doria family — but it was not the utter catastrophe for Spain that some historians have made it out to be. By 1561 Philip had rebuilt most of the ships he
had lost, and though, as John Guilmartin points out, he lost a good number of
maritime experts at Djerba, Aguareles notes that Spanish prisoners were ransomed quickly, if at great cost.[2] Doria was quickly replaced as admiral-in-chief
by his adopted son, Marco Antonio Carretto Doria, who "hoist[ed] his flag
at Naples where he will sail with the whole fleet in search of Dragut."[3] That
same year we read in passing that "Spain has thirty-one galleys, and four of
the Duke of Savoy's had gone towards Naples from Civita Vecchia to join

the twenty-two which are there. Marc Antonio Carretta [*sic*] is general of all the army, having aboard the galleys three thousand Spaniards, which will be employed against Tunis."[4] (It didn't happen, and Philip was to lose these ships the following year at Herradura to a sudden hurricane — such was life on the Mediterranean — and they would again be rebuilt.)

So Christian galleys continued to sail, and if they did not venture much farther east than the waters around Sicily, they hadn't done so in years anyway. This is not to say that Christendom was complacent. Far from it. Turgut and other Barbarossa protégés were still very active along the Italian and Spanish coasts, and in 1561 "the corsairs have done much harm, especially in Puglia where, landing three or four hundred at a time, they took a great number of persons."[5] Rumors came west that Suleiman's daughter had offered to finance four hundred ships to invade Malta. The same year Pope Clement, "fearing for Malta, has sent thither Ascanio Della Corgna" — not for the final time, as we shall see.[6] Invasion rumors were credible enough again in early 1564 for Valette to order all knights in Europe to report to the island and for all noncombatants to leave. False alarms, in both cases.

Why nothing? Suleiman was again distracted by local problems of increasing population, decreasing food, rising inflation, riots, and plague, which killed off an estimated eighty thousand, including a large number of slave oarsmen, whose absence would make it impossible to dispatch "as many slave [powered] ships as in prior years."[7] A Venetian envoy adds to this list, curiously, love of peace and fear that his son Selim might attempt usurpation just as his namesake, Suleiman's father, had done.[8] Suleiman also was troubled by age — he was now sixty-five. He had outlived his great rivals. Charles V had abdicated in 1556 and died in 1558, Francis I in 1547. There was also the matter of his succession.

+·+·+·+

The process of ensuring a stable Ottoman dynasty was ruthlessly pragmatic — there must be sons, and once a new sultan was named, there must not be living rivals to the throne. The first part was easy: when the urge struck the sultan, one woman was chosen, bathed, clothed, and brought to his bed chamber. Rewards came to those who bore sons, but once they had done so, they were retired from the harem. Suleiman's good fortune had been to be an only child. His own sons were not so lucky. They knew the winner-take-all tradition —

and the fate of the losers. So did their mothers. Foremost among this number was Hurrem, a Circassian Russian, better known to the West as Roxelana.

The French diplomat Nicolay describes her as not classically beautiful but possessing a lively nature and the ability to entertain the sultan with chitchat.[9] Suleiman, still in his twenties, was beguiled. He allowed her to be seen with him in public. She was said to give him political advice. She was believed to "retain his affection by love charms and magic arts."[10] It was all very scandalous, and worse followed. She provided him a son, and though by custom Suleiman should have discarded her, he did not. She, however, refused to sleep with him unless he married her, and in time she got her way.

If she was merely conniving, she played her part remarkably well. She poured out letters to him at his every absence, letters by turns formal, playful, pleading, loving. Over the years, she bore him four more sons and one much-favored daughter, Mihrimah.

As to his successor, Suleiman tried to be scientific about the selection process. He appointed each of his sons as governor of a province, where they could learn the craft of government. Mustapha, his eldest son (but not Hurrem's), proved very capable indeed as sanjak-bey of Magnesia, modern-day Manisa on the east coast of Turkey. By charm, by efficiency, by looks, and by character, Mustapha achieved the loyalty of his soldiers and his subjects. Hurrem's sons did not measure up. Of course, he would have to go.

This took time and careful planning, and Hurrem worked long and hard. Pillow talk alone would not be enough. Pressure must come from outside. Alliances must be cultivated. She arranged for her daughter Mihrimah to marry Rüstem Pasha, a rising official and soon to be the grand vizier. Once he was family, he must become an enemy of Mustapha.

Mustapha's excellence was used against him. Rumors were planted. Why did his mother prefer Magnesia over Constantinople? What did she and her son talk about? Could he be cut from the same cloth as his parricide grandfather Selim?

By 1552, Roger Ascham, writing from the court of Charles V, reports that Mustapha was "given to all mischief, cruel, false, getting he careth not how unjustly and spending he careth not how unthriftily, whatsoever he may lay his hand on; wily in making for his purpose and ready to break for his profit, all covenanants . . . ; he is a seeker of strife and war, a great mocker of mean men, a sore oppressor of poor men, openly contemning God and a bent enemy against Christ's name and Christian men."[11] In 1552 Mustapha was to lead an army against Persia, and the rumors grew louder. What was the son doing at the head of such a large army, an army that Suleiman himself had commanded with such skill in the past? What would the masses think?

Suleiman needed little persuasion. He headed east, arrived near Mustapha's army and set up camp. The son, surprised by this unexpected arrival, hurried to his father's quarters. He never got there. While Suleiman, impassive, sat upright on a cushion inside his tent and listened, assassins garroted his son with a bowstring. On the battlefield, the enemy was put to flight, the Persian crisis passed, but Suleiman was never quite the same. The death was said to have affected Cihangir, Suleiman's youngest child by Hurrem. He was both well educated and clever and thought that since his severe hunchback precluded him from taking the throne, Suleiman might allow him to live; his mother brutally disabused him of this hope, and it was with that knowledge that he died in 1553, some say of grief.[12]

Succession was now between Hurrem's two surviving sons, Bayazid and Selim. It could not turn out well. Busbecq writes that she favored Bayazid, and she may well have done.[13] But Hurrem died in 1558, leaving the matter unsettled. Suleiman placed Bayazid far to the east. Fearful of reprising Mustapha's fate, he rebelled. He lost. Suleiman marched east and crushed his son's followers at the battle of Konya in 1559. Bayazid escaped and wrote to his father, confessing his error, explaining his thinking, and begging forgiveness. The letter somehow never reached Suleiman.

Hearing nothing, Bayazid sought asylum in Persia, and for two years he got it. The shah, however, was in a mood for peace with his Ottoman neighbor and spent those same two years hammering out a treaty with Suleiman. Among other things, the shah would receive the heads of some old enemies then living within the Ottoman borders. In return, he would have Bayazid executed.

Once Suleiman ordered Bayazid's infant son killed, all Selim had to do was wait.

+·+·+·+

Meanwhile, the Knights of St. John under Valette were flexing their muscles. With only a handful of ships, they had made it their business to savage Muslim shipping in the Levant. Commanders such as Guimeran and Giou, La Motte, and above all, Romegas were becoming notorious throughout the Mediterranean. These men, whom Suleiman might have expected to have disappeared in 1522, were proving to be a singular piece of unfinished business.

Certainly the Order needed the money. The costs of fortifying Malta on top of making good the losses at Djerba required a special levy of thirty thousand scudi on all foreign possessions, payable within the year 1563.[14] When not taking part in the Habsburg Empire's military operations, the knights and a large number of licensed Maltese corsairs sought out whatever infidel cargo came within their considerable reach. These attacks should not be overly romanticized. Ships generally carried the mundane stuffs of commerce — grain, cloth, rope, oil, and wine. Treasure ships were a rare occurrence and notable, such as Turgut's taking the gold that was to finance Valette's Tripoli. The most common high-margin commodity was prisoners, and one of the more reliable sources for these was the steady supply of vessels filled with devout Muslims making the Hajj. Those with money were ransomed for what they could get. Captives with no influence were sold in the bustling slave markets of Malta. Hurrem is said to have hounded Suleiman relentlessly on the subject, leaving at her death money to fund an expedition against Malta and the men who sailed the ships.

The most successful of these was Fra Mathurin d'Aux de Lescout, called Romegas after the lands owned by his grandfather. Born in 1519 in Armagnac, he joined the Order at age eighteen. He rose swiftly, proving himself a capable, courageous, and most important, a productive sailor — he never returned to port without a prize in tow. Brantôme, who knew him, refers to the knight as "generous, splendid, magnificent and liberal."[15] Brantôme had a fairly florid pen and was lavish with his fellow countryman, but he was not alone. Blaise de Montluc, a marshal of France, Romegas's distant cousin and commander in the wars against the Huguenots, and he, a soldier as brave as any that period produced, considered Romegas "a courageous person, more than any other I know."[16]

Romegas also was lucky. On a September evening of 1555, a freak storm swept across Malta; a water spout, tidal wave, and high winds barreled through Grand Harbor, crashing boats against one another, lifting some onto shore, simply overturning others at their moorings. The storm lasted only thirty minutes. The next morning the bay was strewn with the remains of broken ships and the floating corpses of knights, sailors, and galley slaves, this final group still chained to their benches. Some five thousand people died.

Eventually a small boat wove a course through the floating wreckage. As it approached the upturned hull of Romegas's ship, crewmen heard the sound of tapping. They paddled over and began to hack at the wood with axes. They managed to break through, and instantly a terrified monkey, the knight's pet, leapt out. Behind the monkey was Romegas, who, together with the animal, had spent twelve hours in total darkness, head just above the water line, not knowing if the wreck might shift at any moment and drown them both. His hair had turned white, and from that day forward, Romegas's hands trembled.

This tremor did nothing to diminish his abilities as a sailor. Valette thought highly enough of Romegas to put the knight in charge of his, Valette's, own personal galley. Thinned ranks presumably helped the survivors hoping for promotion, but this kind of high favor turned on talent. One notable encounter was with Yusuf Concini, a Calabrian renegade. Their ships fired on each other, and finally the Christian galley crashed his bow into the corsair's galleot. Romegas leapt on board, shouting, "Concini, you old bastard, where are you? Romegas is here." "And here is Concini, son of the devil!" yelled his opponent, rushing forward with cutlass in hand.[17] They fought on the bloody deck until Concini slipped and fell onto the benches, where the oarsmen, two hundred Christian slaves, tore him to pieces, taking his bones as souvenirs. Romegas roared out a threat to the remaining Muslims that he would throw them to the oarsmen as well if they did not yield. They chose to surrender, adding to better than a thousand Ottoman prisoners taken in the course of his career.[18]

If Romegas was a long-standing irritant to Suleiman, 1564 was the year he became insufferable. In the spring, he and his colleague La Motte were cruising off the coast of Alexandria and came across a carrack too high walled to be stormed. The merchantman also had 150 soldiers on board. They were, however, becalmed, making it easy for Romegas and La Motte to fire, retreat, reload, advance, and fire again. They managed to punch holes into her hull, destroy her rudder, and take down her main mast. The knights won the fight and would have been rich with its cargo — but they had gone at it a little too hard and the vessel was sinking. They contented themselves with the nearly six hundred living passengers, including the governor of Cairo, who was ransomed for eighteen thousand *zecchini*, Venetian gold ducats.[19] Also aboard was the onetime nurse to Suleiman's favorite daughter, Mihrimah. Despite her age (a hundred years, according to Balbi), she was still able to write a bitter letter to the sultan on his inability to protect a pious woman such as herself.[20] She was soon to die in captivity in Malta, her pilgrimage unfulfilled, her ransom unpaid, her story the subject of outraged sermons in Constantinople and a reproach to the sultan.

A few days later Romegas took another galley, this one carrying the governor of Alexandria. Weighed down with booty (three hundred captives above and beyond the wretches pulling the oars), he dragged his prizes back to Malta and set out yet again.

His next target was the *Sultana*.

❖·❖··❖·❖

In the spring of 1564, the population of Suleiman's seraglio, the various concubines, the head eunuch Capigias (aka Qapu Aga) and his underlings, and Mihrimah, bought a large quantity of silk and other luxury goods, which they intended to sell in the markets of Venice. The cargo was valued at eighty thousand gold pieces; the expected profit would be handsome. Presumably through the influence of Mihrimah, they were able to transport the goods in the hold of the galleon *Sultana*, personal property of Suleiman, armed with twenty brass cannon and a crew of Janissaries, as well as a few to ward off anyone reckless enough to approach her.

It was still a risky venture. Constantinople was as given to gossip and rumor as any port, and word of this cargo and its owners was well known long before the ship set sail. And for all the influence that the Ottoman navy (and the Venetian navy at this time) had over the sea lanes between the Bosphorus and the Adriatic, there were still men able and willing to take up a challenge even of this size.

The knights of Malta, alert to rumor, were now among that number. To take on the *Sultana*, they brought together the full seven galleys of the Knights of St. John, two belonging to Valette and commanded by Romegas, five belonging to the Order and commanded by Chevalier de Giou. The flotilla headed east. Various Greek and Venetian merchantmen claimed to have seen a large galleon carrying some two hundred soldiers and decked with twenty bronze cannon, some lesser guns, and with a *caramusali*, a small oared cargo ship, in attendance.[21] They advised the knights to let it pass and look for prey closer to their own size. On this information, Romegas put himself between the straights of Zante and Cephalonia in the northern Adriatic, calculating that the *Sultana* most likely would choose that route to come back home. One more time, he was lucky.

The *Sultana* had had an uneventful cruise until the galleys hove into view. The caramusali took off to find help, but for the *Sultana*, flight was not possible — the galleys were far too quick — and the *Sultana*'s captain did not try.[22] He readied his two hundred arquebusiers as the seven galleys steadily drew closer, and Giou let off a gunshot that invited surrender or battle. The *Sultana*'s crew fired back their refusal, then raised their pennants "to show that they were men of war."[23] It was to be a fight, the more numerous Christian sailors having the task of laying siege to the high wooden walls of what was in effect an extremely well-defended and well-armed floating fortress.

The men of the seven galleys were practiced in this sort of thing. They slid their vessels forward to flank the ship, forcing her captain to split the defenders port and starboard. The galleys waited just out of range until Romegas gave the orders, when there followed a series of twinned assaults against the *Sultana*, each galley darting forward, firing the guns on the bow, and retreating to let the next galley follow.

The *Sultana* was strong and carried enough firepower to give back some of what it was taking. Scattershot from large-bore guns killed and maimed the knights and their crew in large numbers. Small arms did the same, one man at a time. Hot cannon fire splintered chunks of ship's lumber, creating a nasty form of shrapnel. Incendiaries exploded on decks. Smoke and the ringing echo of cannon fire lingered in the air and ears, further degrading sight and sound and making coordinated action progressively more difficult. In time, Romegas believed Giou had been killed. Giou believed the same of Romegas.

Romegas finally sensed that the time had arrived to end the fight. He ordered his galley to head toward the *Sultana*'s stern. As it approached the galleon, his bow gun sent a barrage of shot, clearing the space of enemy soldiers. His men swung grappling hooks onto the poop, rapidly pulled the two ships fast, then began to swarm up and over the rails and onto the *Sultana*'s bloodied decks. Ottomans struggled to climb over their own dead and dying to repel the invaders. The sound of metal striking metal rang out as the men finally got a chance to fight hand to hand. Other galleys now joined in, grappling where possible and pouring new soldiers over all sides of the *Sultana*. These men pushed forward, hacked, and thrust their way down the center of the ship, killing large numbers of the crew, and finally pulling down the Turkish standard.

Five hours after the fight had begun, the *Sultana* was taken, its Muslim crew in chains, its Christian slaves freed. Romegas and his men towed the prize back to an astonished Malta, where the cargo was now examined, tallied, and divided. The vessel itself was a notable prize, and it graced the wharf for the next year. It was a near-run thing for the knights — the English ambassador to Venice wrote from home on July 29, 1564, referring somewhat enigmatically to "the seven galleys of Malta, which had taken a Turkish ship, being nearly surprised by Dragut Reis, with difficulty saved their prize in Syracuse."[24]

Back in the seraglio, the reaction was understandably violent. Bad enough that the honor of the sultan had been smirched — so had the pocketbooks of the women and eunuchs. Their chief and Mihrimah herself goaded the sultan, reminding him of his obligations to his family, his empire, his honor, and his religion. "Is it possible that you, my Lord, who have much power find it so difficult to destroy these disturbers of our sea, whose only home is a rock?"[25] Outside the palace the imams and citizens also were calling for revenge against the knights.

Age, experience, responsibility, and loss had caught up with Suleiman; he was now a dour, solemn man concerned with his legacy and his god. He had abandoned his old pleasures of listening to a boys' choir and orchestra, had exchanged his silver dining service for clay, forbade the import of wine, which, although forbidden to Muslims, had traditionally been permitted to Christians and Jews living within the empire. Even ten years earlier, his face had been powdered with red dust, probably less from vanity — he had little — than to suggest a younger, healthier circulation. The defeat of the knights forty-two years before had proven to be a job half finished; his magnanimity at Rhodes was now a rebuke.

Spanish and Italian histories cite the taking of the *Sultana* as the triggering event for the expedition; Pallavicino Rangone, in a postsiege report to the pope, states that the knights brought it on themselves with their sheer greed for pirate treasure.[26] This is true as far as it goes, but other issues would have made the attack inevitable. The French ambassador Petremol suggests that Don Garcia de Toledo's 1564 taking of Peñon de la Velez and the growing size of the Spanish fleet were a consideration.[27] Viperano, writing in 1567, claims that the knights' forefront in any military action against the Turk was reason enough for the Ottoman to go to war.[28] Unlike the Venetians or the French or almost anyone else in Europe, the knights would not be bought off, negotiated with, or frightened away. Suleiman's only course was to destroy them, and on this topic he was blunt. To Hassan ben Khairedihn in Algiers, he wrote: "The island of Malta is a headquarters for infidels. The Maltese have already blocked the route utilized by Muslim pilgrims and merchants in the East Mediterranean on their way to Egypt."[29] (A somewhat petulant Valette, writing to a fellow knight, construed Suleiman's reaction to the Order's recent activities as almost a matter of spite: "Not content with kicking us out of Rhodes . . .")[30]

There were also larger strategic concerns. Conquering Malta would make the island firmly Ottoman, and only Ottoman. It would not be a fiefdom or a client state like Algiers or Tripoli, the loyalty of whose leaders and people could waiver. A powerful Ottoman fortress in their midst would stiffen Muslim resolve throughout the Maghreb. The eastern Mediterranean would be more secure, the western, certainly from Spain's perspective, in greater peril. The idea was seductive. Sicily and even Malta itself had once been parts of the caliphate; Granada was lost to Islam within living memory. With God's favor, they might be regained.[31]

Balbi fancifully quotes Suleiman as saying, "My intention in the taking of Malta is not for the sake of the island itself but rather for its utility in other even harder and greater enterprises."[32] His previous schemes with Francis I back this up.[33] Specifically, he wanted Sicily, then Apulia and Calabria, the heel and toe of the Italian boot, perhaps the rest of Italy, perhaps beyond. He could envision a pincer movement into central Europe through the Balkans and past the Alps. It was an ambitious plan, no less grandiose than Charles V's stated hope of retaking Constantinople back in 1538. Certainly Valette believed that Italy was next after Malta — or at least said as much, possibly to catch the attention of Spain. In a letter to Philip in February, Valette assures him that his spies, "always very truly informed," had told him that the Ottomans had targeted Malta in 1565 as a springboard to Italy.[34]

Back in Constantinople, a council was called to discuss the matter. The knights were an offence against Islam, true, and the world would be better off without them. But was now the time? Malta was not Rhodes. It was far from any Ottoman base and surrounded by uncertain allies at best, its land too poor to feed an invading army, much less supply it with water. Conversely, the Order could draw on the religious sympathies and material aid from both Rome and Philip II. The current crop of knights was stronger than those who had abandoned Gozo and surrendered Tripoli. Suleiman should recall the Order's stubbornness at Rhodes and consider that he had had shorter supply lines there. Moreover, the season, which had worked against the Christians at Rhodes, would work against the Ottomans in Malta. In a bit of flattery, Mohammad Pasha pointed out that at Rhodes, Suleiman himself had been present, and was not to be at Malta.[35]

The war party was anxious to move. Two spies had gone to Malta disguised as fishermen and taken the measure of its defenses — interior design, elevations, angles, walls, capacity of the port.[36] Time was passing. Given the island's current state and Valette's sudden rebuilding campaign, this might be the last chance before it was all but impossible. Then there was the matter of Turgut — he was now eighty and had the most experience of any man alive of raiding Malta, and he owed the sultan some gratitude for coming to his side at Djerba. Turgut had a working relationship with Piali Pasha, whom he saw as a "dear son" (*caro figlio*), and who was also the best man, possibly the only man, who could galvanize the Barbary corsairs.[37] It was enough to make Suleiman opt for Malta.

✦·✦·✦·✦

By custom, Renaissance powers prepared for war in winter and prosecuted it in spring and summer. Siege guns needed to be cast, men enlisted, campaign supplies gathered. In the campaign of 1565, a fleet needed to be raised and a commander named. Suleiman tapped Kızılahmedli Mustapha Pasha of the Isfendiyarid Dynasty, an exact contemporary and a cousin (they both were grandsons of Bayazid II) and allegedly a descendant of Khalid Ben Walid, robe carrier to the Prophet Mohammed.[38] Mustapha had entered the army at an early age and served in various campaigns, including the siege of Rhodes. He made a name for himself in Persia and Hungary, and had been appointed governor of Rumeli in 1555, then promoted to fifth vizier in 1561.[39] An Arab ambassador judged him to be "a venerable person with charm and good nature."[40] Bosio says that he was "robust, and in command, very determined."[41] This last point at least comports with what the Ottoman chronicler Selaniki says of him, that he was "possessed of such heroism that it cannot be described." However, Selaniki also writes that "as long as [Mustapha] was vizier, he was suited to the post; once appointed *serdar* (field marshal), they say that he lost his wits."[42]

His reputation apparently did not reach his opposite numbers in the West. Intelligence reports from Constantinople had little concrete to say of him, dismissing him as "a man of some authority but little experience in war."[43] (The same report refers to Turgut by name only — that man's history and reputation were unquestioned.)

Command of the navy went to Piali Pasha, now married to Selim's daughter, Suleiman's granddaughter — a reward for his service at Djerba. Selaniki records his letter from Suleiman: "I have decided to order an expedition to be undertaken. You will therefore prudently and energetically gird yourself to gather all military means, and with care and diligence prepare sufficient powder and munitions, and losing no time be ready and prepared [to set out]. We hope that, with the infinite aid of God, we shall defeat the enemy of the faith and that the soldiers of Islam will be victorious."[44]

It had not been certain that Piali would get the position. He had some taint of corruption, having accepted bribes from the Genoese in exchange for not attacking Bastia in 1558.[45] There was also the story that after Djerba and before his marriage, Piali Pasha had secreted the son of the Duke of Medinaceli at Genoese-held Chios in the hope of getting a suitably large ransom from the family. This was presumptuous — all booty technically belonged to the sultan — and Suleiman got wind of it. He ordered a search for the child, but the boy died before this could happen, either of plague or by an alarmed Piali. Until Selim and the chief eunuch could talk Suleiman into granting him a pardon, Piali stayed on his ships, nervously cruising the Aegean while awaiting word from the palace. Suleiman needed him alive more than dead and was content to let him live out his natural life, after which, he said, "May God, the just avenger of crime, inflict upon him the punishment he deserves."[46]

The sultan also called upon the corsairs who lived in Galata (a section of Constantinople), experts in maritime arts, astute and famous men of the sea who were specific in their requirements: "What is needed is nothing less than three hundred ships, twenty cannon capable of bombarding the fortress with ninety-pound projectiles, one hundred and twenty columbrines and siege guns, five mortars, twenty thousand quintals of powder ... forty thousand projectiles, ten thousand spades, picks and oars, fifty ships armed with cannon, barges to carry horse, provisions, victuals, and hardtack ready for the Muslim soldiers. Give us what we demand, hold back nothing. Let us take the contest upon ourselves; victory will be in God. However much more is provided through war and battle, that much greater will be the strength of the soldiers' hearts."[47]

Once more, woodsmen of the Black Sea cut down old growth trees for new vessels. Hawsers, cook pots, grain, olives, swords, arquebuses, canvas, pitch, powder, ladders, pennons, water butts, sail, chickens, all these and more besides began to flow from the farther reaches of the empire into the chandleries and armories of Constantinople. All that autumn and winter, the noise of the arms makers sounded from the armory just north of the city. Suleiman came by daily to watch as his shipwrights sawed and shaped and joined the myriad pieces into a new fleet of galleys, galleots, foists, mahones, and barques.

Most spectacular of all, there was the casting of the behemoth siege cannon needed to bring down the heavy walls. Gun casting was a recent and still developing technology, an art as much as a science and one that captured the attention of the age. It was also inordinately dangerous, all the way from melting the bronze to firing the end product. Evliya Chelibi in his *Book of Travels* has left a detailed account of casting the great guns, a process so important that infidels, however skilled (and it was from Europeans, chiefly Germans, that the Turks learned the craft), were forbidden access to the final stages "because the metal when in fusion will not suffer to be looked at by evil eyes." Instead, viziers, muftis, and sheiks were called to the sweltering foundry to pray repeatedly, "There is no power and strength save in Allah!" Workers added tin to the molten brass, and the head founder ordered the guests to "throw some gold and silver coins into the brazen sea as alms, in the name of the True Faith!"[48] When the pour was ready, viziers and sheiks put on white shirts and sacrificed sheep on either side of the furnace. These were not men to leave anything to chance.

✦·✦·✦·✦

The rhythms of sixteenth-century war between Christian and Muslim, or more specifically between Ottoman and Habsburg, went on against a backdrop of continuous East-West trade. And as this was a regular event, the only question was whether the sultan's armies would head east to Persia or west to Hungary. Suleiman could make this decision at any time. Only when the army was ordered to muster, either on the northern or southern side of the Bosphorus, would people know for certain whether it was going to Europe or Persia. There might, however, be clues in the run up.

In the winter of 1564–65, foreign agents of the Germany's Fugger banking family noted the activity and carefully reported back to their Augsburg headquarters, from where the communiqué would continue to other branches and incidentally to the pope. The Fuggers were not alone. Antoine Petremol, the French ambassador to the court of Suleiman, kept his own masters informed regarding events in Constantinople, and his was not an encouraging picture: "The great preparations for the Sultan's navy continue and increase day by day, such that it is likely that this army will be ready to depart this coming March 12, and will be far larger than any force that the Turkish ruler has ever launched in terms of galleys and other large vessels, guns and artillery."[49] Venetian spies reported much the same, though Venice voted on March 24, 1565, not to share this information with the outside world.[50] Spies reported that the king of Tunis had collected a good deal of raisins, dates, honey, oil, and other food for the Ottoman fleet, in return for which Turgut had exchanged bolts of silk and small bronze cannon. Rumor stoked anxiety all over. English ambassador William Fayre writes from Madrid that "the Turk is much feared in Sardinia, Sicily, and Corsica."[51]

Some held that the target might even be Cyprus or Crete or someplace in the eastern Mediterranean, but Valette was not one to take chances. Valette had spies even in Constantinople, Italian merchants who, whether for money, for piety, or for both, wrote in lemon juice — invisible dry, but dark when exposed to heat — between lines of business correspondence.[52] An unnamed Greek knight is also noted as Valette's informant, a man who had gone to Constantinople at the time of the buildup and "penetrated with his industry, fluency, and banter (*plática*) as far as the chamber of the most principal pashas, and not without great risk to his own life."[53]

What Valette really wanted were hard facts and firm numbers. What was the target, what was the force? Viperano wrote that it was well known "from the letter received from Alexandria, Dalmatia and Constantinople of their preparations and their intentions retailed by fugitives and deserters all this apparatus of war was ordered used against the Knights of Malta."[54] For once, common knowledge was correct. The Ottoman archives have confirmed that Suleiman was trying to enlist his North African allies as early as October of 1564.[55] Turgut in Tripoli and Hassan, Suleiman's proxy in Algiers, were ordered to prepare their own men and however many other corsairs as could be persuaded to take part in the expedition against Malta.[56] (Suleiman also assured Hassan that it was his reportage of Christian activity in the west that convinced him to take arms against Malta — a bit of flattery possibly designed to sweeten the beylerbey.)[57] The sultan also requested — it was hard to order these men — that the Algerian corsairs leave French ships alone, hoping that France might at least remain neutral. On April 8, 1565, he informed Mustapha Pasha that he had appointed Mustapha Reis commander of the Muslim pirates, to reinforce the imperial fleet, though he seems to be more hopeful than certain they would actually get into the spirit of the thing ("I believe they will besiege the island of Malta").[58] Nevertheless, as late as December the French ambassador was throwing around huge numbers — thirty to forty thousand spahis (Ottoman cavalry), fifteen thousand Janissaries exclusive of any other men — and professing ignorance of the final target.[59]

The corsairs should have been quick to sign up for this enterprise. The knights had made considerable trouble in their lives, and the treasuries on Malta were presumably packed. Moreover, any knight taken alive ought to be worth a considerable ransom. There were profits enough for all, even if this was primarily an Ottoman operation. (The financial rewards of success were presumably on Suleiman's mind as well. According to Selaniki, "The fleet had taken a great toll from the treasury and it had not been enough."[60] The shortfall was borrowed from senior officials.)

Alone, the knights would be hard-pressed to resist a force of this size. They would need help from Spain, now ruled by a decidedly ambivalent Philip II. To persuade him, Valette would need a very strong advocate indeed. Fortunately, he had one in the person of Don Garcia de Toledo.

7

+·+·+·+

DARK CLOUDS
IN THE EAST, 1565

+·+·+·+

The same day the fleet raised anchors and departed
from Beshiktash; passing in front of the Seray, the troops made
their salute, the guns fired with such force that it rang to the skies
and was heard across the world.

Selaniki

Don Garcia de Toledo was one of the great figures of the era, honored and praised in his own time, but maligned or all but forgotten by posterity.

He was born in Villafranca di Bierzo in 1514, the son of Pedro de Toledo Zuniga, viceroy of Naples; the nephew of the duke of Alba; husband to a Colonna of the Roman aristocracy; and brother-in-law to Cosimo I de' Medici. His portrait shows a man with a long prominent nose, hooded eyes, receding hairline, and a full beard half covering full lips. Watchful and intelligent, he might have passed for a Dutch burgher. In life, he managed to combine in one person the talents of a skillful general, a patient diplomat, a perceptive strategist, an imaginative engineer, and a bold sailor. Emotionally, he could be proud, petulant, and if his numerous letters on the state of his health are to be believed, he was of fragile physical condition. Bosio describes him as "grave, judicious, and experienced."[1] He was also thoughtful, farseeing, conscientious, and loyal to his king, his soldiers, and his faith.

Family connections got him his first job, serving on and soon commanding galleys under the tutelage of Andrea Doria himself. Talent saw him rise. At the age of twenty-one, he became captain general of the galleys of Naples, in which role he commanded six galleys at the 1535 battle of Tunis. In 1540–41 he took command of Doria's land forces at Monastir, Susa, Mahomet, and Calibra. He was also present at the 1541 catastrophe at Algiers. Two years later he and his fleet were cheered in Messina as he towed a treasure ship belonging to Barbarossa himself. But it was his ingenious work at Mahdia, his mounting of heavy cannon on a makeshift catamaran and thereby destroying the wall from seaborne cannon, that solidified his reputation.

The two decades at sea, however, had their effect. By 1552 he wanted out, and asked an intermediary to plead ill health for him — "the sun by day and the damp at night, along with other miseries, have destroyed his health and could possibly carry him off."[2] (Coincidentally, this was the same year he married.) He was instead made a colonel of Spanish foot in Naples, and in the following year, he led twelve thousand imperial troops against Franco-Sienese forces at Siena.[3] Among his fellow officers were the one-eyed *condottiere* from Pavia, Ascanio Della Corgna; the Tuscan nobleman Giovan Luigi "Chiappino" (the Bear) Vitelli (a favorite of Garcia's brother-in-law Cosimo de' Medici); and Don Álvaro de Sande, all of them respected veteran commanders. He also served in Flanders and Italy. In 1560 he was slated to replace Medinaceli as viceroy of Sicily if the latter did not return from Djerba. By February of 1564 Philip had named him Captain General of the Sea (Andrea Doria's old title), and when others (including the Djerba veteran Sancho de Leyva) had failed, ordered him to take the Moroccan pirate stronghold, the Peñon de Velez de la Gomera.[4]

Peñon de Velez, like Mahdia, was an example of the care with which Don Garcia mounted a campaign. It also demonstrated, again, his ability to manage an international force. His resources included Spanish, Portuguese, Italian, and German soldiers, as well as the galleys of the Knights of St. John. Among the commanders were Chiappino Vitelli, Leyva again, and the young Gianandrea Doria. After an involved two-pronged attack, victory: "About 3 A.M. on Wednesday, two Turks came from the fort, and told the general that a great number of runagates [renegades] had abandoned the place, and that such as remained had agreed to render it."[5]

The ill health that had plagued Don Garcia in recent years had not abated. At age fifty, he was suffering from rheumatism and gout — his old friend Chiappino Vitelli had sent him a medicinal elixir in 1563 — and he might have been expected to settle down to a quieter life among the fountains, statues, gardens, and orchards at his villa at Chiaia, with honor and thanks and without the chains of office.[6] He did not. He saw the threat of Islam to Spain and Christendom, and not without cause, saw himself as almost uniquely capable of doing something about it. And if he was to defend the empire against the full force of the Ottoman fleet as well as their Barbary allies, he would need as much authority as he could get. In addition to his title of captain general, he asked for, and got, the position of viceroy of Sicily, which combined authority made him the most powerful man in the central Mediterranean.[7] He had his work cut out for him. "It is impossible to describe or imagine the condition in which I found the fleet," he wrote to Francisco de Eraso, the king's secretary in August 1564.[8] Corruption was rampant, and he was not shy about saying so.

It was, however, external threats in the upcoming year that were his greatest concern. Rumors were coming from the east; and in 1564, Garcia cataloged various possible targets, noting each city's strengths and weaknesses, the reasons Suleiman might (or might not) wish to attack them, and the kinds of preparation that should be taken in each case.[9] This report was long and meticulous, but it was essentially superfluous. Without doubt, Malta was the target of choice, with Goleta a possible second.

He laid out the threat in the starkest possible terms: "If Malta is lost, not only would there be the loss of those who are therein, which would be great, but it would be simply like having the kingdoms of Sicily and Naples with a chain around their necks; and joining hands with Tripoli, [our enemies] could at any time gather together all the forces of Barbary."[10] When that failed to move Philip to action, Toledo wrote to the king's secretary Eraso pleading with him to "for the love of God, expedite these matters."[11]

Spain was in an awkward position. The treasure ships from America this year were not enough to finance the horrifically expensive wars Spain waged and the fleets she tried to maintain. Philip had petitioned the papacy for money to help defray his military expenses, just as it had given France large sums to quash the Huguenots. Don Garcia, on his way to his new position in Sicily, went in person to Rome to press his case. Pope Pius IV was by nature a genial man, certainly a good friend to the knights and deeply concerned with the Muslim threat, but he was irritated with Philip. As of February 1565, revenues from Spanish parishes were being diverted to build sixty new galleys, and the pope thought that Philip should lead the armada in person, as his father would have done. Don Garcia endured a lengthy harangue in the gilt and marble halls of the papal palace, and afterward, in a nice bit of understatement, wrote to Philip that the pope "had his eye on [them]."[12]

Nevertheless, the pontiff did come through, as did the Duke of Savoy, as did Toledo's brother-in-law, Cosimo de' Medici of Florence, as did the narrow-eyed bankers of Genoa, as did most of the others whom Don Garcia visited on his way to Messina. Malta was, after all, a good deal closer to home than Rhodes had been, and the ramifications of an Ottoman victory were a good deal easier to imagine.[13] His rounds finished in April of 1565, Don Garcia sailed into Messina to settle into his new offices.

+·+·+·+

While Don Garcia was still working to gather the Spanish fleet, the Ottoman armada was ready to sail. One hundred and ninety ships — war galleys, carracks, galliots, galleons — filled the harbor of the Bosphorus.[14] Crowds of civilians — idle beggars and busy merchants, young children and old men — drifted down to the waterside to see this spectacle of imperial might, gawked at the ships, and cheered the soldiers and sailors. The galleys' sterns were decorated with moons of hammered gold, with various paintings in the Turkish ornate style. The imperial galley had three lights, and instead of the normal standard it flew a banner of green silk.

Preparing to board were spahis, light horsemen and archers who lived off of small land holdings called timars, granted by the sultan for good service (much as Roman soldiers were granted land in exchange for service, a practice that required an ever-expanding empire); Janissaries from Anatolia and Rumelia, crack soldiers and the sultan's personal guard, who dressed in red coats and tall white turbans topped with the white feather that marked them as a military elite; Iayalars, religious fanatics intent on death, both of the enemy and of themselves, dressed in animal skins; and corsairs from the Black Sea, adventurers who cared very little for rank and a great deal for a fight, the more one-sided the better. Finally, there was the subsidiary army of support personnel — engineers, armorers, tent makers, cobblers, ditch diggers, physicians, sailors, caulkers — unheroic men, but vital to the success of such enterprises. And of course, there were the merchants who follow any army, ready in this case to pay cash for any slaves the army might pick up along the way.

Long lines of porters had carried all the matériel that any large army needs from the quays and onto the ships and into the holds. Every spare corner was packed with rope; canvas; grain; arquebuses; tents neatly folded, bound, and labeled; pikes; a seemingly endless supply of iron and stone cannonballs in all sizes from egg-sized (scattershot, suitable for maiming a crowd of men quickly) to six-hundred-pound granite stones thirty inches in diameter (capable of knocking down walls). There were eight thousand kegs of powder to launch these missiles, and the mammoth bronze siege guns, so large they needed separate ships to carry the two halves.[15] All the impedimenta of war caused the ships to ride ever lower in the water as the oarsmen awaited the order to push off.

Above it all, Suleiman sat on a raised dais with a clear view of his fleet and the army that was boarding it. The grand vizier led the two commanders to the platform to get his final benediction. He tried to set a light tone: "These two are known to enjoy a bit of *kif*, and here we are sending them to two islands just made for that. And on two ships loaded with coffee and opium!"[16] Ottoman historians later condemned such frivolousness. They thought it ill omened.

Suleiman presented Mustapha with his own standard and a jeweled scimitar. Apparently concerned that there might be an unhealthy rivalry between the two, he ordered Mustapha to treat Piali Pasha as a beloved son, and Piali to honor and revere Mustapha as a father, and both men to work in unity and harmony.[17] Petremol, who was the French ambassador in Constantinople at the time, writes clearly that Suleiman named Mustapha Pasha as "chief of the enterprise."[18]

The sultan encouraged the both of them:

"The armada joined for you is the largest ever created — the army numerous, the soldiers hand chosen, the matériel more than sufficient. Nothing more is required other than courage and zeal. The prophet will aid you in this most just war, from which you must not think to return until you have swept Malta clean, destroyed all as an example to these pirates and to the ages."[19]

Left unspoken was the injunction that they wait for Turgut to arrive at Malta from Tripoli and to do nothing without first consulting him. He had, after all, invaded the shores of Malta repeatedly and thrown the knights out of Tripoli. He had the trust and respect of the Barbary corsairs, and the corsairs were a vital part of this expedition.

One can imagine Mustapha's feelings about that. His reputation was high, but nothing so high as Turgut's — or perhaps even the young gun, Piali's. Add to this the fact that Turgut and Piali had a highly successful working relationship of long standing, and Mustapha, although nominally in command of this enterprise, was looking more and more like the odd man out.[20]

The crowds cheered, cannon fired, drums beat, trumpets blared, flutes whistled, cables were unbound, and the armada set off. For several hours the galleasses, mahones, galleots, bastardas, and foists all jostled their way from the wharves of Constantinople, heading westward to whatever fate God had ordained. With them, at least for part of the way, was Grand Vizier Semiz Ali Pasha, who disembarked and returned to Constantinople just before the galleys reached the wider waters. He was not happy. The Ottoman historian Selaniki quotes him on his return:

"My Pashas! They believe that Malta is a cake and wish to eat it. They do not go to me to decide their actions and I have not approved of them; for all that has been spoken, they have no intention of heeding me. May God grant a good end to this enterprise. May I not see their ruin. God alone knows if we should succeed!"[21] He died the following June 28.

It was the custom of mariners setting out to sea to journey up the Bosphorus to the tomb of Khairedihn, there to acknowledge the greatness of the admiral, invoke his spirit, and pray for a successful outcome to whatever their purpose might be.

It is said that both commanders neglected this particular custom.[22]

+•+•+•+

Malta may have been the likeliest target, but ships are mobile and emperors capricious. The merchants at Genoese-held Chios briefly assumed they were the target as the armada rested for a short time at anchor outside their harbor — in fact, the ships wanted only tar.[23] Fretful senators in Venice were covering all bets. The Serene Republic had both supplemented their normal defenses at Cyprus, Corfu, and Zante, and collected gifts (velvet, satin, sugar, glass, etc.) for Mustapha and Piali should the two men pass near any Venetian outposts. Venetian sailors were warned to avoid any unfortunate incidents with the armada. France was less concerned. A week after the fleet's departure, the French ambassador Petremol was able to assure his king that Suleiman had no quarrel with friends of the Grand Porte. The ambassador had, however, no light to shed on the armada's final destination. To the best of his knowledge, the target was up to the judgment of the commanders, but would be either Malta or La Goletta, depending on which one they found [le] plus commode, most suitable.[24]

The armada's first leg ended in the various coves and inlets along the coast of Greece. The holy month of Ramadan was approaching, April on the Christian calendar. Fasting would be mandatory from dawn to dusk, with all the enervating effects the practice entails; and although the Janissaries, members of the Bektashi strain of Islam, were generally more elastic in their religious observance than others might be, it was better to have this obligation over and done with before any possible encounter with the enemy.

In this quiet period, part of the armada anchored in the bay of Navarino, where conscripts assembled from mainland Greece. The commanders examined these men just as they would a slave or a horse, enrolling the promising candidates and weeding out the lesser. (Balbi claims that reluctant soldiers "paid money freely to be quit of the obligation"; these bargains were a moneymaker for the mustering officers, and perhaps even for the empire.)[25] The commanders also waited for volunteers, who were not long in coming — on top of the chance for looting the riches of Malta, Suleiman had offered free pardon to any Levantine pirate who signed up for the expedition. Some, like the spahis and Janissaries, were already looking past Malta and on to the riches of Italy.[26]

Any enterprise this large will have setbacks. Mustapha's began now. While being towed through the channel of Nauplia, without warning and for no obvious reason, one of the troop carriers suddenly capsized. Seven hundred highly skilled spahis struggled in the water and, in their allotted time, slipped under the surface and drowned. Soon they were joined by a number of large cannon stowed on a second boat. The captains and essential crew in both of these vessels somehow managed to survive, a fact that the remaining landlubbers could not fail to notice. At the very least, it could be taken as an omen.[27]

+·+·+·+

As spring awoke on Malta and shrugged off the winter chill, Valette began to make preparations. For whatever reason — fear of expense, hope that the armada would target Goletta — he had left the matter later than was strictly prudent. Don Garcia had arrived at Malta in February with three thousand solders and offered to leave some behind; Valette turned down the offer in case the armada should target someplace else.[28] For the time being, he was content to call for the knights to come from Europe. This he did on February 10, a delay that would have consequences later on.[29]

Still, by April the Knights of St. John began to make regular trips to Sicily, three days' journey in good weather, importing "rods and hoops to make gabions [wicker baskets filled with earth to absorb gunfire], great quantities of hoes, of picks, of spades, of iron tools, of baskets, of nails, and other items to work on the fortifications and make necessary repairs. They also carried bread, cloth, leather, drugs, medicine, wine, salted meat and other provisions, all as much for the defense of these fortresses as for the sustenance and lives of men in case of siege."[30] Most important, they brought knights, soldiers, and adventurers who had gathered from all over Europe in Syracuse. The return voyage from Malta carried off useless mouths — the very young, the very old, women, dubious foreigners, prostitutes — all of whom were to wait out the conflict where they would not be in the way of the fighting or, more important, a drain on limited resources. At least, not on Maltese resources. Don Garcia ordered the Sicilians to treat them with courtesy, *como buenos vezinos*, like good neighbors.[31]

On April 9, Don Garcia arrived once more, leading twenty-seven galleys manned with nearly a thousand foot soldiers.[32] The grand master came down to the dockside as the sailors brought the viceroy's ships along the quay. Bad news. Malta would be getting one hundred and fifty men at this point; the rest were bound for La Goletta.[33] Don Garcia assured Valette that Philip took a keen personal interest in Malta and that further Spanish foot were being gathered. Unfortunately, this might take several months, during which time the island would be largely on its own. Don Garcia was outwardly hopeful, however. To Philip he reported that Malta was well positioned and that La Goletta was even "more difficult to attack, and easier to defend, and if [the Ottomans] go to that island, I firmly believe that they will depart with little honor and great injury."[34]

The two men had the same goal of keeping Malta free of the Ottomans, but each had long-standing grievances against the other's nationality. Valette and a large part of the Order were French; he would associate Spain with such troublemakers as d'Amaral, the possible traitor at Rhodes; D'Homedes, who lost Tripoli; and La Cerda, who failed to retrieve it. For his part, Don Garcia would recall that France had allied itself with Suleiman and given Khairedihn hospitality. As brother-in-law to Cosimo de' Medici, the viceroy likely would have heard that man's indignation when Valette declined the free offer of the Tuscan military engineer Baldassare Lanci to put Malta's defense works in better order in 1562, an oversight the more galling now that he could see firsthand just how ill prepared Malta was for a siege.[35]

All this was water under the bridge for the moment, but it would serve to color their relationship from here on out. The viceroy had one last offering. He presented his bastard son Faderigo to Valette. Faderigo, a beardless youth just twenty years old, had traveled with Don Garcia from Messina with the stated intention of joining the Order, and it is a testament either to Valette's regard for the boy, or for the father, or for own his need to oblige the viceroy, that rules requiring four aristocratic grandparents (often loosely defined) were in this case set aside.[36] Certainly the young man was an eager soldier, which could only be welcome. Faderigo was enrolled in the Spanish *langue*.

Valette took this occasion to introduce Don Garcia to the commanders who would lead this defense. In addition to Romegas, there was Sir Oliver Starkey, Latin secretary to Valette. Starkey was the last of his countrymen to represent the English *langue*. (Henry VIII, the great champion of L'Isle-Adam, had had a change of heart in latter years. He quashed the Order on his island and stripped it of its considerable remaining assets.[37]) There were Luigi Broglio, the aging, fat commander of Fort St. Elmo; Juan d'Eguaras, *bailo* of Negroponte and second to Broglio; Melchior d'Eguaras, a captain of cavalry and Spanish secretary to Valette; Dom Mesquita of Portugal, another septuagenarian and commander of Mdina; Marshal Coppier, commander of the horse; Fra Vincenzo Anastagi, who would act as a conduit between Valette and Don Garcia; and Giou, Gimeran, and others, some of whom Don Garcia would have fought alongside on previous campaigns.

As the men gathered in the council chamber at Fort St. Angelo, they could review past history and guess at Mustapha's general strategy. Malta had suffered many quick raids in the past thirty years, chiefly from Barbary corsairs, but her strongholds had been avoided. This time would be different, not a harvesting of peasant slaves, but an all-out attempt to take the main island in its entirety. How then should they allocate their defenses? An unsigned and undated letter exists, probably the work of Don Garcia, in which the author suggests that the core of the defense should be made in Senglea and Birgu.[38] Useful as far as it went, but all options needed examination, and so the council members began their discussions.

For Mdina, some five miles from the grand harbor, there was little that could be done. Its walls had been untouched since Roger of Normandy expelled the Saracens in 1090 and would not be able to stand up to any serious artillery. Although the capital of Malta, it was now little more than a closed city whose inhabitants, old nobility of no power and a great antipathy toward the knights, had largely packed up and left for Sicily. For Valette, however, the city's loss would be a serious matter. Besides its nominal value as capital of the island — a propaganda point if nothing else — Mdina served any number of tactical ends for the Christians. It was a staging point for any communications between Messina and Malta. It would soon headquarter the cavalry units, useful for hectoring Ottoman patrols. It would also be the temporary refuge for any relief efforts, those that found their way onto the island from the west.

Valette's main concern, however, mirrored Don Garcia's. The greater effort should go into the area of the Grand Harbor, the chief entry point to the island. The peninsula of Mount Sciberras was like a tongue sticking out of the harbor's mouth with Fort St. Elmo on the tip, and Senglea and Birgu, two long teeth sticking up from the bottom jaw and holding Fort St. Michael and Fort St. Angelo. Looming over these, ranging from east to west, were Mount Salvatore, Mount Margaritas, Mount San Giovanni and Mount Corradino, and Sciberras across the bay. Against these, geography provided three lines of defense behind which the knights could rally, and Valette led the viceroy to inspect all of them.

Slaves, civilians, and even soldiers were busy pulling the stones from quarries and using them to bolster the defending walls of Birgu, Senglea, and not least of all, Fort St. Elmo. Here the Christians had one remarkable advantage. Their spies in Constantinople had filed a report of the Ottoman strategy sessions held the prior winter, discussing how best to take Malta: "On the fifth [of December 1564], a divan was arranged wherein all the old captains were present, because they were called to discuss the enterprise of taking Malta. The plan is to first take Castel San Ermo [sic] so as to command the port, and insert the better part of the fleet to spend the winter and then take Castel San Angelo by siege."[39] It says something of Spain's intelligence network that they might have this kind of access, and it helps explains why Toledo was so concerned about bolstering the defenses of Fort St. Elmo in particular.

Fort St. Elmo presented its own peculiar problems and had been a concern for many years. Turgut's raid in 1551 had underscored the need for defending the area, and in 1552 a committee was formed and engineers engaged to discuss the matter.[40] Money was tight that year and the question became, what was the least they could get away with? Grand Master D'Homedes insisted that no project be undertaken that could not be finished before the following fighting season. The result was a plan for the relatively small Fort St. Elmo with its four spurs overlooking the entrance into Grand Harbor. The rest of the budget went to bolstering the bastions of Provence and Auvergne, and to Senglea, another small fort on the hill of St. Giuliano.

Work began in 1552. When the Sicilian laborers proved insufficiently diligent, native Maltese, who had a vested interested in the matter, were hired instead. Barracks were constructed of Sicilian wood, the ditches excavated, and some walls put up so that by April of 1553 the knights were able to fire a salute to galleys entering Grand Harbor. As a further precaution, a heavy chain that rose "two or three palms above sea level" was ordered from Venice, enough to block unwelcome ships from the inlet between the head of Fort St. Angelo and Senglea peninsula.[41]

Still, Fort St. Elmo in 1565 had shortcomings. It was at the lowest elevation of the Sciberras Peninsula, at the end of a plateau measuring about a hundred paces. Guns placed on the higher elevation could fire down on its weak landward side. The solution, already in place, was a cavalier, a short tower built on the seaward side, solid enough to anchor heavy guns and fire a considerable distance into the water. Its guns could also fire back over the fort if need be. The tower was connected to the main fort by a drawbridge over the ditch that surrounded the fort. One startling oversight was the total lack of embrasures or crenellations, slits where defenders could fire outward with some degree of cover, rather than rise up and present enemy sharpshooters with a silhouette.

Don Garcia's greatest concern, however, was the north face. The wide angle of the spurs provided no opportunity for protective crossfire. It was also dangerously exposed to the water. After his own success at Mahdia, Don Garcia was acutely aware of the possibilities of a seaborne cannonade. To solve both problems, he suggested that a ravelin be built, a detached counterguard that allowed for crossfire and a defense against waterborne cannon fire.[42] Workers were diverted to the purpose. It was a sound idea, but implemented too late. By the time they had finished, the ravelin's height was modest, which was to have serious consequences later on.

On the eve of Don Garcia's departure, Valette reminded the viceroy of Charles V's old promise to aid the Order against all enemies. He was preaching to the converted. Don Garcia promised aid "on his honor and his conscience through all the month of June."[43] With that said, and having gone over and critiqued the island's defenses with some care, the viceroy could offer little more than advice learned from his years of practical combat.

Valette must, he said, maintain utter control over the men. He might seek their advice, acknowledge their concerns, and listen to their suggestions, but in the end they must understand that his word was final. He must at all costs preserve his person from harm, since an army without a leader can easily fall into confusion and despair. However compelling the urge to join his men in battle, he must never become a casualty of war. All good advice, but this last, given the nature of the man and the nature of the times, was as good as useless. Honor would scarcely allow Valette not to become part of the fight.

The following morning, Don Garcia boarded the viceregal galley heading for La Goletta. The next ship, he promised, would bring more soldiers and equipment, and his sincerity on this cannot have been doubted. Nor his courage — he was heading into Barbary waters and was concerned both for Turgut's twenty galleys and the three more that Uludj Ali was bringing from Constantinople.[44] It was April, early days yet. Slaves, civilians, and soldiers could continue to pull stones from the quarries and improve the defending walls of Birgu, Senglea, and not least of all, Fort St. Elmo. Even the peasantry worked the quarries when required. Some of them were still convinced that the Turk would not show up this year at all.

PART TWO

·•·•·•

Objective:
St. Elmo

8

+·+·+·+

FIRST BLOOD

+·+·+·+

If we are to predict the outcome based on the beginning,
we can expect only confusion worse confounded.

Petremol, French ambassador to Constantinople

Today, all the soldiers were assembled in and around
Pasha Hazretleri's tent and the imperial letter of command conferred on the
pasha was read out loudly. Prayers and praises were raised to the Sultan.
Even the Pasha himself bestowed many favours upon the soldiers.

1565 Ottoman Malta Campaign Register

On the morning of May 18, a single cannon shot rang out from Fort St. Elmo.
An answering shot came from Fort St. Angelo (a thousand meters across the
still water of Grand Harbor), quickly followed by the sound of church bells
in Birgu. Ships, too many to be from Sicily, had begun to crowd the eastern
horizon, indistinct dots on the glittering water, multiplying not quickly, but
inexorably, until they formed a single arced line. Any lingering hopes that Malta
might be spared were now over.

The Ottoman's imminent arrival created new problems for Valette. The ten
thousand men that Don Garcia was hoping to raise could not now manage
to pierce the Turkish cordon and would have to stay in Sicily.[1] Worse, far
too many old, young, infirm, and unsoldierly noncombatants would remain
in Malta, as they could not now be evacuated. As word of the approaching
armada spread, some twenty-four thousand peasants, the inevitable refugees
of all wars, began to clog the roads from the countryside to the safety of Birgu
and Fort St. Elmo.[2] Viperano writes uncharitably of the "fear and anxiety in

the souls of the Maltese, who are by nature timid and scarcely accustomed to war."[3] These people were now Valette's responsibility. Valette ordered the lightly inhabited peninsula of Senglea, site of D'Homedes's old pleasure garden, to be made available to them. It wasn't much, but at least it was on the right side of the walls.

(Viperano's take on the Maltese is repeated elsewhere, but it was nonsense even at the time. Fifteenth-century surveys, taken years before the knights arrived, show native cavalry on the island. Maltese companies had served at Algiers in 1541 and Tripoli in 1536 and 1551, and Maltese corsairs at this time worked under license of the knights in exchange for a hefty 75 percent of their profits, later reduced to 9 percent.)[4]

As the sun rose, anyone not better occupied came out to watch the approaching fleet. Don Garcia had reported to Philip a total of one hundred and sixty Ottoman vessels at Modon as of May 3, but who could say if that number was accurate?[5] Valette now ordered Romegas and Giou out on the waters for a closer look. The mission was strictly exploratory — any threat of engagement and Romegas was to break off and return to port. As it turned out, the grand master need not have worried. The Ottoman commanders had no interest in Romegas's tiny squadron and certainly no reason to disguise their strength. Ships by the dozen, soldiers in their thousands, could only terrify the islanders. Malta would crack all the sooner once she understood that the fight was hopeless.

A single galleot lead the sultan's fleet, its crew repeatedly dropping a lead line over the side, taking soundings. Romegas had learned what he could (not much) at a safe distance and headed back to Fort St. Angelo. The question then arose, where would the enemy attempt to land? By midday, the ships were close enough to shore that individual figures could be distinguished — soldiers, support personnel, the naked oarsmen, and the watchful coxswains who kept them in line. As the armada bore south, Valette ordered Marshal Guillaume de Coppier's cavalry to shadow the armada's progress along the island. Horses would not be staying in Birgu once the siege began in earnest anyway (too little water), and this foray was a preliminary to sending them to Mdina for good. Coppier commanded a hundred knights of Lieutenant Medrano, Colonel Pierre de Massuez Vercoirin (aka Colonel Mas), with part of Captain La Motte's company and that of Captain Juan d'Eguaras, a thousand men in all.[6] They mounted, the gates to Birgu squeaked open, and the men headed down the coastline, parallel to and maintaining the same speed as the ships.

By late afternoon the armada was rounding the southern points of the island near Marsaxlokk bay. This was the logical choice for a landing — a large, circular inlet, shallow, suitable for offloading the numbers of men and equipment the Ottomans had brought. Moreover, there wasn't much chance of harassment from the Maltese or their allies — the surrounding terrain was flat and offered little in the way of defensive cover. Coppier's men reached a good spot to survey the ships' entry into the bay. They waited in vain. The wind shifted, and this, combined with the lateness of the hour, made landfall impracticable. As the fleet passed between the cliffs outside Zurrico and the small island of Fifla three miles offshore, the knight Ramon Fortuyn counted a total of 193 ships.[7] The final total was closer to 380.[8] (By contrast, the Spanish Armada of 1588 totaled 130 ships.)

It was this report that Valette gave to Giovanni Castrucco for delivery to Sicily. Castrucco's small boat paddled out of Grand Harbor and headed north, alone, while the great Ottoman parade continued toward the south and past Marsaxlokk until, as dusk arrived, it finally stopped and dropped anchor off the rocky west coast, forming a magnificent and alarming silhouette against the dying sun.

After sundown, Coppier's horsemen regrouped at Mdina. The Turks, they knew, would not offload their army at night, but they might land a few scouts. Valette would appreciate a few captives, and between the dark, the unfamiliar terrain, and their still feeling the effects of a long voyage, the odd Muslim patrol should be relatively easy to catch. Coppier ordered a small patrol and headed some two miles northwest to Torre Falca, a landmark mill north of Mdina and a high point from which it became clear that Ottomans had indeed landed. Further reconnaissance required stealth, which in turn required smaller groups. He ordered Captain d'Eguaras to lead a detachment of one hundred foot and two hundred and fifty horse. D'Eguaras proceeded another two miles, then stopped in his turn and sliced off a yet smaller squad of a dozen chosen men — knights and Maltese guides, all with horse — to approach the shoreline.[9] They were to find a well-sheltered position and wait for a stray Turk to come to them. Should they run into real trouble, they were to fire their weapons and d'Eguaras would come to their aid. D'Eguaras put Adrien de la Rivière, onetime page (*trinciante*) to Valette, in command, wished him luck, and watched as the men mounted and disappeared quietly in the dark.[10]

There is nothing harder or more typical for a soldier to do than to wait. These men, agitated by the sheer size of the armada and the knowledge of how few Christians were on Malta, could sit still, listen for unexpected sounds carried on the offshore breezes, peer into the dark horizons and up at the night sky, imagine what their comrades were doing, when they would come back, and what the rest of the spring and summer was going to bring.

Meanwhile, La Rivière's expedition walked their horses across the rocky ground, alert to sound and movement — little enough, despite the night's silence and the nearly full moon. After about two miles, they heard voices. La Rivière found a stone outcropping, ordered his men to settle in the stone's lee and waited and listened. Uncertain sounds came and went, until he heard the clip-clop of a lone horse walking across the rocky ground. It was coming from behind them. La Rivière raised his head. What he saw was a man on horseback, clearly Christian, clearly lost. Shouting out would have been foolish; letting the man wander away would have been irresponsible. La Rivière mounted his own horse, exposing himself to the faintest of early morning light, and rode toward the interloper.

The rider was Vendo de Mesquita, a young nephew of the governor at Mdina. What did he want? Nothing more than to be part of the mission, and to that end he was wandering, unauthorized, just as aimlessly as the Ottomans he hoped to encounter. Foolish of the boy, but if he wanted excitement, he was about to get it. The Turkish patrol La Rivière had detected earlier now saw these two silhouettes against the creeping dawn and opened fire. Mesquita's horse was startled by the noise and bolted, leaving La Rivière and his men to face the enemy alone. The Ottomans were just yards away, and their numbers were growing quickly, as they, experienced soldiers, were attracted to the sounds of shouting and gunfire. La Rivière took the initiative. He wheeled his horse about and charged a knot of men. According to the Ottoman campaign register, one Mehmed ben Mehmed managed to get La Rivière off his horse and capture him alive.[11] One of the enemy raised a long arquebus, leveled the weapon, and fired a bullet square in the center of La Rivière's breastplate. The armor saved his life, but his horse reared and La Rivière slipped off the animal's backside. He was alive, but flat on his back, the wind knocked out of him, unharmed but helpless.

La Rivière's outnumbered comrades were firing back now. One of the Maltese broke cover and attempted to drag La Rivière to safety. But the knight was heavy, the more so with armor on, and after several attempts, the task proved too much for one man. The Maltese saw no advantage in their both being captured or killed. "Forgive me, Sir, that I can do no more," he said, and retreated to fight another day.[12] The firing died off, the Christians melted away, and La Rivière lay alone on the ground. He might have fought to the death, but did not get the chance. The enemy, more interested in a live prisoner than a dead trophy, surrounded the knight, hoisted him up, and carried him off. They also had managed to snag a Portuguese serving brother, Bartolomeo Faraone, who failed in a last-ditch attempt to save his commander.[13] (Elsewhere the Ottoman records claim: "Mehmed ben Mustafa . . . when the fleet arrived in the island of Malta and some horsemen on the side of the infidels put up some resistance . . . overturned one of the horses and captured the horseman riding it alive.")[14]

Later that morning, Maltese scouts found Vendo de Mesquita propped up against the side of a farmhouse some miles away, stone dead. He had gotten his cuirass off, but to no purpose. An Ottoman bullet had hit home, and he had bled to death. He was the campaign's first casualty.

✦·✦·✦·✦

D'Eguaras did not get a Turkish prisoner, but he did get a Neapolitan renegade, a young man who had managed to jump ship and stumble his way into the Christian lines. One renegade pawn was a poor trade for three knights, but he was better than nothing and, as a Christian, deserving of refuge. And he had information. The fleet, he said, carried fifty thousand fighting men and enough supplies for six months.[15] He also reported bad blood between the commanders. According to this man, just as the fleet was approaching Malta, Mustapha pulled out a *firman* from the sultan giving him ultimate power, and thrust this toward Piali Pasha, which started a serious shouting match.[16] The *firman* was unlikely to have changed the line of command as laid out in Constantinople, but the story encouraged the defenders.

Bad news followed good. Some time after midnight, thirty-five ships of the invasion fleet had broken off and headed back for Marsaxlokk where, unopposed, they off-loaded three thousand men.[17] By morning, these exploratory troops had marched on and entered the villages of Zeitun and Zabbar.

Detachments of Coppier's remaining cavalry had harassed them as much as possible, but to no great end. When Valette learned of the situation, he ordered all infantry back to Birgu and all cavalry to Mdina. Coppier and his men may have been eager for revenge; Valette wanted to keep his force at full strength.

In the meantime, the defenders could do little more than pray, which the bishop of Malta did with a general procession, including the grand master, the knights, and the people. A Capuchin preacher prayed aloud for forty straight hours.[18]

The size of the opposing forces is largely educated guesswork. Contemporary reports take the Ottomans from a high of 80,000 to a low of 24,500 — the latter figure being part of a report late in the siege. The figure of 35,000 men, 12,000 of them trained soldiers, is likely about right. That is against the 6,100 to 8,655 Christian defenders, of whom perhaps half were professional — at best a three to one advantage.[19] On May 21, two days after they had arrived, the remainder of the Ottoman fleet glided into the shallow waters of Marsaxlokk, now fully secured, and prepared for the arduous task of landing an army and all its equipment on the beach.

✦·✦·✦·✦

The prisoners La Rivière and Faraone were brought to Mustapha, who could only have been delighted. First blood to the Turks; two knights captured, one probably killed — it was a good start. He might be able to learn how far the defenses of Birgu had progressed since previous reports.

The barriers to the peninsula of Senglea were a set of bastions, the so-called Post of Carlo Ruffo (later called the Post of Robles), the Post of Italy, followed by the Post of de Medi and the Post of the Maltese. The wider expanse of Birgu was defended by the Post of Aragon, the Post of Provence, of France, of Auvergne, of the Genoese, and where the walls met the water, the Post of Castile. On the water of Kalkara Creek were the Posts of Germany and England, all named for the *langues* assigned to defend them.[20] There could be no question that Valette had been working hard these past six months to reinforce all of the defense works, but inevitably there would still be weak spots. Mustapha would find them in time, but how much easier it would be to learn it firsthand and thereby expedite the inevitable. Interrogation was hurried along with torture. The Ottoman standard (and Spanish, for that matter) would be the bastinado, whereby a skilled man took a heavy stick and, starting at the feet, methodically shattered all the bones in a man's body. Death would come slowly and painfully from internal bleeding, and in theory a man would reveal anything his inquisitors wanted to know.

La Rivière suggested this was pointless: "What will you get by torturing me? You will never learn anything other than that you will never take Malta, because it is very strong and well provisioned, its captain is exceedingly valorous, its knights and soldiers valiant, and as is their obligation, they would sooner die for their faith and their Order than to show weakness."[21] Mustapha might have taken the last comment as bravado — admirable but irrelevant. Still, he held off torture and even sweetened the deal by offering La Rivière freedom if the knight revealed the weakest part of the Christian defense.

9

+·+·+·+

SIZING UP
THE ENEMY

+·+·+·+

When the war waxed hote: the Master of the order
thought good to certifie Garzias of Toledo the viceroy of Sicile,
that he might make haste to come with his fleete.

Celio Secondo Curione (Thomas Mainwaring translation)

On May 21, 1565, Mustapha and seven thousand men gazed down on Birgu from the heights of St. Catherine, prevented from coming any closer by Christian artillery. As they watched, soldiers, slaves, and civilians were pulling down the stone houses of Bormulu outside the walls, to deny the invaders any cover. Women and children gathered up the loose detritus and carried it inside Senglea and Birgu. Once the Ottoman guns started firing, these stones and sacks of dirt would be vital to repair any damage to the defense works, or could serve as weapons — stones dropped from a height of twenty feet can easily crush a man's skull.

Other than this controlled destruction, there was little more the defenders could do, and accordingly, they did little. Valette would not risk his soldiers, many still green, this early on, as failure to rout the Ottomans would end the campaign before it even started. He did, however, allow Coppier's horsemen to ride out in search of targets of opportunity. They found work enough. By nightfall they had returned to celebrate the feats of the day. Souvenirs and trophies of the day were brought out and displayed to inspire fellow defenders. A Monsieur de Montal la Prade and an unnamed Spanish soldier took joint credit for seizing a Muslim standard, soon to adorn the Church of St. Lawrence. Others carried the heads of dead enemies. In the Auberge de Provence, Jean Antoine de Morgut of Navarre was showing off a talisman, *una piastra d'oro*, taken off the right arm of a richly dressed Turk. Arabic script covered the surface, its message simple and to the point: "I come to Malta not for gold or honor but for the sake of my soul."[1] No doubt there was truth to this, just as Christian adventurers were encouraged by the papal indulgence Rome had attached to this operation. Faith mattered. One of Valette's anxieties was that La Rivière might reveal to Mustapha just how many of Malta's defenders were *soldati pagati*, mercenaries, who might cut and run if things went badly, or be open to a higher bidder.[2]

On May 22, the last of the invasion fleet had settled into Marsaxlokk, and the invasion force had begun to snake its way toward Grand Harbor, taking advantage of abandoned property along the way, chiefly in the form of livestock. Not all peasants had had the time or the foresight to get their cattle and oxen to safety, or the discipline to slaughter them. Mustapha Pasha, by contrast, ordered that these animals "*grandissimi*, most large, like those of Sicily," according to the Genoese spy Bregante, not be slaughtered.[3] These animals were soon hitched up to the invader's yokes and pulling carts laden with tents, cannon, food, ammunition, and other impedimenta over uneven roads.

By midday the Ottomans occupied Zeitun (St. John), a small village midway between Birgu and Marsaxlokk. The first serious assault could wait, but the day ended with one more fight, and a crucial one. It concerned water.

This was a resource worth dying for. Water, or rather the lack of it, had decided the siege of Djerba, and no general could afford to overlook this resource, not in summer and not at that latitude. A corps of water bearers was part of the Ottoman army. The invaders knew about the springs of the Marsa — the main water source for Birgu and environs — and were anxious to take control of them. Coppier, still angry over the loss of La Rivière, was determined that they should not. The two factions came to contest the matter on May 20, raising a din that carried across the waters to Fort St. Elmo, where several hundred soldiers were busy digging defense works. The sound of battle was catnip to these men, and they and their commander, Juan de La Cerda (a Spanish captain, not the former viceroy), hearing the sound of battle, felt their blood rise. These men had come to Malta to kill Turks, not lay stones, and now Turks were being killed, and not by them.[4] Fra Broglio, in charge of St. Elmo, directed La Cerda's men to down their tools, pick up weapons, and head off to join the fight. Broglio then waited for news, listening to the sounds of distant battle, wondering if he had lost the Spaniard and his men for good.

He hadn't. Some hours later, La Cerda returned to Fort St. Elmo, caked in blood and victorious. The incident should have been remembered when, as we shall see, his bravery was later called into question.

Brave or not, soldiers were too valuable to risk when there were other, cheaper ways of denying the enemy water. Soon after this scuffle, Valette ordered Camillo Rosso, *protomedico* of the Order, to gather whatever filth and poisons he could and spike the cisterns and wells outside the walls, causing "serious illness and even death to a great number of the Barbary infidels."[5] They would eventually be forced to travel as far away as Gozo in search of the stuff. (Regarding water, the Ottomans appear not to have done their homework. According to the military engineer Laparelli, "You cannot prevent the enemy from obtaining water; anyone who digs a hole 4 *palmi* deep on the plain [of Marsa] will find fresh water and in abundance."[6])

Water was a concern for the defenders as well, and comes up repeatedly in Valette's letters to Don Garcia. Food stores he had, but with only three cisterns inside the wall for a swollen population, he was forced to economize. Two knights were dedicated to finding new sources within the walls. Just as at Djerba, all remaining oxen and cattle were slaughtered — better to let them rot in the sun than to swill the daily gallons they needed. Valette also ordered all dogs put down, starting with his own hunters (and presumably, the pet lion he kept in his quarters). Their howling at night, it was said, distracted the sentries. More likely it was their thirst, not as extreme as the larger animals, but constant.

◆·◆·◆·◆

By the morning of May 21, the Ottoman's brilliant multicolored tent village covered the hills of Santa Margarita, sprung up overnight like desert wildflowers after a sudden rain. The army corps of tent minders had unpacked and unfolded and erected the place in a matter of hours. Camps for Ottoman armies were designed along the lines of small cities, concentric circles of cotton, broadcloth, canvas, brocade, and even silk tents, each dedicated to private, semiprivate, and official use — latrines to bathhouses to hostels to conference rooms, smithies, workshops, and hospitals. Decorations hung from the walls, carpets softened the floors, stools and storage filled empty space. Chimneys rose out of some tents. Flags and pennants with emblems flew above them all, indicating what each one contained. Guylines crisscrossed the gaps and alleyways between the structures to keep traffic slow. Soft walls for hard men — orderly, tranquil, and clean. Busbecq knew these camps, and he knew their European counterparts: "Anyone who is familiar with conditions in our camps will scarcely believe it, but the fact remains that there was utter silence and calm . . . there was the complete cleanliness, no dung heaps or rubbish, nothing to offend the sight or smell."[7]

Comfort and order were important to the Ottoman campaigners. So was food. Janissaries would have understood Napoleon's dictum of armies marching on their stomachs. Their entire hierarchy was laden with culinary terms; the corps itself, the *ojark*, translates as "hearth."

The soup cauldrons were the emblems of the various regiments within the corps' battalions, as important as the standards and pennons carried into battle, and the colonel of any given regiment carried a soup ladle as a symbol of his authority. Officers were called *shorbadji* (soup makers), *çörekçi* (bread makers), and even *karakullukçu* (pot washers). When the Janissaries revolted, as they did from time to time, they indicated their displeasure by overturning the regimental cauldrons.

For the moment, the invaders could be upbeat and eager to get past the mundane aspects of camp administration and on to more substantial matters. "All the soldiers were assembled in and around Mustafa Pasha's tent and the imperial letter of command conferred upon him was read out loudly. Prayers were intoned and praise declaimed to the Sultan, and Mustapha Pasha himself bestowed many favors upon the soldiers"[8]

They could now look down on a defensive system of good modern design, but it was still a work-in-progress.[9] To reach the walls, the Muslim soldiers would have to cross over a flat expanse littered with the half-destroyed houses that had recently made up the suburb of Bormulu. Beyond this was a deep ditch, traversed at intervals by drawbridges. The walls themselves were traced in the current designs of pointed spurs, which allowed for crossfire against any invader. It was formidable, but these men had seen worse. Even now they could gaze down on the defenders in the suburb of Bormulu, gathering up the last of the old broken stones and beams. The Ottomans were not overly concerned. For them, it was a good time to strike a little terror.

+·+·+·+

Mustapha ordered the musicians out. Kettledrums, tambours, trumpets, bagpipes, and brass horns began to shrill and wail down and across to the Christian defenders.[10] Only then did Valette order the work halted and the demolition crews back inside. Some were reluctant. Soldiers stood at the ramparts watching all this, many seeing an enemy for the first time, most eager to fight. Valette himself was never one to shrink from a challenge; best to let his men loose. Veterans could get back the feel of battle; greenhorns would learn what they were really up against; civilians could get over the initial shock of seeing the bleeding dead and wounded being carried through their streets.

Valette ordered his own musicians to reply to Mustapha, then called Lieutenant Medrano, Colonel Mas, Captain d'Eguaras, and Romegas to the wall. Their orders were simple. They were, he said, to take a few hundred arquebusiers outside, draw up a defensive line, and fire on the enemy. Minutes later, the gates opened and the men trotted out, took positions, and took aim against the enemy. Music on both sides was soon drowned out by the sounds of gunfire and shouting soldiers. The battle was on and still had room to grow. Giou and La Motte came out and bolstered the Christian forces with another four hundred foot. Valette noticed the Ottomans watching from Mount Salvador and Calcara, some five hundred meters southwest of Senglea and Birgu. He ordered Captain d'Eguaras, still smarting from his initial failure days earlier, to take the cavalry out and engage the enemy once more. Horsemen passed through the gate and passed by the infantry and galloped headlong for the Ottoman lines. Valette stood at the gate, pike in hand, holding back anyone else who wanted to get into the fight. However eager his soldiers might be, Valette was still determined to show he was in charge.

The rank-and-file discipline of the European armies, rooted in the almost machinelike Greek and Roman phalanx, was not the Ottoman way. The sultan's troops were greatly disciplined, but their fighting was of a looser nature.[11] In formal battle, they followed a crescent formation that dated back to Hannibal at Cannae and Khalid at Walaja, and would come down to Ntshingwayo at Isandlwana. The center line of cannon and Janissary arquebusiers, flanked by spahi cavalry, was curtained by stolid Azap infantry. The spahi's task was to excite the enemy and retreat, drawing the enemy in toward the Azap. These men could fight and then part in order to give an open field to cannon and Janissary arquebusiers. Spahis then enveloped from the flanks.

Spahis, skilled horsemen, would therefore have to make war on foot. This was not too much of a handicap. On or off their horses, they were practiced archers who disdained guns as dirty, loud, inelegant, and unmanly; their nomad ancestors had perfected the composite bow, carefully and patiently built from layers of wood, animal horn, sinew, and glue. These graceful weapons had a range of up to five hundred yards, and its arrows fired en masse could find unprotected parts of any soldier (something that arquebus fire could not always achieve). Mounted spahis, even at a full gallop, could hit moving targets. Even unhorsed, however (and the historian Cirni tells us they brought no horses to Malta), they were formidable opponents and excelled at close-quarter fighting.[12] As d'Eguaras and his men now rode into their ranks, the sound of sword hitting scimitar, much like a smith pounding hot iron, almost pleasing in any other context, carried across the field and back to the respective camps.

Elsewhere, the respective arquebusiers had spread out and were engaged in a slug match marked by the familiar pattern of load, prime, fire, and reload. Christian guns had shorter barrel lengths, enabling their owners to fire more rounds per minute, but at the cost of accuracy. The Ottoman arquebus was a longer weapon, harder and more time consuming to load, but once loaded, it was, in the hands of a skilled marksman, unnervingly accurate. Each weapon had good and bad points — for the Janissaries, the accuracy allowed snipers to hold down an enemy behind walls. For the Christians, the ability to reload quickly made it easier to defend a specific area — a breach in a wall, say — against mass attacks.

As the Christians stood and fired, a Spanish knight called Sésé, commander of the Post of Bormla, strolled about in the stink and smoke with a keg of powder and a sack of bullets, replenishing the troops' ammunition as needed and shouting out encouragement. His constant movement made him difficult to hit, but his vital role made him all the more desirable a target. His time came. A hot bullet pierced the keg, ignited the powder, and sent Sésé and some dozen of those around him to a better world.

The day wore on, the sun rose higher, the fight dragged on; men fell at random as unseen bullets hit their arms, legs, chests, or heads. Men negotiated the spaces between the dead and dying. Among the horsemen, fighting was up close and vicious. D'Eguaras was struck in the thigh and turned over command to his adjutant Antonio Varese. Turkish infantry edged down from the slopes for hand-to-hand combat. Valette was now overseeing the fight on the Post of Provence on the walls of Birgu, highly visible and "exposing himself to great danger."[13] A soldier standing nearby was struck and killed. Soon after, the grand master's page was also hit. Given the notorious accuracy of Janissary marksmen, it is tempting to think they were ordered to avoid hitting any white-haired gentlemen. Valette alive would make a nice prize either caged or in chains during the inevitable triumph in Constantinople.

Out on the field, the Christians were beginning to flag, their formations to fragment. Accidents occurred. A misfired cannon killed several gunners and burned nearly all of Faderigo de Toledo's face (the report to his father Don Garcia downplayed the damage and commended the young man's valor, assuring all that the boy would make a "fine knight").[14] The battle had lasted some five hours — enough for one day. Valette ordered that retreat be sounded and finally, steadily, perhaps reluctantly, perhaps not, the men pulled back into the gates. The day's fighting had seen twenty-one defenders killed and a hundred and fifty wounded. The Turks had lost over a hundred men, including an unnamed sanjak-bey.[15]

The Christians might have viewed that day as a victory since more Muslims than Christians had died. The Ottomans used other measures. Back in the camp, Mustapha wrote his report back to Suleiman that the first battle had gone to the Ottomans and all was well; he had, after all, seized the Marsa, a "place of water" for his campground.[16] (He does not mention the state of the water, though whether from neglect, from ignorance, or because the *protomedico*'s work had not taken, is unclear.) And whether victorious or not, Mustapha still had his prisoners to deal with.

At some point prior to the fight, La Rivière had singled out the Post of Castile in front of Birgu as being the weakest, and in consequence Mustapha had thrown the better part of his effort against it. The weaker outer wall was backed up inside with a new inner wall, strengthened until it was the "strongest of the chain, and enforced by iron."[17] Mustapha understood that he had been duped. La Rivière was dragged off to an Ottoman galley, where his executioner was waiting for him. Over the course of the next few hours, his bones and internal organs were expertly and painfully shattered.

He died before morning.[18]

❖·❖·❖

Suleiman had ordered that no action be taken without consulting Turgut Reis.[19] Turgut still had not arrived. Some thought that he was not coming at all — he was old, and strange things happen at sea. There was no reason to hold up all operations on his account. Spain was a formidable power, moreso now that they were not distracted by wars in the Lowlands and against France. They were quite capable of launching a relief force to trouble this siege, and intelligence suggested that, under the guidance of the new and capable viceroy, they were in the process of doing so. Best then to get on with the operation and hope that Turgut would show up sooner rather than later.[20]

The leading commanders gathered in Mustapha's tent to decide what to do next.

In theory there should have been little to discuss. The strategy had been laid out months earlier in Constantinople, aided by a scale model of Grand Harbor built on the report of two Muslim spies posing as fishermen.[21] The plan was to take out Fort St. Elmo and so control the eastern-facing deep waters and the secure bay of the Grand Harbor, better protected than Marsaxlokk from the spring's strong gregale winds that could sweep down from the northeast. In so doing, the Ottomans could maintain a supply base close to the army's center of operations, thus simplifying the demands of logistics. All future matériel arriving from Constantinople or North Africa would not have to be hauled the eight miles overland from Marsaxlokk, a wearisome task at best, and a dangerous task so long as there were Christian marauders about — as, in fact, there were until the very end.[22]

Mustapha had his own ideas. A veteran of wars in Hungary and Persia, Mustapha was accustomed to long marches over rough terrain — what was an eight-mile trek to him? Concede Grand Harbor to the knights, he thought, and St. Elmo becomes a Christian liability, a place they would have to defend while the bulk of Muslim soldiers were wearing down the main objectives elsewhere. His proposed order of operations was for Piali Pasha to take ten thousand men and ten guns and seize the lightly defended capital of Mdina at the center of the island. This would be both a psychological blow to the Maltese and a boost for his own men, and it would serve to protect the army's rear from Mdina's cavalry raiders and any possible Spanish relief forces. Once Mdina was taken, he could then attack the bulk of the enemy's forces at Birgu and Senglea, and finally, almost as an afterthought, seize the island of Gozo. His vision went further, offshore and into Piali's area of authority. He suggested a new disposition for the fleet, that it be divided into three parts: one to blockade Grand Harbor, one to remain in Marsaxlokk, and one to patrol the channel between Malta and Sicily.

It did not go down well. Piali Pasha reminded the council that his responsibility was to meet the needs of the sultan's "powerful and invincible armada" and to guard the island from any Christian warships.[23] (After his attempt to swindle Suleiman out of some ransom after Djerba, he was also on his best behavior.) Piali wanted the eastern-facing deep waters and secure bay of the Grand Harbor. To get this, they would need to take out the defensive Fort St. Elmo. The council, many of them navy men, concurred with Piali.

Compelled against his better judgment to target Fort St. Elmo, Mustapha wanted to know how long it would take to capture the place, and he sent out engineers skilled in this kind of calculation to make an estimate. They got as close as they dared, and came back with a mixture of good news and bad. The good news was that the shortcomings Don Garcia had criticized were all in place. The bad news was that the stony ground, while suitable for trenches, was useless for digging mines. As to siege artillery, that was simply a matter of getting cannon down the steep length of Mount Sciberras and into position opposite the fort. The engineers were confident that the Ottoman army, fresh from their voyage and ready for a fight, would be able to bring down the walls and take the fort in under five days. With luck, they might be able to present the first victory of the campaign to Turgut when he eventually arrived.

Mustapha gave in. His May 23 report to Suleiman notes the divided opinions and the final proposed course of action; it does not, interestingly, indicate what he thought.[24]

Balbi describes this squabble in some detail, based on the gossip of two more renegades who had, they claimed, stood guard outside the tent. (In camps famed for their silence, shouting commanders were presumably easy to hear.) Gossip or not, an overjoyed Valette reacted swiftly. His spies in Constantinople had reported that St. Elmo was to be the first target, but he could not be sure. Initially he had entrusted its defense to the aging and unwell Fr. Broglio and a small contingent of Spanish foot. From his command center in Fort St. Angelo, he now ordered the French knight Pierre de Massuez-Vercoirin (aka Colonel Mas) and two hundred of his men, as well as sixty-five volunteers from the knights, dispatched to bolster the three hundred and thirty-five soldiers already in Fort St. Elmo.[25] He cautioned them, however, to make self-preservation their priority, to not engage the enemy in any unnecessary skirmishes.

+·+·+·+

The day saw one other small victory for the Christians. Pierre Antoine de Roquelaure de St. Aubin, a knight of the Order, was commanding a galley that had been scouting the north African coast for intelligence. As he approached his home port, guns began to fire at him from Tigne point on the northern entrance of Grand Harbor. Damning the cannon, he headed full speed forward in hopes of running the gauntlet and rejoining his comrades at Fort St. Angelo. Piali in turn called six captains, led by Mohammed Bey, son of a onetime governor of Algiers, and ordered them to seize the interloper. Six Ottoman galleys progressed toward the bay's entrance, and a large audience of both Ottomans and Christians at St. Elmo gathered to see what was about to happen.

St. Aubin was bold, but he was no fool. When the six Ottoman galleys debouched from the mouth of Grand Harbor, he knew any battle would be hopeless. He quickly reversed course away from the island and north toward Sicily and safety. Despite having the advantage of fresh crews, five of the six vessels failed to close the gap with St. Aubin; soon only Mohammed Bey had any chance of overtaking the Christian. A galley of this sort with low draft can reach speeds of up to seven knots by oars, but only in short bursts. (Under sail, it can reach up to eleven knots.) Mohammed Bey was closing in on St. Aubin, when St. Aubin made a surprising move. Without warning, he ordered the galley stopped, came about at 180 degrees and suddenly was directing his own guns at the oncoming Ottoman vessel. St. Aubin had now become the challenger in an even fight.

There was a well-understood protocol of galley warfare. Two vessels charged each other and fired the bow guns, larger first, smaller second, at the last possible moment, after which the stronger boarded the weaker and the fight played out on a blood-soaked deck. The crucial question always was who fired first. The time it took to reload the guns made one shot the only shot, thus making the galley joust into a primitive game of chicken. Fire first and you were then at the mercy of your surviving opponent's remaining strength. Fire second, preferably at the very moment of engagement, and you had the momentum of your shot to carry your men onto the enemy ship. This was the goal of any captain, and it took strong nerves to pull it off.

The alternative was simply to break off the fight, and it was that option that Mohammed Bey chose. While there was still a large gap between the ships, the Ottoman commander ordered his vessel to pull up short, turn around, and head back to the safety of Grand Harbor. St. Aubin, triumphant, set course for Sicily.

It was no surprise that cheers went up from behind the walls of Fort St. Elmo. It was a bitter humiliation for Piali Pasha, but more so for Mohammed Bey. The admiral had the disgraced captain brought to him, berated the fellow, and finally, spat in his face. This is the last we hear of Mohammed Bey.

10

+·+·+·+

PREPARATIONS

FOR A SIEGE

+·+·+·+

What matters is that if Malta is not helped now, I believe it will fall.

Don Garcia de Toledo to Philip II, May 31, 1565

The governing council of Mdina, the Università, was concerned about the state of the city's defenses, and with the blessing of Governor de Mesquita they sent one of their own, Luca de Armenia, to confer with Valette. Armenia arrived at Fort St. Angelo at dusk on May 24 and had to wait some hours while the grand master inspected the troops.[1] He is likely the same Armenia who had written, just prior to the siege, a short paean to his country and city, expressing doubts as to its fate:

> Alas, we flee our native land, we leave the city by herself
> Dispersing each one according to each one's fate
> Sorrowful city, farewell, for a second and a third time farewell
> We are left to our tears and grief. No other city will be like you, farewell[2]

The Università had a simple request — permission to send their excess citizens to Birgu, or failing that, to get more soldiers, mercenaries, artillerymen, and powder sent to Mdina.[3] If the grand master could arrange the latter course, Armenia assured him that the remaining citizens of Mdina would do all they could in defense of their homeland. Valette was in no position to welcome more people in the already overcrowded Birgu, and Armenia could hardly point to any imminent danger to the old city. Nevertheless, Valette agreed to send more men, and Armenia appears to have roused himself from his melancholy. By the end of the siege, the soldiers he commanded could take credit for having killed over a thousand Ottomans.[4]

At about this time, Valette received mail from Don Garcia that gave Valette some cause for anxiety.[5] While it was true that the viceroy was gathering men as quickly as possible, he also made it clear that he was anxious for boats. Malta had boats, arguably the best in the Mediterranean.[6] Don Garcia requested that the grand master send him however many he could, to help in the transport of the forces gathering at Messina, while also removing noncombatants from the island. All of this, he noted, would be much more difficult once the Ottomans controlled the entrance to Grand Harbor.

Valette wrote back to say that he could not spare the galleys, but again urged the viceroy to come as quickly as possible. He gave the letter to the Perugian knight Vincenzo Anastagi and, as he promised the Università, dispatched him with sixty soldiers to reinforce Mdina.[7] With them went horses, the last in Senglea and Birgu. Cavalry, useless in the city, was ideally suited for the fast raids and reconnaissance missions that would come out of Mdina. (Two days earlier, Valette had also sent a letter directly to Philip II, voicing confidence that they could win not just at Malta, but also at Goletta.[8] Clearly he knew his audience.)

Now certain that the first target was to be Fort St. Elmo, Valette had all the civilians who had taken refuge there brought over to Birgu. The boats that carried this last group out of harm's way returned with powder, lead, rope, incendiaries, hardtack, wine, cheese, lard, oil, and vinegar for the five hundred men inside. He also ordered Colonel Mas and 150 of his men to swell the ranks.[9]

If Valette expected caution from the men at St. Elmo, he had sadly misjudged them. Inspired by the knowledge that Ottoman siege guns were being towed down the peninsula, Colonel Mas and Captain La Cerda led a number of their men out of the fort and headed for the enemy. The ensuing fight, the last direct fighting they were to enjoy for some time, was a short and spirited affair, but the handful of men killed on both sides did not materially slow Mustapha's progress.

It appears, however, to have prompted him to position sharpshooters within range of Fort St. Elmo. Janissaries were notorious for the efficiency of their snipers, "most excellent marksmen."[10] These men could lie in wait for hours at a time in the hope of blowing the head off anyone who, from curiosity, might peek over the top of the parapet, however briefly. From that time on, the Christian defenders were trapped inside the fort, with only the sound of Muslim sappers digging trenches outside the fort and enemy gun carriages moving closer and closer.

The defenders, however, were able to fire cannon from seaward facing cavalier cannon fire that was supplemented by Valette's men across the water at Fort St. Angelo. The footsoldiers might feel superfluous in such circumstances. These were experienced warriors who knew what went into a proper fort, and Fort St. Elmo was not the best example of the military architect's art. Personal bravery notwithstanding, the men of Fort St. Elmo could calculate odds as well as any Ottoman engineer, and they knew the power of the wall-smashing guns that in a day or so would be brought to bear.

✦·✦·✦·✦

On May 24, Mustapha was ready. His guns were set in three ranks facing the landward side of St. Elmo. Defensive gabions, boxes filled with cotton, now created a wall through which ten guns capable of firing eight-pound balls poked out toward the fort. A second tranche that boasted two culverins, guns capable of lobbing sixty-pound shot, backed them up. Finally, on the rise overlooking the fort was one of the so-called basilisks, its vast cyclopean eye staring down on St. Elmo, a huge weapon capable of throwing a stone ball of a hundred and sixty pounds. More guns would follow, and from different emplacements, but these would do for now. Sacks of powder were shoved down the bronze gullets, with stone balls lifted in as a chaser. Engineers sighted targets and adjusted angles of fire. Each gunner prepared his slow match and blew the tip into a bright orange glow, loose sparks flying off and crackling as they expired. Mustapha himself stood behind them, waited until all was ready, and then gave the order to fire. The artillerymen lowered the linstocks to the touchholes, and in a storm of sound, fire, and smoke, the first volleys slammed into the walls of Fort St. Elmo.

The effect was devastating, so powerful that even in Birgu the houses shook.[11] The infantry huddled inside the fort, unable even to watch the enemy. Throughout the day, Turkish artillery smashed against the walls, pulverizing and knocking off chunks of stonework and beginning to fill the ditch. Of necessity, trained soldiers became journeyman masons of the crudest sort, reduced to reinforcing the walls as the ground shook and stonework crumbled, their swords and guns and all thoughts of fighting now shelved. Men such as La Cerda could only seethe at this misuse of their talents.

The Christians of St. Elmo were not, however, fighting completely alone. Valette had ordered the guns on Fort St. Angelo to fire on the Ottoman sappers and cannon, and they did so with good effect. One of these shots dislodged a stone that struck Piali Pasha's head and knocked him senseless. He was unconscious for about an hour, prompting rumors about his death — premature, as it happened. He had, they said afterward, his turban to thank for his life. Mustapha's reaction to this news is unrecorded.

The entire day passed in ponderous rolling thunder of cannon fire, smoke, and dust quivering in midair. The very ground trembled in response to this pummeling. Finally, night fell, the cannon ceased, and the men at St. Elmo considered the situation. It was clear to them that the fort could not hold up under this kind of abuse, and since the defenders could not even fight back, the best option, the only option, was to abandon the fort entirely, return to Fort St. Angelo, and bolster the fighting force there.

If someone was to suggest this course of action to as stern a man as Valette, best that it be a reputable commander who was not a member of the Order of St. John. The job went to Captain La Cerda.

On the night of May 24–25, La Cerda slipped into a small boat and under a moonless sky was rowed across to Fort St. Angelo. Valette was there to greet him and in a public square asked him how matters stood at St. Elmo. The grand master presumably expected a bluff-and-hearty answer to the effect that they were holding their own and eager to fight. He got the opposite. La Cerda answered that matters were exceedingly bad.

It was a straightforward, honest, and heartfelt answer, but as the chronicler put it, one that "he should have kept secret and in chambers, so as not to frighten the populace."[12] He was quickly hustled into the council room before he could blurt out anything more. The grand council sat in tall back benches on either side of the room, unsteady candlelight wavered over the stones and wood, and the commanders asked him to explain himself. La Cerda didn't hesitate. Fort St. Elmo was, he said, "a sick man in need of medicine."[13] Its walls could not hold, and the soldiers, his soldiers, were being condemned to die without hope of fighting back. Let the place be mined and abandoned so that Turks could enter and be blown up in the process. Let the Christians rejoin their fellows at Senglea and Birgu, and let the real fight begin.

The council might not have expected good news, but this kind of talk, this early on in the campaign, was a shock, the more so given the source. La Cerda was no raw recruit who flinched at the first sound of gunfire. He was a veteran of the 1543 siege of Tlemcen, on the Barbary coast, in which battle he had been wounded in his shoulder.[14] His actions on Malta so far had been aggressive, even rash, but undeniably brave. Given his position and experience, his word must carry some weight, both with the council and with his own men.

How did Valette react? Accounts differ. However displeased the grand master might have been, the chroniclers Balbi and Cirni record a relatively temperate response. The encyclopedic Bosio, however, writes that Valette was scathing.[15] He thanked La Cerda for his report. Did the men in the fort truly have no confidence in their abilities? Very well, they were free to go. Valette did not wish to have anyone in whom he could have no confidence, and clearly he could have no confidence in them. He would replace the men now in the fort with better men, braver men, men headed by Valette himself.

It may have been stage anger or the real thing, but regardless, the threat had its intended effect. The council protested that as grand master he must not leave. If more soldiers were required at St. Elmo, they could be found. Valette agreed in the end and called up Lieutenant Medrano, a subordinate to Captain Miranda (who was recovering from an illness at Messina) and ordered him to take his company of two hundred men across to Fort St. Elmo.[16] Proving that good things come to those in whom Valette did have confidence, the grand master also promoted him to captain.

Not to be outdone by the Spanish volunteers, a French knight, Captain Gaspard de La Motte, stepped forward and offered to take a number of his own men to bolster the defenders of Fort St. Elmo.[17] Would Valette agree?

He would. Ardent men, he said, were exactly what was needed. To top off the rebuke to La Cerda and any others at Fort St. Elmo who thought the place not worth defending, Valette also offered some sixty pressed convicts (*forzati*) their freedom if they would agree to act as ferrymen for the soldiers.[18]

The sky was still dark. Captain Medrano, La Motte, and two hundred fresh troops (along with the humiliated La Cerda) embarked stealthily into the small crafts and under the last sliver of the old moon crossed the waters back to the crumbling fort. Valette wrote to Don Garcia that the fort's complement was eight hundred men, though perhaps he was exaggerating a bit when he said "all were resolved to do their duty."[19]

If nothing else the incident demonstrates the degree to which auxiliaries, especially the Spanish soldiers like La Cerda, considered themselves to be the equals of the Order in terms of authority. Vertot, a seventeenth-century French historian for whom Valette could do no wrong, derides the Spaniard as someone "whom fear made eloquent."[20] The charge is ludicrous and ignores La Cerda's logic, which in this instance was both simple and direct. He was on Malta to kill Muslims. In St. Elmo he was not killing Muslims. Better, therefore, to abandon a slaughter pen and take the fight to the enemy elsewhere. This was perhaps an admirable view, but impractical for Valette. The grand master's was not a split command, much less command by consensus. Dissent was already a problem in the enemy camp, and Valette would not have it in his own.

And he did not let the matter drop. He quickly informed Don Garcia, who raised the matter with the king: "Juan de la Cerda and his lieutenant . . . have shown great baseness (*vildad*), and attempted to persuade the Grand Master to abandon the fort and mine it, because it was no longer possible to defend the place."[21] Don Garcia suggested that beheading would be suitable punishment, and the king, who took a minute interest in all details of his empire, did not object: "If what you say is true, that Juan de la Cerda and his lieutenant wanted to abandon Sant Telmo, you are to give orders that they be punished according to what is just."[22] Philip's letter is dated July 7 — it is a little touching that the king could imagine that he was addressing a situation static enough that his advice would be meaningful. Nothing further seems to have come of the matter, and as we shall see, La Cerda's fate would be more complex than a simple execution.

+·+·+·+

It took Captain Medrano just two days inside Fort St. Elmo to understand La Cerda's frustration. Sitting around while the walls around them were toppled and pulverized was no way to fight a war. He and Colonel Mas discussed the situation. What was needed, they decided, was to give the Ottomans a sharp kick to remind them that the Christians were not a bunch of passive cowering bricklayers. Night would be a good time to take the fight to the enemy.

Turkish sappers worked all hours in shifts. By day, Muslim sharpshooters held down the Christians and allowed the ditchdiggers to work in safety. But at night the Janissaries retired, and it was at night that two companies under Mas and Medrano girded themselves in steel breastplates, strapped on greaves, snugged morions on their heads, and gathered weapons. The moon was two days into its first quarter and in no danger of giving them away. The two companies slipped out from a sally port and approached the dull sound of pick and shovels in the near distance.

The Turkish sappers, grateful for the cool of the night, off guard on the presumption of safety, and unarmed except for their tools, continued their spade work. This was the soft shift, free from the unspeakable Maltese sun and any possible danger of a stray Christian missile. Certainly they were luckier than the soldiers who, once the ditches were finished, would actually have to attack the fort. Comparatively speaking, their lot was a happy one.

Weird shadows appeared above these happy men, and Mas and Medrano's columns fell on them with speed and violence. The Spaniards, too long unable to take the fight to the enemy, were releasing a long overdue fury against the almost defenseless foe. If there was little glory in this kind of one-sided slaughter, there was satisfaction in the knowledge that it would delay Ottoman progress. Swords and pikes sliced open the enemy; sharp edges cut deeply into their torsos or limbs, or took off their hands or feet. The sappers fell quickly but not quietly, and the Janissaries soon awoke to what was happening. Rising from their beds, they seized their own weapons and guided chiefly by sound, rushed to close with Mas and Medrano's men. Now the real fight began and the Christians no longer held the advantage.

The sounds of shouting, clashing metal, and gunshots carried across the water to the sentinels at Fort St. Angelo; thus alerted that some kind of fight was under way, they could only stand at the edge of the bay and wait, and listen, and watch the darkness sporadically illuminated by the yellow spit of gunfire. There was no telling how the battle might be going, though every Christian knew how the numbers stacked up. Any fight between soldiers of equal skill — and the Janissaries were as good as any soldiers on earth — is weighted to the side with the most men. All surprise spent, the Christians' only hope was in a timely retreat to the relative safety of the fort. The men across the waters at St. Angelo waited anxiously and prayed that their comrades were giving worse than they got.

It took some hours for the sounds of battle to die down. Dawn gradually broke and a light wind carried off the last of the smoke as the men at Fort St. Angelo strained to see across the bay.

Christians still held the fort. The Muslim crescent, however, now waved over the counterscarp, with just the ditch below separating the attackers from the walls of the fort itself.

11

A FATAL
OVERSIGHT

✦·✦·✦·✦

Whoever intended to carry out the plans of the original designer
of fort [St. Elmo] modified the design or added new features to it. But these
men were incompetent and, regardless of their motives, their work did not
strengthen the fort and nor was it faithful to the original plan. The masonry
walls were built too high and then the cavaliers were built even higher
although they would never be able to challenge enemy artillery positions
on the high ground. Excessively high walls are dangerous, for to expose too
much masonry to the enemy gives him the opportunity to fill the ditch with
their ruins and then to climb over the rubble into the defenses.

Gian Giacomo Leonardi, 1557

Turgut arrived on June 2, two weeks late. He brought with him a flotilla of
thirteen galleys and two galleots filled with fifteen hundred corsairs and volunteers.[1] These men were independent minded, volatile, and dangerous, and
unlike the army under Mustapha and Piali's command, they were not slaves
to the sultan. Barbary corsairs were willing to give lip service to the Ottoman
Empire but were too far away from Constantinople for their allegiance to
be much more than theoretical and voluntary. In the end, the corsairs would
serve only under leaders they respected and would slip away the moment their
leaders, or the mission at hand, became unworthy of respect. They were brave,
at times alarmingly so, but they served their own interests and expected to be
paid. The Ottomans recognized this and factored it into their calculations —
according to a Venetian ambassador, "[The Ottomans] don't trust them much

and employ them the same way doctors use poison, that is, in small doses and intermixed with the rest of the fleet."[2] Turgut's stature among the Christians defending Malta, however, was high enough that Anthoine de Cressy, a French knight who served throughout the siege, thought that he was essentially in charge ("il commandoit tout").[3]

Why should Turgut be so late? Tripoli is, after all, much closer to Malta than is Constantinople, and Turgut had been invited months earlier. He was now eighty years old, of course, and had been ill the previous year, but as events were to prove, he was still an energetic man. He was said to have been disappointed that the target was not Goletta, and his delay might have been an opportunity to remind the two commanders that he was no man's errand boy. (Neither, for that matter, were the corsairs themselves, and coordinating them may well have been like herding cats.) There is also the fact that years before a fortune-teller had predicted that one day he would die on Malta.

Turgut's official mandate as recorded in the Ottoman state archives is fairly limited: "You should help Mustapha Pasha at sea and you should protect our navy against the enemy's navy, which could set out from other countries to help Malta."[4] Ottoman historians, however, claim that Suleiman ordered his two commanders to do nothing without consulting the old corsair, as he "knew everything concerning Malta — knew the direction from which to strike the fortress, and where to raise the shelters. [Mustapha] was ordered to conform to his opinion."[5]

As Turgut showed up late, obeying this mandate would have required a delay of fifteen days, with no guarantee that he would appear at all. Still, arrive he did and Piali Pasha at least seemed eager to see his old comrade in arms. The rendezvous was to be at St. Paul's Bay, a few miles north of the Grand Harbor. Hoping to make an occasion of things, Piali lead his eighty vessels out of Marsaxlokk to greet the corsair, and while passing by the Grand Porte ordered each galley to fire on Fort St. Elmo. The sound and fury were impressive, but the end result was something of a pratfall — several of the volleys flew over the beleaguered Christians and struck and killed a number of Mustapha's gunners. Worse, the fleet was close enough that the Christians were able to fire back. They sank at least one galley.

Turgut's appearance was not well timed. The fight for St. Elmo, projected to take five days, was now on day nine, with no end in sight. Worse, it turned out that Turgut agreed with Mustapha's abandoned strategy completely, and said so: "'Of what use is it to take Saint Elmo?' he asked. 'Even if you had ten Saint Elmos, until you take Malta [i.e., the rest of the island], you cannot be conquerors.' Thus having spoken, he immediately wept."[6] They should, he thought, have gone for Mdina and Gozo, the easy targets, the mother to the child St. Elmo.[7]

It was too late now, though the endorsement of Mustapha's plan, added to the soldiers killed by Piali Pasha's guns, cannot have helped relations between Mustapha and Piali. It was best to look forward. Having received a full run-down of how matters stood, the aging Turgut immediately went out to the end of the peninsula to see firsthand what steps had been taken and what things could be improved. Turgut's first concern was for the safety of his troops. He noted that the southward part of Sciberras was clearly visible from the walls of Fort St. Angelo. Given the expectations of a quick victory, Mustapha had had no reason to spend too much time in masking their actions. By now, however, Christian gunners from across the water had been able to calibrate their fire on sappers and artillerists, making the Muslims' work both difficult and short. This interference had to be stopped. Turgut ordered a makeshift screen to be erected between Fort St. Angelo and the Turkish part of Sciberras. Blind the gunners to specific targets and they would be wasting shot and powder on empty space.

The men now relatively safe, Turgut turned his attention to the fort itself. A devastating bombardment was in order, and from as many directions as possible. Turgut ordered new artillery emplacements on Tigné point, the north tip of the harbor mouth. This would allow the Turks to fire on St. Elmo from three sides and force the defenders within to spread out their repairs. He was particularly interested in neutralizing the raised cavalier whose cannons faced back on the Ottoman lines at Mount Sciberras. Finally, he considered the matter of the Christians' nocturnal relief boats. These vessels, all but invisible under the nearly moonless sky, had until now been largely unmolested. The moon, however, was waxing, and with each passing day, the Christians lost another sliver of advantage. Turgut was determined to end the fort's cycle of slow bleeding and regular infusions, and just finish the fort off once and for all. The guns — thirty of various caliber — were to begin firing that night.

+·+·+·+

The chroniclers considered it something of a miracle that the fort was still standing at all. One reason for its survival was distance. Large, wall-smashing guns work best at close range, a fact the Ottomans were happy to exploit. More than that and they lost significant power. Whether from reluctance to bring out the heavy guns against this smaller target, or as Hughes suggests, because the geography prevented their pulling anything up to point-blank range, Mustapha kept his largest cannon a full 180 yards from the fort.[8] The discharges were inevitably both dramatic and loud, but they did less damage than they might have done had the guns been closer. Large cannon, moreover, took a long time to prepare. Smaller bored pieces, if not as destructive, could at least be fired and reloaded in fairly quick order. The knight Fra Girolamo Pepe Napolitano, with little else to do, lay back and counted the shots and "calculated that a day did not pass in which six or seven hundred cannonades were not fired against it."[9] Anthoine de Cressy claims that on one day, no less than fourteen hundred *coups de canon* struck the fort, and that by the end it would endure nineteen thousand.[10] The numbers should not be too surprising. The chief object of the cannonade was to chip away a wall faster than the defenders could repair it. Strictly speaking, proper rebuilding was impractical if not impossible. The best that could be done was to buffer the edges with earth or cotton-filled gabions, crude barrels made of rush, that would absorb the blow of the next day's cannonballs. It was a job best done at night when the sharpshooters were sleeping. Come the morning, the artilleryman's first order of business was to sweep this padding away as quickly as possible and get back to chipping away at the stone structure itself. In addition, and depending on available material, the defenders could build a secondary wall inside the fort that would come as a surprise to anyone rushing through the breach.

However necessary all this preliminary work might be, in the end taking the fort would depend on sheer grit. Any given breach favors the defender insofar as it concentrates the attacking force. It took outstanding bravery to rush the small opening and become an easy target for prepared men. A single cannon of scattershot would cut a wide swath through the attackers. Where a few dozen men might charge, none might survive. The Muslims made these attacks over and over, and each time to no end other than filling the ditch with their dead and dying.

It is the mark of a good leader that his men want to go out of their way to impress him. Turgut had this quality. When the Janissaries demanded that they be allowed to take the breach, the corsair forbade it, commending their zeal but noting that the opening was still too small, and that if they gathered to make a charge, they would present Christian gunners and the fast-loading arquebusiers a single, concentrated, easy-to-hit target. He wanted better odds.

Not to be deterred, a squadron of Ottoman engineers set out in the predawn hours to see if there were any new weaknesses they might exploit. One place they explored was the north-facing ravelin, the heightened defensive spur that had so concerned Don Garcia de Toledo. Under the pale light of the first-quarter moon, these men scurried down to get a closer look. The ravelin loomed in the dark ahead of them. They approached, ready for the sudden pop of gunfire that would send them back into the shadows, but they heard nothing.

The reasons for this are obscure. Some have suggested that the designated sentry had nodded off or been killed by sniper fire, or that the complement of soldiers was unexpectedly small, only forty men, none of them Knights of St. John.[11] Whatever the case, the Janissaries soon realized that this was a target ripe for the taking and wasted no time in getting word back down the line. They consulted (or not) Mustapha for instructions and were ordered (or not) to hurry up and take advantage of this rare opportunity.[12]

Accounts of what followed are somewhat confused. What is nearly certain is that before dawn a number of Janissaries trotted back to the ravelin, threw up scaling ladders, then flowed over the sides of the ravelin and through its embrasures (low enough that a man standing on the shoulders of another man could easily get in), and started to butcher the Italian and Spanish soldiers inside. The luckier defenders awoke in the early half-light of dawn only to see their commanding officer lying dead and an ever-increasing number of highly agressive, brightly gowned, scimitar-wielding Janissaries looming above them. In a panic they scrambled up, abandoned their arms, and ran back onto the causeway toward the fort. Fortunately, the ravelin's defenders were backed up by fifty men under the command of a Neapolitan knight Francesco di Guevara. Guevara's men were stationed in a trench that blocked the passage between the ravelin and cavalier; and now alerted by the shrill cries of the Janissaries and the shouting of their comrades, they climbed over their barricade down the causeway toward the plank bridge (wood, easy to destroy in an emergency) to take up the fight. Arquebusiers fired on the Ottoman ranks, helping to slow the sudden incursion until more help could arrive.

Which it did in short order — the knight Vercoiran, along with his brother Colonel Mas, Captain Medrano, and the Spanish knight and *bailo* of Negroponte Juan d'Eguaras came out of the fort, across the drawbridge that spanned the ditch, and on through the causeway with the aim of repelling the Turks from the ravelin.

Despite their best efforts, it was too late to repel the Turks; word of the impromptu battle had quickly flowed back to the Ottoman camp, and fresh waves of exultant soldiers had rushed to join their comrades. As Guevara and his men hacked away on the narrow confines of the causeway and the wooden plank bridge that connected it to the ravelin, more and more Ottomans had been climbing into the ravelin itself. Soon an excess of Muslim troops was spilling over into the ditch, bringing their force up to the face of the ramparts themselves. Curione, writing in 1565, mentions ladders too short to top the ramparts, but even with that disappointment, the taking of the ditch, even at the cost of five hundred men, was worth it.[13] Because of the fort's wide angle and the lack of embrasures or crenellations, it was impossible for the Christians to cover all approaches in the ditch except from the tower, and even that had dead zones where the Ottomans could crouch next to the fort's wall in near total safety. From here, they could both fire on the causeway and work on destroying the foundations of the fort itself. Along the causeway, the battle grew and the sun came up to illuminate the brawl, and for five hours men fought hand-to-hand, chiefly with blades.

The Christians had one advantage in the person of Fra Francesco Lanfreducci, who commanded two artillery pieces on the heights of the cavalier. By repeatedly sending scattershot into the mass of Ottoman troops, he was able to clear Ottoman soldiers from the traverse and even, temporarily at least, within the ravelin itself. A great multitude of flags had marked the Ottoman's taking of the ravelin, but all were blown away in an instant by Lanfreducci's guns. The attackers, however, were not to be deterred, and Lanfreducci could fire his guns only so often before they overheated to the point where they might themselves explode. Moreover, where the fighting was hand to hand, any shot the gunners let loose risked killing as many Christians as Muslims. As a final problem, early on Lanfreducci was short one of his key cannoneers, lost to a well-aimed arquebus shot.

The battle lines wavered over the morning hours, and from time to time, there was some hope that the ravelin itself might be recovered. The Ottomans, however, were already putting their own defense works — wooden fasces, earth-filled gabions, bales of wool — in place against any such attempt. Force of numbers eventually told, and the mass of Ottomans was able to push the defenders across the traverse and back toward the drawbridge that gave access to the fort itself. Guevara, wounded in his arm, and Louis Vercoirin, the brother of Colonel Mas, commanded the retreat, which was so closely engaged that the defenders were unable to raise the bridge.[14] The Turks were on the verge of breaking through, those in front being pushed forward by the men in back, when the defenders on the parapets began to bombard them with a storm of rocks and burning pitch. The defenders also likely used trumps.

Trumps were an unpleasant weapon consisting of a metal tube strapped onto long wooden poles. The tubes were filled with a mixture of bitumen, tar, sulfur, and other incendiary material, the stuff the ancients called Greek fire, and all too similar to modern-day napalm. Once the material was ignited, the tubes became flamethrowers, particularly useful for defending narrow spaces, such as the entrance to Fort St. Elmo. Defenders would wave these against the men pressing the entrance. The weapons, once given a chance to warm up, spat out sticky gobs of burning naphtha, which clung to everything it touched. From the changed quality of the screaming, it took only a short time before the men at the back realized what was happening and fled backward, allowing their less fortunate comrades to run from the bridge and throw themselves into the dust or farther off into the water. Dust might have extinguished the matter, but water would not — according to contemporary sources, only vinegar or urine was proof against the stuff.[15]

The attacks stopped entirely at about half past noon. The ravelin was now firmly in Ottoman hands, as was the greater part of the ditch. The cost to the Ottomans had been high — five hundred men killed on this day, and as many as two thousand killed since the assaults on St. Elmo had begun (a figure received from runaways). The defenders had lost about twenty knights, and sixty soldiers were killed and many more wounded.[16]

Valette ordered boats to bring the dead and wounded back to Fort St. Angelo, and it is a testimony to Turgut's effectiveness that not one of these vessels escaped unhit. Valette sent Coppier over to determine if the ravelin could be retaken. The answer was immediate and negative. Worse, Coppier had to inform Valette that the Turks were already hoisting goatskin sandbags onto the ravelin in order to raise its heights above the walls of St. Elmo. Balbi, in describing the action, laments the failure of Fort St. Elmo's design, even going so far as to defend La Cerda's objections.[17]

Mustapha was happy to report this success back to Constantinople and put it down as a matter of careful preparation rather than luck.[18] For Valette, the day's failure had to be particularly bad news, and not something he would wish to report to Don Garcia, the ravelin's chief proponent. The situation was all the more galling since the ravelin's commander was a corporal in La Cerda's company — the same La Cerda who had suggested the entire structure be mined, handed over to the Ottomans, and then detonated. Cirni suggests that his men, "having lost heart," simply and dishonorably (*vilmente*) abandoned the ravelin as more trouble than it was worth[19] — in effect, a strategic retreat decided on the ground without waiting for possibly inconvenient orders from on high.

If so, they paid a high price. Among the day's wounded was a lieutenant (*alferez*) to La Cerda. Valette, conscientious about greeting all casualties from the fort, saw this man with the others, judged his wound insufficiently grave, and ordered him thrown into prison. The offence cannot have been too egregious, and the man's presence must have been too valuable for him to stay in jail for long — he was released within days. But Valette had made his point about who was in charge on Malta. (Curiously, La Cerda's own whereabouts at this time are not recorded.)

12

+•+•+

THRUST
AND PARRY

+•+•+

If Julius Caesar had been alive and
seen such a perilous situation,
he would never have thought to
allow such valiant men to die.

Antoine de la Roche

In the early morning hours of the day after the battle, Valette's guards on the far side of Fort St. Elmo became aware of a small boat quietly heading toward the rocks below them. Fearing a night attack, the guards fired on the vessel, fortunately without effect. One of the passengers called out, explaining that he was the knight Salvago, back from Sicily, and with him was Captain Juan de Miranda, commanding officer of Lieutenant (now Captain) Medrano.[1] Just weeks before, Miranda had been heading to Malta when he fell ill at Syracuse, and rather than delay the expedition, ordered Medrano and his men to continue on without him. Once recovered, he had taken the opportunity to join Salvago on one of two of the Order's ships heading out of Syracuse for Malta, and run the blockade in a smaller boat.

Miranda appears to have been the kind of openhanded, optimistic officer whom men instinctively like, and the few trivial orders he gave were immediately carried out. He was also generous in the matter of Medrano's promotion, saying that a gentleman so excellent and valorous deserved that much and more; and as the man was now well settled into the post, Medrano would have a better understanding of how matters lay and what could be expected of both the enemy and the veteran defenders.

Miranda's immediate task, moreover, was to report to Valette, and so he and Salvago were soon being ferried across the water to the grand master, who greeted the pair warmly. The news they brought from Sicily was less welcome. The viceroy had so far been unable to gather as many men as he had hoped and now could not send relief before July 20, and in the meantime, he asked that Valette send the Order's remaining galleys back to Messina. This seemed an impossible request, and certainly Valette took it that way, or as an excuse by Don Garcia for not providing the aid he had promised. Valette wrote back, declining to send the galleys, and asking for twelve to fifteen thousand men. He explained that preserving Fort St. Elmo had cost him two hundred Christians, but that the Ottomans, in their failed attempts to take it, had spent six to seven thousand Janissary and spahi lives.[2] Impressive figures, and one wonders if Don Garcia actually believed them.

Valette now returned to the matter of the fort and Miranda's brief and dismal assessment of it. The grand master made it clear that he did not like this kind of news. Was Miranda certain that everything they had said was true? It would be best that they go back and confirm their findings before Valette made any decisions. They obeyed, and returned before dawn. They were lucky to get back this second time alive — Turgut's snipers had potted one of their crew members as the skiff crossed the water.

The fort, they learned, was marked by breaches and near breaches, by enemy troops a stone's throw away in the ditch, and by few places to shelter from their gunfire. Worse, the Ottomans were making rapid progress on building up the ravelin, and would soon be able to fire down into the fort's central piazza. Miranda added that, having now seen the fort, he was unhappy with its design and regretted that the ravelin had not been mined prior to its capture, as La Cerda had recommended.

He firmly agreed with the grand master, however, that the fort's importance as a means of keeping the Ottomans busy and away from Birgu and Senglea was paramount and that a premature evacuation would be a grave mistake. New troops, Miranda said, should be rotated into the fort, and he volunteered to go himself, an offer to which Valette immediately agreed. Since the grand master had already promoted Medrano to Miranda's old job, Miranda was offered overall command, superior even to the ailing Broglio. Miranda declined, making a joke of the whole matter: "Heaven forbid that I should take charge of such a hopeless task! Afterwards people might say that it was I who lost the fort!"[3]

Valette's offer made a good deal of sense. Miranda was clearly a man whom soldiers trusted, and he already had a history with his former company. The Spanish soldiers needed someone to inspire them, and what greater endorsement of Spanish ability could the grand master make than to put one of their own in charge? Even though Miranda turned down the offer, news of it would quickly have made the rounds. As for the knights, their mandate was obedience to the grand master, and if Valette chose to delegate authority to a worthy outsider, they were obliged accept the fact and carry on accordingly.

As Miranda was preparing to head back to St. Elmo, Valette asked if anything else could improve matters at the fort. Miranda said that the men should be given their pay. The suggestion was a little surprising. These men were on the front line, there was nothing to buy or sell — what possible use could they have of cash? A little dicing and cards, presumably. Miranda suggested that an influx of money would do no great harm, but that it would give an illusion of normality and therefore a measure of hope. He also suggested providing a few casks of wine. Valette agreed to all of this, tapping the bishop of Malta for the funds, and Miranda returned to the fort the following night, along with the provisions and over a hundred new soldiers and knights. Although officially he had turned down command of the fort, he did not hesitate to ring the alarm just to check the soldiers' state of readiness, or to give orders where he thought they were warranted. Presumably the wine and money that he brought with him made this the more palatable.

However inspiring Miranda might be, his fellow captains were still pessimistic. They had tried, and failed, to recapture the ravelin. Valette had been especially keen on this goal, and had sent Marshal Coppier and Don Costantino Castriota to see if it could be done. They said it could not and that the only hope for St. Elmo was a steady supply of men and matériel for as long as possible. In keeping with the tradition of the fog of war, dispatches to Queen Elizabeth reported that the ravelin had been retaken and that the defenders were in the process of demolishing it.[4] The fort indeed stood for the moment, but it was ultimately doomed.

❖·❖··❖·❖

The end was coming, but there remained the question of how it would play out. The ravelin continued to rise as the Ottoman workmen topped it with sandbags made of goatskin, and it would in due course command the parade ground. Meanwhile, Ottoman engineers were at work on a bridge to span the ditch between themselves and Fort St. Elmo. Excess galleys, superfluous as the invasion force died off, were being dismantled and reconfigured to this end. Spars were planted in the ground, supports tied in crisscross patterns to give them stability, flat planks laid horizontally on top, and dirt thrown on the whole to prevent the Christians from tossing incendiary grenades and setting the structure on fire. The passage was wide enough for eight men to advance abreast, and it looked as if it would be ready by June 5.

The night before, however, a squad of Christians stole out of the fort with buckets of pitch and began to paint the bridge's supports. Noise, or the perhaps the smell, alerted the Ottomans still awake, and although the defenders were able to torch three of the five supports, they left the job half finished. Discovered in their task, the Christians scuttled back to the safety of the fort while Mustapha's men did their best to put out the blaze. By daylight, the fire was out and the bridge was still standing, but sufficiently weakened so that the Ottomans did not wish to risk using it in a general assault. If the Christians had not stopped the Ottomans cold, they had at least bought themselves some more time.

By now, Broglio had lost confidence in his ability to command. Seventy years old and fat, he did not carry his age as lightly as Turgut, or Valette, or Mustapha. During his tenure at Fort St. Elmo, according to Curione, he had repeatedly told Valette that the fort was in fine shape, its men superhuman in their energy and faith.[5] His own, however, had fallen short. He offered his resignation to the grand master, which was accepted. D'Eguaras was also in bad shape, suffering from an arrow wound to his hand. His request was to remain with his men, even if that required his taking a lesser role. Overall command of Fort St. Elmo, something of a hot potato, was ceded to Colonel Mas.

✦·✦·✦·✦

The guns kept chipping away at the fort, the defenders kept patching it, the tally of dead and wounded on both sides increased, and the bridge lately damaged was soon almost whole again. A renegade managed to cross the lines and bring Valette welcome news from the Ottoman camp. Turgut had been ill and confined to bed for a few days. The seventy to eighty galleys that patrolled the approaches to the island were beginning to put a strain on manpower.[6] Valette countered by redeploying Giovanni Vagnone and a hundred of his men from

Mdina to St. Elmo, proof of his determination to hold onto the fort and keep faith with the men inside it.

By contrast, the men inside the fort were losing confidence. The dead and, worse, the scattered parts of the dead — the arms, legs, and shredded viscera — lay stinking in the hot sun, blackened and fly-covered for lack of opportunity to retrieve and bury them. Detritus from the smashed walls flowed into the ditch, lessening its usefulness as a defensive structure and setting up a pathway for the inevitable assaults. And the guns kept firing.

Miranda, Broglio, and d'Eguaras all now agreed that remaining on the peninsula was a pointless gesture, even a strategic error, a poor trade-off of brave men for an inevitable defeat. The case for holding on might have made sense earlier, but no longer. One more time Medrano crossed the night water, past gunfire that was now taking a considerable toll on Christian boats, and one more time clattered through the narrow streets to the council chambers at Fort St. Angelo. He found Valette alert — the grand master didn't sleep a lot these days — and ready to discuss the situation. The two spoke together first in private, and Medrano was persuasive enough to get a hearing with the entire council. He gave an affecting account of the men's gallantry and endurance.

The spirit was willing, but facts were facts. Medrano reported on the quick work of the Turkish sappers, of the ditches they were filling in, the bridge they had constructed. He described walls scarcely worthy of the name, crumbling faster than could be repaired, the heavy casualties among those making the repairs. He spoke of the wounded and exhausted men, of the frightening accuracy of the Janissary sharpshooters, of the ravelin now mounted by two cannon capable of firing into the fort, of the sudden necessity of digging trenches within the fort because there was no other place of safety. He told of the cavalier that swayed under the constant force of cannon fire, of the two remaining guns on the eastern spur (they would be knocked out and their crews killed the next day). The fort, he said, was doomed, and the men with it unless the council permitted them to return to Fort St. Angelo.

The report was all very compelling, but except in the details, it was not news; and ultimately, it was not as compelling as Valette's need for more time. Malta was the last bastion before Sicily, the last outpost of the Order, which in his own lifetime had lost both Rhodes and Tripoli. Malta was the last chance for an international force of Christian men to show that they could come together against the expansive embrace of Islam. Just as Malta was the shield for all Europe and as such for all Christendom, Fort St. Elmo was the shield of Malta. The longer Valette could tie the Ottoman forces down on this small piece of real estate, the longer he would be able to bolster Senglea and Birgu, the longer Mdina might survive as the main supply route for information and reinforcements, and the longer Don Garcia would have to gather and launch a relief force. Valette believed that he had no choice. The job of the men at St. Elmo was to make the taking of it long, expensive, and painful to the Ottomans. He urged Medrano to go back and convince his colleagues to hold on just a little bit longer, with the cold promise that Don Garcia had promised relief soon — as indeed he had.

Valette understood what the wretches on St. Elmo were going through. As a veteran of Rhodes, who better? But however much he sympathized, he wanted these men to realize that they, and everyone else under his command, were dedicated to Malta's preservation. The soldiers at St. Elmo might die in its blasted ruins — and in fact probably would die there. But all men must die, and few are given the chance to do so for the sake of such a greater good. Valette was firm. Fort St. Elmo must be defended to the last man.

Medrano left Fort St. Angelo in the predawn half-light and made the trip back across the bay. As he appeared on the parade ground of Fort St. Elmo, all those who could get away from their posts gathered around him, eager to hear what the council had decided. The message did not go down well. While the older officers and men accepted obedience and blood, the younger saw nothing but pigheadedness in Valette's decision. The latter argued that the grand master was not here on the ground, facing incessant cannon fire and arquebus bullets, he had not grappled hand to hand with Janissaries and corsairs, only barely keeping the fort under a Christian flag — how could the grand master possibly appreciate what they were going through?

What they were going through was about to get a good deal worse. At daybreak, the Muslim cannons started up their usual gunpowder symphony, slowly chipping away at the walls and almost incidentally taking Christian lives. This was routine. What was not routine was the sudden crescendo of both artillery and small arms fire just as the sun hit midday, followed by the shrill ululating voices of a thousand Muslim soldiers preparing to overrun the fort en masse. The defenders could not risk a glance over the wall to see what was coming, but they could hear the enemy approach. A wave of intense loose-robed men passed over the bridge and scrambled up the unsteady slope of collapsed masonry, shouting at and cursing the men of St. Elmo; Christian arquebusiers rose just enough to lay down a heavy cross fire into the enemy's flanks, killing those at the van and leaving a low wall of dead and dying soldiers to slow those coming behind. Christian arquebusiers worked in teams, one man at the ridge firing, a second reloading and passing up fresh guns, and so increased the rate of fire. Those Muslims who managed to stumble over their fallen comrades and loose rubble, who dodged bullets and ignored the minor scrapes or punctures, and who got to the breaches were met with a sharp, agitated hedge of steel pikes and battle-axes. One after another the Ottomans saw the expert, almost balletic, moves of grim Spanish professionals, the swift flick and twist that propelled the razor-sharp edges and hooks of those elegant weapons. An unfortunate Muslim soldier, dressed for mobility and heat rather than for personal safety, might find a hand or a foot sliced off, his face or torso flensed, maimed for life rather than launched to paradise.

And yet they pressed on. Charge followed upon charge; no Iayalar or Janissary was willing to admit defeat against such a weak defense. Each assault failed in its turn, and the slopes that led down to the ditch were painted in blood and littered with scores of dead Muslims, and a lesser number of dead Christians. Those still alive breathed in a rank mixture of burnt sulfur, sweat, blood, viscera, and human waste. The ebb and flow of repeated assaults went on for a full seven hours, a showcase of unspeakable cruelty and astonishing bravery. Balbi praises the supreme valor of the defenders, and then adds that it was equaled by that of the enemy. He singles out Juan de La Cerda, noting that the Spanish captain had received a gunshot wound, attended to it once the enemy had fallen back, and then "with great courage removed his bandage and returned to his post as soon as the alarm was sounded again."[7]

By the end of the day, the defenders had lost forty men; the Ottomans, five hundred.[8] As exhausted soldiers on both sides prepared to settle in for the night, a Spanish renegade called out from the Turkish lines: "You have done well today, knights. But tomorrow you will have the general assault you've been yearning for."[9]

13

+·+·+·+

FRESH RESOLVE

+·+·+·+

*The immense number of flares and incendiaries used by
both sides meant that there was no darkness . . . the gunners
in St. Angelo and the other positions had no difficulty
in laying their guns by the light of the enemy's fires.*

Balbi

The threat of a general assault, following on the heels of the day's fighting and
the hard line taken by Valette, proved too much for the defenders. Despite the
greater number of Muslim casualties, the exhausted Christians doubted they
could take another fight like today's and saw little point in trying. Not that
they feared dying; or at least, so they said. Among those who most wanted
to abandon the fort was the "recently accused (*poco tacciato*) . . . Captain Juan
de la Cerda: who nevertheless resolved to die valorously and honorably while
fighting for Birgu."[1] The Spanish soldiers already had petitioned to abandon
the place. Now for the first time, they were openly joined by fifty-three of the
Knights of St. John. The members of the Order came together in the fort's small
chapel and by candlelight drafted a letter for the grand master and the council:

> Most Illustrious and Very Reverend Monseigneur:
>
> When the Turks first landed on Malta, Your Highness ordered the present
> knights to repair to this fortress and defend it. We have done this with fullness
> of spirit and to the best of our abilities and with some good outcome, as we
> believe Your Highness is aware. In the doing we have shirked neither fatigue nor
> danger. Now, however, the enemy has brought us down to such a state that we
> can neither injure them nor defend ourselves. They now hold the counterscarp

and the ditch. They have carved steps into the very ramparts. They have built a bridge by which they can come and go at will. They have tunneled beneath the walls, leaving us to expect an explosion at any moment. They have raised the ravelin so high that it overlooks the entire fort. In consequence, our sentries are killed as quickly as they take up their positions. We are reduced to such an extent that we are no longer able to use the piazza at the center of the fort. We have lost several men there, and only the chapel provides any measure of safety at all. The soldiers are dispirited, and their officer can no longer get them to man the walls. Perfectly aware that the fort is doomed, they prepare themselves to swim for safety. We likewise see ourselves as at the end of our rope, and because we can no longer execute the obligations of the Order, we are determined, absent Your Highness's sending us boats tonight in which we can withdraw, to rush out and die like proper knights.

Do not send further reinforcements, as they must surely die as well. This is the determined resolution of us the undersigned. We also point out to Your Highness that [Turkish] galleots have been cruising past the end of the point. Accordingly, thus resolved, we kiss your hand and keep a copy of this letter.

— Dated from St. Elmo, June 8, 1565[2]

Fra Vitellino Vitelleschi of Corneto (modern-day Tarquinia) had the thankless task of crossing to Fort St. Angelo and delivering the letter. Balbi, ever tactful, says only that Valette was "deeply troubled" by the letter, largely because of the number of knights who signed it.[3] Well he might have been. These were not outsiders, but brothers in faith, men sworn to obedience, and their letter was tantamount to insubordination bordering on mutiny. The threat of a quick suicidal attack might have been bluff, or might not. The signatories had no leverage (other than surrender) but the threat to cut the siege of St. Elmo short, which to Valette was unthinkable. If it was true that the Spanish soldiers were no longer willing to stand their ground, then St. Elmo might well be a lost cause.

How to respond?

The grand master had Vitalleschi wait as he wrote out his answer. First he chastised the petitioners for questioning his lawful orders and declared dishonorable the very thought of an unauthorized suicide attack on the enemy. The knights, he reminded them, were bound by vows of obedience, and he, as their superior, had determined that they would best serve the Order and their God on Fort St. Elmo.

He then softened, if only a little. Proud men, after all, can be pushed only so far, and if even his own knights had reached this extreme, how much worse must it be for the others? Valette was willing to demonstrate good faith and hoped that it would buy him at least a little more time. He determined to send over three senior knights — from Spain, Don Francisco Ruys de Medina; from France, Antoine de la Roche; and from Italy, Costantino Castriota — and have them make a full and impartial evaluation of the situation. Any further decisions, whether to remain or to retreat, would follow from their reports, which he expected before sunrise. It was one more delay, which is the least Valette wanted, and by calling their judgment into question, he might cause the knights to reconsider whether things were quite as bad as they thought.

At three that morning, the boat carrying the trio of knights bumped up against the rocks below St. Elmo, and Vitalleschi led the way up the steps to the fort. What they found was a low-rimmed crater filled with a confusion of unexpected activity. The signatories had been so confident of their case that they were already shutting down their operation. Despite the disapproval of Colonel Mas (whose alleged feelings did not seem to translate into any effective action), the defenders of St. Elmo were breaking swords and arquebuses, and tipping cannon shot into the sea. All leftover gunpowder they planned on using, as La Cerda had long ago suggested, to blow up what remained of the fort, preferably while a large number of Turks were inside it.

The soldiers stopped long enough to hear Valette's short message. They were not pleased. Filthy, tired, wounded, insulted, and clearly sensing prevarication, they said no, there was nothing to discuss. Repeated requests, from the most blunt to the most reserved, had failed to move Valette and his council, yet a blind man could see that the fort was beyond hope. Let the envoys discover what the defenders of Fort St. Elmo had endured these past weeks and see for themselves if the demands were reasonable.

The three knights were then led past the dust-covered, truculent men who defended scarcely maintainable posts. By starlight, these envoys saw the broken walls, the shattered cavalier, and peered at the lost ravelin; from over the wall they heard the sounds of Ottoman spades thudding into the hard ground, pushing the enemy ominously closer. The three knights quickly came to their conclusions. The Spaniard agreed that there was no hope and that immediate withdrawal was the best course. The Provençal gave it a few more days, but in essence agreed.

Castriota, the Italian who on an earlier trip to St. Elmo had declared the ravelin hopelessly lost, was made of sterner stuff. A middle-aged, collateral descendent of the Albanian hero Skanderbeg, he had probably seen more action than any other man present, serving and suffering wounds in the Italian wars of Charles V (Capodorso, Turin, and Naples). He had come late to the Order (1561), "hounded by the court, a stranger to my family, abandoned by my friends," after a multifaceted career as a soldier, diplomat, and perhaps a spy.[4] Under the pen name of Filonico Alicarnasseo, he had also made a name for himself as a noted literary scholar (his treatise *De Cavaglieria*, coincidentally was dedicated to Don Pedro de Toledo, father of Don Garcia de Toledo). Given his background and his possession of a "robust and ferocious mind," it was logical that he should have been chosen as one of this small party.[5] He was the last to speak, and it would have been better if he had kept silent.

Things were not, he said, nearly so bad as some had claimed. True, the outer defense works were lost and the main walls were in terrible shape, and the men were tired and clearly strained. But there was all around them an abundance of stone and masonry. The soldiers might build a secondary wall behind the breaches, a curtain from which they could continue the fight for a good while longer. Abandoning the fort just now would be unnecessary, even foolish, and he could not in good conscience advise the council otherwise. He went further. He said that, should Valette put him in charge, he would be able to hold out at the very least until Don Garcia himself arrived.

It took a brave or foolish man to say such things in such circumstances, and if Castriota's summing up was an insult to the foot soldiers, it was a slap at the commanders as well. The mood turned ugly, and the men began to shout. Had this interloper not seen how small the fort actually was, how useless the materials he expected them to use? Had *he* experienced the terror of Ottoman guns, of Janissary arquebusiers, of a wild-eyed Iayalar assault? The more hard-hearted, or just sarcastic, suggested that Castriota should spend a full day there to get a true sense of just how things stood. "Since you claim it possible, you can stay and show us the means and together we can defend [the fort] to the death."[6]

Castriota claimed obedience to his warrant and said that Valette had ordered him back that same night. In response, an angry Colonel Mas ordered the gate that led to the water's edge be closed. Ruys de Medina and Antoine de la Roche, the two dissenting knights, pointed out that it was only Castriota who proposed holding on, and the Council must surely favor the opinions of two men against the one.

The impasse was suddenly broken when the chapel bells began to ring, the signal for all men to report to their stations. Remarkably, like trained border collies, they all did so. Soldiers ran into the far dark corners of the outer walls, alert to whatever might be coming, and in an instant the parade ground was entirely cleared.

It was d'Eguaras who had sounded the alarm, not because there was an actual attack, but because he saw the distraction as the only way to break the standoff. The last thing he wanted was a knock-down, drag-out fight between his men and a trio of de facto diplomats. Having scattered the mob, he came from the chapel and urged the envoys to go down the steps to their long boat immediately and return to Valette to describe all they had seen.

One more time, the council met to hear testimony and debate the destiny of Fort St. Elmo. Valette was unmoving. The fort would be defended. He would use shame, anger, guile, ridicule, and whatever else he could to keep men there and fighting. In this instance, he was backed up by Castriota, who took the occasion to do a little grandstanding. The Italian repeated his belief that the fort could be maintained, and further requested that he and his company be allowed to return to the peninsula to fight, even if others would not.

Dawn brought new surprises. A swimmer arrived from Fort St. Elmo, carrying a cow horn sealed with wax, inside which was mail. The letter was from the rebellious knights, their demands for pulling out now replaced by demands for more men and more equipment.

The explanation for this turnabout was simple. On hearing about the knights' petition the night before, senior members of the various *langues* had dispatched letters of their own to their countrymen at Fort St. Elmo, chastising the rebels for the shame they brought to the individual *langue* and to their fellow knights. If knights of the Order of St. John could not be counted on for obedience and bravery up to death if required, what could be expected of other men? What did this kind of disobedience say to the outsiders, the Spanish and Italian soldiers who had volunteered to join them in defense of an island and an Order not their own?

If the point needed to be underscored, the senior men also had informed the defenders of St. Elmo of Castriota's offer to return to St. Elmo with five hundred men. They added that his was not simply an offer to fight to the end, but to do so as the overall commander of all forces within the fort, an offer that the grand master could all too easily be expected to accept. For the knights, the dishonor was too great. They would as soon stay alone and die as the brave men that they were.

But Valette, having regained the upper hand over the men on St. Elmo, was not going to let go easily. In a communiqué laced with regret, he informed the knights still at St. Elmo that he was relieving them of their post. That such once-brave men should have lost heart was unfortunate, the more so as this was in violation of their vows. If, however, any knight on St. Elmo wished to leave, Valette would not stand in his way. Indeed, he would prefer not to have anyone there on whom he could not rely, and as there were four or more eager volunteers for every soldier currently at the besieged fort, it would be no great hardship to fill the gaps. He announced that he was granting Castriota his request, and that the gentleman had already raised his banner, sounded his drum, and inducted volunteers. The bishop of Malta had promised another two thousand ducats to encourage new recruits. It seemed that Castriota's common soldiers would do for money, the bishop's money, what certain knights of St. John would not do for honor.

The letter was delivered by Don Melchior de Monserrat, who had been making trips back and forth between the forts for some time now, and who had some credibility with these men that Castriota did not. He and Miranda — who had received a separate letter from Valette reminding him of the confidence the grand master had in him — both exhorted the defenders to remain, and the spoken and written words, combined, had their intended effect. Word of their capitulation spread throughout Fort St. Angelo and Birgu. The men had come back into line, discipline and determination had been restored. Valette had won. More supplies and a hundred more soldiers were now readied and could come across; Castriota, clearly unwelcome at Fort St. Elmo, was reassigned, no longer expected to defend St. Elmo. The wounded Broglio needed replacing, however, and Valette asked Monserrat to take command of the fort, to which Monserrat, who had repeatedly said that the fort should not be abandoned, agreed.

To help consolidate the soldiers' new determination to stay and fight, Monserrat took along the Capuchin monk Friar Robert of Eboli, a man with a talent for fire-breathing rhetoric. This peculiar cleric, for nearly ten years a slave in Tripoli after being kidnapped by a nephew of Turgut, had been living in Malta only a year, but seems to have become an institution. On the second day of the siege, he had taken it upon himself to embark on a forty-hours' adoration before the Blessed Sacrament, a first on Malta, and greatly comforting to the island's inhabitants.[7]

He now stood before the half-dead men in the dust of the ruins and, with the power of the truly inspired, made his sermon "uplift, confirm, and renew the spirits of the said knights with spiritual consolation." His rhetoric had moved two newly converted Jews (Valette had recently allowed Jews back on the island) to come "to die in the faith of Christ."[8] For his work during the siege, his presence was considered as providential. He stayed on at St. Elmo, going from man to man at each station, crucifix in hand, encouraging, comforting, as needed until the night of June 13, at which time the friar accompanied the exhausted Broglio back to Birgu. Fort St. Elmo would endure for a little while longer.

At least one modern scholar suggests that there is an element of wishful thinking in this story. He notes that the men on St. Elmo were in no position to get back to Birgu without Valette's cooperation, and that the grand master's dispatching fresh volunteers was simply a means of defusing the situation. Men will, of course, volunteer to join their comrades in hopeless causes if the emotional draw is sufficient.[9]

+·+·+·+

On June 10, the sixteenth day of the siege, Mustapha had scheduled a night assault on St. Elmo. Surprise was not part of the plan — rather, he intended to stretch the enemy both physically and emotionally before the men attacked. Bombardments lasted into the third night watch, at which point Mustapha judged the Christians sufficiently exhausted. He halted the cannon and sent his men forward into the darkness with scaling ladders.

The downside of his plan was that the defenders were all wide awake and clearly prepared for the attack. Here Balbi mentions fire hoops for the first time.[10] These were wooden rings curved to a diameter large enough to encircle three men. A length of cloth infused with pitch and other accelerants was wrapped around the wood. More cotton, more pitch, and so on until the item was about as thick as a man's leg. When a heavy press of soldiers appeared on the far side of the wall, the hoops were set alight and tossed horizontally in a murderous game of ring toss. The Turks and their allies were in the habit of wearing loose cotton, which, in the torrid heat of a Maltese summer, was far more comfortable than the leather jerkins and steel plate armor that the Christians wore, but which burned readily. Balbi attributes the greatest number of Muslim casualties to this device.[11]

Whatever advantage Mustapha might have had by timing his assault at night was obviated by the extensive use of fire on both sides. Indeed, the gunners in St. Angelo and the other positions were able to lay their guns by the light of the enemy's fires. It was not just the hoops that turned night into day. The defenders lit torches, while the Janissaries hurled *sachetti*, friable clay pots filled with Greek fire that were intended to break on Christian armor and roast the enemy alive. In preparation for these, the defenders had filled a number of deep tubs with water.

By dawn the fight was over. More than fifteen hundred Ottomans were dead, and only sixty Christians.[12] The only activity that morning was a massive cannonade that lasted from dawn till noon.

Turgut had been kept busy as well. Some time earlier, cavalry under Coppier had managed to disrupt his gun battery at Point Tigné. Within a day, he replaced four heavy guns on that point and manned them with enough soldiers to ward off any further attack. Valette countered with new gun emplacements at Fort St. Angelo, and he was able to take out a number of enemy batteries on Mt. Sciberras before they were removed to less vulnerable positions. He also sent over another one hundred and fifty soldiers to St. Elmo, and more ammunition, baskets, mattresses, and rope.[13]

The situation inside the Turkish camps was becoming grim. A Janissary was captured outside the capital city. The man reported that casualties were unexpectedly high and had included Curtogli, aga of the Janissaries, killed by cannon fire while observing St. Elmo from the forward trenches. Six vessels carried Ottoman casualties to Tripoli, and it was common knowledge that the wounded were not recovering as they should. Illness, most likely dysentery, was rampant, and biscuit rations for the laborers were now down to ten ounces a day. There was more talk of friction between the pashas and the Janissaries, a notably independent sort, who could not have been pleased with the loss of their commander. For their part, the pashas could only note that in over two weeks these elite troops had failed to take a fort in a siege that was supposed to have required no more than five days.

14

+·+·+·+

BULLETS
WRAPPED IN SMOKE
AND FIRE

+·+·+·+

Clearly the fortress is
under God's special protection.

Jean de Valette

On June 12, Ottoman soldiers managed to grab a prisoner, who gave them the encouraging news that a cannonball had destroyed the bakers' oven inside Fort St. Elmo, forcing the defenders to rely on Fort St. Angelo for bread. This intelligence was improved upon by a Spanish deserter, a piper, who informed Mustapha that, given the fort's architecture, they needed to raise the ravelin just a little bit more to have total command of its interior piazza. Mustapha thanked the piper but, having been deceived before, assured him that if his report proved untrue, the man could expect the same bastinado treatment that had been meted out to La Rivière. While sappers redoubled their efforts on the ravelin, the piper had time to consider the various fates that threatened him. Should Mustapha be dissatisfied with the ravelin, the Ottoman camp might not be the best place for him; returning to St. Elmo, however, was out of the question. He slipped off again, this time to Mdina, where he presented himself as an escaped slave. Alas for him, he was recognized, and so, after some time on the rack, was the lie. Governor Mesquita turned him over to the citizens, who tied him to a horse's tail and then stoned him to death.

Perhaps the sudden disappearance of the piper caused Mustapha to try to reason with his enemy. On June 14, a trumpet sounded, a white flag went up, and a herald trotted over from the Ottoman lines and offered parley, an offer the defenders refused. The herald withdrew. A little later, the defenders heard an Italian voice call out from the trenches, informing them that Mustapha would graciously allow the Christians to sleep that night and that anyone inside the fort was free to leave in peace. If they continued to resist, however, the Ottoman soldiers would cut them to pieces.[1] In response, the Christians let loose a volley in the Italian's general direction, which ended any further talk of surrender.

There followed a day and a night of sporadic raids, cannon volleys, the sound of shouts and music that sometimes preceded attacks, but often did not. Mustapha's technique was that of a picador at a bullfight: the administration of modest irritants to keep the defenders off balance, sleep deprived, and confused. There was little the commanders at St. Elmo could do other than petition Valette for more men, more ammunition, and more supplies. He complied and loaded the night boats with the fire hoops and powder and biscuits and ammunition needed to defend the fort. That these small convoys were able to make their nightly runs was a significant failure on the part of the Ottomans, and lack of moonlight notwithstanding, we can only conjecture why they were allowed to proceed. Once arrived, these goods were shifted to points where the fighting, once it came, would be fiercest.

The real attack came on June 16. Two hours before sunrise, the defenders of St. Elmo could hear the Ottoman mullahs addressing the gathered Muslim force and the full chorus of the soldiers' response. The pattern of call and response, measured by the slowly rising light to the east, seemed interminable, but the meaning was clear — the soldiers were cleansing themselves of sin and preparing themselves for death. Then silence, as the four thousand men carrying arquebuses padded to their stations. Having called up the dawn, the Ottomans ringed the fort at the counterscarp, west, southwest, and south, facing into the rising sun that at dawn would silhouette anyone who looked over the walls. They were also girding themselves mentally for the fight. They knew how tough the Christians were.

Defenders lined the cracked rim of the fort in a regular pattern — three soldiers, then a knight, three more soldiers, another knight, and so forth. Monserrat, Miranda, and d'Eguaras commanded three bodies of reserves, stationed in the piazza and ready for deployment wherever the enemy threat proved greatest. Support staff prepared wine-soaked bread to refresh the hungry and thirsty —

and to comfort the wounded and dying. Guns, pikes, swords, grenades, and stones all lay within easy reach of the men on the front. Fra Roberto da Eboli had returned to the fort and was in his element: "If God is with us, who will be against us? . . . recall the ancient kings of Israel, Joshua, Gideon, Samson, Jefte, Delbora, Jehosaphat, Ezekiel, the brothers Maccabee whose zeal and valor you, sacred knights, must now emulate. . . . In this most sacred sign of the cross we shall prevail."[2] Not far away, Mustapha reminded his own men that Muslim prisoners inside the dungeons of Fort St. Angelo were counting on them: "Perhaps you have not heard the cries and entreaties of captives from that fortress, people joined to you by blood and bound by hardest chains, enduring a life sadder than death itself, immersed as they are in squalor and sorrow?"[3]

Then the artillery barrage began. This time Piali Pasha had brought gun-mounted galleys to fire in concert with the land batteries. Cannon fired from the ravelin, from all platforms, and from ships offshore, throwing "around a thousand shots with such force that not only the Maltese, but also the neighboring Sicilians were dumbstruck with horror."[4] The bombardment stopped an hour later, as suddenly as it had begun, leaving the men's ears ringing. A few of the defenders snatched glances over the rubble to see what was coming next. The farsighted could make out Mustapha, upright, determined, the green standard fringed with horse tails significant of the rank given to him by Suleiman himself. He stepped forward the better to be seen and drew his scimitar from its scabbard. The roar of eight thousand Muslims filled the air. The assault was on.

The Iayalars, religious fanatics, came first, "dressed in the skins of wild animals and the feathers of birds of prey" and with "blue tattoos of various characters on their faces."[5] A good number of these alarming men managed to cross the ditch and scrabble up the loose rubble toward the breach, where they were stymied by an "infinity of caltrops," sharp spikes welded in such a fashion that one point will always face upward and impale the foot of anyone unlucky enough to walk on it.[6] While the Iayalars contended with this new hazard, Christian arquebusiers rose up and fired into their ranks, killing many outright, wounding others, but failing to turn the tide.

Soon enough the fighting drew closer, as guns gave way to pikes and halberds, then swords, stones, and finally knives, poniards, and fists. Fortune seemed to favor the Muslims; a westerly breeze drove smoke from incendiaries into the defenders' eyes, and more fortunate still, as the Iayalars had filled the breach, the entire store of the Christians' firepots somehow ignited, exploded, and covered those nearby in flaming pitch. Christians and Muslims alike screamed, ran, rolled on the ground, and threw themselves into the water barrels or the sea.

Their bravery notwithstanding, the Iayalars, exhausted, withdrew soon after this incident. Mustapha now sent in his dervishes. This new strain of religious fanatic made their way over the dead and dying bodies of their coreligionists and took up the fight in a dry fog of powder smoke and the increasingly scorching heat of Malta's July sun. The Christians managed to push the enemy back down to the counterscarp and would have pushed farther if Monserrat had not ordered them to remain in the relative safety of the fort. Zeal was all well and good, but the numbers were against them, and Monserrat wanted his men to prepare for the third wave of attackers. It was the turn of the spahis. Another charge at the breach, another failure to take it. Mustapha now turned to the warhorses of his army, the Janissaries.

The Janissaries targeted the post of Colonel Mas. Valette, watching from Fort St. Angelo, saw the attackers bringing scaling ladders to the wall, and ordered his gunners to shoot them down. Precision was wanting. Their first volley landed too far to the right and killed a mixture of the enemy and eight Christians, "putting with this misstep the fort in greatest danger of being lost."[7] Frantic signaling had the artillerists correct the error. Their next shot was better. Twenty Turks died, but no Christians. The remaining Muslims were few enough for the men at St. Elmo to push back successfully with pikes and trumps.

The next wave included a crew heading specifically for the cavalier. Burning hoops repelled some, and a good number were seen rushing down to the water to extinguish the burning gelatin that clung to their flesh. For seven hours "spears, torches and stones flew from all sides," until Mustapha and Turgut finally called it quits.[8] The defenders, once they realized they had bought another day, jeered at the retreating Muslims and heard the cries taken up by their comrades across the water in Fort St. Angelo. Mustapha's report to Suleiman was philosophical. He wrote that he had suspended operations "because all things are tied to their destiny and marks of victory are unavoidable."[9]

Regrettably for him, destiny in this case had decreed a thousand Turks and only a hundred and fifty Christians should lie dead on the edge of the fort. Two Muslim standards, one belonging to Turgut, the other to Mustapha Pasha, were now in Christian hands. The battle had exhausted both sides, and veterans of the fight believed that the Turks would have been able to take the fort if they had made just one more assault. Balbi writes, in a left-handed compliment, that convicts, oarsmen, and even the Maltese fought "as if [they] were [men] of superior reputation," *persona de mayor estima*.[10]

Among the dead was Medrano, having received a bullet through the head as he seized one of the Muslim standards. Miranda had led the final counterattack and was wounded (broken leg) but not, according to him at least, incapacitated; he ordered that a chair be brought up and positioned near the big guns. Let the enemy come again — the Spaniard would stay with his men. He could, he noted, fire an arquebus from a sitting position and even kill with a sword if his enemy had the nerve to approach. Other defenders, burned, cut, maimed, of lesser birth and therefore of whom less was expected, did not stay. These, along with Medrano's body, were ferried back to Birgu; senior among them was the badly wounded Juan de La Cerda. The force was down to some three hundred men.[11]

Outside the battle zone, the Ottomans were on the move. They had now struck camp at the village of Zeitun, their halfway point between Marsaxlokk and Mt. Sciberras, and burned the remains — they would soon be settled closer to the fighting and bring their ships into Grand Harbor. The endgame was under way. St. Elmo would be annihilated shortly.

Valette would no longer order any more men into Fort St. Elmo, though he would accept volunteers. Three hundred men of Birgu and thirty knights stepped forward and presented themselves for service across the water.[12] They were targeted by Turgut's sharpshooters on Tigné, whom Valette had Coppier chase away until the boats could make it across. On June 17, Valette reported these events to Don Garcia in terms meant to encourage him to get on with sending some aid. The entire Ottoman fleet, he said, had moved from Marsaxlokk at night so "we should not see his weakness" and from "fear of your fleet," thus leaving Marsaxlokk free for any Spanish relief force.[13] Bombardment of Fort St. Elmo had slackened, morale was high even though supplies were low, and Valette was certain that just a few more men, even just the two triremes of the Order now in Messina, would be enough to hold the fort indefinitely. "Our safety lies in your hands; after that, our hope remains in God."[14]

The siege was in its twenty-fourth day. The Ottomans kept up a desultory bombardment of six guns on the southern spur, but spent the better part of their day in recovering and burning their dead. As the smoke rose and then bent back and covered the island, Mustapha and his lieutenants considered why Fort St. Elmo had not yet fallen. Exasperated at the tenacity of the enemy and eager to get the operation over with, he was ready to listen to all sides. Theories were fielded, argued, weighed, and finally reduced to three. First, the Christian gun on the fort's eastern flank was disrupting any mass attacks on the right side. It must be taken out. Second, the guns on Fort St. Angelo had found their range and were interfering with operations on the southern side of Sciberras peninsula. They must be neutralized. And finally, the steady flow of fresh troops from Fort St. Angelo kept the defensive manpower at an insuperable level.

This last point was key, and Turgut had already begun to address it. In addition to his cannons, Turgut had placed sharpshooters on the peninsula of Tigné. Men without pity, they fired on the small boats bringing the dead and wounded back to Birgu.

✦·✦·✦·✦

Turgut and the Ottoman high command began the morning with a tour of the various trouble spots with a view toward improving offensive capabilities. They also reconsidered the terrain. Turgut ordered that the counterscarp of the ditch facing St. Angelo be extended down to where the relief boats from Birgu entered Fort St. Elmo. The project had been more trouble than it was worth back when the siege was estimated at five days, but reality was forcing their hand. Sappers were already pushing the Turkish trenches forward, and sharpshooters should be able to fire not just on the skiffs that ferried men across the water, but at the subterranean entrance to Fort St. Elmo. Other sappers completed the curtain wall that hid the Turks from the guns of St. Angelo.

Turgut and Mustapha and their staffs, all dressed in the brightest robes possible, were inspecting the new arrangements. Balbi writes the Turgut was dissatisfied with a Turkish gunner who was aiming his cannon too high.[15] He told the man to lower it. Still too high. He ordered him to it lower still more, but this final time the trajectory was too low, with disastrous consequences. The ball glanced against a trench and chipped off a stone that ricocheted back and hit Turgut in the temple.[16] Turgut's turban absorbed some of the shock, possibly preventing him from being killed outright, but the shock was severe. Blood flowed out of his mouth, perhaps even his ear and eye, and he lost the power of speech. Staff officers, appalled, quickly covered the still breathing Turgut and carried him back to Mustapha's own tent at the Marsa, worried that news of his injury might spread and alarm the men. Ever the professional, Mustapha continued the inspection, and with his remaining staff oversaw the emplacement of four new guns aimed at the watery route to Fort St. Angelo.

15

+·+··+·+

A PLEA TO GOD

+·+··+·+

*Forasmuch as the Isle of Malta . . . being as it were the key
of that part of Christendom, is presently invaded with a great Army and
navy of Turks, infidels and sworn enemies of Christian religion, . . . it is our
part, which for distance of place cannot succour them with temporal relief,
to assist them with spiritual aid: that is to say, with earnest, hearty,
and fervent prayer, to Almighty God for them.*

Liturgies and Occasional Forms of Prayer Set Forth
in the Reign of Queen Elizabeth, *June 19, 1565*

News of Turgut's injury marked the beginning of a small winning streak for
the Christians. The day after the corsair was hit, Grugno, the knight in charge
of the cavalier, was able to lay cannon fire into knots of the enemy and kill
the aga (commanding officer) of Turkish ordnance.[1] The Ottomans' reaction
to this — piercing howls of grief — encouraged Grugno to strike out at other
brightly uniformed men. To do so, he had to expose himself more than was
strictly prudent. A Muslim sharpshooter soon winged him, and he was sent
back to the infirmary at Birgu, replaced by a Fortunio Escudero, a knight of
Navarre who was even more troublesome than his predecessor. The Muslims
eventually trained thirty-four guns on the cavalier, he had become such a
nuisance.[2]

There was some encouragement for the Ottomans as well. On the evening
of that same day, across the waters they heard a massive explosion, the more
surprising as they had not been firing in that direction. A cloud of dust and
smoke hung over the area, and only later did they learn that it had been the
powder mill at Fort St. Angelo. Two kantars — about a hundred kilos — of

powder were lost along with ten workers.[3] The Turks cheered the display "with their bestial voices," which Valette answered with a volley of cannon fire across the waters.[4] Fra Sir Oliver Starkey was appointed to investigate the matter (possibly Valette was handing the Englishman a vote of confidence; before the siege, he had been charged with accepting bribes).[5] He determined that the explosion was accidental, but it was unnerving nevertheless, and that much powder was hard to lose. Valette sent word to Mdina asking them to make up the shortfall and to provide some twenty-three more kantars besides. With St. Elmo nearly ready to fall, he would need them.

Turkish guns surrounded the fort and kept firing the entire day, though almost to no purpose — at some points the bombardment had reached bedrock, and only the ditch lay between Christian and Turk, a ditch the Ottomans were doing their best to fill up with brush and rubble and whatever else came to hand. As the inevitable climax approached, the defenders of Fort St. Elmo seemed to have fallen into a calm acceptance of what was to come, which in turn encouraged daring and insouciance. The night of June 19, Pietro di Forli had himself lowered into the ditch, where he hoped to torch the bridge. He could not — the Ottomans had packed it with wet dirt (*terra ben bagnata*) and its defenders soon noticed him and began to shoot.[6] Di Forli managed to return to the fort, where his companions followed up his efforts by dismantling a section of wall and firing chain shot at the bridge. This turned out to be a waste of powder, as they were unable to depress the angle of fire enough to actually hit the structure. However futile these efforts were, they at least gave proof that these men had by no means lost their spirit.

By now the space between Fort St. Elmo and Fort St. Angelo had become a watery no-man's-land, but somehow Ramon Fortuyn, the knight sometimes credited with the invention of fire hoops, was able to cross over from Fort St. Angelo without incident to get a sense of how things stood. Miranda, more or less in charge despite himself, seemed a little surprised to see him and assured Fortuyn that it would be simple cruelty to send more men to die. Those remaining officers on St. Elmo — d'Eguaras, Monserrat — all said the same. Fortuyn would better serve the island by returning to St. Angelo and readying himself for the fight that would soon begin again at Birgu. All that remained was prayer. Accordingly, Fortuyn went back to Fort St. Angelo along with two Muslim standards captured in the last assault, standards that he ceremoniously presented to Faderigo de Toledo as a proxy for Don Garcia and King Philip.

Fortuyn's report clearly disturbed Valette, and the grand master followed up the next night by dispatching a second emissary, the Chevalier de Boisbreton, along with an Italian brother Ambrogio Pegullo. A dangerous trip — the moon was just past full and the Turks were vigilant. Fra Ambrogio's head was taken off by a cannonball. Boisbreton's arrival must have stirred new, if unreasonable, hope within these men — why else had he been sent if not with good news? But nothing had really changed. The fort, they agreed, might be able to hold off one more Muslim assault, but no more. If they did hold off such an attack, and no help arrived from Sicily, it would be best to evacuate the fort at that time.

This was wishful thinking at best. Boisbreton managed to bring the news back to Valette, but only barely. Turgut's engineers finally had extended their trenches to command the grotto from which Fort St. Elmo anchored its lifeline to Fort St. Angelo. By the same token, it would be impossible to get enough boats to ferry the men in St. Elmo safely across the water. In Turgut's words, Fort St. Elmo, the child of Birgu, was now cut off from the mother's milk and must soon fall and die.[7]

June 20 also appears to be the last day that anyone in the Order had enough leisure to compose a daily situation report.

✦·✦·✦·✦

June 21, the feast of Corpus Christi. Soldiers, civilians, and men, women, and children lined the streets of Birgu. Inside the Church of St. Lawrence, the priest intoned the liturgy, raised the monstrance containing the host above his head, and then solemnly carried it into the daylight and through the streets — a demonstration to the faithful that God was not confined to the inside of a church but was everywhere with them. Valette and other knights, trading the red-and-white cloaks of martyrdom for the black-and-white of devotion, raised the poles to hold the canopy that shielded the container from the sun or rain. At the conclusion, Valette, "carrying his staff, served food to thirteen poor men," as did others of the Order, replaying the message of love and charity at the core of the Order's mission.[8] To the sound of distant cannon fire, the procession trod the narrow stone streets among the people of Birgu, solemn, but with a care for current dangers — the route deliberately avoided those areas most at risk of Ottoman artillery.

Across the water, Ottoman forces had managed to create a breach on the scarp walls of the cavalier and hurried to exploit this bonanza. Quickly erecting a barricade against the gunfire and fire hoops of the Christians above them, they brought up four or five small culverines (capable of firing sixty-pound balls) and began to fire down into the central piazza.[9] It took the men inside a few minutes to realize what had happened, and when they did, they fired back with small arms. When that failed to discourage the enemy, Monserrat ordered one of the few remaining cannons wheeled about. The gunners knew their business. They stuffed the barrels with scrap iron and stone, fired on the tower, and silenced the enemy position — at least, for the time being.

The end, however, was getting near. The sun went down, and as the exhausted Christians lay and waited, the cool night air carried the sounds from the Ottoman army of "the same prayers, rituals, and acts of superstition and false religion that had been heard the night before the previous assault."[10] There was no sleep, and so the defenders made the best use they could of the dark. Fifteen men under the Rhodian Pietro Miraglia (emulating the Italian Pietro da Forli) slipped into the ditch and attempted (unsuccessfully) to set the Ottomans' bridge on fire before being chased back to the fort. The rest of the night was spent listening to the enemy's prayers and chants as both sides prepared for the morning.

The attack came just after dawn and on every side. The Ottomans threw scaling ladders against the walls and were met by flying *sacchetti*, gunfire, trumps, and pikes. For six hours of repeated assaults, they chipped away at the defenders, never quite getting the upper hand. Several times the Ottomans planted their standards on the parapet, and each time the Christians pulled the banners down. On one occasion, the Muslims succeeded in mounting a portion of the wall, only to find that the siege cannon had left the masonry so unstable that it collapsed under their weight, throwing them down into the ditch below. From across the water, the guns on St. Angelo fired on the wooden bridge leading to the post of Colonel Mas. This was welcome help to the Christians inside the fort, who were running low on powder and soon forced to defend the breaches with steel.

Janissaries had also retaken their position near the cavalier and were again firing into the fort proper. Monserrat ordered the same gun that was so successful the day before to prevail again. For Monserrat it was a personal victory, and his last. Seconds later a bullet struck him in the chest, killing him instantly. The still-living were saved the trouble of burial when moments later cannon fire brought down a wall on his remains. After the siege was over, survivors "dug through the ruins of the fort and found his body, fully armed, his hands joined as if still in prayer to God."[11]

With Monserrat gone, rumors spread among the foot soldiers that d'Eguaras, Miranda, and Colonel Mas, all three of whom had not been seen since the last assault, had also been killed. This was easy to disprove. The three were all badly wounded, struck by bullets, arrows, and artificial fire, but still alive, or half-alive. They dragged themselves into view to encourage their men and to restore some sense of order. Mas and Miranda returned to their places on the line; d'Eguaras returned to his command post at the center of the piazza. Those still alive had neither the time nor the energy to bury the dead. Instead, they stacked the bodies against the walls to bolster the defenses. Even this gruesome expedience might delay the enemy and cost them a few more casualties, which was some consolation to the survivors.

Seven hours after the assault had begun, five hundred Christians lay dead, one hundred others wounded.[12] They comprised the last of the fort, and yet, against all logic, the Turks still fell short of victory. Balbi claims that all Christian officers were now killed.[13] The men waited in what is described as a day as hot as any fire.[14] The next attack could come at any time, on any side, on all sides. Anyone not utterly incapable was at his post, weapon in hand. Mustapha toyed with these men, launching a series of feints, so many that no one bothered to keep a tally. Nightfall provided welcome relief from the sun at least, and time enough to tend their wounds, many of them serious.

All stocks of gunpowder were now empty, and the surviving defenders were forced to scavenge the powder horns of their dead comrades. They were able to get out one last communication to Fort St. Angelo. A single light swift boat shot out from the grotto under St. Elmo and managed to elude ten heavier Muslim craft. As backup, an unnamed Maltese swimmer followed suit, navigating a good part of his trip underwater. They reported that in St. Elmo "almost none healthy remained, and of those who were still healthy, all were exhausted, all soiled and stained by the blood, brains, marrow, and viscera of the dead colleagues and the enemy they had killed."[15] That the defenders would have only cold steel to fight with — Cirni refers to picks and spades — was almost an afterthought.[16]

Men trapped in situations that must end in certain death can inspire a strange envy in outsiders. Having heard the last testimony from the fort, of its remaining defenders with their broken weapons, a large number of knights, soldiers, and citizens stepped forward to join the chosen few certain to die the next day.[17] Romegas himself volunteered to lead them. Valette, who had masked his emotions with bluff heartiness and further talk of Don Garcia's imminent arrival, refused to allow it. He did, however, agree that they might carry supplies to the beleaguered men, the first supplies in three days.

In the event, it didn't matter. The moon was full and the Ottomans were on highest alert; and while a lone swift boat might, with some luck, successfully dart its way through, there was no hope of five cargo-laden boats lumbering over the water between St. Angelo and St. Elmo in safety. Piali Pasha, already humiliated by the last vessel out of St. Elmo, was in no mood to let another one back into the fort, and now led the flotilla to prevent any action in person. Romegas, outnumbered sixteen to one and target of a furious storm of cannon fire, gunfire, and arrows, chose to return back to Fort St. Angelo.[18]

The chosen few remaining at Fort St. Elmo were now utterly alone. Without hope for victory, for rescue, or for mercy, they could only prepare themselves for a good death. "Seeing that all hope of survival was broken, being already certain, clear, and secure that they were to be taken and killed, and their fate delayed only so far as the hour of dawn; with great contrition they confessed to one another, asking forgiveness of God for their sins, and with his Divine Majesty, they devoutly reconciled themselves with no Sacraments other than a shared fraternal and devout embrace."[19]

Along with the soldiers, two friars, Pierre Vigneron and Alonso de Zembrana, one French, one Spanish, remained at St. Elmo. The two had tasks of their own to fulfill before sunrise. They entered the chapel, which now served as a hospital for the most grievously wounded, and delivered what last rites they could. This accomplished, the two brothers prised up a large paving stone and, putting it to one side, dug a hole in the earth below. Into this cavity they laid the gold and silver chalices and candlesticks and a reliquary containing a bone of St. John the Baptist. With the stone back in place, they proceeded to gather all remaining sacred objects — the tapestries that covered the walls, the wooden crosses and cloth vestments, the sacred books. All these they carried out of the chapel, piled up in the center of the fort, and set on fire. The Turks took this as a signal fire calling for help.

The pair made the circuit of the fort. They took confession from and conferred absolution on all those who remained alive in Fort St. Elmo in anticipation of imminent death. Then they, too, waited for the dawn.

16

+·+·+·+

THE END
OF THE
BATTLE

+·+·+·+

The castel of St. Elmo is taken and
all within it hewn to pieces.

Phayre to Cecil

June 23 was the eve of the feast of St. John the Baptist. Fort St. Elmo had held
out for twenty-nine days, and the Ottomans were impatient to be done with
it. Throughout the night, their thirty-six heavy guns fired from three points
on land and several of Piali's ships on the water, illuminating both the sky
and the fort and proving if nothing else that they still had a vast amount of
ordnance to waste. Dawn broke. The Muslim soldiers on Sciberras gazed up
at the smoking ruins and saw the white-and-red crossed flag still flying, still
defiant. Presently they made themselves ready for what would have to be the
final assault. Across the water, the men at Fort St. Angelo, all too aware of what
was coming and helpless to stop it, stood and watched the final act play out.

Inside St. Elmo scarcely sixty men remained, scattered among the breaches
and placed in the remains of the cavalier, outnumbered by the dead, who lay
where they had fallen. Few of those left alive had escaped injury; all were determined to hold on to the last instant.[1] The captains were focused on a hard
fight, a good death.

One more time the kettledrums pounded, brass horns shrilled, men shouted,
and the order to advance was given. Mustapha reported to the sultan that his
troops, "shouting 'Allah, Allah!' and accompanied by the souls of the martyred,"

began to charge the walls.[2] Janissaries, spahis, and their corsair allies, impatient for victory, crossed over the rubbish pit of stone, earth, and broken weaponry, climbed over the corpses, scrambled up the incline toward the breaches, and braved a single, weak volley from inside the fort.

If they expected the job to be easy, they were disappointed. The first Muslims into the breach were met with a hedge of sharp steel, pikes, swords, lances, and a hail of stones. An hour passed, and although men on both sides fell, the fort did not. Another hour passed, and the attackers fell back, re-formed, came forward again, and again were held off by the stubborn Christian line. Both sides licked their wounds and dragged their dead away. From time to time there followed small diversionary attacks of no particular consequence, each a prelude to the next general assault.

When the final assault came, the first Janissaries to cross the rise found, to their astonishment, Captain Miranda, strapped into a chair and gripping a pike. The commander was maimed and bandaged, but still possessed of the soldier's skills of thrust and parry. Even now in a position of weakness he managed to slash and gut a handful of enemy soldiers before his fellow Christians were able to repel the attackers one more time. The Muslims, however, managed a final parting shot that killed Miranda.

Command now devolved on d'Eguaras. His leg had been shattered, and so he too was confined to a chair. Seeing how the number of his men had dwindled, he thought to improve the odds by consolidating his remaining forces. He ordered the gunners on the cavalier to fall back and join their comrades inside the fort. This move was a boon for the Muslims, who quickly moved to fill the cavalier with sharpshooters. From its heights they could look down inside the shattered fort and signal to their comrades just how diluted the Christian force truly was.[3] All tactical advantage now lay with Mustapha. Marksmen on the ravelin and on the cavalier could fire down on the Christians from the rear while Muslim infantry could attack from the front and flanks. (Oddly, Balbi says that the Muslims confined themselves to throwing stones.)[4]

A little past eleven that morning, the final assault began. Janissaries, corsairs, and anyone else who wanted to be in at the kill, drew their blades and over-topped the crumbling edge of the fort and poured into the main piazza. The area soon resembled a Roman amphitheater in the final stages of a gladiators' show, a confused mass of desperate men fighting in separate brawls "in which there ran rivers of blood from the multitude of the dead and the wounded on all sides."[5] D'Eguaras was among the first to die. Knocked from his chair, he managed to raise his sword and limp toward four Janissaries. One of the four brought a scimitar down on his neck and severed his head, which Mustapha would later order stuck on the end of a pike.

With their comrades gone, not wishing to survive them, unable to see beyond the moment or to hope for a life in this world, the remaining Christians lashed out with a superhuman fury at any Muslim who came within reach. At the door of the chapel, Chevalier Paolo Avogadro swung a broad sword with both hands and soon created a half-circle of Muslim dead around him. It took a volley of arquebus fire to put an end to this slaughter, and the dying knight collapsed on top of the pile of men he himself had killed.

The few small fights were winding down as force of numbers made good the Ottoman effort to leave no man standing. Colonel Mas, last of the commanders and also confined to a chair, swung a two-handed sword until he was himself cut down. Fortunio Escudero, last gunner on the cavalier, headed a small group of soldiers wielding broadswords on the crest of the fort, clearly visible from across the water at Fort St. Angelo, until he and they too succumbed to greater Muslim numbers. Official reckoning was now only minutes away. Mehmed ben Mustafa, who had captured La Rivière on the first day of the invasion, had the honor of seizing the knights' ragged banner for his general as well, after which he "entered the bastion of the infidels and chopped off some heads."[6] The end was marked when a wounded knight, Frederico Lanfreducci, went to his post at the marina and gave the final agreed-upon smoke signal (*una fumata*) that the fort was lost.[7] Moments later he was taken prisoner, becoming one of nine Christian survivors captured in Fort St. Elmo's last battle.[8] A handful of Maltese, able swimmers, were able to escape.

The fight was over. It had taken four hours.[9]

✦·✦·✦·✦

"After having occupied that post for several days, [Mustapha] bombarded Fort St. Elmo and attacked night and day with heavy formations, then, following the attacks, with a uniform and impatient force, and with the help of God, the fort was taken."[10]

So wrote the Ottoman historian Selaniki in his brief account written years after the fact. In the days after the taking of St. Elmo, Mustapha appears to have commissioned forty-two lines of poetry extolling the Muslim troops,

Suleiman, and Mustapha himself.[11] Piali Pasha is mentioned, but not named, and due respect is paid to Turgut Reis. Composing this kind of poetry was a common practice in the Ottoman army, and Mustapha may have hoped that it would soften the harsher realities of the campaign.

The taking of St. Elmo, the proposed work of well under a week, in the end cost the Ottomans thirty-one days, four thousand men, and eighteen hundred rounds of artillery.[12] Mustapha's initial reaction was one of horror and dismay: "If this is what such a small son has cost us, what price the larger father?"[13] The fort's new occupants busied themselves with hauling up a new collection of pennons and flags. Mustapha Pasha's men were relieved that the worst of it was over, and cheered as Piali's fleet sailed into the safety of Marsamxett Harbor.

Mustapha's final report was prepared and a fast ship ordered to Constantinople with the good news, along with a collection of various Christian guns, small trophies from a small fort too hard won. Mustapha could only hope that these (and the poem) would mollify the sultan when he read the casualty reports. Royal displeasure in the sultan's court could cost a man his head, and this knowledge would weigh on both Piali and Mustapha. In his report, Mustapha refers to "one hundred galleys of the imperial fleet that guarded and impeded the Maltese barges and caiques from bringing reinforcements to the defenders of St. Elmo" — a measure of overkill that might have led some to wonder why the siege had taken so long.[14] He also had his engineers draw up a map of the siege to accompany news of the victory back to Constantinople. This chart is brightly colored and minutely detailed, and gives a recognizable outline of the area and each side's deployments. It is (like some of its Christian counterparts) somewhat out of proportion, suggesting to the observer a more formidable target than a strictly accurate illustration might.

The corsairs concentrated on the search for loot. There wasn't much — broken weapons, the cannons, some of the coins that Captain Miranda had had brought over to boost the men's morale. More mundanely, there was leftover grain and three cisterns of water.[15] There were also a handful of Christian survivors. Always on the lookout for a business opportunity, the corsairs gathered those unhappy few who might be worth a ransom and protected them against the Janissaries, who still had spleen to vent. Mustapha settled the matter by paying the corsairs four gold zecchini a head, whether as living trophies or as a capital investment is uncertain, though we do know that Lanfreducci was set free in Constantinople six years later at a crippling cost to his family.[16]

As for the Janissaries, they found an outlet for their lingering rage among the surviving defenders too far gone for the slave markets. Soldiers they killed and hacked to pieces. Those identified as knights had their legs bound and were hoisted upside down through a ring in the roof of the chapel normally used for the chandelier. The victims were then gutted like cattle, their hearts ("still beating" according to the chroniclers) torn out, their heads cut off.[17] A quartet of these heads were stuck on poles and lifted up to gaze back over the waters on their comrades at Fort St. Angelo — a grisly attempt at intimidation. The victims were assumed to be d'Eguaras, Miranda, Medrano, and Mas, but at that distance, who could tell? It scarcely mattered. The four heads, covered in flies and quickly turning black in the scorching heat, were emblematic of all who had fought and died at Fort St. Elmo.

Meanwhile, a messenger was sent back to the Turkish camp. He hurried to enter Turgut's tent, then leaned down and gently whispered to the semiconscious man that Fort St. Elmo was theirs. Hearing is the last sense in the dying to go. Moments after the words were spoken, Turgut Reis, Drawn Sword of Islam, lay back on his pillow and died, faithful to the soothsayer's prediction. Four galleys carried him back to Tripoli for burial, and Uludj Ali, the onetime Calabrian peasant, now became the city's governor. Mustapha and Piali would have had another reason to regret Turgut's death. Ottoman historian Kâtip Çelebi wrote that the noncorsair "should consult corsairs and listen to them" in naval affairs, one reason being that should an enterprise fail, this will "save him from being the only one to bear the blame."[18] (Mustapha took the opportunity of Turgut's death for his "gold coins, his money, his personal belongings and six *kula* infidels, his horses, his mules etc." to be listed and if possible brought over for the use of the siege.)[19] Bosio ends his chapter on St. Elmo with an extended peroration on the wickedness of Turgut and the debt owed by Christendom to the knights who finally killed him. Balbi refers to him as *el perro*, "the dog," a rare bit of abuse from this normally generous man, but leaves it pretty much at that. Cirni, ever one for the humiliating detail, notes that his "tongue was lolling out."[20] The English made no editorial comment; his stature was enough that this death needed only one line in the reports sent to Queen Elizabeth: "Torgut Reis is slain."[21]

For Mustapha, the victory was Pyrrhic. Soldiers want easy victories, and they value and admire the leaders who arrange them. Mustapha's engineers had promised that St. Elmo would be a walkover. For superstitious men —

and both soldiers and sailors can be exceedingly superstitious — this broken promise was a bad omen. Why should they respect Mustapha? Not only had he failed to bring quick victory, but his unwillingness to press his case against Piali was the only reason they were at St. Elmo in the first place. Instead the supreme commander of the army had allowed himself to be browbeaten by his junior in a quarrel over strategy. And it was no comfort that the legendary Turgut had agreed with Mustapha's original plan to leave Fort St. Elmo until last, or that the plan was probably sound — both facts merely underscored this failure. No doubt if the old corsair had shown up earlier, *he* would have won the point and might still be with them, bringing victory.

Certainly the news did not go down well in Constantinople. The French ambassador to the Grand Porte wrote home to say, "I will only tell you that the death of Torgut Reis has brought great sadness to Suleiman and even taking Malta would not bring him pleasure, if it comes at the price of so valiant a captain. Yesterday morning, by the arrival of a courier, we wanted to believe that Malta had been captured."[22]

Nevertheless, Suleiman's next letter to Mustapha was an order to "encourage the army and the Janissaries to fight against the enemies and you should conquer the island of Malta. I trust that you and everybody else will succeed in this feat."[23] From now on, it would be uphill work for Mustapha to regain the respect of his men.

✦•✦•✦•✦

Valette moved out of the grand master's palace. Common gossip held that he could not bear to see the Muslim banners flying over St. Elmo, though it is just as likely that he wanted to be closer to the next phase of the operation. A new hardness came to him. The dead would not be allowed to undermine Christian resolve, and so long as the enemy was still on the island, grief was a luxury. Valette ordered no public mourning for the husbands, brothers, or sons who had died. Instead all Christians were to mark the feast of St. John, which occasioned the weird phenomenon of two enemies engaged in twin celebrations, since the Ottomans as good Muslims also held St. John in "great reverence" and noted the occasion with "large bonfires and great firing of artillery."[24]

After three weeks of almost constant cannon blast, the sudden quiet the following day must have been both welcome and eerie. Any psychological respite, however, would be short-lived. Valette's injunction to leave the dead unmourned was about to be put to the test. The morning after the fall of St. Elmo, watchmen on the walls of Fort St. Angelo saw four pale objects floating in the water. Eyes can play tricks on even the most farsighted, especially where water is concerned, but as the currents brought the objects closer, there was no doubt as to what the watchmen were seeing. They called for Valette. Gently bobbing like so much driftwood toward the tip of Senglea were four large wooden crosses on which were nailed the supine remains of as many dead Christians.

The pallid, sea-washed bodies, skin white as marble, had had their chests slashed twice in a grisly imitation of the red cross on their order's uniform (possibly as a subtle suggestion that Mustapha had no quarrel with the Maltese, only with the knights). The corpses were gently pulled ashore with the reverence due to martyrs and brothers, and where possible, identification was made by those who knew them best. It was a ghastly and wholly unnecessary excess, "contrary to all law of war and all humanity."[25] Piali Pasha himself is said to have protested the action, and Mustapha reproved him for doing so.[26] Mustapha had a point to make, both to his own men and to the holdouts across the bay.

The sight of their butchered comrades was distressing even to the hardest veteran, and Valette spoke at some length to the soldiers, seeking to calm their fears and reinvigorate them for the rest of the siege. The fall of Fort St. Elmo, he said, should not dismay them, but rather should cause them to redouble their courage. Death comes to all men, but those who died at Fort St. Elmo exited life gloriously, sacrificing themselves nobly and of their own free will in the name of Jesus Christ, than which there was no finer or more desirable death. They were Christian soldiers fighting against impious barbarians, valiant warriors fighting against ignoble brutes, skilled soldiers fighting against undisciplined hordes.

Even for an accomplished public speaker, his was a weak response, and no words could really measure up to this horrid action. Outrage must answer for outrage. Valette, his speech done, went to Fort St. Angelo and ordered all Muslim prisoners to be brought out of their cells. When they emerged from the dark, blinking at the bright sunshine, he gave the order that they were all to be executed and their heads thrown over the wall in front of Birgu. He ordered the same to be done at Mdina.

Modern historians starting with Vertot have embellished the story by having

Valette stuff the heads into cannon and fire them into enemy lines.[27] Contemporary records, when they mention the affair at all, state only that heads were cut off and thrown at the enemy camp (*capita versus hostium castra iactata sunt*).[28] The story seems excessive on the face of it. Aside from the question of how well a human head might weather that kind of treatment, there is Valette's need to husband powder, exacerbated by the recent explosion of his powder factory. (There is no record of what happened to the bodies; their treatment is unlikely to have been in accordance with Islamic law or tradition.)

Cannons or not, later writers, Porter chief among them, have tut-tutted Valette for this act, "unworthy of his character as a Christian soldier," which shows little appreciation of just how desperate his situation was.[29] In addition to the need to prove his own ruthlessness to a ruthless enemy, there is the plain fact that these prisoners were, like horses, cows, and dogs, useless mouths whose presence required valuable food, water, and the manpower needed to keep an eye on them. They were, moreover, a potential danger. Hostile prisoners (led by a Knight of St. John) had, after all, broken out of their prison and guaranteed the 1536 conquest of Tunis. To chastise Valette for this act, given all that had gone on before, is to ignore the utter barbarity of war in general. Unquestionably, the gesture sent a strong message to the Ottomans. Until now, the invaders could assume that capture did not mean certain death. It's a comforting thought in war, where comforting thoughts aren't all that thick on the ground. Piali, objecting to the slaughter in Fort St. Elmo, seems to have realized this. With all assurance of chivalry gone, the Muslim foot soldier had one more incentive to leave, and one more reason to doubt his commander's ability. Conversely, as Mustapha hoped, they might have one more reason to stay and exact revenge from the infidel knight Valette.

Regardless, both sides had shaken off the trammels of tiresome humanity in order to expedite a fight. The devil had pitched a tent on Malta.

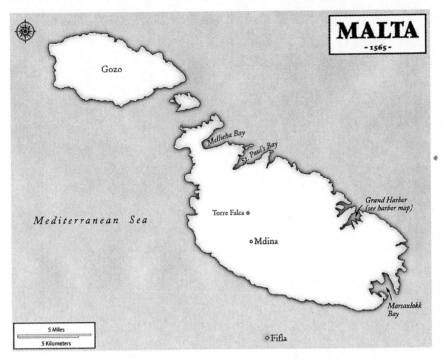

Map of Malta and Gozo, by Chris Erichsen.

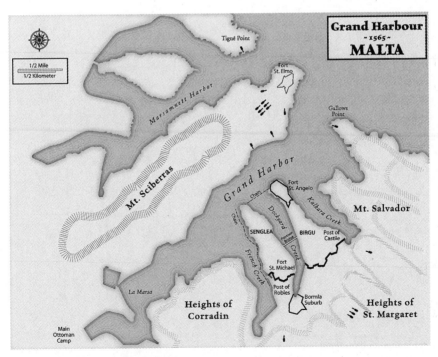

Map of Grand Harbor, by Chris Erichsen.

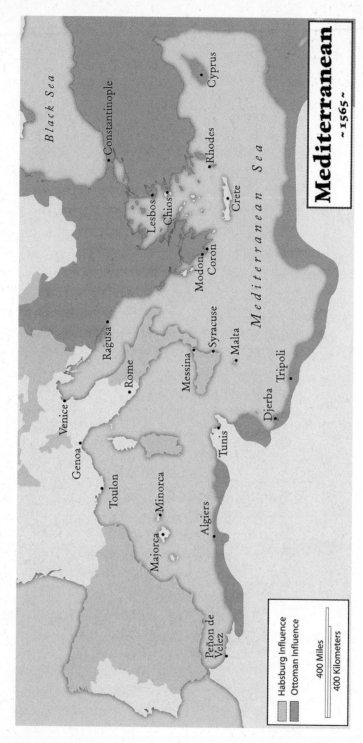

Map of the Mediterranean, 1565, by Chris Erichsen.

Mediterranean
~ 1565 ~

Black Sea

Constantinople

Cyprus

Rhodes

Lesbos
Chios

Crete

Mediterranean Sea

Modon
Coron

Ragusa

Syracuse

Rome

Malta

Messina

Tripoli

Venice

Djerba

Genoa

Tunis

Toulon

Minorca

Algiers

Majorca

Peñon de
Vélez

Habsburg Influence
Ottoman Influence

400 Miles

400 Kilometers

Philippe de Villiers de L'Isle-Adam.
Anonymous etching.

Suleiman the Magnificent. Anonymous
Venetian woodcut in two blocks, ca. 1532,
in William Stirling-Maxwell, *Examples
of Engraved Portraits of the Sixteenth
Century* (London, 1872).

Charles V of Spain. Oil portrait by Juan
Pantoja de la Cruz, El Escorial, Madrid.

ABOVE LEFT Khairedihn
Barbarossa. Engraving from
André Thevet, *Les vrais pourtraits
et vies des hommes illustres* (Paris:
Kervert et Chaudière, 1584).

ABOVE RIGHT Sinan Pasha.
Etching by Giacomo Franco,
*Effigie naturali dei maggior prencipi
et più valorosi capitani* (Venice:
Giacomo Franco, 1596).

RIGHT Jean de Valette. Etching
in M. Manger and J. Praetorius,
Atrium heroicum Caesarum regum,
(Augsburg: Custos, 1600).

IOHAN · VALETTA · MAG · RHOD · MELITENSIS · MILITIÆ · MAGIST

Te, pulsis Turcis, Melite defensa Magistro,
Te nulla folli morte, VALETTA, sinit.

LEFT   Philip II of Spain. Oil portrait after a painting by Alonso Sanchez Coello, Pollok House, Glasgow.

BELOW LEFT   Gianandrea Doria. Etching in M. Manger and J. Praetorius, *Atrium heroicum Caesarum regum* (Augsburg: Custos, 1600).

BELOW RIGHT   Don Garcia de Toledo. Etching in Cesáreo Fernández Duro, *Armada española: Desde la unión de los reinos de Castilla y de Aragón*, vol. 2 (Madrid: Sucesores de Rivadeneyra, 1896).

ASCANIVS · CORNEVS.

RIGHT Ascanio Della Corgna.
Etching in William Stirling-
Maxwell, *Don John of Austria*
(London: Longmans, 1883).

BELOW Vicenzo Anastagi.
Oil portrait by El Greco,
Frick Collection, New York.

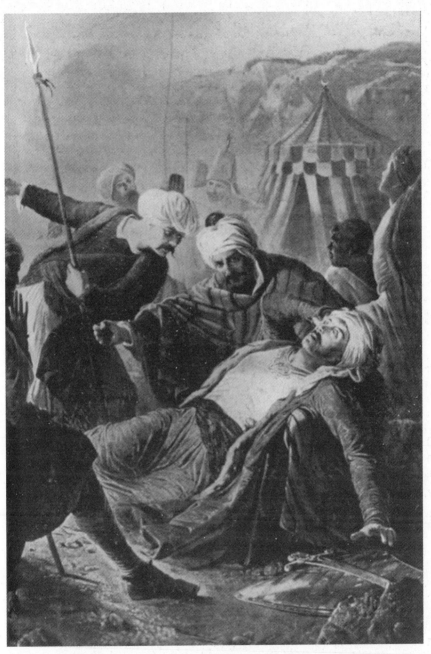

The Death of Dragut. Oil portrait by Giuseppe Calì, National Museum of Fine Arts, Valletta, Malta.

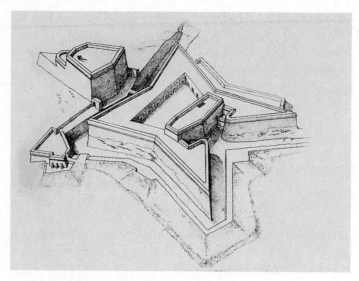

Fort St. Elmo. Rendering courtesy of Stephen C. Spiteri, *Fortresses of the Knights* (Malta: Book Distributors, 2001).

Fort St. Elmo after the loss of the ravelin on the left. Rendering courtesy of Stephen C. Spiteri, *The Great Siege: Knights versus Turks, MDLXV: Anatomy of a Hospitaler Victory* (Malta: Gutenberg Press, 2005).

Fort St. Angelo. Rendering courtesy of Stephen C. Spiteri, *The Great Siege: Knights versus Turks, MDLXV: Anatomy of a Hospitaler Victory* (Malta: Gutenberg Press, 2005).

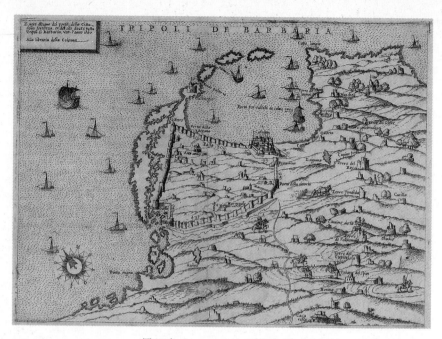

Tripoli. Anonymous etching, 1567,
courtesy of Barry Lawrence Ruderman Antique Maps.

Fortress near Humt Suk, Djerba. Wood engraving, 1886, by Fortuné Louis Méaulle,
from a drawing by T. Taylor.

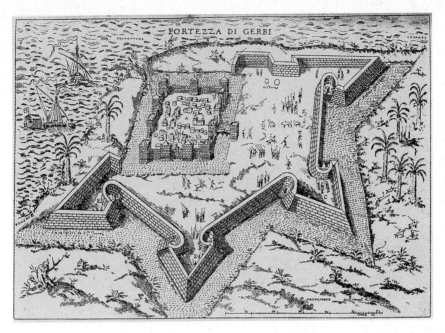

Djerba fortress. Anonymous etching, 1599.

The Tower of Skulls (Djerba). Steel engraving, 1841, by E. Benjamin,
from a drawing by Sir Grenville T. Temple, Bart.

Sixteenth-century galley. Anonymous etching.

Galley of Knights of St. John. Etching by Jacob Custodis in Joseph Furttenbach,
Architectura Navalis (Ulm: J. Saurn, 1629).

PART THREE

·•·•·•·

Honor
Bought
with
Blood

17

＋·＋·＋·＋

PICCOLO
SOCCORSO

＋·＋·＋·＋

The men of St. Elmo have shown the Turks
what we're made of.

Valette

Since early spring, knights and soldiers and adventurers had been gathering
from all over Europe at Messina. Once arrived, they sat. The waiting was made
all the worse by the knowledge that just over the horizon fellow Christians
were engaged every minute of every day in a hard-fought battle that they
looked all too likely to lose. The men had come this far; it was maddening to
have to stop now.

The man holding them back was Don Garcia, and if he was holding them
back, it was with good reason. As overall military commander, he had to weigh
the strength of the Turks already on Malta against the strength of his own
fleet. He repeatedly had told Valette that he would send a force when, and only
when, there were sufficient soldiers to overwhelm the enemy. Valette, in a letter
of June 29, downplayed the threat, dismissing the enemy ships as "the trifling
guard that the enemy is putting up."[1] Don Garcia would not be moved. The
Ottoman armada was formidable and circled the island like a jealous dragon,
watchful, dangerous.

Nor was Malta the only battleground that summer. In July, Don Garcia was
reported to have "fought with forty galleys, and taken twenty-five and sunk the
rest."[2] Algerians were, according to rumor, again laying siege to Spanish-held
Oran, due south of Cartagena (unsuccessfully in the end).[3]

Always, Don Garcia had to consider the wishes of his king, who, like Suleiman, above all wanted to preserve the fleet. Suleiman was generally more aggressive than Philip, in part because he had no one else to answer to. In Philip's case, the concern over his ships was stronger both because he had lost so much at Djerba and because his current fleet was largely funded by the generosity of the pope, who expected results. A navy was hideously expensive, and having recently borrowed two hundred thousand ducats from his Genoese banker Nicolò Grimaldi, "il Monarca," he could not afford to lose another.[4] If Philip's galleys should be lost, the situation would be suddenly and drastically worse for Malta, Italy, and Spain, a point his father had taken some pains to drum into him.[5] Philip said outright that his ships' "conservation was more important than the relief."[6] (Giovanni Battista Adriani, court historian to the Medici, makes an offhand comment about Spain's "customary slowness" (*l'uso loro tardissime*).[7]

There was also the question of tactics. Amphibious landings have always been a difficult business. Attempting one against a strong opposing force, and factoring in the sixty galleys patrolling the island, would be disastrous.[8] What success Don Garcia had enjoyed in the past — and he was more successful than not — had been due to meticulous planning and a precise calculation of the odds.

The knights, understandably, didn't want to hear any of this. Their position was simple. Their brethren were dying. They wanted to fight. This man was preventing them. In consequence, they hounded him. They reminded him of the service the knights had performed when he, Don Garcia, had taken the Peñon de Velez de la Gomera. They questioned to his face his strategy and his nerve.

It was not, however, as if Don Garcia had done nothing. Two other relief efforts had been sent out earlier, only to turn back in the face of Piali's fleet.[9] Moreover, the viceroy was dealing with a somewhat skittish monarch and had to convince him that the situation of Malta in general and Fort St. Elmo in particular might be worrisome, but not so dire that they should give up entirely: "And even if San Telmo [*sic*] were lost, I do not consider that loss the worse for Malta so long as the other [forts] are retained, because any fleet that [the Ottomans] will put in the port that lies under San Telmo is still subject to whomever is master of the island."[10] Philip meanwhile kept coming back to the situation at La Goletta. Did it have enough men, should they send more, had Don Garcia considered the thoughts of the locals?[11] Don Garcia had repeatedly assured him that La Goletta was relatively safe, a "part of the world most difficult to attack, and easiest to defend, and if the Ottomans do go to that island I am certain that they will leave with little honor and a great deal of harm."[12] The king continued to fret, and Don Garcia replied with a tact that at times gave way to impatience: "If Your Majesty only knew how our enemies were now engaged on Malta."[13]

Whatever the troops badgering him at Messina might think, the viceroy's primary concern was with the island, and he had sent a long and detailed letter to Philip explaining the various risks of confronting the Ottomans on Malta ("putting people on the ground there is a lot of work") or fighting the armada at sea.[14] Curiously, Don Garcia's brother-in-law Cosimo de' Medici had taken upon himself to write directly to Philip, regretting that the knights had failed to prepare for this siege years earlier, but then suggesting that a few small relief forces sent in sooner rather than later could do good service while the larger relief for later that summer was being prepared.[15] Whether this was done with or without Don Garcia's knowledge or approval is impossible to know.

In the end, however, he did act. A small force of some forty-two knights and six hundred men, dubbed by history as the *Piccolo Soccorso*, the "Small Relief," was slated to try where two other attempts had failed. It was still a risk — any force that reached the island could easily find itself caught between Piali's ships and Mustapha's army — but less a risk than sending everyone who wanted to go. Don Garcia, still unaware that Fort St. Elmo had fallen, was under no illusion that such a small number of soldiers would make much difference; at best, these men could be a temporary boost to morale, a show of good faith, and a means of disarming his critics.[16]

The boats would be commanded by Don Juan de Cardona, the land forces by Melchior de Robles, a highly charismatic Spanish knight of the Order of St. James and *Maestro de Campo* for Sicilian Tercios. In the past he had served as a soldier in Hungary and less dangerously as *Gentilhombre de Boca* for the Emperor Ferdinand.[17]

Don Garcia set down one condition — if they learned that Fort St. Elmo had fallen, the expedition was to be called off. The logic is clear enough. Their chances of reaching Birgu were better if Mustapha was still occupied with St. Elmo. If St. Elmo had fallen, the Ottomans most likely would target Birgu, making it impossible to reach. In that event, the relief could only be safe at

Mdina, where they could do little good while eating and drinking stuffs that the locals could ill afford to lose. Don Garcia's strategy all along had been to avoid any relief that was not overwhelming, and this exception needed exceptional justification. Bolstering Birgu and only Birgu was justified; bolstering Mdina, at this stage, was less so.

The *Piccolo Soccorso* arrived at Malta on June 29, too late to help Fort St. Elmo.[18] There was, somewhat surprisingly, no interference from, or even sightings of, Muslim ships along the way. The galleys anchored most of the day a few miles offshore and behind the small island of Fifla. They sat there bobbing in the water for the better part of the day and night and only at dawn headed toward the western shore, where the lookouts saw the dull light of a nearly exhausted campfire. It could belong to Maltese fishermen; it could just as easily belong to Ottoman sentries. If the boats were discovered now, either from sea or from land, the expedition would be over before it had even begun.

Cardona brought his ships as close to shore as he felt prudent, then had a skiff lowered onto the water. Robles and two others climbed in and rowed toward the island. Among the party was Quincy, a French knight who spoke both Maltese and Turkish. Once the boat was dragged on shore, Quincy approached the fading campfire, around which was gathered a small group of Maltese peasants. He called out to them, explained who he was, and asked about Fort St. Elmo. The islanders regretted to inform him that the great fort had fallen with serious losses to his fellow knights and other brave soldiers. A tragic day for Christendom, and they prayed that the Turks could still be repulsed. The word also was that Valette, unlike Don Garcia, was eager to have any men regardless of the state of Fort St. Elmo. Quincy thanked the men for the information, got up, and returned to his comrades. His duty was clear and he did not hesitate. Fort St. Elmo, he said, still held out.

In short order, the men began to climb over the sides of the galleys and onto the longboats that would carry them to the shore. As they milled about along the beach, still beneath a black night sky, the ships had turned and, oars dipping rhythmically, disappeared into the dark. Cardona could not risk being caught in broad daylight in galleys stripped of their fighting men.

The *Piccolo Soccorso* was at risk so long as they were out in the open. Any stray foraging party, any patrol, might discover them and report their presence to the Ottoman command. The new arrivals needed to reach Mdina and safety as quickly as possible. At this point, fortune (*miracolosa providenza Divina*) favored them.[19] A mild wind ferried in heat and moisture from North Africa, slowly but steadily, and in so doing conjured up an enveloping mist. It was and is an unusual midsummer phenomenon on Malta, and rarely so well-timed. Cloaked by this soft shield, guided by the coastal Maltese, the long train of soldiers ghosted its way across Malta's short hills to the gates of Mdina, where it was welcomed with some surprise and great happiness by Dom Mesquita and the rest of city's inhabitants. They would remain there while Toni Bajada, dressed like a Turk and fluent in their language, made his way through the lines, contacted Valette, and discovered what the grand master wanted them to do.

Mesquita was worried enough about word of their arrival getting out that he posted extra guards at all gates. It wasn't enough. After sundown, a small boy at Mdina saw a man slipping out of the city. The boy cried "Turk, Turk!," alerting a nearby sentinel, who saw the fleeing man and managed to capture him.[20] Torture persuaded the renegade, a Greek, to confess that he had intended to report these new arrivals to the Ottoman invaders. He was taken out and quartered.

There remains the question of Don Garcia's curious condition, so casually dismissed by Robles, for going forward only if St. Elmo still held. The answer was a matter of hard logic. As long as St. Elmo stood, the Ottoman army would be preoccupied. Until they could turn their attention to St. Michael and Birgu, Ottoman lines were as stretched and their mass as diluted as it would ever be. Don Garcia knew that messengers could get through the Ottoman lines, if with some difficulty. Once the enemy began to concentrate on Senglea and Birgu, those gaps would quickly shrink, or even disappear. Certainly they would become too narrow for any moderately large force to make its way to Valette. Don Garcia had managed this calculation with a nicety that his later detractors were to ignore. He assured Philip that "I didn't consider sending these galleys except with a wide margin of time before St. Telmo was lost."[21]

✦·✦·✦·✦

Men die, other men replace them. Turgut's successor as governor of Tripoli was Uludj Ali, whose first duty was to carry back the body of the old corsair and return with the city's munitions that Turgut had refused to bring. Turgut was honored as befitting a man of his stature. No anonymous mass grave for him — the old corsair was wrapped in cloth and laid to rest inside Tripoli's al-Saraya al-Hamra (Red Castle) mosque that he himself had built for the city. It can still be seen. Fittingly, Turgut shared his last journey with soldiers wounded in the several assaults on St. Elmo, men who would otherwise cram the already overflowing Ottoman hospitals on Malta. Uludj Ali set off on June 25. He missed the *Piccolo Soccorso* by forty-eight hours.

Uludj Ali (variously known as Uluch Ali, Kiliç Ali Paşa, El Ulucchialim, and to the Italians, Occhiali), born in 1519 as Giovanni Dionigi Galeni, the son of a Calabrian fisherman, was the last of Khairedihn's great commanders. Calabria, the sharp, rocky toe of Italy with its many inlets and coastal villages, had been a natural haunt for pirates and smugglers since before the days of the Greeks; and if there was little enough treasure to steal, there were always people to kidnap. Galeni was snatched in one of the too frequent slave raids. Rumor — since proven untrue but persistent to this day — held that he was a failed Jesuit, or that he was at least intended for the church, when he was taken by Muslim corsairs.

Galeni was short, squat, scabrous, shrewd, loud-mouthed, and apparently fearless. He was hustled on board the corsairs' galley and chained to the rowing benches with the rest of the miserable Christians. It was a common enough story of the time; and with no family connections and no money, his only hope of freedom was that a Christian pirate, or the Knights of St. John, might seize the vessel. Until then, endurance, faith, and patience were the chief allies of a galley slave. Galeni may have had all those qualities, but he did not have tact. Where others would row in silence, Galeni spoke out loudly and often, freely criticizing the way the captain and crew were handling the ship. A cruder man might have taken offense at a slave's backtalk, but Chaifer Rais, who owned the galley, was fascinated by the Calabrian. Something might be made of a man like this.

The story goes that Chaifer Rais brought his ships back home to Egypt and Galeni into his house. He made the Calabrian a proposition. If he would accept the blessings of Islam, his master would take him on as a business partner and give him command of one of his ships. It was a generous offer, and it took a strong man to turn it down. Galeni was never anything but strong, and his Christian faith was still powerful enough to send him back to the oar bench.

What the captain could not force, Galeni's own temper made inevitable. One day a fellow oarsman, presumably tired of this man's mouth, insulted him, one guesses grievously. Galeni lashed out and struck him dead. Under the laws of his master, the slave Galeni must pay for a slave with his own life, and suddenly a dogged adherence to Christianity held less attraction. Galeni immediately professed Islam and claimed its protections. The captain considered the matter. As the dead oarsman was a Christian slave with few rights that a man of faith was bound to respect, the matter could be ended then and there. Galeni was free from the oar bench, free to join his master's enterprises, free to marry his master's daughter.

Now reborn as Uludj Ali, he began his rise to greatness. He started out as an able-bodied merchant seaman and soon became one of Barbarossa's protégés. By 1560 he was sailing in tandem with Turgut, and as we have seen, played a significant part in the fight for Djerba. When he arrived at Malta, just before Turgut, he brought four ships, three hundred Levantine fighters, and three hundred Egyptians skilled in digging tunnels. Just the sort of man Mustapha could use. Unfortunately, although his own luck would hold out, his contributions at Malta would be plagued by bad timing.

◆·◆··◆·◆

Mustapha, his spleen vented on the dead of St. Elmo, now had a harder nut to crack in Birgu and Fort St. Michael. In theory, taking St. Elmo had been a worthy endeavor, but the cost had been horrendous, more than he cared to count, more really than he could afford. Even now he was preparing Suleiman for lowered expectations. He wrote that he hoped for victory, but that, in his judgment, it would prove more difficult and time consuming than previously believed.[22] Balbi goes further, stating that Mustapha reported home "his small hope of actually taking Malta."[23] Suleiman, in a letter that must have been both encouraging and alarming, acknowledged the taking of St. Elmo and the loss of Turgut, then added that "you should encourage the army and the Janissaries to fight against the enemies and you should conquer the island. I trust that you and everybody else will succeed in this feat."[24]

Mustapha could comfort himself with the belief that the worst was over. The Christians had put on a brave show, an astonishingly brave show, but one that had cost them as much if not more than it had cost the Ottomans. The cream of the knights had died in defending St. Elmo; those who remained might just be willing to accept peace with honor. Protocols of war, though much abused in this siege, still had meaning, and Mustapha would have to make the offer. It would be irresponsible, unchivalrous, and contrary to the laws of Islam to do otherwise. Worse, it would be unbusinesslike. Mustapha would rather take a walled city fully intact than plant his standard on a second pile of blasted rock.

On June 29, a small party overseen by a man on horse approached the walls just outside St. Michael under a white flag of truce. One of their number declared that he was a fellow Christian, a Spaniard, thirty-two years a slave of the Ottomans, and that the party wished to discuss terms. There was some consultation behind the walls, and after a time, an answer came down. The Christian might approach and enter. The others should stay where they were. Minutes later the old man was hustled inside, searched, and his eyes bound. He was then frog-marched through the stone streets of Birgu to the Piazza del Borgo, where his blindfold was removed. He blinked in the sudden glare, and he found himself face to face with an unsmiling Valette.

Mustapha, the slave told him, was proposing an honorable finish to this affair on the same terms as his master Suleiman had offered at Rhodes. The knights would have to leave, of course, but unmolested, and they might take their belongings with them. The Maltese were welcome to stay, their lives spared, their property and religion respected, and their safety guaranteed. Peace would be restored, lives saved, and honor served. The Order was even welcome to return east, to an (undetermined) "larger and better island than Malta, paying a light and fair tribute, allowing each one to live according to their own laws," where they might "practice their skills as Hospitallers."[25] There could be no shame in accepting these terms. The alternative was the grisly fate of St. Elmo; worse, even — all killed and the grand master marched in triumph through Constantinople.

Valette listened to the envoy in silence, and when the terms had been laid out, he spoke. He ordered the guards to kill the man, in sight of the enemy, to make an example to others who might come to him with similar offers. The old man broke down. He was a good Christian, he said, an unfortunate who had been captured by these infidels and forced to serve them all these many years, but a man whose true faith had never wavered. He was here by order and hoped only to save the lives of fellow Christians through his mission. For the knight and a man of God to execute a poor wretch such as him would be a sin.

Valette let the man babble on for a while, then, at the urging of his knights, appeared to relent. He pardoned the envoy, but told him not to try this again, since he, Valette, would not entertain further offers from such barbarous men (gente tan barbara) and would hang anyone who brought them.[26] He ordered that the Spaniard's eyes be bound again, then led those present out of the chamber. They tramped down the hot echoing streets and into a stone-covered passageway, down some steps, then stopped. Again the blindfold came off. The slave looked about him, again adjusting his eyes in the bright sunlight, and found himself at the bottom of the ditch between the enemy lines and the defensive walls by the bastions of Provence and Auvergne. Valette let him take in the sight.

Mustapha, said Valette, might have Malta, but not before he had filled this ditch with Muslim dead.

The whole affair had been a well-planned piece of theater, but the dramatic setting and the blunt talk had a powerful effect on the slave. He said that the Turks would never take Birgu. He was not, however, going to risk uncertainty in his own life — faith could only take a man so far. He chose instead to return to the Ottoman lines, presumably to a familiar and comfortable station in life. He is hereafter lost to history.

The next day, Mustapha sent his envoys to Mdina with much the same message, slightly altered to play to this different audience. Suleiman, they declared, had no wish to make war on or in any way harm the ancient and pacific capital of Malta. His quarrel was with the knights, old enemies and constant troublemakers in the sultan's domains. An alliance, or at least an understanding, was suggested, though on what terms we are not told.

It was an interesting approach, and the aristocracy of Malta, those old Italian families who had lorded over the island before the knights arrived, might have been tempted by the promise of renewed, if largely nominal, power on the island. That was the hope, in any event. Mustapha, however, was negotiating in a vacuum. The elite of Mdina had left the city before the Ottomans ever arrived. The envoys got their answer from an unnamed prefect, foursquare with the defense: "Those who are enemies of the Knights of Rhodes are also enemies of the Maltese, nor will I ever permit such an alliance."[27] Turgut might have talked his way into Tripoli. Mustapha would not be so lucky.

18

+·+·+·+

RELIEF

INTO BIRGU

+·+·+·+

If the fort is on the water, there must be stones and stakes emplaced
around it to render its approach secure, so that the sea borne machines
of war should not be able to advance within close range.

Giovanni Battista Alberti, De Re Aedificatoria

The enemy is laboring with all diligence to dig trenches
all around Senglea, and although the Pasha and his Janissaries have
not yet moved from the Marsa, they will not delay long, perhaps tomorrow,
having already established many emplacements above Santa Margarita . . .
It is desirable to send some vessels to hearten our people.

Valette to Don Garcia, June 29, 1565

The offer and refusal of surrender was as much a matter of protocol for Mustapha as it had been for Valette. Mustapha, however, also had a practical reason
for ending the siege now. This was not Rhodes, close to the center of Ottoman
power. If he should manage to seize Malta, it would need walls. Anything that
was destroyed on Malta, particularly any defense works, would have to be
rebuilt. Even as his heralds had raised white flags, he had been arranging his
guns before Senglea and Birgu. Four new platforms rose on the grand master's
garden in the Marsa, readying the army for the next phase of operations — the
battle for Senglea and Birgu.

On the morning of July 2, a lone man dressed in red robes stood on the shore
across the Spur of St. Michael. The clothing suggested a figure of some conse-

quence, and for some reason he was waving his hands at the defenders, trying to catch their attention. Someone shouted over to him, asking his business. He called back that he wished to join them but had no way of getting across. Could they send a boat over to fetch him? The ranking officer hesitated. A boat over would require lowering the massive chain that defended the water between Senglea and Birgu. He needed permission from Valette for this and sent a runner to get it. It would, however, take some time and the man was advised to swim, if he was able, and wait for Christian swimmers if he was not.

This conversation had been carried on over a thousand feet of water, and although it was far from the Ottoman activities, it could not escape notice for long. Armed Muslim soldiers from Coradin began to run down Sciberras toward the man in red. There was only one way out. The defector threw off his cloak, tied his shirt around his head, and stumbled and flailed into the water. As the Muslims drew closer, the men on the ramparts of Fort St. Angelo were able to provide covering fire. In the water, the renegade managed to reach the halfway point before he began to founder. Three Christians — a Maltese, a Provençal, and a Sicilian — managed to reach him and haul him back to Fort St. Angelo.

Once the rescue party and their charge returned, Balbi himself and Don Jaime de Sanoguera escorted the shaken guest to rest in the room where Valette once kept his lions before being led to the grand master.[1] His Turkish name, he said, was Memi Celebi, but he was born Philip Lascaris. This would have raised an eyebrow among the knights. Lascaris was a name with roots deep in Byzantium's imperial history, and included two emperors and a small army of court officials. When Constantinople fell to the Ottomans in 1457, his family had been largely humbled. He had, he said, been taught to despise the faith of his ancestors. The logic was simple enough: Allah had permitted Islam to seize Constantinople, proving itself better favored than Christianity.

In submitting to Islam, Lascaris found opportunities almost as dignified as any that he might have enjoyed in Christian Byzantium. The fifty-five year old had been a spahi and close to Mustapha Pasha. But the example of the Christian soldiers at St. Elmo had moved him and, as Bosio writes, "The Holy Ghost touched his heart . . . to return to the sacred Catholic faith" (ignoring that the Lascaris family had been born Greek Orthodox).[2]

This conversion was no small thing. As an apostate of Islam, Lascaris had bound his fate entirely with that of Malta. If the island fell, he would be executed immediately, and so more than most he needed to see the Ottomans fail. Fortunately, he had a wide and intimate knowledge of the Ottomans' strategies, troop levels and dispositions, morale, intelligence, and supplies. He was able to tell Valette that an attack was imminent, and a serious one, and that it would come by land — no great secret there — and by sea. The bulk of the attack would, in fact, be aimed at the relatively weak western flank of Senglea, and to get the ships past the guns of Fort St. Angelo to the inner harbor, Mustapha would take a page out of Turgut's playbook. He intended to drag his ships overland around the base of Mt. Sciberras.

Lascaris had other news as well. He was also able to explain recent anomalies, such as the smoke and flares that Valette had seen since June 24 at Mdina, but which Valette could not interpret. Lascaris said that this was a signal that the Spanish relief had arrived, a fact, he added, known only to him. (How this could be, we are not told, but if true, it might have factored into his decision to switch sides.)[3]

Confirmation that the *Piccolo Soccorso* had arrived came the next day with the arrival from Mdina of Toni Bajada. Valette pondered his options. St. Elmo was gone and had taken nearly a quarter of his entire force with it. His soldiers had bought him time, but that time was now up. The Ottomans were redirecting their guns against Fort St. Michael and Birgu. They were also redeploying around those walls, making it more and more difficult to get in and out of the peninsula. A few hundred fresh soldiers would be useful both militarily and as a morale raiser for the general population on Malta.

But could it be done? Bajada made frequent trips back and forth between Mdina and Birgu — as had others — but always alone, always at night, and always with a native's instinctive knowledge of the area. Even those trips were dangerous. Getting a train of that many men weighted down with heavy clanking armor and metal weaponry through lines increasingly thick with enemy soldiers would seem nearly impossible.

Valette and the council discussed the matter with Bajada and Lascaris present. Lascaris noted that the Ottomans were at their most lax in the depression below Mount Salvador, opposite to the Post of Castile. Even a force as large as the *Piccolo Soccorso* might, with the grace of God, be able to follow the coastline, skirt the enemy pickets, and be brought to safety. Bajada could not do this alone; he needed guides who could navigate the terrain at night and keep a line of men this large moving quickly and quietly. Lascaris himself volunteered. He might not know the land as well, but he did have a native's command of the

Turkish language and the army's habits, in case they were challenged. Others were quietly lined up, though not told what for — Valette could not risk word leaking out — then sent off to Mdina under Bajada's command.

In short order, Robles assembled his troops and, just an hour before sundown on July 3, they began to march. Seven hundred men, many armored and some on horse — the silence could not have been total.[4] The moon was entering its first quarter, too dark to be seen clearly. The closer they came to Birgu, the more Turks were in evidence on the ground. Several times the column passed "within a stone's throw of the Turkish line"; not once did any sentry or watchman challenge them.[5] The sheer unlikelihood of a Christian relief force was its protection. What the Ottoman sentries could not imagine, they would not investigate. Robles was not taking undue chances, however, and before he got much closer, he had his riders dismount and the horses sent back to Mdina. It was to be pure marching from here on in.

Some six hours had passed from the time Robles and his men had left Mdina. With just two hours of darkness left, they arrived on the outskirts of Birgu and filed north to the rendezvous point at the water's edge. One of the guides descended into the glittering surface and silently disappeared toward the defenders' bolt hole. Several minutes passed before the first of six longboats glided into view and settled near the shore. Then they began the steady feeding of the Christian defenses. For the next hour the boats brought the six hundred on the final leg of the journey, just as they had carried men back and forth from Fort St. Angelo to Fort St. Elmo. Their luck held to the end, when Robles allowed himself to be the last man out of 521 ferried across.[6]

Those members of the expedition leading the horses back to Mdina were not so lucky. Ten or twelve men under the command of Commendatore Fra Girolamo di Gravina, knight of Catania and Capitano d'Arme of Mdina, seem to have lost their way in the dark.[7] They were discovered at first light and hauled before Mustapha. Gravina confirmed that the unfamiliar pennants now flying from the walls opposite were the calling cards of new soldiers, proof that Europe had not abandoned Malta as it had Rhodes and Djerba. It can be argued that the *Piccolo Soccorso*, more than any other strategic decision, determined the outcome of the entire siege. Even Balbi — who credits God rather than Don Garcia — notes that, had they not arrived, "Birgu would have been taken at the next assault."[8]

+·+··+·+

The Ottoman response to the *Piccolo Soccorso* was a cannonade aimed at Birgu proper. The purpose was pure terror. It also meant repair work had become more dangerous. Valette directed that the Order's slaves take this duty, both to keep Christians out of danger and in the hope that the Ottomans might be reluctant to fire on their fellow Muslims (who were, in addition, expendable mouths for Valette to feed). It was a vain hope. Even assuming he knew the sappers were Muslim, Mustapha was not going to spare any lives so long as victory was on the line. Besides, Muslims killed in this manner would go straight to paradise. The benefits were most likely lost on the slaves themselves, some of whom, to avoid the assignment, chose to cut off their own ears. (How effective this tactic was is not, unfortunately, recorded. Given Valette's nature and the desperation of the defenders, one can guess not very.) Over five hundred Muslim slaves (*los pobres*) would die under the Ottoman guns.[9]

As for the Christian response to the *Piccolo Soccorso*, Don Garcia wrote that "the Grand Master's joy was such that I cannot write about it without tears."[10] The new arrivals were, however, a mixed blessing. Although they had brought themselves and their weapons, they had not brought much in the way of provisions, and no water. Those still alive behind the walls, already headed toward strict rationing, were now allotted that much less, a serious problem on a dry, hot summer island with no wells, and with the rainy season still two months away. Geofrè de Loaysa and Iacomo Coloroti had still come up with no new sources.

If morale was low at this time, there was no record of it. Certainly the men of the *Piccolo Soccorso* were upbeat. Fresh and full of high spirits, they confronted the Ottomans the first day and "killed a great number."[11] The armories were running full tilt, forges blazing in the creation of more weaponry, slaves put to work making the slow matches for the arquebus. The bombardments became routine, and one can become accustomed to routine, however frightful. Slaves and civilians scrabbled at the collapsed houses and other unoccupied shelters in Birgu and recycled the stones and roof tiles to fortify the walls. It was in the open-air lee of these walls that many of the dispossessed civilians now slept.

Mustapha, however, was just warming up. On July 6, even as he was sending word out to Modon that he was greatly concerned about his diminishing supply of powder and cannonballs and ordered that more be sent, along with fresh fruit and "other things," he was, as Lascaris had promised, pushing six Muslim vessels deep inside Grand Harbor, outside gun range.[12] The next day there were six more and the day after more still. But forewarned was forearmed, and Valette had opened the question of how to improve Senglea's shoreline defenses, and fast. The walls, only about ten feet high, fronted onto a stretch of flat beach. They held two gun emplacements capable of crossfire on the shoreline. How well this could hold off a massive, dedicated, and sustained assault was unknowable. In thirty years, no invaders had ever gotten this far.

A partial solution came from an aging captain who had clearly read his Alberti. This man advised an adaptation of the chain barrier that protected the inlet between Senglea and Birgu. The shoreline did not possess a pair of anchor points from which to string a chain across; it did, however, have sand. Sappers should be able to get out into the water, drive wooden piles deep into the silt and mud, and settle the ends just below the water level. It would then be merely a question of stringing a barrier chain from post to post.

The difficulty was in the doing. The Ottomans had arrayed sharpshooters on the far shore of Corradin, six hundred paces away, too close for anyone to expose himself in safety. Construction would have to take place at night. Maltese, adept at water work, again came forward. Under cover of darkness they dragged the piles out fifteen feet from shore, and in a feat of astonishing strength and virtuosity, somehow drove them deep into the seabed, underwater, at fifteen- to twenty-foot intervals. On the final day they mounted the chain, and where the sand or silt was insufficient and the space between the posts exceeded fifteen feet, they tied the chain in place with floating logs. A barrier now stretched between the point of Zanogara on Senglea's tip to the so-called Post of Robles at the wall.

The Ottomans had monitored this painstaking labor and the men who had bobbed in the water and nighttime chill, sinking the posts and stringing the links. The day after that work was finished, the same Maltese heard the sharp tap-tapping of metal on metal. Ottoman swimmers had crossed the narrow strait and were taking axes to the poled chain. The demolition team was working in full daylight and under the protection of Ottoman sharpshooters, who would pick off gun crews, making certain that Christians did not fire on the sappers.

The gunners may have been cautious, but the men who had installed the chains were not going to let their hard work be destroyed without a fight. Four of them grabbed knives, rushed out a sally port, ran across the strip of land between wall and water, plunged in, and headed straight toward the Turks.

There followed a series of fierce hand-to-hand struggles. Steel blades and wet skin glinted in the sun, and dark water turned a shade of purple as the Maltese and Ottomans began to draw blood. Men slashed and gouged, held their opponents under the surface, burst up and gasped for air, were pulled down again, never certain that they would ever come up again. The Ottoman sappers realized that their choice was between destroying the defenses or preserving themselves. In the end, they paddled back to their own line, the poles and chains remained as they were, and the Maltese returned to Senglea and safety. Not one of the Maltese was injured, testimony to their skills as swimmers and as fighters.

Later that day, the Ottomans made one more attempt on the chain. This time a single Ottoman swimmer carried a hooked line to the chain, threw it across, and returned to his comrades. The cable was attached to a winch, the purpose of which was to pull out the entire line with the mechanical advantage it conferred. A lone Maltese ran across the short beach, swam out to the chain, cut the cable, and the Turks never tried again.

Ottoman records of July 11 cite one Salih ben Mahmud as having "rendered outstanding services by cutting one of the booms laid by the infidels in the sea in front of the suburb of the Malta fortress," for which action he was duly rewarded.[13] The Ottomans recognized bravery and honored those who demonstrated it, whatever the final outcome.

Meanwhile, in sight and still out of range, the number of galleys kept growing.

19

+·+·+·+

BRAVI D'ALGIERI

+·+·+·+

I don't know if the likeness of Hell could be more accurately
described than by putting on canvas or recording on paper this crude,
horrible, frightening, and cruel fight.

Bosio

While the Maltese were installing their maritime chain and accommodating
the men of the *Piccolo Soccorso,* the Ottomans were welcoming reinforcements of their own, chief among them Hassan ben Khairedihn, also known
as Barbaroszade (son of Barbarossa), beylerbey of Algiers, son of a Moorish
woman from Granada and of Barbarossa himself. Hassan seemed to have
inherited the better part of his father's abilities. Suleiman named him to his
post at Algiers two years before his father's death in 1546, which post he held
on and off for ten years. When not in Algiers, Hassan was a kind of special
envoy of the Grande Porte. Suleiman dispatched him repeatedly to outposts
in North Africa with an eye to keeping Ottoman protectorates from becoming
too free-spirited.

Now Hassan and his lieutenant, the Greek renegade Candelissa, another
veteran of Prevesa, rowed into Grand Harbor with twenty-five hundred
Algerian corsairs, so-called *bravi d'Algieri.*[1] If Hassan carried his authority
over them lightly, it was because he, just like Barbarossa, just like Turgut, just
like Uludj Ali, had little choice. Corsairs were men of some independence
and a great deal of élan, men who followed their own inclinations, men who
carried themselves with a swaggering confidence that spilled over into arro-
gance. They wore the trophies of their thievery, the bright and rich clothing
and jewel-studded weapons, and would follow a commander only if he had a

good chance of obtaining more. Hassan voiced his regrets that they had not arrived earlier, and hoped that they would have the opportunity to perform "something noteworthy."[2]

Mustapha had just the thing. He invited Hassan to consider Fort St. Michael, bulwark of Senglea. High walls, a low ditch, strong defense works. The prospect doesn't appear to have alarmed Hassan, and he and his men joined with Mustapha in preparing for the assault. It would begin, as usual, with bombardment, two days and two nights' worth, starting on July 12. When cannons finally did retire for the night, their sound was replaced by a full-voiced cleric who began a chant to which others would reply with shouting and screaming "con gran vozeria y gritos monstruosos."[3]

In the predawn hours of July 15, the Ottoman forces could be heard across French Creek preparing for battle. Their imams had been chanting the entire night, inspiring their own, unnerving their enemy. One hundred boats of many sizes, padded with sacks of wool and cotton against gunfire, were lined up on shore opposite the Senglea peninsula.[4] On board, the attacking force was ready, three thousand Ottoman troops and the cream of Hassan's army, "not a man among them who was not dressed in scarlet tunics, cloth of gold, cloth of silver, crimson damask, carrying muskets of Fez, scimitars of Alexandria and Damascus and fine bows."[5] Smaller vessels elbowed their way through the ranks of larger and pulled up in front of the line.[6] The boats carried imams, "men with very long beards," "strangely clothed, wearing large green hats, and many holding open books."[7] To the accompaniment of kettledrums, bagpipes, and tambours, the readers now stood up and faced the attack force and read out suitable Koranic verses, which Christians dismissed as fortune-telling: "Avian echado las suertes."[8]

The prayers came to an end. The imams, superfluous to any actual fighting, returned to shore. There was a pause, a signal, then the oarsmen dipped their long oars into the water and began to pull, propelling the boats across the water, gaining speed the while. Cannon fired on them and sank many, but not enough. Those that made the passage ran straight into the chained logs, hoping to break the barrier and eventually reach the walls with their feet dry. It didn't happen. No matter. Led by Candelissa, the Muslims poured out of the boats and into the water and, waist deep at best, sloshed their way toward the Christian shore, shouting all the while.

Besides the ranks of arquebusiers lining the relatively low walls of Senglea, the defenders had one advantage: two repurposed naval guns that together from their single embrasure covered the traverse and which, by firing sequentially, could slaughter an enemy en masse. Don Jaime de Sanoguera, nephew of Captain Don Francisco de Sanoguera, was deputed to ensure that the two guns would fire unimpeded.

The guns failed to fire at all. Balbi, who was present at the wall, claims there was no time, but also notes that "some say" the failure was the gunner's fault.[9] The Algerians were able to cover the space between the water and the wall with few casualties. There were other, smaller guns, but even their combined effect was negligible against the oncoming tide. Once having arrived at the base of the walls, the Algerians set ladders firmly in the ground, then arced them up over and against the low-lying defense works. Muslim arquebusiers at the base of the wall fired upward to clear any defenders who dared put their heads out beyond the wall's edge, then the first of the corsairs scrambled upward into a thicket of sword and pike and axe.

Bad luck continued to dog the Christians. Before the battle had begun, thirty thousand incendiary grenades had been distributed to the various front lines.[10] A soldier named Ciano, unpracticed with the weapon and presumably agitated by the approaching enemy, held his spluttering grenade right next to a basket of more incendiaries. A stray spark or drop of flaming naphtha landed in the container and set off the entire store into a sudden bonfire, seriously burning Ciano and several of his comrades, and depriving the Christians of more weapons than they could afford to lose. They tried to make up for it with stones, apparently to some good effect — Balbi says better than had they used only incendiaries — but inevitably, through tenacity and sheer force of numbers, the Algerians were able to get onto the wall. Now arrows, arquebus, and incendiaries largely gave way to knives, rocks, and eventually even fists.

Don Francisco, intent on inspiring his outnumbered men, stood at the very edge of the wall, as close as he could to the fight, dressed in bright armor — a natural target. A bullet struck his breastplate. He fought on. A second bullet, fired from the base of the wall, threaded a chink in his armor, entered his groin, and killed him. Rejoicing Muslims now tried to drag this high-ranking corpse from the parapet as a grim trophy. Balbi and others were just as determined not to let them. The result was a grisly tug-of-war, Spaniards pulling his arms and Muslims his legs, which ended with the Spaniards keeping the body of their commander, the Algerians, his shoes.

In other spots, the Algerians had reached the top of the wall. The question then became, could they hold on and head inward?

As Candelissa was leading his men onto the western walls, Hassan had opened the second phase of the attack against the landward-facing walls of Fort St. Michael. Robles, commanding the defense, had his eye on the flat shoreline before him and watched as Hassan launched a sea of eight thousand white-robed Algerians.[11] These men swept forward with shouts and yells, oblivious to the steady fire Robles's men were laying down upon them. Here and there along the wall, grapeshot and chain tore great holes in the tightly packed masses of oncoming attackers, holes that were quickly filled as the Muslims kept on coming, stumbling over the bodies of comrades, some dead, some wounded. Commanders were as much at risk as foot soldiers. Piali Pasha had mounted a horse to oversee the course of the battle. Artillerymen on Fort St. Angelo saw him and fired. They missed, but "the shock waves lifted the turban from his head and threw him on the ground, and he remained stunned for several days."[12]

Those Algerians who first reached the foot of the wall planted scaling ladders, longer for the greater height of Fort St. Michael, and began the suicidal first climb. From atop the wall, men poured thin streams of hot pitch and Greek fire on those below, and the screams changed from battle cries to agony as their flesh began to burn. Those who made it up the ladders then faced an armory of cold steel: longswords, pikes, and knives, all slashing and thrusting at the intruders. Weapons began to hit their marks, blood began to stain the outer wall scarlet in splotches and streaks and rivulets. The defenders kept the ramparts free of the enemy, and yet despite this the human tide just kept on coming.

The enemy was now swarming on two sides of the peninsula, and all Christian soldiers and by now civilians who could be spared were present, firing arquebuses, lunging and gouging with blades, dropping stones over the walls, and even so just barely holding the line.

And then Mustapha launched his third and final line of attack.

As the defenders of Senglea were now fully occupied with the ongoing assaults along the western shore and at the landward walls of St. Michael, ten Ottoman vessels quietly appeared on the water. These were headed not into the chain that had stopped the earlier boats, but farther north, to the tip of the peninsula, just at the point where the chain began. Ten galleys of eighty men each, Janissaries and Levantines, advanced against a position with little to no immediate defense and almost no chance that further reserve troops could be sent there in time, if indeed there were reserve troops on hand. This squadron's successful arrival would open a third and decisive front on an already hard-pressed position, and had every chance of winning the battle then and there.

(Balbi suggests that this ancillary attack was improvised, based on the other boats' difficulties in getting past the chains.[13] It is possible, however, that one or the other of the Ottoman commanders planned the move from the outset. Hold one area while striking a second is an ancient tactic; to hold two and strike a third is not a great stretch.)

The progress of this flotilla did not go wholly unnoticed. Below the stone walls of Fort St. Angelo, just at the waterline, well removed from any of that day's fighting, Chevalier Francisco de Guiral was at his post, looking out through a set of five embrasures. His post was a recent creation, designed to protect the chain that protected Dockyard Creek, and therefore vital to the defense. That it was vital to the defense was small comfort to Guiral. As he and his men sat behind this low wall, the two greatest assaults of the siege were going on, and he was as far away as possible, forbidden to take part, unable even to know how the battle was going. His only view was of the gentle lapping water of the Grand Harbor and the far shores of Sciberras. The one thing he could not have expected to see was this small flotilla coming across the water and directly into his line of fire.

Guiral knew his business. His view was clear; he had his gunners sight the oncoming squadron, gauge distance, and prepare their guns. Oars rose and fell, dipping into the water and moving briskly toward their goal. He watched, waited, and the boats, ignorant of the danger they were in, pressed forward until they were perfectly aligned in his sights. Guiral gave the order to fire. Gunners lay slow matches onto touchholes, which sputtered briefly; then four of five cannons let loose a single volley of stones and iron and scrap, which billowed across the water.[14]

The manmade storm crashed into the vessels — so carefully shaped and joined back in the shipyards of Constantinople — which now exploded into a gale of splinters, killing and maiming the better part of the passengers. Hundreds of men, many of them injured, most unable to swim, flailed in the water, grasping at any piece of floating wreckage they could reach. Nine of the ten ships were now sinking, and the commander of the tenth, quick-witted and recognizing a mismatched fight, ordered his boat to withdraw as quickly as possible, leaving the bobbing survivors to whatever fate they could manage.[15] In most cases, this was an acceptance of death by drowning. One by one, the struggling heads slipped beneath the water's surface and cries for help diminished to silence.

Guiral's men immediately reloaded and fired again, but the process was long and the surviving ship was quick. There Muslim command was in brief disarray. When Uludj Ali rallied his boats for a second attempt, not only was he met by Guiral's, but according to an official report, they were helped by a battery "from the Castle of St. Angelo whose artillery sank I do not know how many boats and killed many soldiers."[16] By then it didn't matter. No other vessels would dare to attempt that landing, not on that day. Guiral, confined to a secondary position, had his one shot; and by this one action, he and his men almost certainly saved the peninsula.

+·+·+·+

Back on the western shore, the fighting grew hotter, and the numbers of dead grew larger. Don Jaime de Sanoguera and Faderigo de Toledo, recovered enough from his facial burns to fight, had together and against orders crossed the pontoon bridge from Birgu to get closer to the front line. The two had been standing on the wall and taking in the scene when a single cannonball tore through them both. Back in May, Melchior d'Eguaras had written to Don Garcia that Faderigo was "full of virtue and will make a fine knight"[17]

At least it was a quick death. Others were not so lucky. One soldier had three fingers torn off by a flying piece of armor. The wound turned septic, and he died ten days later. And if imams had the luxury of encouraging their coreligionists from a distance, Christian prelates often did not. A monk stood on the wall of Senglea, cross in one hand, sword in the other, a single breastplate covering his brown monk's robe, shouting at the men to hold the line. He was shot from below and died at the top of the wall.

The day dragged on, and both sides exhausted themselves on the walls of Fort St. Michael. Slowly Hassan's Algerians began to withdraw for good to the safety of their camps. They at least had the option. On the western shores of Senglea, the Muslim attackers had nowhere to run except to the waterline and the boats that had carried them into battle. Of these boats, however, some had foundered, others had withdrawn, and none seemed in any hurry to rescue the desperate soldiers. Christian writers claim this was done deliberately to ensure that the men would fight.[18] It briefly had that effect, but the final Muslim assaults could not overcome the guns from St. Angelo, Senglea, and Sanoguera. The space between Senglea's walls and the water became a killing ground, and Christians had the upper hand. The onetime defenders now launched a counterattack, filing out of the bastion through a sally port and firing into the enemy at point-blank range. Candelissa's Muslims, exhausted by fighting and trapped in the narrow strip of land, had no choice but to push back or throw themselves on the mercy of their opponents. "*A buona guerra, o Christiani!*"[19]

Mercy was not a quality easily found in that parched season. The fate of Fort St. Elmo was too recent, and the Christians were not in a forgiving mood. They began to scream, "*Ammazza, ammazza, pagate St. Elmo, pagate St. Elmo, canaglia!*" "Die, die, pay for St. Elmo, pay for St. Elmo, bastards!"[20] A few Muslims were spared, but found little to celebrate. Fra Federico Sangiorgio, whose brother had died at St. Elmo, somehow managed to seize two Janissaries alive and brought them back to the Borgo, where he thrust them into a crowd of "peasants and women."[21] The mob tore them to pieces. Valette's timid Maltese had become accustomed to war.

Meanwhile, desperate men forced back to the water flailed wildly in an attempt to reach the far shore. "Dressed like women" in various fashions and colors, living and half-living bodies stained the water pink and sank beneath the waves.[22] Turkish gunners on the far side of the water, unable to help their comrades, did the next best thing—they fired indiscriminately at the melee. If the Muslims were going to die anyway, there was no reason not to take out as many Christians as possible. God would welcome His own.

Among the Christians, the commercially minded stopped fighting and began plundering. Some of the more foresighted carried ropes with which to tie up slaves—useless planning, as only four Muslims survived the bloodbath. More plentiful were the Algerians' gold clothes, scimitars, and gold and silver embossed arquebuses, worth thirty and forty scudi each, now scattered the ground, rich rewards for anyone with stomach enough to take them. Christian commanders gathered the six enemy standards. Less sentimental men hacked off and saved Muslim heads. Maltese, swimmers by birthright, crossed over the strewn battlefield, leapt into the bloody water, and swam down among the sunken boats and bodies to see what they could find. Besides the jeweled weapons and clothes, they found supplies of food—proof, Balbi infers, that the enemy had every intent and expectation of camping on Senglea that night. More bitter, they found coins that had lately belonged to the men of St. Elmo— St. Elmo's pay, blood money now returned with some interest.

There were also quantities of *afion*, which the contemporary historian Salazar notes "gives one unaccustomed zeal, and causes one to feel no wound, however serious, nor to fear any grave situation or danger." Some modern historians identify the drug as hashish, but this seems unlikely. Persian physician Avicenna (980–1037) notes that patients come to doctors for two reasons: "One is pain. The other is fear . . . *Afion* may relieve both." Welcome stuff for any soldier heading into battle. High-grade opium is not the soporific that its processed cousin morphine (Morpheus, bringer of dreams) is; people lightly intoxicated with opium can function quite well. This was Dutch courage for the attackers, much like the amphetamines German soldiers were issued during World War II, and a partial explanation for the insane fury and bravery of some of the suicidal attacks.[23]

Five hours had passed from the time of the first signal from Sciberras to the final Muslim withdrawal in front of Fort St. Michael. Four hundred Muslims had died and two hundred Christians. At least that many had been wounded. Four Turks were allowed to live and be questioned by Valette.[24] The Ottomans let their surviving soldiers rest and heal and returned the burden of attack to the artillerists, who kept a steady stream of cannon fire on Fort St. Michael. They worked alone. The boats that had failed to take Senglea, those that Christian guns had not destroyed, were now dragged back over the ridge of Sciberras. There would be no more naval assaults on Senglea.

20

+·+·+·+

ENDURANCE

+·+·+·+

The noise of the shot of the ordnance and battery
of Malta not having been heard in Italy
for three days, it is thought that all is lost.

Phayre to Cecil, August 6, 1565

Even before the assault, Mustapha was writing desperate, even threatening, letters to the governor of the Ottoman-held port of Modon, insisting that he send more gunpowder as quickly as possible.[1]

Supplies were not his only problem. His troops were now falling ill with "bloody flux, putrid fever [typhus], and illnesses of great mortality."[2] The hospitals were filling with "as many wounded (of which there was already a good number) as sick," a curious departure from the norm, as the Ottoman military was famous for its clean and orderly camps.[3] Rank determined which of three locations a casualty ended up in. Soldiers were sent to hospital at the Marsa, support personnel to the rear ends of ships. Christians and slaves were put between the banks of oars on the galleys, an area notorious for filth. (Between washing decks and benches every two days, the standard method for deep-cleaning a sewage-laden galley was to scuttle the hull for a few days and let seawater drift over and dissipate the waste.)

Conditions behind the Christian lines were significantly better. Even before the invasion, the knights had built a sizeable working infirmary, two stories covering nearly a third of an acre, an area that expanded during the course of the siege as adjacent buildings were requisitioned and repurposed. There was also considerable space carved into the earth below, in anticipation of a siege like this. The halls were large and airy, the linens washed regularly, and tableware for even the lowest patient was of silver.

Moreover, the Order's physicians had refined medical practice over the centuries. They were familiar with battle wounds and what contemporary weapons could do to a body and what human ingenuity could do to hurry the natural healing process. Blade wounds, where a limb was not wholly severed, might be clean and if so could often be repaired. A lead bullet could shatter bone, requiring amputation; cannon firing scattershot or rubble could lacerate a man, carve out large sections of flesh, or simply cut him in two; Greek fire caused severe burns.

If military technology had created more horrific wounds, medical science had done its best to keep up. Prior to battle, surgeons and orderlies cleared tables and prepared the tools of their trade. Long, thin, dramatic probes, clamps, and retractors enabled them to search deeply for arrowheads and bullets and whatever else might wind up inside a combatant's body. Boiling pitch was used to cauterize open wounds, herbs and medicines to dull pain and pro- mote healing. The Order's medicine jars carried a wide assortment of curative herbs and unintentional placebos, ranging from mallow to St. John's wort. The Order also kept a good supply of a moss peculiar to the island of Gozo that was remarkable for its antiseptic qualities. Onion and salt was a popular sixteenth-century treatment for gunpowder and other burns; salt water was for immediate relief.

As far as they could, both sides followed prudent basic steps where the dead, and body parts of the maimed, were concerned. They buried their own men as decently as they could, which after some battles could only mean mass graves hurriedly dug and filled in. The enemy dead were burned as befitted their de- graded status, with the occasional exception made for heads, better employed in gracing the ends of pikes. Even so, in the latter days there were body parts and whole corpses abandoned to the swirl of sun, smoke, dust, and flies.

+·+·+·+

By July 18, Ottoman engineers were all but finished with a bridge across the ditch to Fort St. Michael. It would have to be destroyed by hand, and Valette's nephew, Henri Parisot, volunteered to lead an attempt. Engineers chipping away from inside the stone wall opened a small sally port through which he and several others rushed out in the hope of setting the structure afire. His uniform, gold-chased armor, marked Parisot as worth a bullet, and Turkish snipers killed him before he or his men could even begin the job. With some difficulty his comrades managed to bring the body back inside the walls. Valette came to view the body, and when someone tried to console him for the loss of a family member, he replied that all knights were equally as precious to him as his nephew.[4]

True or not, it was a wise statement. Nearly every family on Malta had lost a relative, or a home, or a livelihood, or all three, and Valette could not allow his charges to give in to despair. Civilian resolve had cracked at Rhodes with disastrous results, and he was not going to let that happen here. If this meant containing his own grief, then so be it. He encouraged rumors if that would buy his people a few days' strength. July 25 is the feast of St. James, patron saint of Spain. Don Garcia was a member of the Order of St. James. Clearly Don Garcia would choose this day to bring relief. An anonymous diarist notes, "On that day we all waited for the armada to arrive."[5] When it did not, Valette directed the people's attention to a higher power. God had preserved them thus far and would ever do so. All present were Christians and should remember that they were fighting for their faith, and could expect no greater mercy from a victorious Ottoman army than had the defenders of St. Elmo.

Harsh justice to the enemy helped. One of Anastagi's lieutenants had captured five Turks and one Christian renegade and dragged them to Mdina. Bad luck for them: "On Friday, the twentieth day of July, [the Turks] were cut into pieces by our people in revenge for the cruelties inflicted at St. Elmo. And the renegade, having been strung up on the gallows by one foot, was given a miserable death by having a small fire set beneath him."[6] It wasn't just active participants against the siege who were at risk. Robles tried and hanged a Genoese soldier for calling the siege "hopeless."[7] On June 1, Marietta de Modo, wife of a onetime captain of the garrison of Fort St. Angelo, was dragged before the Inquisition, accused of having prayed for a Turkish victory. Her son, it happened, was possibly the third man in a robbery masterminded by two knights the year before. The knights were executed; this man escaped to Alexandria, converted to Islam, and sold his intimate knowledge of Maltese defensive works to the Ottomans.[8]

There was also good news. Before they were cut to pieces, the Turkish prisoners said that the two pashas were again at odds, with Piali sleeping aboard his ship at night (this for three consecutive nights). Better still, they reported that rebellion had broken out in Tripoli and that Uludj Ali had been forced to return there to deal with it.[9]

Best of all, and closer to home, the water managers Geofrè de Loaysa and Iacomo Coloroti had found a spring (*una vena d'acqua sorgente*) in the house of Doctor Cadamosto, "putting to an end our fear that we should die for lack of water."[10] Clearly God was once again smiling on the Christians.

Valette slept little and only in snatches. His waking hours he spent in a round of inspection, constantly moving from one position to another, encouraging here, advising there, always making himself known to the people defending the island, and by the force of his own willpower forcing them to bear up. He lengthened the workday. Until now, reveille had been blown an hour before sunrise. Hereafter, it was two hours; Valette wanted no surprise attacks. Whether the new routine prevented any such attacks is unknowable, but the Christians were able to see off a few predawn scouting parties that otherwise might have caused trouble. Any victory, however small, was a further boost to morale.

Physical labor was a distraction, and there was plenty of it. In places, notably around Fort St. Michael, the defenses were crumbling faster than they could properly be restored — not surprising when a single basilisk (and the Ottomans had four of them) could pound a hole through twenty feet of earth. This mattered, as the walls were not solid blocks or true concrete, but rather loose agglomerations of small stones connected with mud. All kinds of makeshift work were brought to bear against the problem. Carpenters dismantled ships so that their timbers could be recycled for defensive works. Tailors and seamstresses turned cloth from dead slaves and awning material into sandbags. In the armory, iron bullets and cannonballs were still being forged; powder was still being mixed. New incendiaries were being devised, one of which involved cotton sacks of powder covered in pitch. Even the stone houses half-broken by Ottoman cannon were further broken down to be hurled on the enemy.

+·+·+·+

Back in Sicily, Don Garcia understood that the Small Relief had disobeyed orders in landing at Malta. If this bothered him, there's no record of it. His next move, in fact, was to send more men and ships. Plans were made for Don Juan de Sanoguera to join his uncle Don Francisco and brother Don Jaime and other family members on Malta. By chance, Gianandrea Doria had arrived at Messina, where there was little for him to do other than to read Valette's letters. The younger man, whose respect for the grand master went at least as far back as events at Djerba, and who perhaps felt obligated to make up for that disaster, was very moved by what he read. He approached the viceroy and offered to go to Malta with his own three galleys. He would, he said, underwrite the cost of the galleys himself, and would even take two more companies of Spaniards and chosen papal troops. The galleys, he declared, would carry only Christian crew, who then might trade oars and benches for swords and shields. In a final dramatic gesture, he requested that Don Garcia see that his debts were paid in the event he died.

The offer was initially accepted, then rejected. We can assume political interference at work. The papal troops, which Pope Pius had dispatched only by June (after initially sending insubstantial good wishes), were under the command of Pompeo Colonna, a cousin of Don Garcia's wife. Colonna was best known for having killed his mother-in-law two weeks after having married her fourteen-year-old daughter. Condemned to death, excommunication, and a ten thousand ducat fine, he saw his sentence suspended when he joined his father at the 1554 Siege of Siena, after which it seems to have been forgotten. The reason given for rejecting the offer was that "such a young man" as Gianandrea Doria was not to be exposed to so much danger, and therefore Andrea Provana di Leyní (who had been with Don Garcia at Peñón de Vélez de la Gomera in 1564), captain of the galleys of Savoy, was sent instead.[11] Three triremes transported Colonna with six hundred of the pope's chosen men from Rome and a good number of chosen Knights of St. John from diverse places.[12] They were to work off signals from Valette indicating whether it was safe to enter the harbor. In the event, the naval blockade was too much to overcome, and this expedition came to nothing — but Don Garcia was trying.

＋·＋·＋·＋

So was Mustapha. Starting on July 22, he ordered sixteen guns, two basilisks, and two *morlacchi* to begin five days of continuous bombardment, so loud that it could be heard in Sicily, with smoke so thick that "like clouds they blocked out the sun light."[13] Some shots were directed against the curtain walls, in particular those between the posts of Castile and Germany, in the continuing effort to break them down; others were lobbed into the town itself to kill and terrorize the inhabitants. In addition to cannon fire, Mustapha launched repeated sallies against the walls, sometimes real, sometimes fake, to keep the defenders exhausted and off balance. Streets within Birgu were now visible to Ottoman gunners, and Valette had walls thrown up to protect those inside.

It helped, but in truth there was no place of greater safety, and sudden death could come by day or night. Nevertheless, the Christians continued to resist everything the Ottomans could throw at them.

Anastagi and his cavalry raiders from Mdina continued to harass the Ottoman foraging parties, in particular those searching for water. Balbi describes one such encounter in which sixty Turks were killed against only one Christian[14] — good numbers for the side that had lost nearly a quarter of all its soldiers in the defense of Fort St. Elmo.

At the end of July, the commander of the Janissaries approached the Post of Robles with a white flag and asked for a parley. All combat ceased as he flattered the Christian for his service in other campaigns and suggested that the fight be ended without further effusion of blood. As he went on in this manner, spectators behind the wall noticed some of the rubble at the foot of the wall shifting, and even a spear point protruding — a Muslim digger presumably trying to gauge if they had reached the stone walls. This was a clear violation of the spirit of truce at the very least, and the Christians reacted with anger.

Andres de Muñatones, Robles's lieutenant, immediately rushed to the spear point with his own sappers, who furiously began to dig an opening into the Ottoman tunnel. (Likely the Ottoman sharpshooters were under orders not to fire for the duration of the parley.) Muñatones had thought to bring three or four fire grenades with him and tossed one inside, after which he himself jumped in. Three of his men, armed with arquebuses and swords, followed suit and together they began to chase the enemy back down the tunnel. Once satisfied that he had seen them off, Muñatones retraced his steps and then ordered masons to block off the tunnel, but to leave loopholes so the Christians could fire on anyone who thought to try again.

For this, Valette awarded Muñatones a gold chain worth three hundred scudi (the soldiers received a few ducats each), munificence unparalleled in the accounts of the siege.[15] Valette was under no illusions concerning these men. Money had boosted morale at St. Elmo; it would do the same here. Muñatones clearly snatched the gold ring in this carousel. However much piety might inspire the hired men, it was cash that told in the end, and the defenders knew that the Ottomans could pay handsomely for a good soldier of whatever faith. They were already profligate with cannonballs, firing essentially at random — at houses, at inside walls, even overshooting into the harbor, "as if to show us that they could afford to waste ammunition."[16] No wonder then that by the end of a five-hour battle on August 1, Marshal Robles gave thanks to God for the victory, then immediately turned to address the soldiers who did the actual fighting:

"Gentlemen, here and before God I award you ten extra scudi, for I saw your actions today and if Don Garcia should not be prepared to pay it, then I promise that I will pay it myself, if I live. But I have faith in the munificence of our king who, learning of your valor, will not only confirm this award, but will provide even greater."[17]

Valette, desperate for intelligence and doubting that another Lascaris would jump the lines, was now offering fifty scudi to any man who could get him a Turkish prisoner. Romegas, always game for a challenge and distressed at Valette's anxiety, offered one hundred scudi above and beyond that sum, and this from his own pocket.[18] That same night, August 1 and 2, Romegas's men slipped out of Birgu on small boats and headed toward Turkish lines. The expedition, however, was quickly scotched when they ran into a Turkish brig far in excess of anything they could hope to fight. They were forced to alter course, then to abandon ship and arms, and swim back to the fort with only their lives. The Ottomans were far from defeated.

Money worked in the other direction as well. On August 6, Francisco de Aguilar, a Spanish soldier with a wife and family on Gozo, deserted.

He apparently had been planning this for some time, contriving to get himself into the good graces of senior officers, to be present in the main conference rooms when strategy was being discussed, to tour the various posts and positions, watching and chatting with the soldiers about the various states of preparedness. If he had gone too far, it was in quizzing Toni Bajada about the various routes he took when carrying messages between Mdina and Birgu. This was valuable information. Several of the couriers had been captured already, and it was getting harder to find people willing to take the risk. Bajada observed that if he, Bajada, had not known Aguilar to be a trustworthy fellow, then he might feel inclined to report him to the grand master.

It was unfortunate that he did not. On the night in question, Aguilar went to the post of Provence, gun in hand, and began chatting with the men on duty. He put it out that he wanted to kill a Muslim. This was perfectly all right with the soldiers, and they let him settle near a suitable embrasure to try his luck. He lit the slow match on his arquebus, gazed out over the landscape, and complained, "I can't see any of those dogs."[19] Having set the stage, he waited a considerable time for his moment, long enough for his fellows to get bored and relaxed. Then suddenly he slid through the opening, landed in the ditch, and ran headlong to the Ottoman trenches. The Christians, startled, dismayed, and angered at being duped, cried out and tried to shoot him, but failed to hit their mark. Aguilar was brought straight to Mustapha, who was pleased at this turn of fortune.

If there was any good news for the Christians to be had from this event, Aguilar would, as others had in the past, "tell the pashas how determined we were to die rather than to surrender."[20] Small comfort. He would also tell the Ottomans that there were fewer than five hundred combat-ready soldiers behind the walls and that these were "exhausted, weakened, and badly battered"; besides them were only civilians (*genti*): old women, children, the ill, wounded, and maimed.[21]

Valette would now have to discredit Aguilar. One trick was to bring out all men with guns to line the walls and, an hour or so after dusk on August 6, have them "load and fire four times, so as to make the enemy think we had many men, as our shooting made it appear that our five hundred men were five thousand arquebusiers."[22] How effective this was is unknown. In any case, with what soldiers he could, he redeployed to the Post of Castile and Fort St. Michael. He also sent boat crews to build defense works behind the spur of St. Michael, where the walls were largely razed. He saw to it that the posts were provisioned with arms, powder, incendiaries, trumps, and cauldrons of pitch kept constantly at the boil. Finally, he had his armorers improvise caltrops, nails driven through large planks, then flipped and laid down where the enemy was most likely to leap over and land feet first. All that could be prepared was prepared. The timing proved providential.

21

·+·+·+·

ONSLAUGHT
OF THE
OTTOMANS

·+·+·+·

They assaulted St. Michael and the Post of Castile
together with such noise and the sound
of martial music that we would have been astonished
if we had never heard it before.

Balbi

An hour before dawn on August 7, several Ottoman columns marched down from Corradino to the walls of Fort St. Michael.[1] Aguilar apparently had convinced Mustapha about the state of defenses there. What had failed before must succeed now. Twelve thousand men, virtually the entire Ottoman army, were arrayed for the day's battle, eight against Fort St. Michael, four against the Post of Castile — an unnerving presence, full of menace. The sun rose, and gray shadows slowly took on color. On the ramparts, Christians stared out at the assembled mass. Scattered along the wall at the ready were unlit fire hoops and cauldrons of bubbling pitch. Supplies of bread and wine and vats of water to calm burn wounds were only steps away. Men fingered their weapons nervously, muttering prayers for their own safety and salvation, and death and damnation to the Turks.

Mustapha surveyed his army, waiting for the tension to build. The thin, piercing wail of brass horns and thudding of the kettledrums sounded, agitating the troops and releasing adrenaline into their bloodstreams. The order to attack came down, a shout went up, and the first wave rushed forward toward the post of Marshal Robles and Bormla. Gunners on the wall pumped scattershot and arquebus fire into the mass, with as much effect as pebbles thrown into a wave. The men kept coming, rising from the trenches, and were caught in the crossfire of two traverses. Guns fired on both sides of the attacking column, slowing them, but not stopping them. Wild-eyed Algerians scrambled up the heaped rubble or threw scaling ladders against the walls. Fire hoops sailed gracefully from the ramparts and over the thickest parts of the crowd, then dropped on the crush of men in threes and fours, setting their light cotton clothing on fire and preventing them from dropping and rolling. Men scrambling up scaling ladders looked straight up to see cauldrons of thin, sticky, scalding hot pitch being slowly tipped over the wall's edge.

Their leaders were with them. Candelissa was again in the vanguard, the first to reach the parapets. He was immediately killed by a bullet in the chest.[2] Other men took his place and pushed forward, closing the gap between Muslim and Christian. The fighting became close ordered, blade to blade and hand to hand. On the ground below, Mustapha watched all parts of the assault, eager that this should be the killing blow. Piali Pasha meanwhile was waiting with four thousand men before the Post of Castile, expecting the grand master to rush troops to St. Michael.[3] Valette disappointed him, and after an hour, Piali made his move. Ottomans charged toward the walls, crawled up the shattered battlements, and entered a hail of fire and steel and stone and lead. The oncoming troops faltered, fell back, then pushed forward again, earning some admiration from the Christians, as "the assaults that day were very brave and well fought on all sides with much blood and cruelty."[4]

Valette had spent his morning in a piazza, ready to lead the reserves to wherever they were needed. Eventually the call arrived. A knight ran up and said that the breaches at the Post of Castile were being overrun. Quickly grabbing his helmet and a pike, Valette called to his entourage, "Come, my knights, let us all go there and die! This is the day!"[5] He went as far as the gate that led to the breach, where Romegas and other senior captains urged him to stay back. He refused and began to climb to the spur of Castile to take on the Turks who had seized that position. It was, however, too much, and he was persuaded to another spot, the battery of Claramonte, where he took an arquebus and shouted, "There, boys, there!" (*Alla, alla, hijos*) firing upward at the enemy.[6] It worked. The defense stiffened, and Christians began to push back the Muslims with fire and stone until the immediate danger was over.

The Ottomans may have fallen back, but they were far from calling it quits. Mustapha himself was in the middle of the force attacking Fort St. Michael, urging his men on, leading by example. Fighting takes its toll on even the most fit men, and Mustapha was steadily cycling in fresh troops for each new surge. A dozen separate assaults that morning were broken by short, welcome intervals when monks and priests and old men and women and children carried bread and wine to refresh the exhausted, brought water to extinguish fire and soothe burns. Soon enough, and to the extent they were able, this support staff joined in the fighting itself.[7] There was no question of the defenders breaking off and letting reserves take over for a time. There were no reserves.

"The dead made the fight more difficult for the living, and many Turks were killed and injured while falling among them: and so too were the Christians, though not in such great number. Some wore the blood of their enemies on their arms and shoulders, others were bathed in their own, and with great pain and determination the souls of the dead set themselves free, some commending themselves to God, others to Mohammed."[8]

The sun kept rising and the attacks kept coming. The outside slope glistened red, then mat black with dried blood. The dead and wounded Ottomans littered the ground, bodies "without heads, arms or legs, burned or with their limbs torn to pieces."[9] Suleiman's standard was seen over the top of the Post of Castile, hauled down, and replaced with another green pennant until it too was toppled. The stink of burnt powder and flesh, of blood, guts, and human waste, clogged the air. Men were fighting hand to hand, close enough to breathe in each other's air and feel the heat of each other's blood. The defenses frayed a little more with each attack. The most severely wounded were dragged off to the uncertain comforts of the infirmary, and each time the remaining men were a little less able to throw the enemy back. Another push, maybe another two, and the green banners of Islam would fly over the ramparts.

And then the cavalry came.

+·+·+·+

There is a 1570 portrait of Fra Vincenzo Anastagi by El Greco now housed in the Frick Collection in New York City. At first glance, the subject doesn't appear all that remarkable. He is wearing dark green, inflated pantaloons typical of the period presumably to showcase fine legs; we can only judge his calves, which appear overdeveloped and befitting a soldier. His helmet rests behind him, his arms and chest are protected by a black cuirass, and a sword hangs from the sash across his right shoulder and breast. He has prominent fleshy ears, a sharp nose, and a heavy close-cut beard. His hairline is receding, his temples are touched by gray, lines mark the corners of his eyes, and his head appears a trifle small for such large hands and legs. This is a man who has seen a lot, a steady man, watchful and intelligent, perhaps tending slightly toward melancholy.

Anastagi was born in 1531 and was inducted into the Order in 1563 at age thirty-two — relatively late in life. His early years are not recorded, but there is the note in his application referring to him as "an expert in military matters for many years and consequently of great utility to the Order."[10] Where exactly he might have come by this expertise and over what period of years is not given, but he clearly was a skilled, brave, and resourceful soldier, and gifted in the art of cavalry raiding.

A large part of his job was as an intelligence officer. This was not limited to interrogating prisoners. Mdina was the transit point for letters between the grand master and Don Garcia. One such message arrived at a time when communications into Birgu were impossible. Seven couriers failed to get the note to Valette, and none volunteered to be the eighth. Unable to forward the message and suspecting its importance, Anastagi set about decoding the cipher. It took him sixteen hours, but he succeeded — it was a message from Don Garcia that he was sending three ships to enter Grand Harbor by night and that Valette was to set up signal lights warning them off in case of danger. The Ottomans had in fact blocked off the harbor with ten ships, and so Anastagi undertook to ride out several nights running and light the signals when needed, and in so doing saved the ships from potential catastrophe.

Anastagi believed that there would be a large attack in early August. He lacked only a date. From the final night of July and the eight nights following, he gathered his horsemen and led them out as close as he could to the Marsa. There was a depression about a mile from the Ottoman camp where even a squadron of horse could be hidden. They came, they waited, and when nothing significant happened, they returned to Mdina, only to repeat the process the following night. So it continued until August 7 when the assault finally came. The all-too-familiar sound of battle carried from St. Michael as Janissaries and spahis and corsairs fell against the wall, scrambling upward in their desperate attempt to take the city. Anastagi waited among his men, their restless horses pawing the ground, everyone painfully aware of the battle raging just a short ride away. All the while, their commander stood listening, waiting, gauging by some unknown personal calculus exactly when he should act.

At the wall of St. Michael, the Ottoman armies continued to lose men, but so did the defenders. Wave followed wave, and Mustapha showed no sign of letting up. He felt sure, with apparently good reason, that this was to be the final battle. Halfhearted measures would not do. Mustapha was at the full flush of battle, the high point of his entire career. His enemy was palpably fading, his men, crawling over the bodies of their comrades, were just moments short of victory.

In his hidden road, minutes had grown into hours and Anastagi bided his time. His men became restless. He did nothing. The sun crept higher, pouring down the impossible heat of a Maltese summer. Anastagi waited. The men fighting on the wall were growing more tired and still Anastagi did nothing. Almost nine hours after the attack began, the Ottoman army had reached its high tide against the walls of Fort St. Michael. Mustapha was urging his men to the final assault that would overflow the tops of the walls. The Christian defenders were flagging, and victory was imminent. Anastagi finally gave his men the order to advance.

Throwing themselves against the Ottoman army would have been point-less — they were raiders, and very few — and so they didn't. Their target lay nearby, and was softer than the blood-spattered men attacking Fort St. Michael.

+·+·+·+

While Mustapha was leading his tidal wave against the remains of Fort St. Michael, the survivors of his previous fights, along with support personnel and camp followers, remained back at the Marsa camp. In large tents there lay scores of injured men in greater or lesser degrees of pain, men whose long days and nights were punctuated by the occasional groan or whimper, by gasped prayers for an end of agony, by regret or relief that they were no longer in the fight; men contemplating their immediate suffering, the fortune that kept them from the audible fight in the distance, a future without the familiar comfort of a hand, an eye, an ear, a jaw, a leg, their wits. Men with charred skin lay motionless, aware that the slightest movement would be torture; other wounded veterans marginally more fortunate shifted positions in the hope that this would alle-viate, or at least redistribute, the pain. The present was bad, the future grim.

The lucky might have families to look after them, a religious shelter to attend to their basic needs; the unlucky were staring at destitution.

They made easy targets. Anastagi's horsemen approached from the south, unsheathed their swords, cried out "Victory and relief!" and began to charge.[11]

There was no defense worth mentioning — a remarkable oversight given the horsemen's record — and the attackers careened around the tents, slashing the guylines. Horse hooves trampled the fallen, billowing canvas, crushing anyone left inside, turning the brightly colored cloth into a lumpy, sticky, glistening, bright scarlet mess. No mercy here. Those who had assumed they were safe from combat were now running "as quickly as healthy men."[12] In short order, fire, presumably from the regimental kettles, spread to some of the tents and sent up columns of smoke.

It took some time for the men engaged at Fort St. Michael to notice the attack, and there was confusion over what it all meant. An Ottoman unit detailed with guarding the fleet was the first to investigate. They didn't see much, but what they did see caused them to rush back toward the boats. Mustapha got a report that all the men in the camp had been massacred. Without orders or permission, men started to withdraw from the trenches before the Post of Castile, which made it easy for the Christians to shoot at their backs. Those still attacking St. Michael froze in indecision and confusion. Wounded refugees from the camp stumbled toward them and swore that a force of over a thousand men was coming. The trenches now emptied as quickly as had those before the Post of Castile. Men defending the Post of Sicily had a vantage point and a slightly clearer idea of what was going on, and began to echo the raiders' cry, "Victory and relief!" Some among the Turks would have understood this and translated it for their comrades.

What did it all mean? Men shouted out speculation, speculation became rumors, and rumors, accepted fact. Piali Pasha's cordon of galleys had failed one more time. The greater Spanish relief, long anticipated, had finally arrived. Unknown thousands of Christian troops had landed on the western shore, unnoticed, just like the six hundred men of the *Piccolo Soccorso*. These new armies, fresh and ready for battle, were now tearing through the camp, destroying food and supplies, trampling the wounded, killing anyone in their path. These new arrivals would soon be attacking the Muslims from the rear, catching Mustapha's armies between two pincers.

Panic breeds panic, but Mustapha appears to have kept his head. Somehow he managed to restore enough order to rally his troops to the high grounds at Santa Margherita, leaving behind him a backwash of dead and wounded before the wall. It was only when he could survey the landscape from these heights that he realized just how feeble the attack on his camp actually had been, and ordered his men to rush back — too late and on foot. When they saw that the Muslim forces had turned toward the camp, Anastagi, considering the mission fulfilled and his men in danger of being routed, ordered retreat. Each horseman hauled up a foot soldier behind him and galloped headlong back to Mdina.

The assault on Senglea was over. Turkish casualties, both before the wall and in the camp, were some two thousand killed "judging by how quickly the enemy retrieved their dead."[13] Of Christians defending Fort St. Michael, sixty were dead.

Not a single horseman was lost.[14]

+·+·+·+

The Mdina cavalry had done their worst, and even if it was unlikely that they would ever manage to pull off a coup like that again, nevertheless, martial pride demanded that Mustapha reply in kind. While the greater part of the army set about putting out the fires, repairing the damage, and attending to the wounded who still survived, he sent Piali in the general direction of Mdina to somehow punish Mdina's cavalry. Three ambush areas were set up in the abandoned village of Zebbug, at San Domingo near Rabat, and in the grand master's wood, all south of Mdina. As a lure to the enemy, Piali dispatched a small number of men to rustle the cattle that still grazed under the watchful eyes of the city. It was a no-lose provocation as far as Piali was concerned, and as he hoped, men under Lugny and Anastagi galloped out of Mdina, chased off the enemy, and began to herd the cattle back within artillery range of the city. They then found themselves being cut off by unseen Ottoman infantry.

The Maltese promptly let the cattle loose and charged the oncoming enemy. In the ensuing scuffle, they managed to kill over fifty Muslims at a cost of twelve of their own.[15] Lugny survived unhurt and returned, alive if not triumphant, to Mdina. Piali followed. He approached the city and was stopped short by the sight of hundreds of soldiers lining the tops of the walls, shouting, jeering, and letting off cannon and small-arms fire. Clearly this was not going to be a walkover. Without proper siege equipment, Piali had no choice but to abandon the operation and return to the familiar problems of Senglea and Birgu.

What he did not know was that these soldiers were in fact civilians in costume. In another trick as old as warfare, Mesquita had dressed the citizens, however old or lame, male and female, and spotted them across the expanse of the wall, firing a few seemingly reckless shots to keep the Ottomans from getting close enough to recognize the swindle.

It could be presented as a victory for the Christians in that more Ottomans than Christians had died. The Christians, however, had initially been outfoxed; and besides losing twelve men, they also had lost nearly a third of their remaining horses, invaluable for raiding and utterly irreplaceable. This was a severe loss for this arm of the overall Christian defense, and Piali, even if fooled by the Potemkin village that Mesquita had arranged on the walls of Mdina, could take some pride in a good day's work.

22

+·+·+·+

TWO GENTLEMEN
OF PERUGIA

+·+·+·+

When I compare our systems to that of the Turk,
I tremble to think what horrors the future must bring. . . .
Once he has made peace with the Persians, he will come
at us with the entire combined armies of the orient —
what our preparedness may be, I dare not say.

Ogier Ghiselin de Busbecq, 1560

Christian warfare has repeatedly been marked by visions, from Constantine's dream of the cross the night before he seized Rome in 312 to the (demonstrably fictional) Angel of Mons in 1914. In 1339, St. Ambrose appeared on the battlefield of Parabiogo, riding a white horse and swinging a cudgel at the enemies of his beloved Milan. In AD 884, St. James arrived to help Christian Spain in its fight against Muslims at Clavijo. He alone killed sixty thousand Moors, and in the doing became the patron saint of Christian Spain. This was powerful help and was paralleled at Malta. Robert of Eboli, recovering from wounds received at Fort St. Michael, fell into an ecstasy and saw Jesus, the Virgin Mary, and John the Baptist. The trio, he reported, had been inclined to chastise the knights for previous bad behavior (and certainly there was no shortage of that), but were impressed by their current valor and return to the path of virtue.[1]

Robert was not the only witness to such visions: "Turks while fighting were terrified by an apparition of a woman robed in white, and several times by a wild man robed in skins, but of divine appearance, and of a white dove."[2] On the vigil of Our Lady's Ascension, "a white dove was seen resting above the miraculous image of Our Lady of Filermo, which for many hours did not fly off; and this made the people pious, and was taken as an augury that they would soon be freed from the siege."[3] Some even claimed that there were manifestations in Constantinople itself.

All this was encouraging, as was the news from another deserter that the aga of the Janissaries had been killed and that the "pasha of the ground troops" was feeling ill.[4] This was encouraging, but it did not kill Muslims. Mustapha had returned to the dull repetitive routine of bombardment. It seemed scarcely worthwhile, as a good part of the walls were as far demolished as they were likely to become. In parts of the town, a single inner wall "about the height of a man" and at places no more than ten to twelve feet thick was the only barrier between Turk and Christian.[5] The men lining the defenses were lying prone on top of the rubble and waiting for the Ottomans either to come within arquebus range or to present themselves for hand-to-hand combat. The Ottoman troops were at least getting a deserved rest.

Robles, leader of the *Piccolo Soccorso*, whose position was less broken down, wanted to know how things stood. It was late in the day and presumably he thought there was enough light to see, but not enough to put anyone in danger. In a moment of absentmindedness, or anxiety, or ill-advised bravado, or of trust in the half-light of evening, or perhaps because it was simply too uncomfortable, he neglected to put his helmet on. An Ottoman sniper instantly put a bullet through his head. He lived through the night, reportedly in great pain, and died the next morning.

At a time where death was commonplace, Robles's fall had a powerful effect on the survivors. All contemporary accounts note that the mourning for this man was extensive and heartfelt. Always "as a devout man, in every assault he carried a crucifix in his hand, encouraging his men to fight in ever greater fury."[6] Soldiers under his command, hard men made harder by the unspeakable horrors of the past two months, could not bring themselves to look at his corpse. Valette ordered the body to be laid out in the Church of St. Lawrence, his casket to be covered in black velvet. The grand master further decreed that Robles should be buried with the honors of a grand cross of the Order, an extraordinary gesture to any man, all the more so since Robles was not a knight of St. John.

+·+·+·+

Letters between Philip and Don Garcia made their three weeks' journey on a regular basis, the viceroy giving updates and explanations, the king offering advice and cautions. He wanted Malta to be helped, but he wanted his fleet to remain intact. He left matters up to Don Garcia's best judgment, but forbade any attack on the Turks. There are times Philip was resigned to the fall of Malta and comforted himself with the thought that it could be retaken at some later date. Indeed, Philip was open-minded enough to allow Fernando Alvarez de Toledo, duke of Alva, to meet with Hajji Murad, an Ottoman emissary then traveling in France. The subject was peace between the empires. Nothing came of it, but the very fact that such a meeting took place was telling.[7]

Whether Don Garcia was aware of this meeting is not known; regardless, he did not let up in his efforts to save Malta. Throughout the summer he had canvassed Europe for volunteers and had quartered and fed those men who had gotten as far as Sicily. He "effected the equipping of triremes, constructing barges more spacious than usual to disembark soldiers, and was gathering from all parts the provender, arms, oarsmen, and however much was necessary to such a mutable war."[8] Already by July 27 Don Garcia could write to Valette that he had one thousand to twelve hundred foot under the charge of Vincenzo Gonzaga, prior of Barletta, and that Gianandrea Doria was en route to Syracuse with twenty-seven galleys and four thousand foot, mostly from Florence and under Chiappino Vitelli.[9] Freebooters and mercenaries were plentiful enough and would fight well if the money was good. Don Garcia was not just trying to gather ships and cannon fodder; the viceroy needed commanders who could lead these men. One man he especially wanted was Ascanio Della Corgna.

Ascanio Della Corgna — nephew of a pope, brother of a cardinal — was a *condottiere*, a contract soldier, and a good one. The sixteenth century was a busy time for men in that trade, and profitable as well, provided one could stay alive. Small wars were plentiful, and Della Corgna's talent was exceptional. He could command a full army, and even after the loss of one eye had destroyed his depth perception, he could take on the strongest swordsmen in single combat. More than three thousand spectators gathered at Pitigliano (Tuscany) to witness Della Corgna's 1546 duel with an insolent subordinate named Giannetto Taddei. Shopkeepers and home owners whose windows overlooked the square rented out the view. Taddei was killed, honor satisfied, and Della Corgna's reputation confirmed. For those who missed it, the bloody event, a matter of short swords and long daggers, is immortalized in fresco on the walls of Della Corgna's palace at Castiglione del Lago.

We get a good portrait of the man from these pictures — a long, thin face, receding hairline and long nose, the full pointed beard characteristic of the era, proud, confident, and utterly effective. (A contemporary bronze bust suggests a rounder head — something for the art historians to ponder.) In an age where distinguished soldiers were reasonably thick on the ground, his name was well known across the continent. An anonymous poet calls him a *vero figliuol di Marte*, a true son of Mars.[10] Don Garcia would have known him (along with Chiappino Vitelli and Don Álvaro de Sande) from their common service in the 1552–1559 war against Siena, one of the interminable power struggles of the Italian city-states. As viceroy, Don Garcia was adamant that this man be put in charge of the major force that he, Don Garcia, was collecting to save Malta.

There was, however, a problem. Ascanio was sitting in a papal jail cell in Rome's Castel Sant'Angelo "on several charges" (*per alcune imputationi*) in Bosio's delicate phrasing, but that others elaborate as theft, rape, and murder.[11] Serious allegations, possibly even true, but they meant nothing to Don Garcia. He wrote to Philip, who wrote to the pope and asked for indulgence. So did Maximilian the Holy Roman emperor. Ascanio's brother, Cardinal Fulvio, also a member of the Order of St. John, argued passionately for his release. Valette also chimed in, noting that such a valiant soldier would do Christendom far more good by fighting the Turks than by rotting in jail.

The argument was hard to deny. So was Fulvio's transfer to the pope of twenty-five thousand gold ducats and two towns in Romagna. On August 3, Pius relented, and twelve days later, with a number of Roman and Perugian gentlemen, Della Corgna was headed to Messina.[12] Don Garcia was "delighted beyond measure and provided him accommodation in his own house, extending him endless kindnesses and always consulting with him."[13] Once having arrived, Della Corgna did not waste time. He wanted a firsthand report on how things stood. And by good fortune, Anastagi, hero of the Marsa battle and effectively the ranking intelligence officer, was a fellow Perugian.

+·+·+·+

It was not only Don Garcia and Della Corgna who were hungry for information. The ongoing events in Malta were being followed with interest throughout Europe, and not just among the political and military captains. Up-to-the-minute reports were published throughout the siege, notably in Paris, of which a handful survive to this day.[14] Even Protestant Europe was paying close attention. On August 27, a pamphlet appeared entitled, *Certayn and tru good nuews from the fyege of the ifle Malta, with the goodly vyctorie wyche the Chriftenmen, by the favorer of God have ther latlye obtained agaynft the Turks, before the forteres of faint Elmo.* The contents are further described as having been "transflat owt of French yn to Englysh," likely by a Flemish printer with an eye for the British market and a shaky grasp of the language. It purports to contain a copy of a letter from Valette to Don Garcia dated June 18, followed by an account of events made by Orlando Magro, who rode the galley into Messina on June 27. It gives a fairly accurate, if truncated, account of the St. Elmo siege and some moving afterthoughts: "Item, that the great mafter was veari forrowful for the death of Capitayn Mirande."

This is not the only such notice in English. There are some pitifully small fragments of a second document, greatly damaged, that relate the final victory, as the pages refer to "the delivuery of Malta." One can imagine the man on the London street grabbing at the pamphlet, reading it aloud at some tavern to his tablemates, heartened to hear the victories of the knights (wicked Catholics though they be), while the more thoughtful wonder what exactly the consequences of a Turkish victory might mean for England. Sympathy for Christendom was also the official line from the English court. Spain's ambassador to England wrote to his king that Elizabeth "expressed sorrow that all the Princes should leave your Majesty alone with the Turk."[15] Not that she was going to pitch in, of course, she having the body of a weak and feeble woman, and there being no princes invading the borders of her realm. Still, the ambassador could report that "great importance is attached here to what is passing in Malta, and the Queen has ordered a general prayer for victory."[16] The interest is not hard to understand. Islam had proven to be a formidable enemy, and the final outcome of this struggle was not at all certain. God's will was obscure, and Muslims could easily summon a sense of entitlement — a great motivator for any army.

✦·✦·✦·✦

Back in Constantinople, Suleiman also wondered how things stood. A letter to Mustapha dated July 17 read:

"I sent you over to Malta a long time ago to conquer. But I have not received any message from you. I have decreed that as soon as my order reaches you, you should inform me about the siege of Malta. Has Dragut, Beylerbey of

Tripoli, arrived there and has he been of any help to you? What about the enemy navy? Have you managed to conquer any part of Malta? You should write to me telling me everything."[17]

Just to make sure that this letter arrived, he sent a copy to the Doge of Venice, a tame neutral who had rejoiced at the fall of Fort St. Elmo, asking that he should forward it to the general, and that he also should send back any news Venice itself might have learned on how things were going.[18]

What could Mustapha say? The best men of his army were already dead, both the fanatics who had questioned nothing in their zeal to eradicate the infidel and the Janissaries who had believed that bravery and skill were enough to take the island. The sick and wounded filled the infirmaries he could not even protect. Many of his corsair allies began drifting away. This was no longer a battle they saw much future in. While they fought the fanatic knights, Christian sailors were cruising the shipping lanes, intercepting vessels carrying staples intended for the Ottoman army. It was galling for the corsairs, impatient at the tedium of a siege and the futility of frontal assaults against hardened positions. Surely their time would be better spent on the water. Janissaries were slaves to the sultan, and Iayalars might wish to die from religious conviction; but the corsairs were mercenaries, and if there were no profit on Malta, the expedition was a waste of their time. Independent men, they had other options. Even among the Janissaries, when Mustapha asked the men to sacrifice more, they began to balk.

Janissaries were a difficult proposition at the best of times. Their bravery and ability were unquestionably first-rate, but they, like any soldiers, needed a reason to keep going. A commander who could not lead them to victory would soon find himself facing a very truculent group of dangerous men indeed. They were not above outright mutiny if circumstances called for it, and they would not hesitate to bring their grievances directly to Suleiman himself. Mustapha ordered them to fight, cajoled, insulted them, called them dogs and unworthy of the name Sons of the Sultan. They wouldn't budge. The impasse was broken on one condition only: the Janissaries would attack, but only with Mustapha in the vanguard.

Mustapha was no coward. He would do it. Time — the siege's and his own — was running out.

+·+·+·+

If Muslim corsairs were trickling out of Malta, Christian soldiers and adventurers were pouring into Messina. Knights of the Order who had failed to get to Malta before the Turks arrived now waited in that city and pestered Don Garcia just as they had before the *Piccolo Soccorso*. Nerves were frayed on both sides and with some reason; Messina can be appallingly hot in August. Already under considerable pressure, Don Garcia, at times a petulant man, at one point took their ranking officer, Louis de Lastic, to task for neglecting to use the viceroy's honorific of Excellency. This was too much for the Frenchman: "If we can come to the aid of Malta in time, most excellent lord, I will call you Excellence, Highness, Majesty, and give you all these high and mighty titles that Your Excellency might ever wish or presume."[19]

Lastic, this "grand old man of much standing," ignored Don Garcia's very real strategic and political concerns.[20] Circumstances had changed to a degree, but were still fluid. Ottoman and corsair fleets still patrolled the waters around Malta, sometimes beyond, and they were still better equipped and larger than anything Don Garcia had on hand. The *Piccolo Soccorso* had been a calculated gamble played in a very specific and limited window of time, and it had been blessed with extraordinary good luck. Its success could not necessarily be repeated — at least, not just yet.

His caution gave rise to the common charge that Don Garcia did nothing. This is, as we have seen, nonsense. Besides the constant solicitation for men and matériel, besides the regular mail couriers that slipped into and out of the island, he had indeed authorized various other attempts to land small groups of soldiers. These failed to reach land either because the ships' captains thought the passage too dangerous, or because the defenders of Malta itself, Valette and Don Mesquita, or as we have seen, Anastagi, warned the approaching ships away. What Don Garcia had always been holding out for was an overwhelming force to go up against an exhausted enemy, and by late August, with sixty galleys, he was nearly there.[21]

On August 21, the viceroy called for a council of war at Messina. By now men could see the end of summer and consider what effect that would have on their options. Factions had formed, and there was heated argument over next steps, taking the same positions men had taken over the Djerba invasion. The season was late, the weather was unpredictable, and the risk to sailing was significant. If there was no immediate threat of Malta's collapse, then relief ships could wait until the following spring, when they could depart and arrive earlier than any ship from Constantinople. Why risk lives and ships when they could do as much good by waiting? Indeed, the Turks might have left already, Constantinople being that much farther away than Sicily. And even if the Turks did succeed in taking the island, well, they would only have a pile of rubble to defend, easily taken, perhaps earlier the following year before they had a chance to rebuild.

Others at the meeting — the knights, of course, and Gianandrea Doria — found that delay only whetted their appetites. Nor was it just youngbloods. Among the knights was yet another octogenarian, the bailiff of Majorca, Fra Nostre de Monsuar, eager to end his life in this grand fight. But even the ambitious acknowledged that there would be difficulties. By mid-August, the Algerians had been ordered to patrol the island perimeter with thirty galleys, basically to keep anyone from reaching there.[22] The island could not supply any relief force with food, and carrying their own would be a significant task. As the men droned on, Don Garcia sat and listened. The respect of the captains required at least the appearance of polite attention, even if the final decision was his. How seriously he was taking their advice — how seriously he was listening at all — is unknowable. He needed to appear impartial. He did, however, have a friend in the audience. Della Corgna now rose to speak.

Della Corgna was among the more forceful proponents of heading on, and his speech was reported at length in Viperano: "Will we have enough grit to take back the island once it is already lost? Do we wish to be spectators to a disaster among our brothers instead of their saviors?" and so on in this vein.[23]

But he had more than emotion to back him up. The envoy Captain Salazar had recently returned from Malta, where he had ridden the countryside in the company of Vincenzo Anastagi. It was Anastagi who wrote "a most particular account on the state of the war."[24] It was this "most particular account" that Della Corgna pulled out and read to the assembly.

The report describes the enemy not as the unbeatable foe that Philip presumably feared, but instead as a weakened, sickly force that was near mutiny and wanted nothing more than to go home. Their ranks were thinned, their powder low, their morale in shreds. Even Anastagi's rampage through the Marsa did not prompt the Ottomans to dig trenches around the camp. Mustapha had arrived with twenty-two thousand men and was now down to only twelve or thirteen thousand soldiers, "of whom the only ones worth anything are the janissaries; the flower is dead, and the survivors no longer dare approach the walls, even though they are forced with cudgel by the Pashas and other captains."[25] They wanted water, food, and sleep. Anastagi then goes on with harder information, including the scheduled routine of the twenty to twenty-five ships (not sixty to eighty) that patrol the islands, and the larger numbers that the Muslims held in reserve. He gives advice on where to land and how the defenders were prepared to help him.

Given that its purpose was to coax an allegedly reluctant Don Garcia into action, the report may have overstated the enemy's weakness — more or less correct in its outlines, but perhaps stretching a point in particulars. How key this single report was in tipping the balance is open to question — Don Garcia had been in regular correspondence throughout the siege and was monitoring the pulse of events from the outset. He had, however, voiced some skepticism of Valette's earlier claims (his June 2 letter to Philip) that the enemy was "always in disorder."[26] Don Garcia tended to keep his own council. If he was already inclined to relieve Malta, then Anastagi's letter may simply have been most useful as a debating point to sway the reluctant. It's solid material from an experienced, intelligent professional, compelling in its details, and sound in its advice. The relief force was, as with the *Piccolo Soccorso*, a matter of timing, nicely calculated and razor thin. Regardless, when Della Corgna had had his say, Don Garcia rose, looked around at the gathered captains, and made his pronouncement. The hour was late, but it was not too late. The fleet, he declared, would rendezvous at Syracuse and then sail to Malta.

✦·✦·✦·✦

Valette hoped for an army. Mustapha would have settled for some food. He had sent Ragusan supply ships filled with grain to Djerba, where it could be baked into biscuits for his troops, and he was still waiting for them to return. While waiting, he ordered another assault on Fort St. Michael — a night attack this time, to be followed the next day by a general assault on the breaches. The three thousand Ottomans were unblooded novices, supported by veterans.[27]

The artillery had done all that could be done in bringing down the walls, and further pulverizing was not going to make much difference. Two months earlier this might have been a walkover. Now, the bravest soldiers were dead or wounded, and the remainder felt truculent and homesick. Many were not even soldiers. Despite this, they were the best that Mustapha had, and his only hope lay in turning them into a facsimile of the real thing. As Don Mesquita had done in Mdina, Mustapha dressed his men in robes of the chosen warriors and put them in conspicuous places. Those who did their jobs properly and survived, Mustapha promised to enroll as proper Janissaries. And when the time of battle came, he also made sure to lead them in person.

From August 16 to 19, there was continuous bombardment, which had little effect since the walls were by now as far destroyed as they were going to be. A few small attacks, by day or night, came to nothing, as both sides geared themselves up for the inevitable. The Ottoman troops were no longer the fire-breathing soldiers of springtime. Some were almost sympathetic. They called out, "Hold on, you dogs, because already there are not many oxen to kill, and only sheep are left and they are not fat. There is not much flour and the next assault you will be free," which the defenders took as meaning that the best of the Ottoman army was dead, replaced by nonsoldiers with little powder, and that the next assault would be their last.[28]

Thin sheep or fat, the attackers were to put up a powerful fight. Mustapha and Piali targeted Senglea and Birgu, respectively, and if Senglea held firm, Birgu, specifically the Post of Castile, very nearly did not. The strategy was to hit Senglea first and hard and wait for Valette to send reserve troops across the pontoon bridge from Birgu. Once those had moved, Piali Pasha was to deploy his four thousand chosen men against the now weakened Birgu.

Valette failed to do his part. Piali eventually lost patience and simply attacked. Initially things went well. His men advanced toward the breaches and soon planted the Ottoman standard, "red, extremely large, with a horse's tail and golden apple capping the top of the shaft," on the post of Don Rodrigo Maldonado, an outcrop of the Post of Castile.[29] Wind carried smoke into the faces of the defenders, obscuring their targets, burning their eyes, and making the shouts of oncoming soldiers all the more frightening. A mine under the wall was successfully exploded and turned part of the wall into a large slag heap, giving Piali's men a breach to enter the town. Women shrieked, thinking the enemy had entered the town.

All this time, Valette had been at chapel, not letting the start of the battle interfere with his devotions. His spiritual duty in the house of God now ended, he and his attendants came outside to the material world, where all hell was breaking loose. A flood of people, civilians and soldiers, rushed from the direction of the wall. White-faced, bewildered, they saw the grand master and shouted, "Monsignor, we are lost! The Turks have entered the Post of

Castile!"[30] Valette, urged to retreat to the safety of Castel Sant'Angelo, instead grabbed one of the young men by the arm and sent him back to the fight. He ordered another to sound the church bell. No one could be spared from this crisis, not these lay brothers, least of all Valette himself. He took his helmet from his page, seized his pike, and made his way to find the enemy.

Valette's crew arrived at what was left of the wall and saw their comrades fighting on the unsteady rubble. The Christians, many still dazed from the initial burst, were getting the worst of the fight. Valette threw himself into the thick of the mob, shouting, "Brothers, my children, in the name of God, let us all go to die together, with weapons in hand — today is our day!"[31] More soldiers streamed toward the breach, pushing the enemy back up the ruined wall, looking for men to kill. Through a fog of light brown dust both sides came at one another. Gunfire from a distance was all but useless as friends and enemies were barely distinguishable. Men pressed forward with steel weapons, close enough to choke on the same clouds of burnt powder and stone as they swung their blades at each other. Convalescents, those who could, hobbled from the infirmary to take up arms, recalling, presumably, the fate of the Ottomans at the Marsa.

Valette was shouting encouragement to his men and defiance at the enemy, thrusting the needle point and sharp edge of his pike at the oncoming Muslims. At some point, a missile knocked off a stone shard that gouged Valette's left calf. Blood began to pour out, and men nearby urged him to withdraw. Don Pietro de Mendosa turned to Valette and said, "Ah, Illustrious Monsignor, would you wish that they kill you and all be lost?"[32] Apparently Valette was indeed willing to risk it and pointed to the crescent flag still standing on a high point in the breach. As long the banner stood, he shouted, he would not leave the fight. A soldier immediately climbed over the slope of rubble toward the offending banner and tore it down, and again his men urged Valette to withdraw. By now the best of the assault was over, and Valette, confident that the Ottomans had retreated for good that day, allowed himself to be led away and have his wound tended to.

Corsairs might have been leaving, but among the Muslims who remained, personal bravery was still found, as if it were shameful to live when so many companions had died. Cheder, sanjak-bey of Bosnia, an old soldier of the Ottoman army, magnificently clothed, "in person being most resolute to conquer or die, came with some of his most ferocious men."[33] He and his chosen spahis fought their way to the Post of Maestro di Campo and planted the standard, then held the position for some hours. It was the bey's misfortune to face none other than Captain Juan de La Cerda.

Whatever La Cerda might have been doing since the fall of St. Elmo has escaped the attention of the otherwise exhaustive chronicler Bosio. Any punishment for his bad attitude is apparently not worth mentioning. His actions this day, however, could not be ignored. He was among those who broke out from the Christian lines and ran headlong toward the Ottoman standard. The sanjak bey's "most ferocious men" were unequal to these mad Spaniards. Within minutes, the cordon protecting the bey had been cut through, the bey himself was dead, the enemy repulsed, and the Ottoman standard taken. All this, however, did not come cheaply. La Cerda was now wounded, and badly; his comrades bore the captain back to the infirmary, where he died ten days later, his honor restored.

Balbi says the two (Bosio counts six) assaults on Senglea lasted a full five hours, as fierce as anything they had yet seen, and it may have been so.[34] But the number of casualties had fallen dramatically from earlier battles. After five hours of fighting, two hundred Muslims were dead. Perhaps it was a reflection of the reduction in soldiers. Certainly it was no reflection on the commanders. On August 20, Mustapha was again in the vanguard "with a most valorous spirit."[35] At some point — we are not told when — a shot from Birgu knocked off his turban and stunned him. He remained in the ditch outside St. Michael for the rest of the day. No one appears to have noticed him or thought him or his corpse worth saving. Hours later, under cover of darkness, he roused himself enough to crawl out under his own steam. We can only imagine the effect of his staggering out of the shadows and back into camp. Perhaps Allah was favoring this expedition after all.

PART
FOUR

+·+·+·+

*A Line
Drawn
in
Water*

23

+·+·+·+

THE GRAN SOCCORSO
AT SEA

+·+·+·+

Up to now I have had no news from you. . . . Have your soldiers enough
provisions and weapons? Is the day of conquest of the Malta fortress near?
Have you sighted any enemy ships? . . . Send me some messages.

Suleiman to Mustapha, August 24

They also say, yᵗ the battrie of yᵉ Turkes hath so spoyled
the walles of the Borgo, and saint Michaels fortresse, that cartes and
chariottes may passe in at the breaches, and that it is great mervayle
that euer our men could kepe them.

Anonymous, September 2

Suleiman may not have been getting much information directly from Musta-
pha, but he was getting regular reports from others. He was careful to include
Venice in all his queries and received reports from them in consequence. A
Habsburg spy in Ragusa, on the Adriatic, informed his masters that "news from
Messina arrives here every ten days, particularly regarding what Signor Don
Garcia, General of His Majesty, is up to. . . . When he so much as washes his
face, word arrives here and then leaves for Constantinople via a Turk."[1] Ragusa,
like Venice, was anxious to prove its worth to the Ottomans.

By late August, the news was not good. The weather began to turn — "the
sun exited the sign of Leo, the heat of the Dog Star was lessened."[2] A cold
tramontana wind stumbled down the Alps, thrashing the Mediterranean and
kicking up high waves. Rain followed close behind. Now the Ottomans were at

a serious disadvantage. Although no longer threatened by firepots, they found that the slow matches on their guns were useless, and their powder turned to paste. Worse, they were unable to use their bows. The Turkic composite bow was a magnificent weapon, perfected over centuries. It was designed, however, for a dry climate. In constant rain, the glues that helped give the bow strength absorbed moisture, grew loose, and robbed the weapon of its effectiveness.

The Christians didn't have that problem. Behind the walls, Valette had raided the armory and brought out crossbows for his frontline men. These weapons, their power stored in taut steel bands, could stand up to the weather, were deadly accurate in even a novice's hands, and had a throw weight sufficient to put a bolt through a sheet of plate armor, much less the wooden shields of the enemy. The test came when one of the Ottomans fell in front of the post of Don Bernardo de Cabrera, and the Ottomans could not, or dared not try to, remove him — something of a scandal for an army that prided itself on taking care of its fallen. Christian defenders sallied out, hacked off the man's head, and carried it back on a pole to decorate what was left of the walls of Fort St. Michael. Encouraging for the defenders, but distressing to the Ottomans.

The Christian soldiers were now cocky enough to take chances they would not have done earlier, making increasingly bold sorties from behind the walls and getting away with them. Where the Ottomans had been attempting to build a wool-and-cotton bastion at the Post of Robles, defenders rushed out, chased the sappers off, destroyed their works, stole their picks and shovels, and again, took the head of a man not quite fast enough to get away.

Lacking his suicidally brave soldiers and a favored traditional weapon, Mustapha now turned to higher technology. His engineers busied themselves for the next few days in sawing, shaping, boring, and nailing together the masts and planks of excess galleys. What they created was a manta, a primitive wheeled armored personnel carrier, covered with damp animal skin, that could carry a large number of troops as close to the front line as possible, impervious to enemy fire until the last few yards. The Christians had seen what they were up to.

They busied themselves with a countermeasure conceived by a Matias de Ribera, *soldado aventurero*.[3] He came at the problem from below. Masons were called, and stonework and rubble near the base of St. Michael's walls were removed until finally there was one large stone between the wall and the outside world. When the manta was close to the wall and could not be missed, the men wrestled the last stone free, pushed a cannon into the freshly created embrasure, and fired off a quick blast of grape, metal chains, and miscellaneous rubbish. The hail of scattershot broke through the body of the manta, tearing the unsuspecting men inside to bloody shreds, and it also finished off some forty or so others who had followed behind. Thus ended the first and last attack of that day.

Even Ottoman successes were turning against them. They had managed to take and hold the salient of the bastion before the Post of Castile. Valette had ordered a mine dug beneath them, and with two barrels of valuable powder, blew up the position and the forty men who were defending it. On August 28, the Ottomans pushed a siege tower toward the Post of Castile, much to the contempt of the defenders. The Christians cried out from the walls, "Rogues! To what end and to what purpose have you brought this pulpit, to preach the Mohammedan religion? For you know that nobody wants or believes in your false prophet."[4] A cannon shot fired into the base caused the structure to teeter and then fall, killing or wounding a good number of men inside and behind it. To add insult to injury, some quick-witted Christian officer had his men quickly exit from the walls and take over the wooden hulk for use as an outer bastion. Again money changed hands as the grand master handed out gold to the men who had brought the thing down.

That night, the Turks began a twenty-four-hour cannonade. It was thought to be a distraction. Those guns that the Ottomans were not firing were being quietly removed from the scene.

The only kind of fighting possible was close quarter and cold steel, and neither side appeared to have the stomach left for it. Morale among the Muslim ranks was so low that the attack of August 29 required officers to bully their soldiers with cudgels to get them to fight at all. A soldier may be willing to die for a lost cause, but no soldier wants to be the last to die knowing that his comrades will soon be packing up and going home. Mustapha himself was rumored to be contemplating retreat. Uludj Ali reportedly talked him out of it.[5]

If mental exhaustion had not quite reached Valette, it certainly had reached his immediate lieutenants. The council of senior knights, alarmed at the state of their defensive works, proposed retreating to the keep of Fort St. Angelo. A hard force in there could maintain the position for weeks, months even. Long enough for relief to come. Long enough to preserve the artifacts and records of the Order.

Valette squelched the idea. It could not be done, he said, without abandoning the common people of Birgu and the wellborn soldiers at Fort St. Michael.[6] Although he himself had pardoned Vallier for abandoning Tripoli, Valette was not about to do the same here. The fort could hold only a small number of people. All others would be at the mercy of the Ottomans. It would bring shame to the Order, just as Rhodes had done, just as Tripoli had done. The council was concerned for the records of the Order? If the knights prevailed, the records would be secure. If they failed, the records would be superfluous. The knights, and everyone else, would remain in Birgu and fight alongside the volunteers and the citizens who had put their trust in God and the Order. To prove his seriousness, Valette ordered the bridge connecting Fort St. Angelo to Birgu destroyed.

Another day passed with no attack. In the lull, a Maltese prisoner was able to escape from the Turkish lines and report back to his countrymen inside the wall on the ruinous conditions of the Turks. There were now, he said, not enough arms for the fleet; sixty galleys were without crew members; sappers were dying of hunger and illness. He might as well have added paralysis at the highest level. Mustapha had made a trip to Mdina, apparently with a view to taking it, but hesitated to attack, "like the proverbial dog caught between two hares who, chasing both, catches neither."[7] He was now acting like a gambler down on his luck and placing bets at random. His nerves cannot have been helped by rumors (true rumors, as it happened) that an emissary from Gianandrea Doria, a soldier named Martinez de Oliventia, had arrived on the island. Don Garcia de Toledo was keeping his word. The *Gran Soccorso* was collected, embarked, and was on its way.

✦·✦·✦·✦

This had not been a sure thing. A week earlier (August 22), the troops of the so-called "Great Relief" gathered at Syracuse. Some ten thousand Spanish foot from Naples, the tercios milled about the town, as well as seventeen hundred mercenaries from Lombardy, scores of Maltese, Italians, Germans, and Knights of St. John, together forming a patchwork of color on the slopes above the city. A fleet of galleys and barges rolled and pitched on the water, ready to take the expedition and its equipment to Malta.[8] Bad weather stopped them.

Don Garcia had heard nothing from Malta since Anastagi's report. He knew, however, that Mustapha would be keeping a sharp eye out for Spanish ships. What the viceroy wanted now was to coordinate his movements with Valette.

Gianandrea Doria, always eager, volunteered to lead an advance party to Gozo. He and Martinez would land on that island to arrange signals for the *Gran Soccorso* — one torch to indicate no enemy ships to westward, two torches for ten ships, three for twenty, and so forth. A man running in the direction of the ships would show where they were. Doria himself would then proceed to Linosa, a small island west of Malta, to rendezvous with the main fleet and prepare for the final invasion. (The suggestion has been made that this was to be a diversion intended to lure Muslims into thinking that Tripoli was the target.)

Martinez and Doria left on Doria's flagship, and the remaining army enjoyed one more night's sleep on dry land. On Saturday, August 25, Don Garcia judged the sky and water friendly enough to risk the crossing. Men in their thousands, land soldiers all, tramped up the gangplanks to the unfamiliar sounds of straining hawsers, lapping water, and creaking timber. For veterans of Djerba — Don Alvarez de Sande and Don Sancho de Leyva were the most prominent — this was a chance for vindication and revenge. Turgut might be dead, and it was a pity they had missed him, but Piali Pasha was still alive, and taking him would be a reasonable consolation prize.

What followed was a ten-day trial of snakes and ladders, and reads a lot like the *Odyssey*. Contrary winds, scattered comrades, skirmishes with enemies, and heavy storms at sea all plagued the expedition. These difficulties were compounded by the needs of the convoy. A fleet could progress only as fast as its slowest member, and each galley, fast or slow, towed a barge stuffed with equipment — biscuit, powder, lead, rope, shovels, picks, and field guns. Worse, they sailed "without lights" (*sin fogones*), which hid them from any passing enemy, but that also made sailing at night highly dangerous.[9] Two leagues out they headed straight into contrary winds. Dawn revealed that they had made no progress at all. They decided to send two galleys ahead on reconnaissance. This pair found a Muslim cargo vessel also heading to Malta. The galleys set out to seize her — they didn't want word of their approach leaking out as it had at Djerba, and a prize is a prize in any circumstances. She must have put up a good fight, since they were still scrapping by the time the armada caught up. It took five galleys to force the merchantman's surrender. The vessel had been carrying food to the Ottoman army in Malta. Bad luck for the captain. Now he, his crew, and his cargo were sent to Sicily in chains.[10]

It seemed auspicious. It wasn't. New and heavier winds kicked up and blew the armada some hundred miles northwest to Pantelleria. Undaunted, Don

Garcia ordered them to try again. On August 28, the weather turned even worse — gray skies turned black, the clouds were ripped by lightning, and cold rain poured in torrents. The barges and galleys twisted and strained and creaked in the rise and fall of the waves; oars and beaks and masts snapped; equipment was jettisoned or fell overboard. The soldiers, unaccustomed to rough seas and fearing a watery death more than the Muslim army, cursed Don Garcia and would have mutinied had they dared. The fleet scattered — no shipmaster with only minimal control of his ship wanted to be too close to the heavy battering rams of his colleagues. Hours passed and ten thousand prayers rose up to the dark sky. By the time this storm died and the sun broke through again, Don Garcia could only gaze across the pacified ocean and wonder just what kind of force he had left.

In fact, they hadn't lost a single galley. Several boats were damaged, some badly, but all eventually managed to limp to the island of Favignana, eleven miles off the westernmost tip of Sicily and 150 miles north of Linosa — testimony both to the power of the storm and these men's ability to weather it. At Favignana, they found a galleot late of Malta and its crew of Turks and Moors, fellow victims of the winds. These men had given up the fight on Malta as unwinnable and gave a grim account of what the Ottomans were suffering. More good news, if not for the refugees — they were immediately sent back to Syracuse as slaves.

Don Garcia ordered the fleet to Linosa, where he hoped to find Gianandrea Doria. Instead he found two of Doria's sailors and a message. Doria had left Martinez on Gozo with instructions concerning the signal fires. He then had continued to the rendezvous point at Linosa, but judged it unsafe in the late gale. He would return in due course for new orders. Don Garcia left some of his own men with a message for Doria, food enough for two weeks, and comfortingly, the promise of ransom should the two men be captured by Muslims. If Doria should show up again, he was to return to Syracuse. As for Don Garcia, he was now leading his sixty-four ships straight to Malta.[11]

There was more bad luck. The main body of the *Soccorso* approached Gozo on September 4, "in the fourth hour of the night"; but as the original plan had supposed the fleet to be approaching from Syracuse, there were no signal lights to guide them.[12] Don Garcia was determined to round the island, in total darkness and heavy seas, and with all taillights extinguished, on account of which tactics those ships pulling up from behind lost sight of the fleet. By dawn, he was able to meet some of them, bemoan the lost opportunity of the night before, and sail back to Syracuse to regroup.

Here they found Gianandrea Doria. After the Genoese had left for Lampedusa in search of water, he got sidetracked in a small scuffle with two small sailing ships — not, he stressed, because he wanted to, but because an overzealous subordinate, Don Pedro de Pisa, had. The fight had gone badly (forty wounded, two killed), though Doria himself reported that he had been in the forefront, rallying his men, retiring only when struck in the face by an arrow (a detail he quietly left off his official report).[13] He took a few days to recover in Lampedusa before returning to Linosa, getting the viceroy's message, and pressing on to Sicily.

Doria's partisans later claim that his volunteering to go to Malta alone with his own twelve galleys had shamed Don Garcia into following. This view assumes Don Garcia was reluctant in the first place, which is at best unknowable. Certainly he would have wanted to know what kind of force he had left. What he had were mutinous soldiers who were tired of all this useless cruising. It took both Ascanio Della Corgna and Leyva, some of the local cavalry, and some loosely held guns to corral the men back onto the ships. On September 6, late in the day, they set out, again from Syracuse, this time in good weather. By midnight they were again approaching Gozo, where the signal fires were visible and positive. Don Garcia had ordered the chickens on board killed in case their noise should give away the ships' presence. Some commanders, anxious for a fight, or at least eager to get off the boats, requested that they land on the big island immediately. It was bold, but Don Garcia had had his share of amphibious landings and respected the kind of trouble they could bring. "Night," he said, "is mother to confusion."[14] He ordered that they wait until dawn, and only then did they enter Mellieha bay, north of the island.

It was a shocking failure by the Ottomans that this was even possible. El Eudj Ali had warned his masters of an enemy fleet in the area. Algerian ships had heretofore been patrolling the entire island regularly. Why special vigilance was not kept at this place and time, and therefore no army lay in ambush for the Christian armada, is a mystery. Perhaps they trusted bad weather to safeguard them. This was a mistake on their part, and within ninety minutes of arriving, the *Gran Soccorso* managed to offload 9,600 men along with 250 horses, mules, and asses to prepare for the next stage.[15]

A runner took off for Mdina to give Don Mesquita the news, and then it was time for Don Garcia to leave. King Philip's orders not to risk the fleet had been clear, and Don Garcia had obeyed them to the best of his ability. He was also under orders not to risk his own person, which gave rise to his dry, even witty ("por manera de donayre") parting words: "Now all that remains is for me to go, and you had best not detain me, if you wish to comply with His Majesty's orders."[16] The response, presumably said jokingly, was that they would not wish to do anything counter to the king's orders. Some contemporaries ridiculed Don Garcia for leaving the island, but he had other good reasons not to stay. By delegating operational command, Don Garcia avoided the potentially awkward question of whether a Spanish viceroy would outrank a grand master on the island itself.

Indeed, the entire question of the relief's command structure was a thicket of regional and political rivalries. Philip had put Sande in overall command, because, says Balbi, Sande was a Spaniard.[17] Don Garcia was a bit more generous, in public at least, citing Sande's "experience and the confidence in which we hold him."[18] His bravery was undisputed — the scars on his face and hands that he carried from St. Dizier were proof of that — but his record as a commander was not inspiring. At St. Dizier, he had lost control of his troops. At Djerba, he was unable to hold the fort together, and rather than standing to the end, he had tried to escape so that, according to Busbecq, others could take the blame for the final surrender.[19] In private, the viceroy had serious doubts, which he shared in a letter to his cousin the duke of Alba: "Although I consider Sande a very good subordinate (ejecutor), I have no faith in his judgment or his ability for high command."[20] For whatever reasons, he had had bad relations with Neapolitan admiral Don Sancho de Leyva at Djerba — "they could not have hated one another more if they had been brothers" — and it seems that the choice did not go down smoothly with the men deputed to save Malta either.[21] Chiappino Vitelli had command of the Italian soldiers, but "has made it clear that he would not serve under Don Álvaro nor della Corgna."[22] Della Corgna was presumably grateful just to be out of prison. He was deputed maestro de campo general — second to Sande was the best that Don Garcia could offer.[23] Don Diego de Guzman, ranking knight of the order, was also to be consulted ("honoris gratia") in operational matters.[24] (A few contemporary historians write confidently that Della Corgna was in overall command — more evidence of just how vague the situation was.[25]) Other appointments included Pompeo Colonna as captain general of the artillery and Paolo Sforza as general of the commissariat. In a clear attempt to rein in Don Álvaro, Don Garcia dictated that no action could be taken without the clear majority of the council voting in favor.[26] This was to last until they could get in touch with Valette, at which time his word would become law.

+·+·+·+

Foot soldiers on Malta, men on opposite sides of the trenches, sworn to kill each other but close enough now to talk, even to shake hands, were exchanging small kindnesses. The Ottomans at St. Michael passed food — oranges and melon, taken from Maltese groves — to the besieged. In exchange and to the Ottomans' astonishment, the Christians gave them fresh bread and cheese. Valette put a stop to this sort of thing since "the courtesy of the enemy must always be suspect," but the point was made — any hope of starving out the Christians vanished.[27] In fact, by September 6, some of the auberges were putting their men on half rations — one and a half loaves of bread and half a *quartuccio* (.14 liter) of wine — but the Turks were not to know this.[28]

Fighting became almost lackadaisical. One man (Balbi ascribes the idea to Valette) rigged up an arquebus to the end of a pole, which he raised above the parapets.[29] By means of a pulley, he was able to ignite the charge and fire down on the Turks. How effective this was is not recorded — one guesses not very — but it probably was unpleasant for the heretofore secure trench dwellers. The Ottomans tried to pull the gun down with grappling hooks, but never succeeded.

The Mdina raiders were becoming bolder, and even Turkish ships were at risk. The crew of a galleot put in to fill their water jugs at the straits between Malta and Gozo. A cavalry group had been waiting near the well, confident that the enemy would have to show up eventually. There followed a violent set-to, and the Christians would have taken the ship itself had two other Ottoman vessels not shown up. If nothing else, it shows how Turkish command of the island was deteriorating, and how badly they were defending the necessary resources still left to them. Despite this, the Turks, or at least Mustapha, were still hopeful. At this late stage a miracle could arrive for either side, and if the Muslim troops had more or less resigned themselves to the unfavorable will of Allah, Mustapha was a man of greater faith. Certainly he was a man with more on the line.

24

+·+·+·+

MUSTAPHA'S
LAST HAZARD

+·+·+·+

*The true strength of armies exists in the first days of a campaign,
and through experience one sees that time only worries, weakens
and consumes them. It creates difficulties, disease, and shortages of
many things without which it is impossible to do anything well.*

Francesco Laparelli

By now the Ottoman army ran on momentum. Muslim sappers put out to the island of Comino to fetch brushwood for more gun platforms and trenches that would almost certainly never be used. Artillery continued to lob cannonballs, though fewer of them, on St. Michael and the Post of Castile, and most particularly against the Post of Provence, where the largest of the remaining Christian standards still rippled in the occasional breeze.

Ottoman gunners had been lobbing cannonballs indiscriminately into the town of Birgu for some days now. The economics of warfare demanded it — the army could not afford to leave munitions behind, and the armada, or what was left of it, needed to travel as light as possible. If stray shots killed more Christians, so much the better. For the first time also, and in another sign that they were preparing to leave, the gunners were firing into the waters between Senglea and Birgu, aiming at the *Sultana*, "the large ship which up until now had not been fired upon, as it was something they had hopes of taking with them."[1] Heretofore, that prize had been inviolate, the one trophy (besides Valette himself) that would most impress the masses — certainly the harem — at Constantinople. Mustapha was resigned to the second-best option, of denying it to the knights. Even this hope backfired, quite literally. An artilleryman on the Salvador platform had not allowed his weapon to cool sufficiently, or perhaps there were stray embers left over from his previous shot glowing inside the barrel, or perhaps the bronze had become as exhausted as the men who tended it. Whatever the cause, the cannon itself exploded, killing the gun crew and turning the metal, so carefully engineered back in Constantinople, into scrap.

The eager and luckless volunteers who weeks earlier would have charged these walls without question, almost without orders, were gone; the remainder saw destiny mocking their dreams. Fatalism had taken root. Other than spite and wounded pride, or shame in surviving where so many comrades had died, there was little point in continuing the siege. The soldiers spoke plainly: "It is not given to us to capture Malta."[2]

For Mustapha and Piali, however, the return to Constantinople was not going to be a happy occasion, and there was no reason to hurry. God was inscrutable. Even at this late day, something might turn up.

What turned up was Uludj Ali and his ships and bad news. He had seen boats, he said, dozens of them, to the north. Mustapha and Piali wavered. They had intended another assault on St. Michael and the Post of Castile. Could they still risk it? How many thousands of Christians might be on those ships, and how many Muslims would be necessary to counter them? How long before these ships arrived?

Piali didn't spend too much time pondering these things. He had his fleet to secure. To that end, he redirected forces from Marsaxlokk and Pietra Negra to the mouth of the Grand Harbor. Piali did not want to be bottled up, in case Spanish ships should attempt a landing. His own victory at Djerba had demonstrated just how badly an unprepared fleet could suffer.

For his part, Mustapha encouraged small skirmishes along the battle line. For the time being, however, he had nothing major in the works — the commanders on both sides were waiting for further developments or new orders. Mustapha still had his original letter from Suleiman, old and tattered and much brooded upon, telling him not to give up the fight.

By nightfall, Muslim soldiers quietly filed out of the trenches before Fort St. Michael and Birgu and gathered around the camps now centered at the

Marsa, near the ships that would take them away from this useless action. Only one day had passed since Uludj Ali's report of ships on the horizon, but nothing seems to have come of it. They would, it appeared, escape any fresh attack from the Spanish relief.

The Ottomans' real failure, whether by Mustapha or Piali, was in not establishing lookouts at all possible invasion zones. Landing on a hostile shore puts an army at the greatest vulnerability and had been Don Garcia's greatest worry. Why Mustapha and Piali neglected this is a mystery.

◆·◆·◆·◆

On September 7, the lookouts at Fort St. Angelo had seen a small galleot enter Grand Harbor and tie up at the end of Sciberras. Across the water they watched as a short man in heavy robes was carried from that boat into a caique to Fort St. Elmo, disembarked, and was greeted by a retinue of men who provided him with one of the few surviving horses on the island. The man managed to get on the animal, fall off, get on again, and fall off again. By now the butt of a low comedy routine, he drew out a sword and slashed at the animal's legs, leaving the unfortunate animal bloody, crippled, and presumably dying.[3] Without a glance backward, the man then trundled his way by foot along the rocky peninsula to the Ottoman camp at the Marsa.

Who he was and who sent him is unrecorded. Balbi infers that he brought orders from Suleiman to withdraw what remained of the armies and return at once to Constantinople. We have no confirmation of this. We do know, however, that supplies were still being forwarded to the Ottoman troops, and according to a September 27 letter from Petremol, that Suleiman had ordered the expedition to overwinter.[4]

Whatever the truth of the matter, what followed is clear. Janissaries and spahis in the trenches were being primed for one more attack. In earlier battles, units had argued over who would have the honor of leading. Now the fight was to hold up the rear. They deferred to their commanding officers the question of who was to face near-certain and certainly futile death. The little man appears to have settled the argument in favor of both of them. Their fate was to live, and there was a sudden rush from the trenches to the ships, each man eager to be the first in line.

Word had finally gotten to the Ottoman commanders that the Grand Relief had arrived, and thirty-five Muslim galleys soon left Marsamxett to block the entrance to Grand Harbor against any Spanish incursion. Bad luck had dogged the Muslim cause again. For some time, Uludj Ali had been stationed with sixty ships in St. Paul's Bay just adjacent to Mellieha. Just hours before the Great Relief, he had moved his fleet to Marsamxett in preparation for another attack on Senglea, and so missed a chance to swoop down on the enemy in a replay of Djerba.

News of the arrival flew overland quickly, but Valette had refused to believe it[5] — not until the entire *Gran Soccorso* passed the mouth of the harbor under full sail and fired off a triple volley of guns in salute, which the Maltese might have returned had they not been so low on powder. Now convinced and with the tide turning in his favor, Valette began to get ahead of himself. He imagined that the invading force would, "following standard tactics" (*segun la razon de Guerra*), wait until dark and then attack the Ottoman camp.[6]

They didn't, and Balbi claims that this was a source of some contention later on. Valette imagined, and others would later argue, that two thousand arquebusiers could have marched from Mellieha, then attacked the Marsa while Don Garcia's armada put in an appearance outside Grand Harbor. In this scenario, the Ottomans would be forced to fight a sea battle (which Don Garcia would of course win), leaving a smaller number of Muslim troops on land for the *Gran Soccorso* to defeat. It was a somewhat grandiose plan requiring a great deal of coordination between land and sea forces and an unrealistic level of hard intelligence as to Ottoman troop strength. Balbi himself is tactful enough to say that second-guessing is easy.[7]

As dawn broke, the Ottoman trenches appeared to be empty. Behind the walls, caution turned to excitement, which finally overflowed to euphoria. Church bells rang out in Birgu, not in warning of yet another attack, but in honor of the Nativity of Our Lady. Valette ordered a High Mass. More good news followed: a renegade from the Ottoman camp appeared at the wall, confirming that the *Gran Soccorso* had indeed arrived. This was cause for rejoicing, and one man, Vespasiano Malaspina dei Marchesi di Mulazzo, unremarkable to this point, did just that. He climbed to the uppermost peak on the post of Captain Fra Don Bernardo de Cabrera and shouted out a Te Deum in thanks for their delivery. An Ottoman sniper shot him in the chest. He was the last knight to die in defense of Birgu.

In Mdina, in the Ottoman camp, and behind the defensive walls at Senglea and Birgu, each man passed the day alone, wondering what his commander had in mind for him.

+·+·+·+

If Ottoman zeal was waning, Christian enthusiasm was on the rise. On September 8, the *Grand Soccorso* tramped south to Mdina. All men were equal, at least insofar as carrying provisions was concerned, and even the captains were hefting food and munitions stored in sacks both "large and difficult to carry."[8] The planned hike was no more than four miles to Bingemma, south of Mgarr, near the Falca gap that separates the northern plain from the outskirts of Mdina. These four miles were, however, under a Mediterranean sun; and early September on Malta, when heat combines with humidity, can be atrocious. Each man was weighed down with thirty days' worth of biscuit (at twenty-four ounces a day) as well as armor, powder, lead, and weapons.[9] The temptation to lighten their load was too much. They began to discard food.

Chiappino Vitelli was bringing up the rear guard and began to see bags of hardtack littering the side of the road. Since the problem of feeding these men had been an argument for not coming at all, this had to be addressed. He sent word to the head of the column. As *maestro di campo*, Della Corgna was responsible for the tedious matter of supplying the army, and he was not going to let this kind of foolishness pass. Anything left on the road could do the men no good and might help the enemy. Della Corgna knew that the enemy, however demoralized, was still undefeated and still dangerous, and that in war, fortunes can change quickly. He brought the entire column to a dead halt. Minutes later, thousands of unwilling hands reached down to hoist the sacks of discarded food and only then did the soldiers retrace their lost progress.

About a mile short of Mdina, they could see two figures approaching on horseback, kicking up dust in the morning glare. Vincenzo Anastagi and Boisbreton were coming down the road in person to intercept the new arrivals. Anastagi pulled up and greeted his fellow countrymen with more urgency than warmth. They should move as quickly as possible — they still had to negotiate the Falca Gap, a pass perfectly suited for an ambush, to get to Mdina, and it was only a matter of time before the Ottomans learned of their arrival. Della Corgna urged the men on, stressing the potential danger that faced them here in the open and promising them that teamsters were coming to help them carry their loads.

And sure enough, as the men of the *Gran Soccorso* came within sight of Mdina, they saw nearly the entire civilian population — men, women, children, and pack animals — streaming down the slope toward them. The two columns converged, and the Maltese began relieving the soldiers of excess baggage and urging them on to the city and safety. (Sande, in his first report to Philip, slights the efforts of the locals — "the Maltese helped us somewhat," *Malteses nos ayudaron algo.*)[10] It would take another day to get all the munitions safely inside the city, and by nightfall, the men had settled down to rest in the shadows of the exterior walls. Their captains met inside to determine the best course of action.

+·+·+·+

Dawn broke on September 9 to reveal smoke rising from the various Turkish gun platforms. Troops were shuffling onto a defensive position on Mount Sciberras, waiting for the relief force to attack. The Ottoman galleys at Marsamxett were being prepared, and men still ashore were busy with last-minute cleanup. Whatever could be carried home was packed up; whatever could be abandoned was abandoned; whatever destroyed, destroyed. Not content with littering the island with their own ash heaps, the departing Muslims also obliterated whatever remaining Maltese houses and fields and goods they could reach. Anything flammable still left at Bormla had been torched the night before, illuminating the sky with an orange parody of daylight. Two thousand Ottoman soldiers oversaw the operation, nursing the vain hope that the outraged Christians would come out to extinguish the fires. None did, but only because Valette forbade it, and by morning those same Muslim soldiers were ordered to the Marsa. The Christians at last dared to creep over the dust and rubble that had once been Birgu to inspect the now-deserted Ottoman trenches. Valette was still not ready to let down his guard. He ordered men into the trenches and to the entrances of the ditches in front of St. Michael and the Post of Castile in case there should be more fight left in the enemy.

+·+·+·+

The *Gran Soccorso* — or at least the officers — was established inside Mdina. Foot soldiers and support were billeted in half-ruined buildings outside Mdina's walls near the churches of St. Paul and St. Francis. The question then was, what next? Della Corgna took a measured view, which happened to mirror that of Philip, who had gotten him out of jail. This strategy — engage only if necessary, and avoid putting any forces at undue risk — applied to land as much as to sea. Expelling Muslims was their goal, and if this could be done with shadow boxing and the mere threat of force, so much the better.

It was a reasonable position, but one that appealed more to Della Corgna and the king than it did to the king's chosen commander, Sande. Philip should have expected as much. Sande and Leyva, both Djerba veterans still chafing from their last encounter with the Turks in general and Turgut's men in particular, had been waiting for this moment for five years.

If Della Corgna wanted to dampen their enthusiasm, he did have the weather on his side. The rainstorms that had dogged the relief at sea had given way to a sudden heat wave. From Mdina to Birgu is some nine miles. The soldiers had already seen what a four-mile march in Maltese heat could do. The prospect of another eight to nine miles, all of it under blazing sun, must have given even the most wild-eyed pause. For the moment, it was probably easy to let them wait for Mustapha's next move. Both factions, the cautious and the bold, agreed to rely on Valette's opinion and to this end dispatched three men on horseback to Birgu. Tagging along, presumably on foot, were about a hundred soldiers — tourists, essentially — who wanted to see Valette in person, to see the damage that had been done to Birgu, and to find out if there was any wine, "as they had brought none with them."[11]

As to the civilians, they apparently did not care. The enemy was elsewhere, the Great Relief had arrived — the Maltese were already thinking of the future. All that day, the men, women, and children of Birgu left the city to scavenge wood from the Ottoman gun platforms to rebuild their houses.

✦·✦·✦·✦

In the Ottoman camp, new quarrels arose between the two commanders. Piali, claimed Mustapha, had been slack in his job. Had he not allowed the Small Relief to sneak onto the island? Had he not then allowed the Large Relief to follow? Had he not missed any number of couriers sailing between Don Garcia and Valette? And who was to say what new dangers were even now just over the horizon? It was difficult enough to stage a siege at the best of times, how much more so when a general could not be certain of his back?

Piali Pasha could respond that he had not only kept the fleet intact, but he had also led various land operations as well. And even if the *Piccolo Soccorso* had landed despite his cordon, the six hundred men had passed through Mustapha's army like water through a sieve. That the island was still in Christian hands was purely the fault of Mustapha, who failed to achieve a victory on land. Further muddying the waters, a renegade now showed up at the Ottoman camp. This renegade assured Mustapha that the numbers were exaggerated — six thousand Christians, not the nine thousand that had first been reported, and not very good soldiers at that. Mustapha could still field sixteen thousand men.[12]

The new intelligence changed everything. There would, Mustapha saw, be a window of opportunity of perhaps four days — more if the weather cooperated — until Don Garcia could return with more men. The matter went to committee. It would be better to stay a little longer. Rhodes had fallen in a winter campaign. Suleiman originally had anticipated a winter campaign, had promised supply ships — they still might arrive at any time. "If," said Piali, "[the enemy] are as few as they say, then you shall be able to defeat them easily and having done so will still have time to conquer Malta."[13] He should, said Piali, at least confirm with his own eyes how large the force was.

For Mustapha, there were also personal considerations to be weighed. The Maltese adventure was almost certain to be his final campaign, the one thing he would be remembered for whatever the outcome. Victory over the knights would be a glorious cap to a long career, defeat an undying disgrace. Defeat also could mean the executioner's silk garrote — a distinguished end for those who disappointed the sultan, but an end nonetheless.

There was one slim reed of hope. With the exception of the first battle in front of Birgu, Mustapha had never met his enemy on the field, not in any significant way. Now that the relief force had arrived, he might just be able to arrange it. If he could defeat fresh, but possibly green, troops on open ground — he had done so elsewhere in the past — then he might still turn the fiasco around. A demoralized Mdina might capitulate; a shattered Birgu, all hope spent, might follow. The knights could retreat into the relatively secure Fort St. Angelo, but without food or water or any hope of another relief, theirs would be a choice of surrender or suicide. Summer was dying, chances were slim that the Europeans would add more soldiers any time soon. The prospect of Mustapha winning just one set battle and then holding the island through the winter months, as Suleiman had ordered, was compelling enough to risk one last throw of the dice.

By day's end they had come to a decision. Piali Pasha would shepherd what remained of his fleet north toward St. Paul's Bay, where they could bring water on board for the return voyage. Mustapha would take what was left of the army and head inland for the last battle. The two forces would rendezvous the following day, and depending on how the day unfolded, they would go, or stay, as God might decide. Ironically, by their very arrival, the *Gran Soccorso* had given the invaders a powerful incentive to drag the matter out.

Malta was back in play.

25

+·+·+·+

THE
GRAN SOCCORSO
AT WAR

+·+·+·+

Let no Turk be left alive!

Don Álvaro de Sande

On the night of September 10, a Genoese escapee from the Ottoman fleet, a man of good judgment (*buen juicio*), appeared before Valette, claiming to have been present among the enemy captains and to have heard that they intended to dispatch five or six thousand men for a fresh assault.[1] Valette believed him. He sent two knights to Mdina with news of the enemy's plans; as predicted, arising two hours before dawn and taking advantage of the cool night air, Mustapha's army was on the march, burning what lay behind them, heading inward and northward, and leaving a trail of torched buildings like so much bioluminescence in the wake of a ship. Valette, still recovering from his leg wound, had been cautious these past few days about letting his guard down. Now that Mustapha was making his move inland and Piali's ships were streaming out of Grand Harbor, the game had shifted to the relief force. Valette ordered the hundred or so visiting soldiers and many of the siege veterans, Balbi among them, back to Mdina as quickly as possible. As a grand gesture, he also ordered Romegas to the ruins of Fort St. Elmo to raise the flag of the Order, the white cross on a red field.

Dawn crept over the horizon. Members of the *Gran Soccorso*, well placed on the heights near Mdina, could see the fires that marked the Ottomans' path.

The men were mustered while the commanders tried to anticipate Mustapha's next moves. It appeared that the Ottomans were not heading toward Mdina, but across the northern fields of the island. The Christian troops were ordered to stand down.

Besides their smaller numbers, the Christians still had a problem with their command structure. The top commanders did not get along. Don Garcia's hopes that Valette might whip them into line were dashed on September 7, when Valette's emissary first arrived at Mdina. Della Corgna asked him to convince the grand master to name him, Della Corgna, as commander in chief. The emissary then ran into Sande outside the city, who presented to him the commission signed by Don Garcia giving Sande full control. Valette chose to confirm the viceroy's decision, but it cannot have smoothed relations.[2]

Ironically, Della Corgna held not only the same strategic views as Philip, but also the same tactical views as Valette. The grand master considered the size of the opposing forces and for the moment agreed with the passive-defensive strategies devised in the gloomy elegance of El Escorial. The numbers were in Mustapha's favor. The siege was very much in the balance and would turn on how this next encounter played out. With no chance of further Spanish reinforcements for some days, Valette advised the relief force to exercise restraint in the face of the enemy. He did not, however, order it.

Before dawn on September 11, Valette had sent Boisbreton to Mdina with word that fifteen thousand Ottomans were heading their way and that the *Gran Soccorso* should show itself, but they should also "take advantage of the situation at hand, while taking all possible precautions for their safety."[3] The first person whom he could find with any authority in that city was Della Corgna. He told Boisbreton that if they stayed inside Mdina, they could hold off up to forty thousand men, and with no risk to the troops.[4] A good answer, but not one Della Corgna as second in command was technically authorized to make. Boisbreton went in search of Don Álvaro, who took a more active reading to the order. He immediately left the city and joined Chiappino Vitelli and three hundred infantrymen in order to get a good look at the army advancing against them.[5]

The Ottomans could be seen in the distance, a huge mass in the middle of which there was a single large banner, heading to the high grounds of Naxxar, north of the city. Mustapha seemed to be taking the same view as Della Corgna. Instead of marching to Mdina and sending an exhausted army up a high hill against fresh troops on a blisteringly hot day, he appeared to want his men to rest awhile on a strong position. If he did so, the two sides would be at a stalemate, each on a hilltop staring across an empty game board at the other, each commander waiting for the other to advance a pawn.

There was also a small hillock near Naxxar. Sande recognized its strategic value and ordered two captains to take the place. Della Corgna, guardian of the king's strategy of caution, came galloping out of the city toward Sande and Vitelli, protesting that he had not been consulted and demanding to know what they intended to do now, as it seemed to him that the Ottomans were determined to march on the Christian position near Mdina, and that it would be more advantageous to be inside the city walls. There was, he said, "more to the military arts than boldness."[6] (Cirni suggests that their meeting was rather more collegial: "What do we wish to do, gentlemen? The Turks appear to be already resolved to come and find us, and so we should stay in place since it is strongest and we are already securely ensconced at this time, and in waiting we shall be most advantageously placed to overcome them.")[7] Don Álvaro, whose experience with a desperate last stand in the fort at Djerba had turned out badly, took a more aggressive view. He countered that putting the entire army and its artillery on display should be enough to scare them off.

While the better part of the Christian force remained agitated but more or less restrained near Mdina, their commanders argued over tactics. The small hillock Sande had ordered to be secured was now being approached by Ottomans as well. Vitelli, who had done some reconnaissance on his own and saw what the Ottomans intended, took matters into his own hands. He cried out to his own men: "Captains, soldiers of honor, this is not the time to tarry and think — Let us go forth with spirit and without any doubt we will carry back the hoped for victory."[8] His men were more terse: "Sant'Iago, forward and at them!"[9] They started running down the hillside and charged the Ottomans, and twice repelled them. Flush with this success, Vitelli then turned his men toward another hill with a house and windmill on it and pushed the occupying Turks off that as well. A small victory, but visible. It got the soldiers' blood up and whetted their appetite for more.

Valette's account to Don Garcia was straightforward and to the point. "Eight or nine thousand marched from Marsamxett to within sight of Mdina, from which exited our forces, and with much skirmishing, closed with the vanguard and without forethought they broke and chased them as far as the armada, killing all those [whom] they caught up with.[10] In his report to King Philip, Sande describes this as a result of his having been warned of an ambush, and of taking it upon himself to seize the hill as "it seemed to me to be a good thing to close with the enemy before he embarked."[11] Sande was, in this reading, in full control at all times, but goes on to suggest that although the Italian troops might well have obeyed (suggesting Italian cowardice, perhaps), the Spanish troops were too hot-blooded. (It should be remembered that Spain had completed the *Reconquista* in 1492, just within living memory.) His men, soldiers who had idled for weeks on the wharves of Messina with no distractions other than to imagine what the infidel was doing over the horizon, who had endured the storms at sea and the final march across the hot island, could now see the smoke rising from Bormla and Senglea; they could see every trace of petty vandalism the Turks had left behind on their final march; they could see the enemy troops responsible for these outrages. And they could see that the Turks had clearly been bested at Torre del Falca. Talk of prudence and caution was no good to them. These were violent men with a serious grudge and a yen for Ottoman blood and wealth. They wanted a fight, the more one-sided the better.

The Christian line became ever more skittish, like racehorses, heads shaking, nostrils flaring, and impatient for the gate to drop. Finally, they could stand it no longer. The Spanish troops under Sande broke free of their line and rushed down at the Ottoman soldiers, shouting, "*Sant'Iago, vittoria, vittoria!*"[12] Della Corgna gave up and joined in the charge.

The final battle had begun.

◆·◆·◆·◆

Ottoman accounts give Mustapha some credit: "After the dawn had turned to midday, he collected the troops and arranged them for combat; the vile infidels, by that courageous act, were stricken with fear and had turned already to escape, when an infidel approached a coward in the Musulman army and struck him and that man began to raise laments."[13]

After this, the fight began to go against the Ottomans. Christian writers claim that Mustapha turned to the man who had promised him that the relief force was trivial and said, "Traitor! Are these the few pathetic and poorly led soldiers you promised me?"[14] Without waiting for an answer, he pulled out his scimitar and killed the man on the spot.

But if the Christians were expecting the Ottomans to cut and run, they underestimated the enemy. Seeing the Christian soldiers pouring down the hillside and even flanking the Ottoman left, the Ottomans, whether by instinct or under orders, rapidly formed a defensive position around the Torre de Falca, north of Mdina. From this superior position they were able to rain fire down on the enemy, and it was around this position that the battle coalesced. The first crew of Ottomans soon were joined by a second wave of two thousand men under Mustapha and Uludj Ali.[15] Although the Christians were still relatively few at the front and had no standards to rally around, their fury began to take its toll. Slowly, surely, Chiappino Vitelli and his Tuscan troops halted the Muslim advance and began to force it back.

Mustapha saw that his van had been stopped. He attempted to gather his men and position arquebusiers to best advantage, but it was clear that he was in retreat. With only a handful of Janissaries and a larger number of his hastily promoted auxiliaries against fresh troops, he was forced to execute that most difficult of military procedures, the disciplined withdrawal while under fire. He did so in heat that Balbi records as being the worst that they had ever experienced during the siege. Some Christian soldiers in heavy armor, padded with leather or heavy cotton, sweating vital fluids, collapsed from heat prostration. Four died of sunstroke.

As the day wore on, discipline among the troops, not the best to begin with, ebbed further. Valette in his brief account to the German knight Georg von Hohenheim stresses that these men were "inspired by Christian piety alone," *sola Christiana pietate commoti*.[16] Clearly he knew better. For all their devotion and blood lust — and there was plenty of both — these soldiers could see a potential windfall in Ottoman gold and silver in danger of slipping away. Spanish troops, thrifty men, stopped fighting long enough to examine the Muslim casualties in case there should be anything worth stealing. The uneven advance helped the remaining Janissaries, the genuine ones, in drawing up a series of defensive lines to hold the Spanish long enough for the next phase of the retreat.

The battle became a jumble of events — a Spanish renegade, engaging some private vendetta, shouted from a distance, "Where's Don Álvaro? Take this arrow I'm sending over to salute you with!"[17] The anonymous missile missed its intended target but struck the commander's horse. Don Álvaro appears to have found the whole thing exhilarating. Turning to his colleague, he called out: "More value here, Señor Ascanio, than back in the fort!"[18] Humiliating enough to be second-guessed, Della Corgna was soon thereafter struck in the face by a stone.

Throughout it all, Mustapha kept his head, directing each section as was needed. Here he showed coolness under fire that, if it did not save the day, at least saved a good number of Muslim lives. Nothing seemed to faze him. His horse was shot out from beneath him. A nameless lieutenant immediately gave up his own mount to the commander. Again and again, Mustapha and Uludj Ali placed their best men at various strategic points to cover the retreat.

Sande writes of a hillock near St. Paul's Bay that aroused his suspicion, enough for him to send four hundred arquebusiers to investigate. They found and drove off five or six hundred of the enemy and "scuttled over four thousand water barrels"—water intended for the Muslims' long journey home, though it would seem unlikely that Mustapha's soldiers would have had time to load them.[19]

The distance between the end of the Turkish line and the Spanish infantry and Maltese militia narrowed. The cavalry only got closer. Mustapha drew up a force of arquebusiers to fire a concerted volley into the Christian horse, and it had its intended effect. Sande was still at the head of this cavalry column, pushing forward, when the volley rang out. He was thrown from his mount (a thing he neglects to mention in his own official report), but survived and managed to re-form his line and again attack the Ottoman ranks. This time Hassan Pasha of Algiers had been given the job of holding the attackers off. Having established his men in their positions, the bey waited for the Christian cavalry to charge, and when they did, he ordered a second volley. Lead shot tore into men and horses. The animals screamed and fell, their riders did the same, and the charge temporarily staggered back. By day's end, most of Sande's fifty horses lay dead on the ground, victims either of enemy action or of excessive heat.[20] Mustapha himself was struck twice by gunfire, and eventually, the Ottomans just cracked.[21] "Then, while the vanguard of the base infidels presented itself, the Muslim soldiers withdrew from the battle and the serdar was abandoned. The base infidels, having seen that the Ottoman army had unraveled, advanced to attack."[22]

At the shores of St. Paul's Bay, northeast of the fighting, Piali and his galleys lay waiting to learn the outcome of Mustapha's work. The sounds of battle, inconclusive and chaotic, came first. That the volume grew louder was a bad sign. Then the first of the retreating Muslims came trickling down to the shore and safety. Piali ordered longboats out to carry the soldiers from the beaches to the galleys. He also had his cannons loaded to discourage any Christians who might chase his colleagues to the water's edge.[23]

By now the Christian infantry had caught up to the remnants of Sande's cavalry and were overrunning Hassan's soldiers, eager to get a piece of the final action. The battle line had come within shooting range of Piali's ships, and Ottoman gunners began to fire onto the shore. The last fighting was touched with the madness that takes over when a battle becomes futile. Men fired guns where they could, blades rang against blades, and once their guns were spent and blades broken, they grabbed at anything that might serve as a weapon.

As the fight approached St. Paul's Bay, all order fell apart. In a scene he had witnessed from the other side at Djerba, Piali Pasha saw an unexpected crush of desperate men who threw themselves into the water, neck deep, rather than wait for lifeboats. "Among those who touched the edge of the sea only those who had the strength to reach the ships were saved."[24] The bravest of the Spanish were right on their heels, pushing the fight to the edge of the water and even, it is said, into it, some reaching as far as the enemy galleys themselves.[25] In so doing they turned the water of St. Paul's Bay pink with blood.

Piali ordered the ships to rush the beaches and pull men directly on board. To the extent they could, the mounted guns on these ships also helped cover the final withdrawal, while just beyond the mouth of the bay, warships waited, on guard against a Christian fleet that might appear at any moment. Don Álvaro and Della Corgna, seeing the danger, called off the attack, with the intention of hauling Chiappino Vitelli's fourteen artillery pieces to the bay to finish the job the next day.[26]

The battle by the shore had lasted an hour or so; the numbers of living dwindled as the surviving Ottoman troops reached the safety of their boats or died in the process. The decrescendo of a dying battle gave way to the drawn-out groans and sudden cries of the injured, the arguing of soldiers over loot, the gasping and panting of the exhausted, and finally to the normal sounds of a late summer day on the seaside, the occasional cry of gulls, the repetitive susurrus of water lapping on shore. The victors could attend to their spoils, the defeated, to their wounds. Twenty-five Christians, according to Sande's report, had been killed. Of the Turks, better than fifteen hundred.[27] The disparity was attributable, we can guess, to the fact that Mustapha was reduced to using exhausted, dispirited, untrained auxiliaries against an influx of fresh, eager, drilled professionals.

The Muslim boats lingered just offshore until nightfall, perhaps stunned, perhaps defiant, perhaps trying to best settle the injured and dying preparatory to leaving, perhaps wondering if Mustapha's remaining hale troops had one last fight within them. The answer to the last question was clearly no. "Having lost many of their oarsmen through deprivations, fatigue and scarcity of necessities, with the armaments of the galleys having been used up in the war to make bridges and war machines against the forts, it became necessary that those galleys better equipped should tow many vessels."[28] After sundown, the wind shifted and the armada departed, Piali's fleet eastward to Constantinople, the corsairs to their several homes to the west and south.[29]

The siege of Malta was over.

26

+·+·+·+

FROM THE
ASHES

+·+·+·+

CATHERINE DE' MEDICI:
Was it really the greatest siege?
Greater even than Rhodes?

ANTOINE DE LA ROCHE, KNIGHT
COMMANDER OF THE HOSPITALLERS:
Yes, Madame, greater even than Rhodes.
It was the greatest siege in history.

The French knight Anthoine de Cressy agreed at least with the first half of this statement, writing to the grand prior of France on September 11, 1565, that "this siege was even more grueling and perilous than that of Rhodes, according to those who had been present in both."[1]

The Ottoman fleet left behind hundreds of dead and parts of the dead to drift onto the water's shallow edges. In the days to come, more corpses floated to the surface as body tissue decomposed and the cavities filled with gas. Unseasonal heat quickly made the stench unbearable, and for some time afterward, the only creatures that would approach the area were scavenging birds in search of carrion.

Perhaps fifteen Muslims, men too dazed or exhausted or unlucky to have made it out with their comrades, were left to be taken prisoner.[2] They were booty as much as the abandoned weapons, armor, and clothing that lay scattered on the field, and were treated as such. An old captain of the spahis was sold to Della Corgna, who, given the ransom he had just paid to get out of jail, must have been grateful for the odd investment opportunity. The spahi was lucky. Balbi writes: "Very few Turks were taken as slaves because through either weariness or cowardice, not a man among them would get up from the ground where they lay, and so they were killed without mercy."[3] Another survivor claimed to be a refugee and told a story that Mustapha in his last moments on the island had torn his beard and cried out, "Allah, Allah, I have today lost two thousand of my men!"[4]

Now that the island was free of the enemy invaders, members of the *Gran Soccorso* became little more than tourists. Those with no more business on the battlefield wandered toward Grand Harbor to see what they, and more particularly, the knights, soldiers, and Maltese people, had been fighting for. They eventually reached the once-high walls of Senglea and Birgu, now reduced to a height more suitable to penning up livestock than to keeping marauding soldiers at bay. Inside these walls were shattered wrecks of buildings. The men of the *Gran Soccorso*, relatively fresh, even invigorated by their one-day slap-down fight, met the exhausted, scarred survivors of the siege at Senglea and Birgu.

(The great irony of Don Garcia's strategy was that the arrival of the *Gran Soccorso* had the unintended effect of encouraging the Ottomans to make one last stand, a stand that, given their superior numbers, they should have been able to win. It was, in fact, the men of the *Piccolo Soccorso* who made all the difference. The numbers tell the story: as of September 9, Birgu and Senglea were defended by no more than six hundred able-bodied men — a hundred fewer than the *Piccolo Soccorso*.[5])

The following day, Valette wrote to the pope and to Philip with news of the victory, thanking God and Spain, and not mentioning Don Garcia at all. Three days later, Don Garcia's viceregal galley and the troops of the duke of Urbino swept into Grand Harbor. The grand master, various knights, and representatives of the *Gran Soccorso* hurried down to Fort St. Angelo to meet them. Whatever recriminations Valette may have voiced for Don Garcia's delay, at this single moment, the two men appear to have been genuinely moved by each other's company, tears streaming down both their faces — though it was the young Gianandrea Doria whom Valette first embraced.[6]

Don Garcia explained that this secondary squadron might have arrived sooner, but when they had first set out, towing barges of soldiers and matériel behind them, they had spotted the Ottoman fleet heading home. He took this as proof that the siege was won, and immediately ordered a return to Syracuse to lighten the load before he rejoined the *Gran Soccorso*. The last thing Malta needed was a few thousand extra hungry and thirsty soldiers.

It did, however, need food. A chicken at that time could fetch two gold ducats (a soldier's gross pay for one month), where chickens could be found. A single egg went for a real and a half.[7] All of which made the feast that Don Garcia underwrote for knights and nobles that much more appreciated.

It was another two days, to September 14, before Don Garcia ordered the fleet to chase the Ottoman armada, not so much with the intention of destroying it—the armada was too far away by then—but of perhaps taking some of the slower-moving cargo vessels. Certainly the Ottomans saw him as a threat. A message (presumably from Mustapha) was sent on September 19 to the *kadi* of Modon that things should be prepared for his arrival and that all "should be aware of the danger coming from the enemy side."[8] No ships were found—possibly none were left—and weather forced Don Garcia to spend a week at Venetian-controlled Kythira (between the Peloponnese and Crete) and to return to Messina on October 7.[9] He might have done better to head westward in pursuit of the fleeing corsairs. De Fourquevaux, the French ambassador to Spain, wrote on November 5, 1565, that "the Barbary corsairs have not six weeks past descended on the lands of Granada and sacked the lands of the Duke of Sesse, some six leagues from the sea."[10] The corsairs were fundamentally businessmen. Malta hadn't panned out—life goes on.

Valette's immediate problem was to rebuild Malta. His concerns were justified. Valette considered the damage to the island's defenses so extreme that the Order might have to abandon the island (or at least, so he said).[11] By December, he threatened to remove his men from Malta to Sicily if more help was not forthcoming. This seemed to do the trick. Toledo, irritated by the Frenchman's ingratitude, had already written to Philip and argued that "even one Frenchman is too much for Syracuse, never mind more than that."[12] By the end of the year, Philip sent Valette fifty thousand ducats, and he promised troops the following year should the putative attack come.[13] More heartening was the sudden rush of those eager to defend Europe from Islam. Applications to join the Order rose substantially.

On the streets of Constantinople, there was grief and outrage directed against any Europeans who happened to be on hand: "I am constrained," wrote Petremol, "by the anger of the people to contain myself and my family in my house."[14] Ominously, Suleiman ordered a headcount of all Christians and Jews, "a thing that had never been done in that city."[15] Suleiman rewarded his soldiers for brave service with promotions and cash, despite their not having taken the island. He did fully intend to try again, and alarmed spies in Constantinople sent reports about the sultan's fury and plans for sending out an even larger force the next year.[16] In the spring of 1566 Suleiman wrote an open letter to the people of Malta, widely translated, demanding surrender and threatening that "yf you will not yeald your selves as wee have said we will roote out the foundacion of your castell upsid down, and make you slaves and to die an evell death according to our pleasure as we have donn to manny others and this be you rightly well assured."[17]

It didn't happen. Piali Pasha set out in 1566 with 130 ships, fewer than the year before and unaided by the Algerian fleet, which had been told that its presence was optional.[18] All spring and summer Europe waited for reports of the armada's progress. Malta, not yet recovered from the siege, braced itself. Piali cruised the Adriatic and made a few raids; the only substantive action he took was to seize Chios from the Genoese. This was no great achievement. The island had been weak for decades, a tribute payer to the empire and of small economic or military importance. A contemporary Ottoman historian claims that the Chians passed on intelligence concerning the disposition of the Ottoman fleet, but as a practical matter Chios was no threat to the Ottoman Empire.[19] Taking the island was more a petulant gesture than a respectable military action, and Piali Pasha is said to have been almost apologetic to the locals he was displacing (as well he might be — Chios had taken care of the wounded and ill after they had left Malta). By August, Valette ordered the defenders of Malta to stand down.

Why was Malta spared? Possibly Suleiman had no generals he felt he could trust. Possibly he worried that the Barbary corsairs who followed Turgut might not have come a second time — a potentially catastrophic loss of face for the self-styled caliph of Islam. Possibly he worried that, were he to take the island, he might not be able to hold it. (Mustapha's guns had been remarkably thorough. The engineer Francesco Laparelli, who came to rebuild what the Ottomans had destroyed, considered Senglea so far gone that it could only be razed to the ground.)[20] Moreover, Malta was simply more valuable to Europe than Rhodes had been. It was the pathway to Sicily, breadbasket to Italy and Spain, as crucial then as oil is today. Europe had shown itself willing and able to mount a rescue of the island in a way they had not done for islands in the eastern Mediterranean.

More likely it was simply a matter of priorities. In its shattered state, Malta almost certainly could have been taken in 1566. But by the same thinking, it probably could have been taken a year after that. In the meantime, Suleiman had unfinished business in Hungary. This (to his mind) vassal state was now under the rule of the new Holy Roman emperor, Maximilian II, who was less accommodating to the Ottomans than his predecessor had been. The Malta summer of 1565 also saw Maximilian waging war on Suleiman's Balkan territories and failing to pay their annual tribute.[21] This kind of insolence, especially after such a great failure as Malta, needed immediate correcting. Malta could wait.

And so the sultan (allegedly at the urging of his daughter Mihrimah) personally led his invasion into Hungary, this time, in deference to his failing health, in a covered panquin rather than on horseback.[22] It was Suleiman's thirteenth campaign, and his last. Aged seventy-six, he died on the outskirts of Szigetvar in Hungary, succeeded by Selim, his remaining son by Hurrem. For the Ottoman Empire, it was the end of their ambitions for the northern Mediterranean.

Selim, called "the Sot" by Westerners because of an alleged taste for wine, had no appetite for Malta. Unfortunately, he also had a reputation to build, for which he would need a contest he could not possibly lose. Genoese-held Chios had been a walkover. Perhaps Venetian-held Cyprus would be the same. Venice was, after all, disliked and distrusted by her fellow Christians, and even if taking the island required breaking a solemn treaty, treaties with infidels could be broken if doing so helped the spread of Islam.

He miscalculated. In defense of Cyprus, Venice joined the pope's new Holy League against the Ottomans, the first since Prevesa thirty years before; and in 1571 this coalition of Spain, the Papal States, the Knights of St. John, and Venice met the sultan's fleet at the battle of Lepanto. (Among the participants were Uludj Ali, Gianandrea Doria, Ascanio Della Corgna, and Romegas. Piali Pasha was absent, temporarily in disgrace.) It was a resounding Christian victory with absolutely no follow-up whatsoever.

For his part, Selim's grand vizier Sokollu Mehmed Pasha tried to dismiss the defeat as inconsequential, and he wasn't entirely wrong:

"In wresting Cyprus from you we deprived you of an arm; in defeating our fleet you have only shaved our beard. An arm when cut off cannot grow again; but a shorn beard will grow all the better for the razor."[23]

It did grow back, but slowly, more sparse, and with gray streaks. Uludj Ali was deputed to rebuild the fleet, but the ships he was able to build were shaky affairs built of green wood, suitable primarily for show.[24] By now, Philip had lost interest in the Mediterranean, and when Selim dispatched 240 galleys to lay siege to La Goletta, Philip forbade his half-brother, Don John of Austria, hero of Lepanto, from taking any action. After five weeks, Tunis, the site of Charles V's greatest victory, fell to the Ottomans, giving Selim the opportunity to boast of his accomplishment in a lengthy poem of praise typical of that time.[25]

It was all but the last hurrah for a struggle that had begun nearly sixty years earlier at Rhodes. Mutual exhaustion and other priorities led Spain and the Ottomans to sign a peace treaty in 1580. This one held. With this matter settled and the quest to reconquer the Holy Lands a dead letter, the Knights of St. John had lost their relevance; at best they were a counterweight to the Barbary corsairs, useful as auxiliaries in the suppression of French Huguenots; but absent a strategy of geographic conquest or ideological persuasion, they were, for survival, left with the increasingly anachronistic role of corsairs.

Anachronistic, but comfortable. Sciberras was built upon and became the city of La Valletta (inexplicably spelled with two l's), "a city fit for gentlemen." The islanders erected storehouses and markets for merchandise, both legitimate and not, that began to find its way to Malta on a scale unimaginable beforehand. Over time, the Order was reduced to a near parody of its former crusading self. Men would join, serve a few years to learn the ropes, resign, obtain a letter of marque from their former brothers, and like mercenaries who build their skills in the French Foreign Legion, set up in business for themselves. (The less ambitious hoped that a few years' service abroad might be rewarded by the sinecure of a commandery at home.)[26] By the eighteenth century, the more adventurous of Europe's Grand Tour set, young men seeing the classical world before settling down to lives of domestic boredom in their home countries in England or Germany, could sign on to a knight's vessel and go a roving on the Mediterranean Sea. Small risk, enough to create a frisson and material to embroider for the folks back home, and who knew? Perhaps one could pick up some booty in the process. On the downside, such voyages could also get them killed or earn them a lengthy stay in a Barbary prison.[27]

The Barbary corsairs, their ties with Constantinople ever looser, continued on in their entrepreneurial fashion, raiding places as far away as Ireland and menacing honest traders from any country, including a young United States, unable to stand up to them. Certainly it wasn't the knights who finally put them down.

The Orders' tenure on Malta ended, as did so many things, with the French

Revolution. Napoleon stopped by the island in 1798 on his way to Egypt, and almost as an afterthought, accepted the bloodless surrender of the current grand master. He also liberated some two thousand Muslim slaves — a nice gesture and a positive selling point to the Muslim world he was about to invade.[28] The American navy fought the good fight against the Barbary corsairs, but it was the French government of 1830 that invaded Algiers and put it under colonial rule, shutting down the slave market for good.

The Order of the Knights of St. John of Jerusalem of Rhodes and of Malta still remains, headquartered in Rome, dedicated now, as nearly a thousand years ago, entirely to the relief of suffering and to healing the sick.

+·+·+·+

Ultimately, however, the Mediterranean was a small stage, too small for a rapidly shrinking world. The Ottoman Empire was doomed to lose its stranglehold on East-West trade. By the end of the sixteenth century, the empire along with Venice had begun their long decline, a pair of fading divas, their time past, soon to be living on memory.

Did they know? One Ottoman writer did: "The Europeans have discovered the secret of oceanic travel. They are Lords of the new world and of the gates to India. The people of Islam are without the latest information in the science of geography and do not understand the menace of the capture of the sea trade by the Europeans."[29]

This was in 1580, year of the peace. History had already turned and had done so with one of those coincidences that mock human ambition. In October of 1565, while Europe exhaled and Constantinople rioted, a Spanish merchant galleon ship glided into the bay at Acapulco on the western coast of Mexico. This was the first of the Manila galleons, vessels packed with porcelain and lacquerware, spices and silks, originating in Philip's other holdings in the Philippines, as well as China and beyond. Teamsters would unload the cargo, carry it overland, and load other ships bound for Spain.

This route would flourish for the next two hundred and fifty years, exploiting the Pacific winds and the economic advantage of ocean vessels for cargo, altering trade patterns and in so doing, enriching those able to adapt and dismaying those who were not.

27

+·+·+·+

VERDICT

+·+·+·+

Rien n'est plus connu que ce siège, où la fortune de Soliman échoua.
(Nothing is better known than this siege, where
Suleiman's fortunes ran aground.)

Voltaire

The first half of Voltaire's quote crops up in just about every history of Malta, the almost wistful point being that now, five hundred years on, the Siege of Malta is anything but well known. This take on Malta's fleeting fame is milked entirely for irony, which, given the source, is not remarkable.

What is remarkable is that the second clause is invariably left out. Yet it is this apparent throwaway line that goes to the very heart of the matter. What fortunes is he talking about, how far-reaching were the consequences of the siege? Were the events of that summer no more than a curtain-raiser for the naval battle at Lepanto six years later? Clearly Voltaire sees Malta as the high-water mark of Suleiman's career. That entire phrase stands alone and with no further context. What exactly did the loss mean to the Ottomans? What was the point of the expedition in the first place?

Did any of it matter?

Certainly it did to the Maltese. They fought for their homeland and for their faith. Rule by the Order might be oppressive, but the knights were at least fellow Christians, soldiers of the pope himself and as such far preferable to those practicing the false religion of the Ottomans.

The knights, by contrast, were fighting not only for their faith, but also for their self-respect, and their possible existence. The failure at Rhodes was humiliating, that at Tripoli alarming. Losing Malta would prove the knights to be three-time losers; and even if Valette survived and avoided being dragged to captivity in Constantinople, would he or anyone else have been able to reprise L'Isle-Adam's role as rebuilder of the Order? Would the knights even have received another offer? Philip was in no great shape financially and far less bold than his father, Charles. The knights' power depended on corsairing and on the rents of their lands throughout Europe. Without a grand master and an independent headquarters, the Order could easily have seen those holdings appropriated by nearby lords and principalities. It had happened in 1307 to the once-powerful Knights Templar, whose fortunes were stolen by Philip IV of France with the connivance of Pope Clement V.

What would an Ottoman victory have meant for Europe as a whole? We step into a contentious area here, but a useful one. Visions of what might have been were exactly what informed the actions of the participants, what made them fight to the last man against such high odds. The fear in Madrid was that had the siege succeeded, over thirty thousand of Spain's Moriscos, closet Muslims, would be encouraged to rise up in revolt, notably in Granada.[1] Even Queen Elizabeth did not like to think about it: "If they should prevail against the Isle of Malta, it is uncertain what further peril might follow to the rest of Christendom."[2]

It was uncertain, but we can imagine some possible scenarios. A victorious Suleiman might have delegated the 1566 Hungary campaign to a proven general, Mustapha Pasha perhaps, and in consequence survived a few more years, placid, without risk of, as the French ambassador feared, "[dying] of anger from his army being repulsed on Malta."[3] With Malta seized, he might have seen no reason to take Chios from the Genoese or Cyprus from the Venetians. Malta under the Ottoman rule could be cleared of the local Christian population (as Muslims were expelled from Spain) and perhaps repopulated with Anatolians (as had happened when Mehmed took Constantinople). As such, it would not be just another traditionally Muslim port city that owed allegiance to a distant Constantinople, but a formidable outpost of the empire. The distinction is not trivial. An Ottoman Malta would show a powerful commitment to the western Mediterranean theater. Corsairs and sheiks of the Maghreb, fair-weather allies who had abandoned the siege when the going got tough, would see a firm exponent of empire on their doorsteps, perhaps with Piali Pasha as its commander. Anyone who doubted the seriousness or the power of Constantinople would have to think twice.

To the degree that the Order lost prestige, Suleiman's reputation would have soared even higher, with significant effects on the psychology of both ally and enemy. France, always pragmatic, would have been encouraged to greater cooperation with their on-again off-again ally in Constantinople. Venice, always eager to avoid trouble, would have continued their commercial relationship. In consequence, any Holy League would have been without their help (or that of the knights, for that matter). Lepanto probably never would have been fought, and if it had been, the inexperienced Müezzinzade Ali Pasha, who oversaw the Ottoman defeat, never would have been in charge of the Ottoman fleet.

Suleiman eventually would pass on the empire to Selim, and the question becomes what would he do with it? Andrew Hess points out that a Muslim *reconquista* of all the Maghreb had been a long-standing strategy of the Ottomans, one that even the disaster at Lepanto did not wipe out.[4] Absent Lepanto and given a successful taking of Malta, the possibilities change dramatically. Sicily, a Muslim holding until 1091, would have been targeted, possibly taken. The Balearics, previously just a harvest ground for slaves and plunder, might have been taken for good, and from there it was a simple matter to help the Moriscos in Spain (a task Uludj Ali neglected in 1567), with what bloody results we can only imagine. There was also the long-term Ottoman strategy to take Rome — the Ottomans were, after all and by their own lights, the torch holders of the Roman Empire. Muslim converts in Bosnia and Herzegovina, along with any number of Christian-born corsairs, proved that not all Europeans were as resistant to Islam as the Maltese were. Battista Mantovano, in *De Calamitatibus Temporum* (1498), reports that Christians living on the Adriatic coast took it as a given that they would soon be Ottoman subjects.[5]

Hess writes: "The battle of Lepanto did not directly set the conditions for the neutralization of the Mediterranean but instead encouraged further warfare until the question of who controlled North Africa was settled in favour of the Ottomans."[6]

North Africa, but not Christian Europe. That question was settled by the men, women, and children who fought to hold on to Malta. The failure to take that island redirected the Ottoman flow away from the Mediterranean's northern shores and back toward Africa. The siege effectively determined that the ocean would divide the two religions. Christendom would hold north and west, Islam east and south. The line drawn that summer continues roughly to this day.

28

+·+·+·+

THE SURVIVORS

+·+·+·+

It seemed a new miracle that those brave knights and soldiers
so few in number and with so many hardships had resisted such frightful
assaults and such a long siege and succeeded in maintaining so many
defense works against so great a force and such excellent warriors.

Adriani

How many brave soldiers drank the cup of martyrdom
and obtained eternal happiness!

Selaniki

Valette lived five more years, not easily. Honors showered down on him, including the offer of a cardinal's hat. His duty, however, lay on Malta. The closeness
of the siege, and the thought that next time the Order would not be so lucky, all
but obsessed him. So did money. By luck or by shrewdness, he sold the Order's
holdings in Cyprus, soon to be conquered by the Ottomans.[1] "He resorted to
wholesale looting of the holy relics of the Order, snatching gold chains from
the necks of anyone he met, melting his table silver and selling the precious
gifts he had received after the siege."[2]

As the Ottoman threat appeared to recede, however, Valette became subject to anonymous and not-so-anonymous sniping. One of the most vicious
examples came from the Italian Pallavicino Rangone, a member of the *Gran
Soccorso*, who for reasons best known to himself took violent exception to
both Valette and Don Garcia de Toledo.[3] It is perhaps Rangone's (secret)
report to Pius V, a man even more fastidious than Valette, which encouraged
the pope to go over Valette's head to appoint the Order's priory of Rome and

various commanderies without consulting the grand master.[4] When Valette remonstrated, Pius refused to allow his envoy to enter the city of Rome — an astonishing slap in the face.

On July 31, 1568, Valette's (illegitimate) daughter was murdered by her jealous husband.[5] It was a blow from which he never quite recovered. Some days later, while attempting to distract himself by hunting partridge with his falcons, he suffered a stroke. As he lay dying, nature rolled out portents suitable in number, drama, and kind to a man of his accomplishments. Thunder clapped in a cloudless sky, "horrid . . . like a great concert of arquebus guns."[6] A school of dolphins beached themselves in Marsaxlokk. One by one, his pets began to die: his ruby-colored parrot; his griffin, a gift from the king of France; and his lioness, who slept at the foot of his bed. He died on August 21, the anniversary of his election as grand master, and was buried in the crypt of the newly built Cathedral of St. John in the town that was to bear his name. His epitaph was written by Sir Oliver Starkey:

> *Ille Asiae, Lubiaeq(ue) Pavor Tutelaq(ue) quondam*
> *Europae edomiti sacra per arma getis*
> *Primus in hac alma quam condidit urbe sepulto*
> *Valletta eterno dignus honore iacet*

> He, onetime scourge of Africa and Asia, and shield
> Of Europe, whence he expelled the barbarians by his holy arms,
> First to be interred in this foster city, whose founder he was:
> Here lies La Valette, worthy of eternal honor.

Mustapha and Piali Pasha sailed to Constantinople with the uneasy knowledge that men were executed for their kind of failure. It speaks something about their characters, or their sense of fatalism, that they chose to return home and accept whatever end the sultan decreed. They were ordered to enter the harbor at night so that their arrival should not excite the masses. Already news of the defeat had sparked violence, as Turkish mobs attacked Christian merchants. What might they have done with the sight of the armada limping back into port to inspire them?

The chill between the two Ottoman commanders as reported by European chroniclers is recorded in Ottoman history as blowing up once they were shipboard and headed home. According to Peçevi, "The two inculpated each other and the Kapudan Pasha turned to the artillerymen and said: 'Take the serdar, put him on the mouth of a cannon and fire.' And the men of the fleet put the blame on the serdar. Thus, after having uselessly lost much treasure and many soldiers, they returned ignominiously to Constantinople, where the serdar was stripped of the post of Vizier."[7] Mustapha might have been grateful that he was allowed to live at all. He died while visiting Mecca in 1568–1569.[8]

In contrast, Piali Pasha was allowed to continue in military office, no doubt because of his blood connections to Suleiman, and later, after Selim took the throne, because of his alliance to the Grand Vizier Sokollu. He was promoted to vizier in 1568, and in 1570 he was among the commanders when the Ottomans invested Cyprus. His insufficient savagery in prosecuting the war and failure to achieve a quick victory saw him recalled to Constantinople. He was not at Lepanto. He died in 1576 and is buried in the Piali Pasha mosque in Constantinople, a building he had commissioned.

Uludj Ali continued as beylerbey of Algiers, where he played off the interests of Spain and those of the Moriscos, who hoped, in vain, to get fellow Muslims from abroad to help them in their final revolt. Uludj Ali accepted what amounted to bribe money from Spain to remain neutral — a stance he was likely to take regardless — while placing no impediment before those who wished to help the rebels in Granada. Indeed, it was a chance for him to get rid of some of the local hotheads — another plus for him.

He commanded the Ottoman left flank at Lepanto and through superior skills managed to feint and to evade the boats under Gianandrea Doria, thus marking the only small upside for the Ottoman fleet that day. Uludj Ali became Kapudan Pasha following Lepanto with the name Kiliç Ali Pasha. He continued harrying the Christian Mediterranean for some years afterward, most notably in recapturing Tunis for Selim in 1576. In time he retired from the sea for good, honored as the last of the Khairedihn Barbarossa's great lieutenants. His death in 1587 is variously reported as the result of overexertion in the arms of a slave girl (against the express advice of his doctor) or, less pleasantly, of poison administered by a Christian slave. Or possibly of a cutthroat razor in the hands of a barber he trusted too much. His estate contained over a half million gold pieces and thirteen hundred slaves, all of which went to the state treasury. He is buried in the Kiliç Ali Paşa mosque in Constantinople, built for him by the architect Sinan. Back in Italy, his hometown of La Castella erected a statue in his honor.

Lepanto was Gianandrea Doria's last significant action. He was later appointed Spain's naval Commander in Chief for the Mediterranean; and to the extent his contentious actions of that day would permit, he enjoyed the glory that all veterans of Lepanto enjoyed. He was in Madrid for a few years, was made a Knight of St. James, and gave generously to the Augustinians. In 1601 he failed to retake Algiers, after which his services were no longer required by Spain. That he had been tolerated as long as he had been was likely because of Philip's worry that he might throw his lot (and that of all Genoa) back with France, a worry that had gone back to Philip's father.[9] He died in 1606.

Don Álvaro de Sande continued to serve his king, who granted him the position of *señorío* of the village of Valdefuentes and later the title of Marqués de Piobera. In the year following Malta, he was sent to defend Oran against any Muslim threats. None appeared. He was in Naples in 1570, gathering volunteers for the Holy League; among their number was Cervantes, soon to fight at Lepanto and eventually to write *Don Quixote*. Sande, like Piali Pasha, was not present at Lepanto. His final office was as governor of Milan, where he died in 1573.

Ascanio Della Corgna did not return to prison — it helped that Pius IV died soon after the Malta siege. Instead, Don Garcia sent him to Madrid, both to claim the respect he deserved and to report on the state of post-siege Malta and what it would need to recover.[10] He was deputed to command a contingent of Germans if the Ottomans had returned to Malta in 1566.[11] He helped create the initial designs for the city of Valletta, but would not live to see them executed. He was the subject of one of many overwrought encomia that came after the siege:

> Had the cruel Scythian, who espied the Pillars of
> Hercules, and, almost as conqueror
> Overlaid our sea with so many ships
> That he filled the world with rumor and fear,
> Not had, against his bold intentions,
> Your ready hand and valor, my Lord,
> He would by now — may all men praise you!
> Have planted the great prize of Malta in Thrace.[12]

In 1571 he was named the Holy League's field master general prior to the battle of Lepanto, a post he held at the time of his death from fever two months after that battle. His body was returned first to Rome, where, at the pope's orders (*mudanza de fortuna!*), it lay in state for six days, then was carried overland to his native Perugia. Bells tolled in each town as the cortege passed by, and when he was finally laid to rest, one of his pallbearers was Vincenzo Anastagi.

Anastagi himself continued to serve the Order in various capacities on Malta and elsewhere.[13] He might have risen very high indeed, but in 1586 he was murdered by a fellow knight, in circumstances that have never been adequately explained.[14]

Romegas seemed poised for greatness as well. He was present at Lepanto, commanding the Maltese contingent, and by all accounts served the order and his religion well. In 1571, Gregory XIII made him prior of Ireland, a post that appears not to have required actually going to that pleasant island. War and such concerns did force him to make the rounds of the Mediterranean by land and sea, notably in attacking the Huguenots in southern France. Politics were his downfall. In 1581, Italian and Spanish knights, alarmed at the strict laws of the new grand master La Cassière, attempted a coup that made Romegas, as second in the Order's hierarchy, the de facto grand master. The pope soon ordered both men and their backers to Rome to explain themselves. The factions were the talk of the city for a season, and the pope eventually ruled in favor of La Cassière. Shortly thereafter Romegas died of a fever (rumors of poisoning naturally arose, but were officially denied). He was buried with full honors in Rome's Trinità dei Monti. Brantôme, who knew him, later wrote: "It was a great shame that this great captain, first among those after Valette, that he was not to become Grand Master, for he would have accomplished great things."[15]

Sir Oliver Starkey fell on hard times. Deprived of English benefices and rent, his lot was one of poverty. A few letters dating from after the siege show pitiful requests for money owed and requests to return home to England (these starting from before the siege began).[16] He appears to have died in 1588, and for centuries it was believed that he was buried in the Cathedral of St. John in the same chamber as Valette, a chamber reserved for grand masters, with Starkey the only exception. As if to toss one more indignity on the man, twentieth-century scholarship has blasted this story as well. His burial site is unknown, but it is said that his spirit still makes itself known in his final home in Malta, now the site of the Russian Centre for Science and Culture.[17]

Lascaris did well. Valette sent him to Rome, where "he arrived the fourteenth day of November, then on the ensuing day he kissed the feet of the Pope."[18] He was also baptized at this time. All this and a papal annuity would see out his unremarkable days. Balbi writes of having visited him outside Naples, presumably to help in the details on the writing of his book. (Balbi also seems to suggest that he was not a genuine Lascaris, but took the name.)[19] A century later, another Lascaris, Giovanni Paolo, would be named grand master of the Order.

Without question the most controversial figure to come out of the Great Siege is Don Garcia de Toledo. In the immediate aftermath of the siege, his reputation was high, but dropped soon after. He had not sought glory, and he didn't get it. In a public address with the Spanish cardinal present, Valette praised God and the knights for victory over the infidel. He did not mention the Spanish at all. In private meetings with this same cardinal, he criticized the viceroy for not having taken the matter in hand sooner. People in the Spanish court were beginning to talk about Don Garcia, and not with affection:

November 8, 1565, Phayre to Cecil: "Don Garcia has come back to Messina without taking so much as an oar of the Turks."[20]

November 17, 1565, Phayre to Cecil: "Don Garcia is at the mouth of the Archipelago with all his galleys waiting for sixty of the Turkish galleys. The strangers say that he will do little good in all his life upon the sea."[21]

December 6, 1565, Phayre to Cecil: "The Grand Master has protested to forsake Malta if by January he be not well succoured. Don Garcia De Toledo has lost almost all his reputation."[22]

Pallavicino Rangone, mentioned earlier, went so far as to tell the pope that he, Rangone, had been so disgusted by the viceroy's pusillanimity in the period leading up to the *Gran Soccorso*, that he had threatened the man to his face with assassination.[23] (If true, this shows either remarkable forbearance on Toledo's part, or serious cowardice. In either case, it shows how freely the man could be abused.)

Among military men, however, Garcia de Toledo ranks high and always has. When the twenty-two-year-old Don John of Austria was tapped to command the Holy League prior to the battle of Lepanto, he actively sought out advice from the aging veteran. Brantôme wrote a glowing encomium.[24] In the later nineteenth century, Jurien de la Gravière, himself an admiral in the French navy and a veteran of Sebastopol, expressed some sympathy for the man's impossible position.[25] Twentieth-century historians have tended to follow suit — Braudel comes down firmly in his camp, and Guilmartin lays out the defense of his action in some detail in his *Gunpowder and Galleys*.[26]

He died quietly in Naples in 1577.

+·+·+·+

A Note on the
Sources and
Acknowledgments

+·+·+·+

Europe followed the siege of Malta closely in the summer of 1565, and reports of greater or lesser accuracy spread across the continent with remarkable speed, and were translated, pirated, retranslated, and eventually and for the most part discarded. The market was proven—sixteenth-century Europe had a fascination with all things Ottoman—and more substantial printed accounts followed soon after the last Muslim ship had left the island. The Frenchman Pierre Gentile de Vendôme published his *Della Historia di Malta* in Italian in 1565, a work that suffers from the haste of its execution. Anton Francesco Cirni (aka Cirni Corso), a prolific author and a member of the Great Relief, based much of his book (*Comentarii d'Antonfrancesco Cirni Corso*, 1567) on his own experiences and on interviews with veterans. Giovanni Antonio Viperano, a Sicilian cleric and literary critic living in Messina during the siege, made his tour of the postsiege island and published *De Bello Melitensi Historia* in 1567. The Genoese spy Bregante appears to have followed the Ottoman fleet and observed events from the Ottoman side, reporting his findings in five crabbed pages for his spymasters in Genoa. His account ends abruptly in July (he would live until 1571) and generally corroborates Western accounts. The most exhaustive near-contemporary account comes from Giacomo Bosio, brother of the influential knight Antonio Bosio, with whose help he gathered the raw material that bolsters the monumental *Dell'Istoria della Sacra Religione et Illustrissima Militia di San Giovanni Gierosolimitano* (1602). The most compelling of accounts, however, is without question by Balbi di Correggio, an Italian mercenary who cobbled his personal experiences and observations into *La Verdadera Relación de todo lo que el año de M.D. LXV ha succedido en la Isla de Malta* (1566 and 1568). There are two English translations, one by Major H. A. R. Balbi (1961) and one by Ernle Bradford (1965).

Ottoman accounts are few, in part because no one likes to dwell on a defeat, in part because the Ottomans were not a print culture (printing presses were banned until 1729). Selaniki and Peçevi, two historians, wrote years after the fact, and Malta was only a portion of their overall work. Both authors are long overdue for translations in full, though happily, relevant sections have made it into Italian.

The siege was the subject of the moment, and as such, mention of it can be found in archives across Europe. Much of the writing is trivial, redundant, or just plain wrong, but there are still small, and perhaps large, gems to be found. Many of those already unearthed have found their way into the secondary literature. Two modern works that have taken great advantage of these nuggets are Fernand Braudel's *The Mediterranean and the World of Philip II* and Kenneth Setton's *The Papacy and the Levant*. In addition to making for compelling reading in their own right, they have provided a treasury of source notes enough for a respectable library of new books. For the siege of Malta in particular, no serious student can ignore Stephen C. Spiteri's encyclopedic account, *The Great Siege: Knights vs Turks, MDLXV—Anatomy of a Hospitaller Victory*. Add to these the many and varied explorations and observations of other scholars, and it quickly becomes clear that the siege of Malta is a story still open for retelling.

For fueling the current effort, I owe thanks to the staff of the New York Public Library, most especially the Rare Book Room; New York University; Butler Library of Columbia University; Rockefeller Library of the Metropolitan Museum of Art; Frick Art Reference Library; Library of the Museum of Natural History in New York; Newberry Library of Chicago; Bibliothèque Nationale de France; the Library of Congress; Valérie Guillot, of the library of the Magistral Library of the Sovereign Order of Malta, Rome; Falvey Library of Villanova University; Alexander Library of Rutgers University; Northwestern University Library; Firestone Library of Princeton University; Walsh Library of Seton Hall University; the staff of Westport (Connecticut) Public Library; Leighann Cazier of Millburn (New Jersey) Public Library;

and most particularly, Patrice Kane and Vivian Shen of special collections in the William D. Walsh Library of Fordham University. For help in tracking down and forwarding some hopelessly obscure material, Fausto Amalberti and Prof. Giuseppe Felloni of Genoa; Stewart Tiley of St. John's College, Oxford; Trent Larsen of Brigham Young University; William Thierens (whose website, http://melitensiawth.com, provides a wealth of Maltese material from rare scholarly journals); Maria Smali and Irini Solomonidi of Gennadius Library, Greece; Thomas Jabine of the Library of Congress; Mary Paris of Amherst, Massachusetts; Barry Lawrence Ruderman of BLR Rare Maps (La Jolla, California); and Pierre Joppen of Paulus Swaen Old Maps (St. Petersburg, Florida).

For help in disentangling some of the more clotted sixteenth-century Spanish, French, Italian, and Turkish, Prof. María Antonia Garcés, Prof. Gretchen van Slyke, Prof. William J. Connell, Prof. Nicola Melis, Adela Jabine, and Andreas Bacalao; for answers to obscure questions, advice, criticism, and general encouragement, Judge Giovanni Bonello, Prof. Steven C. Spiteri, Prof. Geoffrey Parker, Prof. John Guilmartin, Prof. Helen Vella Bonavita, and Andrew Lownie. Particular thanks are due to Niccolò Capponi and Prof. Emrah Safa Gürkan, whose close reading of the manuscript caught any number of errors of fact and challenged a few interpretations. Any remaining errors of detail or of translation are my fault entirely.

For the transformation of the manuscript into a book, thanks must go to Stephen Hull and Susan Abel at UPNE, to the copyeditor Elizabeth Forsaith, and to my agent, John Rudolph of Dystel and Goderich.

Finally, for living alongside the entire project for far too long, all gratitude goes to my wife, Blacknall Allen.

+·+·+·+

Notes

+·+·+·+

INTRODUCTION

1. Porter, *Knights of Malta* (London: Longmans Green, 1883), 340–41.

2. Mustafa Gelal-Zade, in Rossi, "Assedio e conquista di Rodi nel 1522," 26.

3. Lütfi Paşa, *Das Asafname* (Berlin: Mayer & Mueller, 1910), 27.

4. Ibid.

5. Giovio, *Commentario de le cose de'Turchi* (Rome, 1541), 43.

6. Suleiman had wanted to send the grisly object to the doge of Venice, but the Venetian ambassador assured him that Venice, at least, was already quite impressed with him.

7. The Serbian prisoners were especially appreciated for their presumed skills at maintaining waterworks. To this day, that region outside Constantinople is called Belgrade Forest.

I. THE SIEGE OF RHODES, 1521

Epigraph: Brockman, *Two Sieges of Rhodes*, 115.

1. Iacomo Bosio, *Dell'Istoria della Sacra Religione*, pt. 2 (Rome: Stamperia Apost. Vaticana, 1594), 543.

2. Marino Sanuto, *I Diarii di Marino Sanuto*, vol. 33 (Venice: Visentini, 1892), 417.

3. Ibid., 419. Venice seized his goods and charged him in absentia with treason.

4. Iacobo Fontano, *De Bello Rhodio* (Rome: Francesco Minizio Calvo, 1524), 17.

5. Patrick Balfour Kinross, *The Ottoman Centuries* (New York: W. Morrow, 1977), 176.

6. Numbers on the Ottoman side vary wildly. See Kenneth Setton, *Papacy and the Levant*, vol. 3 (Philadelphia: American Philosophical Society, 1984), 205.

7. Luttrell, "The Hospitallers of Rhodes," 88–89.

8. Ludwig Forrer, *Die Osmanische Chronik des Rüstem Pascha*, (Leipzig, 1923), 63.

9. Ibid.

10. Bosio, *Dell'Istoria*, 543.

11. Sanuto, *I Diarii*, vol. 33, 419. (He claims it was 490 ducats.)

12. Jacques de Bourbon, *La Grande et Merveilleuse et très cruelle oppugnation de la noble cité de Rhodes prinse naguères par Sultan Seliman à présent Grand turcq, ennemy de la très sainte foy catholique rédigée par escript par excellent et noble chevalier Frère Jacques Bastard de Bourbon, Commandant de Sanct Maulviz, Doysemon, et Fonteyne au prieure de Paris* (Paris: Pierre Vidoue, 1526), 21r.

13. Eric Brockman, "D'Amaral: Martyr or Traitor?," *Annales de l'Ordre Souverain Militaire de Malte* 24, no. 1 (1966): 18–25

14. Sir Nicholas Roberts to the Earl of Surrey, May 15, 1523, Messina, in Whitworth Porter, *A History of the Knights of Malta* (London: Longmans, Green, 1883), 712–13.

15. Forrer, *Die Osmanische Chronik*, 65.

16. Bourbon, *La Grande et Merveilleuse*, 37v.

17. Sanuto, *Diarii*, vol. 29, col. 391.

18. Hafiz, in Porter, *Knights of Malta*, 378.

19. Ettore Rossi, *Assedio e Conquista di Rodi nel 1522 secondo le relazioni edite ed inedite dei Turchi* (Rome: Libreria di scienze e lettere, 1927), 40. General in Chief Ahmed Pasha held various sacred relics, notably the mummified arm of St. John, for a ransom of other goods worth thirty thousand ducats. Sanuto, vol. 34, 9–11. Even the Ottoman historian Gelal-Zade called him "a bad character" (Rossi, *Assedio e Conquista di Rodi*, 29).

20. Suleiman, in Joseph Von Hammer-Purgstall, *Histoire de l'Empire Ottoman depuis son origine jusqu'à nos jours*, trans. J. J. Hellert (Paris: Dochet, 1841), 41.

2. THE ROAD TO MALTA, 1522–1530

Epigraph: Desiderius Erasmus, *Opera Omnia Desiderii Erasmi Roterodami: Recognita et Adnotatione Critica*, pt. 3, vol. 5 (Amsterdam: North-Holland, 1969), 48.

1. Sanuto, vol. 33, 74.

2. Ernest Charrière, *Négociations de la France dans le Levant*, vol. 1 (Paris: Imprimerie Impérial, 1848), 96–102; Setton, *Papacy and the Levant*, vol. 3, 216.

3. Sanuto, vol. 34, 98. See also Victor Millia-Milanes, *Venice and Hospitaller Malta 1530–1798* (Aldershot, UK: Ashgate/Variorum, 1999), 2.

4. Jean Quintin d'Autun, *The Earliest Description of Malta* (Sliema, MT: De Bono Enterprises, 1980), 30.

5. Ibid., xv. This was partly by choice, Malta having opted in the fourteenth century for the cash crop of cotton rather than wheat. See John M. McManamon, "Maltese Seafaring in Mediaeval and Post-Mediaeval Times," *Mediterranean Historical Review* 18, no. 1 (June 2003): 40.

6. Quintin d'Autun, *The Earliest Description of Malta*, 40.

7. Nicholas de Nicolay, *Dans l'empire de Soliman le Magnifique* (Paris: Presses du CNRS, 1989), 76. Nicolas de Nicolay, "Navigations, Peregrinations and Voyages Made into Turky by Nicolas Nicholay Daulphinois," in *A Collection of Voyages and Travel, Consisting of Authentic Writers . . .*, trans. T. Washington the Younger (London: Thomas Osborne, 1745), 565. Before gaining its independence, Malta would be ruled by both France and England.

8. Bosio, *Dell'Istoria*, vol. 2, 29. See also Victor Mallia-Milanes, "Charles V's Donation of Malta to the Order of St. John," in *Peregrinationes: Acta et Documenta: Carlo V e Mercurino di Gattinara suo Gran Cancelliere*, vol. 2 (Malta: Accademia Internazionale Melitense, 2001), 22–23; and Ettore Rossi, *Storia di Tripoli e della Tripolitania* (Rome: Istituto per l'Oriente, 1968), 126.

9. Royall Tyler, *The Emperor Charles V* (Fair Lawn, NJ: Essential Books, 1956), 20.

10. Rawdon Brown, *Calendar of State Papers and Manuscripts Existing in the Archives and Collections of Venice 1520–1526*, vol. 3 of Setton, *Papacy and the Levant (1204–1571)*, no. 956, 413 n. 229.

11. In June 1525, the pope felt it necessary to send an emissary to Spain "a persuaderlo fazi Guerra contro Turchi," to persuade Charles to make war against the Turk. Sanuto, vol. 39, 102, cf. 130, 157.

12. Ibid., 130. The assumption that this would be Malta, as earlier promised, was alluded to in another letter of June 1525. Sanuto, *Diarii*, vol. 39, 115. Elsewhere it was suggested that L'Isle-Adam asked to go to Spain; Sanuto, *Diarii*, vol. 39, 128–29.

13. Porter, *Knights of Malta*, 14.

14. Sanuto, vol. 34, 9–11.

15. Forrer, *Die Osmanische Chronik*, 67.

16. Minting was a privilege of the Jews of Cairo, and the master coiner Abraham de Castro refused to comply. He instead escaped to Constantinople with the news of Ahmed Pasha's treachery. When Castro's absence was noted, other Jews were taken hostage and would have been executed had not Ahmed been overcome and killed shortly afterward. Ever since, Egyptian Jews have celebrated the Purim of Cairo.

17. Shai Har-El, *Struggle for Domination in the Middle East: The Ottoman-Mamluk War, 1485–91* (Leiden: Brill, 1995), 120.

18. Porter, *Knights of Malta*, 385.

19. Ion Ursu, *La politique orientale de François I, 1515–1547* (Paris: H. Champion, 1908), 31. Cf. Sanuto, vol. 58, 96. Francis's position was, in the best French tradition, both totally logical and utterly contradictory. During the siege of Rhodes, he had been one of the few crowned heads who actually had attempted to relieve the knights. And when, as Charles's prisoner, he was told of the conquests of Granada, he reportedly said, "And these Musulmans? They were not driven out? Then everything is still to be done!" Perhaps he was sincere. Louis Bertrand, *The History of Spain*, 2nd ed. (London: Eyre and Spottiswoode, 1956), 147.

20. Charrière, *Négociations*, vol. 1, 117.

21. Ibid.

22. Ursu, *Politique Orientale*, 33–35.

23. Charles V to J. Hannart, Rome, April 17–18, 1536, in Karl Lanz, *Correspondenz des Kaisers Karl V.*, vol. 2, no. 428 (Leipzig: F. A. Brockhaus, 1544), 223–29.

24. Pietro Bragadino, Pera (Beyoğlu), Constantinople, December 29, 1525, in Sanuto, *Diarii*, vol. 40, 824.

25. Judith Hook, *The Sack of Rome, 1527* (London: Methuen, 1973), 155.

26. Judith Hook believes he knew in advance and even approved of the affair, perhaps without guessing just how far out of hand it would get (ibid.). He disclaimed responsibility for what happened, but appears to have been genuinely shaken. See also, however, Ferdinand Gregorovius, *Geschichte der Stadt Rom im Mittelalter*, vol. 8 (Stuttgart: J. Cotta, 1872), 522.

27. Bosio, *Dell'Istoria*, vol. 2, 54.

28. H. A. R. Balbi, "Some Unpublished Records on the Siege of Malta, 1565," *Institute of Historical Research, Malta*, no. 6 (1937), 16. Bulletin.

3. IN SERVICE TO THE EMPIRE, 1531–1540

Epigraphs: Brantôme, *Œuvres complètes*, vol. 2: *Grands Capitaines Estrangers* (1866), 41; ibid., 67.

1. Jérome Maurand, *Itinéraire de J. Maurand* (Paris: Ernst Leroux, 1901), 153.

2. Bosio, *Dell'Istoria*, vol. 3, 105.

3. English reaction was that the raid would be "either a very great good or a very great evil for Christendom" depending on whether they could keep the city. Chapuys to Charles V. Henry VIII, October 24, 1531, London, in *Letters and Papers, Foreign and Domestic, Henry VIII*, vol. 5: 1531–1532 (London: Her Majesty's Stationery Office, 1880), 228.

4. Edouard Petit, *André Doria: Un amiral condottiere au XVIe siècle* (Paris: Maison Quantin, 1887), 119. Petit claims that Doria was only in it for the money (sixty thousand *écus* annually) and ignored Francis's assurance that he would return to Genoa all its ancient rights and privileges. Fernand Braudel, *The Mediterranean and the Mediterranean World in the Age of Philip II* (New York: Harper and Row, 1973), 500ff.

5. Charrière, *Négociations*, vol. 1, 234; Setton, *Papacy*, vol. 3, 36.

6. Jean Pierre Edmond Jurien de la Gravière, *Doria et Barberousse* (Paris: Plon, 1886), 209.

7. There are other accounts of how Aroudj came to Algiers, accounts involving treachery and murder. See Svatopluk Soucek, "The Rise of the Barbarossas in North Africa," *Archivum Ottomanicum* 3 (1971): 240–51; Andrew C. Hess, *Forgotten Frontier* (Chicago: University of Chicago Press, 1978), 63ff.

8. Francisco López de Gómara, "Cronica de los muy nombrados Omiches y Haradin Barbarrojas," in *Memorial Histórico Español*, vol. 6 (Madrid: Real Academia de la Historia, 1853), 487–88.

9. Kâtip Çelebi, *The History of the Maritime Wars of the Turks*, trans. J. Mitchell, ed. Svatopluk Soucek (Princeton, NJ: Markus Wiener, 2012), 79.

10. John B. Wolf, *The Barbary Coast* (New York: Norton, 1982), 10.

11. Gürkan, *Center of the Frontier*, 147–48.

12. The finer distinctions of this title are discussed in Elizabeth Zachariadou, ed., *The Kapudan Pasha; His Office and His Domain* (Rethymno, Crete: Institute for Mediterranean Studies, Crete University Press, 2002).

13. "Basta decir que él teien cinquenta mancebos y sesanta mancesbas." Our source is Captain Ochoa d'Ercilla, a visitor prior to the siege, who also mentions that he was *mas blanco que negro* (the legitimate heir's mother was a black woman, making him, all else being equal, less desirable as ruler than Muley Hassan) and "effeminate." "Mémoire du capitaine Ochoa d'Ercilla sur les affaires du Roi de Tunis," in *Documents inédits sur l'histoire de l'occupation espagnole en Afrique (1506–1574)*, ed. F. Élie de La Primaudaie (Algiers: Jourdan, 1875), 67–71. Also in *Revue Africaine: Société historique algérienne* (Paris: Challamel Aine, 1875), 268–72.

14. Peçevi, quoted in Svatopluk Soucek, "Naval Aspects of the Ottoman Conquest of Rhodes, Cyprus and Crete," *Studia Islamica*, no. 98/99 (2004): 228. See also Çelebi, *History of the Maritime Wars*, 139.

15. Charles V to Muley Hassan, November 14, 1534, Madrid, in *Memorial Histórico Español: Colección de documentos, opusculos y antiguedades, que publica la real Academia de la Historia*, vol. 6 (Madrid: Imprenta de la Real Academia de la Historia, 1853), 516.

16. Most, alas, already spoken for. Howard J. Ehrlichman, *Conquest, Tribute and Trade: The Quest for Precious Metals and the Birth of Globalization* (Amherst, NY: Prometheus Books, 2010), 198–99.

17. Guillaume de Montoiche, "Voyage et Expédition de Charles-Quint au Pays de Tunis de 1535," in *Collections des voyages des souverains des Pays-Bas*, ed. Louis Prosper Gachard (Brussels: Hayez, 1881), 337.

18. Forrer, *Die Osmanische Chronik*, 93–94.

19. The Emperor to His Sister the Queen, July 26, 1535, Tunis, in *Documents inédits relatifs à la conquête de Tunis*, ed. Emile Gachet (Brussels: F. Hayez, 1848), 35.

20. Montoiche, *Voyage et expédition*, 359.

21. The *Santa Anna* was the wonder of her age. Built in France in 1522, just before the surrender at Rhodes, she was an ironclad carrack, possibly the first of her kind, and was large enough to accommodate five hundred marines as well as the crew needed to sail her. Fifty cannons defended her. On board were three smithies, several bread ovens, and even a windmill to grind flour. She was decommissioned in 1540 by order of Grand Master D'Homedes, possibly out of jealousy over her captain's many successes. Bosio, *Dell'Istoria*, vol. 3, 150.

22. Forrer, *Die Osmanische Chronik*, 94.

23. Charles V to Juan Pardo de Tavera, March 7 and 31, Archivo de Simancas, Valladolid, Colección Estado 638, 77, 81, 95–96, in James Tracy, *Emperor Charles V, Impresario of War: Campaign Strategy, International Finance, and Domestic Politics* (Cambridge: Cambridge University Press, 2002), 172; John F. Guilmartin, *Gunpowder and Galleys*, 2nd ed. (Annapolis: Naval Institute Press, 2003), 77–78.

24. Adrien Berbrugger, "Négociations entre Hassan Aga et le Comte d'Alcaudete, Gouverneur d'Oran 1541–1542," *Revue Africaine* 9 (1865): 379–85.

25. Bosio, *Dell'Istoria*, 204. Hadji Khalifa gives a lengthy account of Charles's demands. René Basset, *Documents Musulmans sur le Siège d'Alger* (Paris: Ernest Leroux, 1890), 39–40.

26. Nicolas Durand de Villegaignon, *Caroli V Imperatoris Expeditio in Africam ad Argieram* (Antwerp: Ioannes Steelsius, 1542), 375r.

27. Basset, *Documents Musulmans*, 23.

4. WAR AT SEA, 1541–1550

Epigraph: Rossi, "L'Assedio di Malta," 151.

1. Maurand, *Itinéraire de J Maurand*, 329.

2. Ibid., 327.

3. *Gazavat-i Hayreddin Pasa* Supplément Turc 1186, fols. 2a–3b, 4b–5a, Bibliothèque Nationale, cited in Christine Isom-Verhaaren, *Allies with the Infidel* (London: Tauris, 2011), 126.

4. Richard Knolles, *The Generall Historie of the Turkes*, 2nd ed. (Oxford, UK: Adam Islip, 1610). Or perhaps they did not. (Knolles said Polin asked the corsair to keep his men at bay to ensure that the Janissaries did not sack the town.)

5. M. Henry, *Documents relatifs au Séjour*, in J-J. Champollion-Figeac, ed., *Documents historiques inédits tirés des collections manuscrites de la Bibliothèque royale* . . . , vol. 2, (Paris: Imprimerie Imperial, 1847), 518–19. Cf. J. Bérenger, *La collaboration militaire franco ottomane à l'époque de la Renaissance*, in *Revue international de l'histoire militaire* 68 (Commission Française d'Histoire Militaire, 1987), 56.

6. Maurand, *Itinéraire de Jerome Maurand*, xxxii. See also Charrière, *Négociations*, vol. 1, 567. For more on their reception, see Ursu, *Politique Orientale*, 146–47.

7. "Ceste flotte à bande ramée / Dont le vent en poulpe est si doulx, / C'est Barbarousse et son armée / Qui vient nous secourir treztous." M. Henry, *Documents Relatifs au Séjour*, 566. See also Christine Isom-Verhaaren, "'Barbarossa and His Army Who Came to Succor All of Us': Ottoman and French Views of Their Joint Campaign of 1543–1544," *French Historical Studies* 30, no. 3, (summer 2007), 395–426.

8. M. Henry, *Documents Relatifs au Séjour*, 566. See also Isom-Verhaaren, "Barbarossa and

His Army," and Aldo Galotta, "Il Gazavat-I Hayreddin Paşa Pars Secunda e la spedizione in francia di Hayreddin Barbarossa (1543–1544)," in *Studies in Ottoman History in Honour of Professor V. C. Ménage* (Istanbul: ISIS Press, 1994).

9. Pierre de Bordeille Brantôme, *Œuvres Complètes*, vol. 2, bk. 1 (Paris 1858–1895), 66.

10. "Barbarossa being cleane gone, the Spaignardes, that wer yn Naples and yn Sardine, comme all ynto Lombardye." Nicholas Wotton to Sir William Paget, July 30, 1544, Camp at Saint-Dizier, in *Calendar of State Papers, Foreign Series, of the Reign of Henry VIII*, pt. 5, vol. 10 (London, 1949), 18.

11. E. Hamilton Currey, *Seawolves of the Mediterranean* (London: John Murray, 1910), 217. Cf. Paolo Giovio, *Elogi degli uomini illustri* (Turin: Einaudi, 2006), 919.

12. Stephen C. Spiteri, *The Great Siege: Knights versus Turks MDLXV: Anatomy of a Hospitaller Victory* (Tarxien, MT: Gutenberg Press, 2006), 220; Bosio, *Dell'Istoria*, vol. 3, 85.

13. Brantôme, *Œuvres complètes*, vol. 7, 248.

14. Antonfrancesco Cirni, *Commentarii d'Antonfrancesco Cirni Corso, ne quali si discrive la Guerra ultima di Francia, la celebratione del Concilio Tridentino, il socorso d'Orano, l'impresa del Pignone, e Historia dello assedio di Malta diligentissimeamente raccolta insieme con altre cose notablii* (Rome: Giulio Accolto, 1567), 37v.

15. Bosio, *Dell'Istoria*, vol. 3, 243. See also Mallia-Milanes, "Frà Jean de la Valette 1495–1568: A Reappraisal," in *The Maltese Cross*, ed. T. Cortis (Malta: University Publications, 1995), 116.

16. The price of slaves, like any commodity, could fluctuate wildly. "And to reduce this Misfortune to a Proverb, some parted with their new taken Slaves for an Onion per head," in Joseph Morgan, *Complete History of Algiers* (London: Bettenham, 1731), 305. Robert Davis puts the market bottom at 1544, following a particularly successful raid on Naples. Davis, *Christian Slaves, Muslim Masters* (New York: Palgrave Macmillan, 2004), 112–13. As to Kust Ali, he got worse than he gave. In 1554 Valette was sailing off the coast of Pasaro in Sicily when he ran into his old captor. A short battle later, Valette had the man chained to a bench, where a few years later he died, presumably of exposure and exhaustion.

17. Bosio, *Dell'Istoria*, vol. 3, 309.

18. Victor Mallia-Milanes, "Frà Jean de la Valette 1495–1568: A Reappraisal," in *The Maltese Cross*, ed. T Cortis (Malta: Malta University Publishers, 1995), 117–29. See also Bosio, *Dell'Istoria*, vol. 3, 255–56, for Valette's petition.

19. Brantôme, *Œuvres complètes*, vol. 2, 68.

20. Cirni, *Commentarii d'Antonfrancesco Cirni* (Rome: Giulio Accolto, 1567), 71v.

21. Setton, *Papacy and the Levant*, vol. 3, 534.

22. Ibid.; cf. Diego de Fuentes, *Conquista de Africa* (Antwerp: Ph. Nuto, 1570), 24v.

23. Setton, *Papacy and the Levant*, vol. 3, 534.

24. Sir John Masone to the Council, May 10, 1551, Tours, France, in *Calendar of State Papers, Foreign Series of the Reign of Edward the VI* (henceforth CSPFS, *Edward VI*): *1547–1553*, 103.

25. Çelebi, *History of the Maritime Wars*, 122. Other accounts say nothing of the stream.

26. Sir Richard Morysine to Cecil, May 12, 1551, Augsburg, Germany, in *CSPFS, Edward VI: 1547–1553*, 105.

27. The quote appears in various forms in secondary literature (Currey, *Seawolves of the Mediterranean*). I have not been able to find its first use.

28. Bosio, *Dell'Istoria*, vol. 3, 237, 369. Turgut had no love for Don Garcia de Toledo either.

The corsair's nephew Hassan Rais Esse had been an official at Mahdia when Don Garcia seized it (ibid., 270).

29. Eugenio Alberi, *Relazioni degli ambasciatori veneti* (Florence: Clio, 1840), ser. 3, vol. 1, 70. Ottoman historian Mustafa Ali in Christine Isom-Verhaaren, "Süleyman and Mihrimah: The Favorite's Daughter," *Journal of Persianate Studies* 4 (2011): 74.

30. Peter Vannes to the Council England, August 15, 1551, Venice, Italy, in *CSPFS, Edward VI: 1547–1553*, 159.

31. Nicolay, *Dans l'empire de Soliman*, 77; Washington, *Navigations, Peregrinations*, 565. Presumably, the bronze Marcus Aurelius statue on the Campidoglio is meant. The garden as a whole is discussed in Vincenzo Bonello's monograph, "Il ninfeo del giardino di d'Omedes," a copy of which his son Giovanni Bonello was kind enough to provide to me.

32. Bosio, *Dell'Istoria*, vol. 3, 254. To give d'Homedes his due, Doria was himself under orders and en route to reinforce Mahdia with arms and men (Setton, *Papacy and the Levant*, vol. 3, 554), which suggests that other targets were always possible, or at the very least that Charles was trying to cover as many bets as possible during that uncertain summer.

33. Setton, *Papacy and the Levant*, vol. 3, 554

34. Roger Ascham, *The English Works of Roger Ascham, preceptor to Queen Elizabeth* (London: White, Cochran, 1815), 372.

35. Nicolay, *Dans l'empire de Soliman*, 76; Washington, *Navigations, Peregrinations*, 565.

36. Andrew Vella, "The Order of Malta and the Defence of Tripoli 1530–1551," *Melita Historica* 6, no. 4 (1975): 367.

37. Dr. Wotton and Sir Richard Morysine to the Council, September 1, 1551, Augsburg, Germany, in *CSPFS, Edward VI: 1547–1553*, 165.

38. Ascham, *English Works*, 374.

39. Ibid., 9.

5. DJERBA, 1551–1560

Epigraph: The phrase is first recorded in Gonzalo Correas, *Vocabulario de refranes y frases proverbiales* (1627; Madrid, 1906), 203.

Similarly, the soldier and poet Garcilaso de la Vega (1503–1536) wrote in his *Eglogo II*, "O patria lagrimosa y como vuelves / Los ojos a los Gelves, sospirando" ("Weeping and sighing, O homeland, / As you turn your eyes to Djerba." He was writing of the 1510 disaster when four thousand men died trying to take the island for Spain. Garcilaso also fought at Tunis in 1534 and wrote of the disaster (see Prescott, *Ferdinand and Isabella*, vol. 2, 455, and Prescott, *History of Philip II*, vol. 2, 327–33).

Nor was it just the Spanish who had problems with Djerba: "An old Maltese nautical term *Taqa'żorba* (the modern day meaning is equivalent to 'find oneself at the lowest ebb of one's strength'), originally seems to have meant 'being driven helplessly to the nethermost part of the Mediterranean.'" Djerba is designated as Zorba on numerous old maps. JosAnn Cutajar and George Cassar, "Malta and the Sixteenth Century Struggle for the Mediterranean," in *The Great Siege 1565: Separating Fact from Fiction*, ed. G. Cassar (Valletta, MT: Sacra Militia Foundation, 2005), 30.

1. Bosio, *Dell'Istoria*, vol. 3, 332.

2. Roger Ascham, *The English Works*, 9.

3. Braudel, *Mediterranean*, 927; Lanz, *Correspondenz des Kaisers Karl V.*, vol. 3, 576.

4. Stanley Fiorini, "Mattew alias Josep Callus: Patriot or Opportunist?" *Treasures of Malta*, vol. 12, no. 3. Also see Godfrey Wettinger, "Early Maltese Popular Attitudes to Government of St. John," *Melita Historica* 6, no. 3 (1974): 255–78.

5. Jacopo Bonfadio, *Le lettere e una scrittura burlesca* (Rome: Bonacci, 1978), 149.

6. Raffaele Bracco, *Il Principe Giannandrea: Doria Patriae Libertatis Conservator* (Genoa: Scuola Graf. Opera SS. Vergine di Pompei, 1960), 91–92. Vilma Borghesi, *Vita del Principe Giovanni Andrea Doria scritta da lui medesimo incompleta* (Genoa: Compagnia dei Librai, 1997).

7. Ogier Ghiselin de Busbecq, *Epistolae Quattuor* (Frankfurt: Andrea Wecheli, 1594), 290; Ogier Ghiselin de Busbecq, *The Turkish Letters of Ogier Ghiselin de Busbecq*, trans. Edward Seymour Foster (Oxford: Clarendon Press, 1968), 231.

8. *Calendar of Letters, Despatches, and State Papers Relating to the Negotiations between England and Spain Preserved in the Archives at Simancas, Vienna, Brussels, and Elsewhere*, vol. 7, ed. Pascual de Gayangos (London: Longman, Green, Longman, and Roberts, 1899), 269.

9. Çelebi, *History of the Maritime Wars*, 68.

10. Seraphim M. Zarb, "A Contemporary Letter Describing the Occupation of Jerba in 1560 by the Christians," *Scientia* 21, no. 2 (April–June 1955): 54–70. The letter is not dated, but it can only have been written sometime in the spring of 1560.

11. Bosio, *Dell'Istoria*, 426.

12. Ibid.

13. Çelebi, *History of the Maritime Wars*, 173.

14. Ibid., 171.

15. Ibid., 179.

16. Alberi, *Relazioni*, ser. 3, vol. 1, 407.

17. Ibid., 189. By 1573, the Venetian ambassador Andrea Badoara referred to him as "a good sailor and valiant soldier." Alberi, *Relazioni*, ser. 3, vol. 3, 365.

18. Busbecq, *Legationis Turcicae*, 224; Forster, *Turkish Letters*, 170.

19. Çelebi, *History of the Maritime Wars*, 163.

20. Ibid., 173.

21. Ibid.

22. Charles Monchicourt, *L'expédition espagnole de 1560 contre l'île de Djerba* (Paris: Ernest Leroux, 1913), 240–41.

23. Alessio Bombaci, "Le Fonti turche della battaglia delle Gerbe," *Rivista degli studi orientali* 19, no. 1 (1941): 207.

24. Setton, *Papacy and the Levant*, vol. 2, 762. He would be ransomed in 1562.

25. Çelebi, *History of the Maritime Wars*, 173.

26. Ibid., 164.

27. René-Aubert de Vertot, *Histoire des chevaliers hospitaliers de S. Jean de Jerusalem*, vol. 3 (Paris: Rolin, 1726), 404.

28. Throckmorton accounts for one boat only. Throckmorton to the Queen, June 30, 1560, Houson, in *CSPFS, Elizabeth*, vol. 4: *1560–1561*, 157.

29. Piali Pasha to Ferhad Aga, 1560, Djerba, in Charrière, *Negotiations*, vol. 2, 612. It is presumably early on, as he is hopeful that the Christians will surrender for lack of water.

30. "There is at Gerbes for general one Don Antonio D'Alvaro, with 2,000 Spaniards and

four months' victuals." Throckmorton to the Queen, June 30, in *Calendar of State Papers, Foreign Series, of the Reign of Elizabeth* (henceforth *CSPFS, Elizabeth*), vol. 3: *1560–1561*, 150.

31. Eugenio Sarrablo Aguareles, "Don Alvaro de Sande y La Orden de Malta," *Revista de Archivos, Bibliotecas y Museos* 61, no. 1 (1955): 54.

32. Alessio Bombaci, "Un Rapporto del Grande Ammiraglio Piyale Pascià a Solimano Sull'Assedio delle Gerbe (1560)," in *Festschrift Friedrich Giese aus Anlass des siebenzigsten Geburtstags überreicht von Freunden und Schülern*, ed. Gotthard Jäschke (Leipzig: Deutsche Gesellschaft für Islamkunde, 1941), 80. Also in *Die Welt des Islams* 23 (1941): 75–83.

33. Zekeriyyāzādé (*The War of Djerba*) mentions two outside wells, a tunnel to one of which Uludj Ali's men discovered, fought over, and filled in. Quoted in Orhan Kologˇu, "Renegades and the Case [*sic*] Ulu/Kili Ali," in *Mediterraneo in Armi* (sec. 15–18), ed. Rossella Cancila, vol. 2, no. 4, *Quaderni Mediterranea: Ricerche storiche Palermo* (Palermo: Associazione Mediterranea, 2007), 530. See also Çelebi, *History of the Maritime Wars*, 164.

34. Busbecq, *Legationis Turcicae*, 226–27; Forster, *Turkish Letters*, 172.

35. Secretary to Cecil, "Intelligences from Sicily," August 22, 1560, Messina, in *CSPFS, Elizabeth*, vol. 3: *1560–1561*, 254. Good intelligence was badly delayed. As late as mid-August, an English diplomat was writing home that "the fortress that the Spaniards keep at Gerbes [Djerba] is yet in their hands, and (as they write from Naples) they doubt not of the keeping of the same. There are other advices that it must fall shortly into the Turk's hands." John Shers to Cecil, in *CSPFS, Elizabeth*, vol. 3: *1560–1561*, 229.

36. Çelebi, *History of the Maritime Wars*, 175–76.

37. Bombaci, *Rapporto*, 83.

38. Commendator Fra Antonio Maria Pagliaro to unknown recipient, August 18, Malta, *CSPFS, Elizabeth*, vol. 3: *1560–1561*, 240.

39. Bombaci, *Le Fonti turche*, 207.

40. The suggestion is there were only six. *CSPFS, Elizabeth*, vol. 3: *1560–1561*, 255. Of the remaining thousand, one hundred and twenty were ransomed in 1562 (in *CSPFS, Elizabeth*, vol. 3: *1562*, 383); many of the rest would be found still pulling oars of the Ottoman navy at the battle of Lepanto. As to springing Sande, Busbecq was not alone: "Salviati, the French Ambassador, has come to confirm the old league between France and the Turk, to whom he presented 100 vestures. A part of his commission is to ransom Don Álvaro Sandi, taken at Gerbes." *CSPFS, Elizabeth*, vol. 4: *1561–1562*, 581. The offer was rebuffed, presumably because Francis was in bad odor since the peace. Cf. Petremol to Charles IX, November 25, 1565, Constantinople, in Charrière, *Négociations*, vol. 2, 562. It was crushing to Sande, whom Busbecq described as a man "of great spirit and of a sanguine disposition and one who knows not fear." Busbecq, *Legationis Turcicae*, 272; Forster, *Turkish Letters*, 216.

41. Uberto Foglietta, *La Vida de Don Álvaro de Sande* (Madrid: Belmonte, 1962), 285.

6. AN ALMOST-PEACEFUL INTERIM, 1561–1564

Epigraph: Charrière, *Négociations*, vol. 2, 75.

1. "Intelligences," August 9, 1561, in *CSPFS, Elizabeth*, vol. 6: *1561–1562*, 241.

2. John Guilmartin, *Gunpowder and Galleys*, 2nd ed. (Annapolis, MD: Naval Institute Press, 2003); Eugenio Sarrablo Aguareles, "Don Álvaro de Sande y La Orden de Malta," *Revista de Archivos, Bibliotecas y Museos*, vol. 61 (1955): 57. English envoys to Venice refer to

120 notables who are returned to Venice in October 1562 (in *CSPFS, Elizabeth*, vol. 4: *1562*, 383). Why they were notable and what their specialized knowledge was is unrecorded.

3. "Advertisements from Italy," August 13, 1561, Milan, in "Elizabeth: August 1561, 16–20," *CSPFS, Elizabeth*, vol. 4: *1561–1562*, 265.

4. "Intelligences," August 13, 1561, Rome, in *CSPFS, Elizabeth*, vol. 4: *1561–1562*, 284.

5. "The Castellan was going into Spain to answer certain information concerning a new fortification about the castle, of great expense, and to small purpose. The corsairs have done much harm, especially in Puglia [Apulia]; where, landing three or four hundred at a time, they took a great number of persons. Visconte Cicala, lately taken by Dragut Rays [*sic*], is well entertained by him, and is put in hope to be shortly dismissed." "Intelligences from Various Places," July 16, 1561, Milan, in *CSPFS, Elizabeth*, vol. 4: *1561–1562*, 194. See also Braudel, *Mediterranean*, 992, and R. C. Anderson, *Naval Wars in the Levant* (Princeton: Princeton University Press, 1952), 14.

6. Throckmorton to Cecil, March 22, 1561, Paris, in *CSPFS, Elizabeth*, vol. 3: *1560–1561*, 34. John Shers to Cecil, February 6, 1561, Venice: "Ascanio Della Corna [*sic*] raises three thousand men to go to Malta to defend that place with the help of the Knights of the Order there, against the Turk's army, which is expected." *CSPFS, Elizabeth*, vol. 3: *1560–1561*, 538.

7. Report from Constantinople to Naples, January 21, 1564 (received March 29, 1564), AGS Estado, legajo 1053, doc. 44 (or 45?), in Emilio Sola, *Despertar al que dormía: Los últimos años de Solimán en la literatura de avisos del Siglo de Oro Español*, Archivo de la Frontera, Centro Europeo para la Difusión de las Ciencias Sociales (CEDCS), 2011, 56–57. http://www.archivodelafrontera.com/wp-content/uploads/2011/07/CLASICOS036.pdf. Report from Constantinople to Messina, March 6, 1564, AGS Estado, legajo 1053, doc. 35, in Sola, *Despertar al que dormía*, 55.

8. Ibid. Another envoy delivered thirdhand gossip ("on good authority") that Suleiman was entering senility: "very old, decrepit and losing his memory, and they treat him like a child." Garci Hernández to Philip II, March 28, 1564, Venice, AGS Estado, legajo 1325, doc. 13, in Sola, *Despertar al que dormía*, 54.

9. Nicolay, *Dans l'empire de Soliman*, 77. Washington, *Navigations, Peregrinations*, 565.

10. Busbecq, *Legationis Turcicae*, 63. Forster, *Turkish Letters*, 49. Busbecq claims to have met a merchant who provided the sultana with love philters derived from unnamed parts of hyenas. The merchant would have had several options. Fifteenth-century philosopher Muḥammad Ibn-Mūsā ad- Damīrī writes that "he" (and presumably she) "who hangs on his person a piece of the vulva of a female hyena will be loved by men" (ad-Damírí, *ad-Damîrí's Ḥayāt al-ḥayawān: A Zoological Lexicon*, vol. 2 (London: Luzac, 1906–1908), 210). Alternatively, Pliny (bk. 28, chap. 27) recommends that women put hyena snout bristles on their lips to attract men.

11. Ascham, *English Works*, 11.

12. Suleiman built a mosque for Cihangir that could be seen from the palace. Caroline Finkel, *Osman's Dream: The History of the Ottoman Empire* (New York: Basic Books, 2005), 140.

13. Busbecq, *Legationis Turcicae*, 97; Forster, *Turkish Letters*, 80.

14. AOM, 91 f78, in Carmella Testa, *Romegas* (Malta: Midsea, 2002), 67. For loss of material, see ibid., 54.

15. Brantôme, *Œuvres complètes*, vol. 4, 129.

16. Blaise de Montluc, *Commentaires de messire Blaise de Montluc* (Paris: Drouart, 1595), 543.

17. Bosio, *Dell'Istoria*, 448.

18. Cirni, *Svccessi dell'armata della Maestà Catolica* (Florence: Lorenzo Torrenti, 1560), 187.

19. Bosio, *Dell'Istoria*, 451.

20. Francesco Balbi da Correggio, *La Verdadera Relación de todo lo que el año de MDLXV ha succedido en la isla de Malta* (Barcelona: Pedro Reigner, 1568), 18v.; Balbi di Correggio, *The Siege of Malta, 1565*, trans. Ernle Bradford (London: Folio Society, 1965), 29.

21. Bosio, *Dell'Istoria*, 471.

22. Ibid., 473.

23. Bosio, *Dell'Istoria*, 471. Balbi (*Verdadera*, 19r.; Bradford, *Siege of Malta*, 29, says the sultana was protected by twenty galleys: "asegurada de veynte galeras"; Bosio (473–74), by twenty cannon: "venti Pezzi rinforzati di bronzo." Bosio seems the more plausible. For a good account of galley tactics at this time, see Thomas Scheban, "A State with an Army—An Army with a State?" in *The 1565 Ottoman Malta Campaign Register* (Malta: Publishers Enterprise Group, 1998), 13–81.

24. "Intelligence from Abroad," Venice, July 29, 1564, in *CSPFS, Elizabeth*, vol. 7: 1564–1565, 183.

25. Cirni, *Successi*, 39r.

26. H. P. Scicluna, "L'Assedio di Malta: Informatione di Malta del 'Rangone,'" *Archivum Melitense* 8, no. 1 (April 1929): 35. Rangone, a veteran soldier and part of the Great Relief of Malta, was also something of a crank. His report, while not inaccurate, was bilious as regards Valette and Don Garcia de Toledo. See Giovanni Bonello, "Pallavicino Ragone: Intemperate Critic of La Valette," in *Histories of Malta*, vol. 9, *Confessions and Transgressions* (Malta: Fondazzjoni Patrimonju Malti, 2000), 58–66.

27. Charrière, *Négociations*, vol. 2, 729. See also Uberto Foglietto, *Istoria di Mons: Vberto Foglietta* (Genoa: G. Pavoni, 1598), 527.

28. Viperano, *De Bello Melitensi Historia* (Perugia: Andrea Bresciano, 1567), 4.

29. Arnold Cassola, *The Great Siege of Malta (1565) and the Istanbul State Archives* (Malta: Said International, 1995), 19.

30. Valette to George Hohenheim, October 9, 1565, Malta, in Porter, *Knights of Malta*, 720.

31. For Ottoman strategic ambitions in the western Mediterranean, see Andrew C. Hess, "The Battle of Lepanto and Its Place in Mediterranean History," *Past and Present* 52 (1972): 543–73.

32. Balbi, *Verdadera*, 22r.; Bradford, *Siege of Malta*, 32. Anton Francesco Cirni, *Commentarii* (40r.) claims that Mehmed II's tomb had inscribed in Arabic and Latin, *Mens erat bellare Rhodum, et superare superbam Italiam*: "His intention was to go to war against Rhodes and overcome proud Italy."

33. For Ottoman ambitions in the western Mediterranean, see Andrew Hess, "The Battle of Lepanto and Its Place in Mediterranean History," *Past and Present* 52 (1972), 543–73 passim.

34. *Colección de documentos inéditos para la historia de España* (henceforth, CODOIN), vol. 29, 54.

35. Bosio, *Dell'Istoria*, vol. 3, 491.

36. Ibid., 490.

37. Ibid., 488.

38. Von Hammer, 103. He should not be confused, though he often is, with Lala Kara Mustafa Pasha, 1510–1580, beylerbey of Damascus, commander of land forces on Cyprus (1570), and briefly, grand vizier. The exalted ancestry is likely bogus.

39. Richard Blackburn, *Journey to the Sublime Porte—The Arabic Memoir of a Sharifian*

Agent's Diplomatic Mission to the Ottoman Imperial Court in the Era of Suleyman the Magnificent (Beirut: Orient-Institut, 2005), 171.

40. Blackburn, *Journey*, 172.

41. Bosio, *Dell'Istoria*, vol. 3, 501. Petremol cites an anecdote on his ill use of a French sailor (Charrière, *Négociations*, vol. 2, 782).

42. Rossi, "L'Assedio di Malta," 148.

43. CODOIN, vol. 29, 345.

44. Rossi, "L'Assedio di Malta," 145.

45. Braudel, *Mediterranean*, 945.

46. Busbecq, *Legationis Turcicae*, 229; Forster, *Turkish Letters*, 175.

47. Rossi, "L'Assedio di Malta," 145.

48. Evliyá Efendí, *Narrative of Travels in Europe, Asia, and Africa*, vol. 1, pt. 2 (London: Oriental Translation Fund of Great Britain and Ireland, 1846), 56.

49. Petremol to Catherine de' Medici, January 20, 1565, in Charrière, *Négociations*, vol. 2, 774. Cf. p. 772 for his information on Turgut's proposed contributions.

50. Setton, *Papacy and the Levant*, vol. 4, 845.

51. William Fayre to Cecil, May 12, 1565, Madrid, in *CSPFS, Elizabeth*, vol. 7: 1564–1565, 365.

52. Cirni, *Commentarii*, 38; Bosio, *Dell'Istoria*, vol. 3, 488. Cf. CODOIN, vol. 29, 38.

53. Balbi, *Verdadera*, 18r. Bradford, *Siege of Malta*, 28.

54. He may have been referring to the intelligence reports to be found in CODOIN, vol. 29, 5ff., which give some remarkably detailed and prescient takes on things to come.

55. Arnold Cassola, *The 1565 Ottoman Malta Campaign Register*, with Idris Bostan and Thomas Scheben (Malta: Publishers Enterprises Group, 1998), 52.

56. Cassola, *Great Siege of Malta*, 15–17. Hess, *The Forgotten Frontier*, 84; C.H. Imber, "The Navy of Suleiman the Magnificent," *Archivum Ottomanicum* 6 (1980), 259. Ottoman records also contain a letter from Suleiman to Turgut confirming the target. Regretfully, the document is undated. "I have appointed Mustapha Pasha as Commander General of the Ottoman Army that is to conquer the island of Malta. I have also appointed Piale Pasha, the beylerbey of the Archipelago, commander of the Imperial Navy and asked him to join in the Siege of Malta. I am also relying on you because of your military experience. You should help Mustapha Pasha at sea and you should protect our navy against the enemy's navy, which could set out from other countries to help Malta." Cassola, *Great Siege of Malta*, 17.

57. Emrah Safa Gürkan, "Espionage in the 16th Century Mediterranean: Secret Diplomacy, Mediterranean Go-Betweens, and the Ottoman Habsburg Rivalry" (PhD diss, Georgetown University, Washington, DC, 2012), 60. (Cf., however, Emilio Sola, *Uchalí, el Calabrés Tiñoso, o el mito del corsario muladí en la frontera* (Barcelona: Edicions Bellaterra, 2010), 111, which suggests that Hassan had bribed court officials to get the Ottomans to attack Malta.)

58. Cassola, *Great Siege of Malta*, 23.

59. Rafael Vargas-Hidalgo, *Guerra y diplomacia en el Mediterráneo: Correspondencie inédita de Felippe II con Andrea Doria y Juan Andrea Doria* (Madrid: Ediciones Polifemo, 2002), 444.

60. Rossi, "L'Assedio di Malta," 147.

7. DARK CLOUDS IN THE EAST, 1565

Epigraph: Rossi, "L'Assedio di Malta," 146.

1. Bosio, *Dell'Istoria*, vol. 3, 494.

2. *CN*, vol. 12, doc. 78; Cesareo Fernandez Duro, *Armada Espanola desde la union de los reinos de Castilla y de Aragon*, vol. 2 (Madrid: Sucesores de Rivadeneyra, 1896), 62.

3. For the defenders' point of view, see Blaise de Montluc, *Commentaires (1521–1576)* (Paris: Gallimard, 1964). Montluc later fought alongside Romegas against the Huguenots, notably at Mont-de-Marsan.

4. Draft in Challoner's holograph, July 29, 1564, Madrid, in *CSPFS, Elizabeth*, vol. 7: *1564–1565*, 183.

5. Report of Captain Francisco De Herazo, n.p., "Elizabeth: August 1564," in *CSPFS, Elizabeth*, vol. 7: *1564–1565*,194.

6. Medici Archives, Florence, doc. MdP 219, doc. ID 16241, fol. 133, 1563. In his portrait, Don Garcia looks quite fit. Chiappino (1519–1575), by contrast, was in middle age widely noted for his immense gut—so large, they say, that a kind of harness had to be fitted about his neck to hold it in place.

7. "Spanish command relationships were characteristically decentralized with the Captain General of the Sea commanding forces afloat and the Viceroy of Sicily controlling the Captain General's main source of manpower and supplies." John F. Guilmartin, "The Siege of Malta 1565," in *Amphibious Warfare, 1000–1700*, ed. D. J. B. Trim (Leiden: Brill, 2006), 165. De Toledo successfully pointed to Ottoman success using such a streamlined method. His powers, however, were not unlimited, and he had to get Philip to order provisions from the viceroy of Naples (CODOIN, vol. 29, 22). Bosio states that Valette himself pushed for Don Garcia's appointment. If true, that suggests a more respectful and trusting relationship between viceroy and grand master than some historians have described, at least initially. Bosio, *Dell'Istoria*, 485.

8. CODOIN, vol. 27, 452, in Duro, *Armada Espanola*, vol. 3, 65–66, in Braudel, *Mediterranean*, 1013 n.: "Your majesty must know that it is indispensable that I have a firm hand with the fleet, in view of its present condition, if I am to do my job properly and safeguard his finances."

9. See Guilmartin, *Gunpowder and Galleys*, 120ff, for a discussion of Don Garcia's report to Philip in fall of 1564. The report itself is to be found in *Colección Navarrete*, vol. 12m, dto 79, fol. 195ff.

10. Don Garcia to Philip, January 18, 1565, in CODOIN, vol. 29, 23.

11. Ibid., 30.

12. Setton, *Papacy and the Levant*, vol. 3, 852. Granvelle, however, writes on January 15, that "Don Garcia de Toledo a esté à Rome fort bien receu du pape; Dieu doint que ce soit le chemin pour rabiller ce du resentement causé sur la prétension de la précédence." Antoine Perrenot de Granvelle, *Papiers d'état du Cardinal de Granvelle*, vol. 8 (Paris: Imprimerie Royale, 1850), 606.

13. There were a few surprise holdouts. The viceroy of Naples declined to help, citing a lack of orders to do so, necessitating yet another begging letter back to Madrid. CODOIN, vol. 29, 22.

14. Petremol to Catherine de' Medici, April 7, 1565, Constantinople, in Charrière, *Négociations*, vol. 2, 782: One hundred and fifty oared vessels, eight gallaces, eight navires, and several other small vessels to carry munitions.

15. Bosio, *Dell'Istoria*, vol. 3, xxiv, 510; Charrière, *Négotiations*, vol. 2, 789–90; Setton, *Papacy and the Levant*, 852; Cirni, *Commentarii*, 42v.; Charrière, *Négotiations*, vol. 2, 782, 783.

16. Hammer, 104. Peçevi has a different view. Rossi, "L'Assedio di Malta," 150.

17. Bosio, *Dell'Istoria*, 501. Cf. Cirni, *Commentarii*, 41v., who says that Piali must be obedient (*ubidiente*) to Mustapha.

18. Charrière, *Négotiations*, vol. 2, 782; cf. CODOIN, vol. 29, 349.

19. Viperano, *De Bello Melitensi Historia*, 190.

20. Charrière, *Négotiations*, vol. 2, 782; cf. CODOIN, vol. 29, 349.

21. Rossi, "L'Assedio di Malta," 147.

22. Balbi, *Verdadera*, 23v.; Bradford, *Siege of Malta*, 34; Cirni, *Commentarii*, 41r.

23. Battista Ferraro, ASG, Constantinopoli Mazzo I.n.g. 2169, *Chius Vincta, or, The Occupation of Chios by the Turks, 1566* (Cambridge: Cambridge University Press, 1941), xciii.

24. Charrière, *Négotiations*, vol. 2, 772–73, 782, 783–84; cf. CODOIN, vol. 29, 38–57. Petremol suggests that the commanders could go elsewhere should Malta or Goletta prove uninteresting. Charrière, *Négotiations*, vol. 2, 785. He did, however, warn that pirates could still be a French concern that season. Ibid., 786.

25. Balbi, *Verdadera*, 24v.; Bradford, *Siege of Malta*, 36.

26. Balbi, *Verdadera*, 24v.; Bradford, *Siege of Malta*, 36.

27. Cirni, *Commentarii*, 45r., says that 150 of the 600 soldiers managed to reach the shore.

28. Balbi, *Verdadera*, 26r.; Bradford, *Siege of Malta*, 38.

29. AOM 430 f., 266v., in Spiteri, *The Great Siege*, 578. After the siege was over, he was ruthless in trying knights (almost all of them French) who had not heeded the call. Giovanni Bonello, "Great Siege, Small Morsels," in *Histories of Malta*, vol. 9, *Confessions and Transgressions* (Malta: Fondazzjoni Patrimonju Malti, 2008), 22–23.

30. Bosio, *Dell'Istoria*, 499.

31. Balbi, *Verdadera*, 27v.; Bradford, *Siege of Malta*, 41. Balbi himself offered to leave. Balbi, *Verdadera*, 38.

32. Valette to Philip, in CODOIN, vol. 29, 348. Cf. Bosio, *Dell'Istoria*, vol. 3, 499.

33. Toledo to Philip, April 11, 1565, in CODOIN, vol. 29, 89. Toledo reiterates this in a May 16, 1565, letter to Philip, referring to two companies of Spaniards. CODOIN, vol. 29, 136.

34. Ibid., 88.

35. Roger Vella Bonavita, "Francesco Laparelli Military Architect at Malta," in *Francesco Laparelli architetto cortonese a Malta*, ed. E. Mirri (Cortona, IT: Tiphys, 2009), 47.

36. Bosio, *Dell'Istoria*, 499. Exceptions were not unknown: Sir Oliver Starkey may not have been technically qualified for his position. See Giovanni Bonello, "Sir Oliver Starkey: Paragon and Victim," in *Histories of Malta*, vol. 2, *Versions and Diversions* (Malta: Fondazzjoni Patrimonju Malti, 2002), 42–54. Nor was Valette necessarily in a position to frown on a bastard child; there is evidence that he had a daughter not much younger than Faderigo (see Giovanni Bonello, "Grand Masters in the Cinquecento: Their Persona and Death," *Malta Medical Journal* 15, no. 2 [November 2003]).

37. Queen Mary had briefly returned them, and Elizabeth was as civil to the Order as she was to anyone who did not directly threaten her—but she was in no position to follow her half-sister's lead. She needed the money. The Order owned the London district of St. John's Wood. As to Starkey, he appears to have had little enthusiasm for the coming siege: "Wrote touching Oliver Starky, Knight of Rhodes, who is in Malta. Men give him a good report both for wisdom and valiantness. But he is poor, and not able without more help than he has of the order there to maintain his estate. He is desirous to return home. If he does come he will conform to their religion." Smith to Cecil, April 10, 1565, Bordeaux, in "Elizabeth: April 1565, 1–15," CSPFS, Elizabeth, vol. 7: 1564–1565, 330.

38. H. A. R. Balbi, "Some Unpublished Records on the Siege of Malta, 1565," *Institute of Historical Research, Malta*, no. 6 (1937): 5–36. Bulletin.

39. CODOIN, vol. 29, 5–10.

40. Roger Vella Bonavita, "The Opinion of Gian Giacomo Leonardi," *Fort, Fortress Study Group*, no. 34 (2006).

41. Bosio, *Dell'Istoria*, vol. 3, 518.

42. Ibid., 499. See Hughes, "How Fort St. Elmo Survived for So Long," *Treasures of Malta* 8 (2002): 115.

43. Bosio, *Dell'Istoria*, vol. 3, 500; cf. CODOIN, vol. 29, 86, 9.

44. CODOIN, vol. 29, 89.

8. FIRST BLOOD

Epigraphs: Charrière, *Négociations*, 784; *1565 Ottoman Malta Campaign Register*, 135.

1. CODOIN, vol. 29,113ff.

2. Testa, *Romegas*, 79.

3. Viperano, *De Bello*, 7.

4. Ettore Rossi, *Storia della marina dell'Ordine di San Giovanni* (Rome: Seai, 1926), 29.

5. CODOIN, vol. 39, 136.

6. Balbi, *Verdadera*, 32v.; Bradford, *Siege of Malta*, 45; Bosio, *Dell'Istoria*, vol. 3, 513. Viperano (7) puts it at 450 men total.

7. Possibly Piali wanted to ensure that no enemy fleets were hidden on the far side of the island. He knew from Djerba what could happen to a disordered fleet caught in a tight space.

8. One hundred and thirty galleys, thirty galleots, nine barges, ten large ships, and two hundred smaller transport vessels. Spiteri, *The Great Siege*, 24. See also Braudel, *Mediterranean*, 1015, for details.

9. Cirni, *Commentarii*, 50v.

10. Bosio, *Dell'Istoria*, vol. 3, 520.

11. Cassola, *Great Siege of Malta*, 64.

12. Balbi, *Verdadera*, 32r.; Bradford, *Siege of Malta*, 47. Bosio says it was a Portuguese who came to aid La Rivière and was captured with him. Bosio, *Dell'Istoria*, vol. 3, 520.

13. Cirni (*Commentarii*, 49v.) gives a simpler story, essentially that La Rivière was wounded and captured in a skirmish, and an unidentified knight killed.

14. Cassola, *1565 Ottoman Malta Campaign Register*, 217.

15. Balbi, *Verdadera*, 33r.; Bradford, *Siege of Malta*, 47.

16. Balbi, *Verdadera*, 25v.; Bradford, *Siege of Malta*, 37. Bosio puts this letter, and the subsequent discord, as happening earlier at sea. Bosio, *Dell'Istoria*, vol. 3, 512.

17. Viperano, *De Bello*, 7; Balbi, *Verdadera*, 33v.; Bradford, *Siege of Malta*, 47; Bosio, *Dell'Istoria*, vol. 3, 521; Cirni, *Commentarii*, 50r.

18. Cirni, *Commentarii*, 50r.

19. For an exhaustive discussion, see Spiteri, *Great Siege*, 70–107.

20. Determining the exact breakdown is somewhat problematic given the source material from the time and the subsequent destruction and reworking of the defense works themselves. See Spiteri, *Great Siege*, 294, for a full discussion.

21. Balbi, *Verdadera*, 33r.; Bradford, *Siege of Malta*, 47–48. Cirni, *Commentarii*, 51v., says only that La Rivière did not know which defense was best ("quel banda era meglio").

9. SIZING UP THE ENEMY

Epigraph: Celio Secondo Curione, *Caelius Secundus Curio: His Historie of the Warr of Malta*, trans. Thomas Mainwaring, ed. Helen Vella-Bonavita (Tempe: Arizona Center for Medieval and Renaissance Studies, 2007), 58.

1. Bosio, *Dell'Istoria*, 522.

2. Ibid., 521.

3. Bregante, ASG, busta I.2169. Gregorio Bregante was a Genoese spy based in Constantinople; he is likely the agent mentioned in Philip Argenti's "Chius Vincta," as going to Malta with the Ottoman expedition (xciii, xciv).

4. *Colección de libros españoles raros o curiosos, Tomo Decimoquinto: Guerras de los Españoles en Africa 1542, 1543, y 1632* (Madrid: Miguel Ginesta, 1881), 98.

5. Bosio, *Dell'Istoria*, vol. 3, 514. Viperano tosses out the figure of eight hundred (Viperano, *De Bello*, 8).

6. *Codex Laparelli*, f. 33v., in Roger Vella Bonavita, "Parere di Gian Giacomo Leonardi, Conte di Montelabbate, sulla Fortezza Gerosolimitana di Malta, 31 Ottobre 1557," *Melita Historica: Journal of the Malta Historical Society* 14 (2004). Don Garcia does, however, express his dismay that the Ottomans might take advantage of the various private cisterns throughout the island, which would make travel to Gozo unnecessary. De Toledo to Philip, May 21, 1565, in CODOIN, vol. 29, 157.

7. Busbecq, *Legationis Turcicae*, 199; Forster, *Turkish Letters*, 150.

8. Cassola, *Great Siege of Malta*, 50.

9. For a detailed account of the fort's construction, see Spiteri, *Great Siege*, 108–19.

10. Cirni, *Commentarii*, 50r.

11. Ibid., 61v.

12. Ibid., 41r.

13. Bosio, *Dell'Istoria*, vol. 3, 523; Cirni, *Commentarii*, 52.

14. Cirni, *Commentarii*, 52. See also CODOIN, vol. 29, no. 2, 380.

15. All figures are notoriously shaky in these accounts. The first comes from Bosio, vol. 3, (524), the second from Balbi (*Verdadera*, 34v.; Bradford, *Siege of Malta*, 50), who does not total up Christian casualties.

16. Rossi, *Documenti turchi*, 318, gives the date as May 22, as does Balbi, *Verdadera*, 36v.; Bradford, *Siege of Malta*, 53.

17. Bosio, *Dell'Istoria*, vol. 3, 524. Cirni claims that La Rivière repeatedly said he did not know which defense was best and leaves it at that. Cirni, *Commentarii*, 51v.

18. Cirni says he was sent to the galleys. Cirni, *Commentarii*, 52r.

19. Peçevi wrote that Suleiman had "expressly commanded that [Mustapha and Piali] not consider nor put into execution, either on land or on water, any plan without consulting with Torgut." Rossi, "L'Assedio di Malta," 150.

20. Rossi, "L'Assedio di Malta," 150. Cf. Bosio, *Dell'Istoria*, 532. "Seeing how late he was in arriving, many doubted, that he was displeased and angry because the Turkish army had stopped first to besiege Malta rather than la Goletta, as he had proposed to Suleiman."

21. CODOIN, vol. 29, 7. The scale model is mentioned in Bosio, *Dell'Istoria*, 525.

22. See Guilmartin, *Galleys and Galleons* and "The Siege of Malta, 1565," in *Amphibious Warfare 1000–1700*, ed. D. J. B. Trim and Mark Charles Fissel (Boston: Brill, 2006), 148, for more on this subject.

23. Balbi, *Verdadera*, 35v. Bradford, *Siege of Malta*, 52.

24. Rossi, *Documenti turchi*, 318. Cf. Curionis, *Warr*, 57.

25. Balbi, *Verdadera*, 37r.; Bradford, *Siege of Malta*, 55; Bosio, *Dell'Istoria*, 525.

10. PREPARATIONS FOR A SIEGE

Epigraph: Don Garcia de Toledo to Philip II, May 31, 1565, in CODOIN, vol. 29, 165.

1. Bosio, *Dell'Istoria*, 516.

2. Carmel Cassar, "O Melita Infelix: A Poem on the Great Siege Written in 1565," *Melita Historica* 8, no. 2 (1981): 149–55. *Heu patrianque* [sic] *fugimus solanque relinquimus urbem / Dispersi veluti sors sua cuique datur / Mesta vale bis terque vale lacrimisque relicti*[s] */ Et gemitu similis non erit illa vale.*

3. Bosio, *Dell'Istoria*, vol. 3, 527. *Gente pagata*, in Bosio's phrase.

4. Cassar, "O Melita Infelix," 151. Armenia is likely to have been one of the few to have remained in the city that long hot summer. The following year, when fear of another invasion was at its height, Valette allowed each household in Mdina to send one able-bodied man to accompany each household of women abroad. All others were to do their bit for the island, which, presumably, they had failed to do in 1565. See Giovanni Bonello, "Great Siege, Small Morsels," in *Histories of Malta*, vol. 9, *Confessions and Transgressions* (Malta: Fondazzjoni Patrimonju Malti, 2007), 24.

5. Bosio, *Dell'Istoria*, vol. 3, 527–28.

6. Viperano, *De Bello*, 29r.

7. Balbi, *Verdadera*, 36v.; Bradford, *Siege of Malta*, 54.

8. CODOIN, vol. 29, 365.

9. Cirni, *Commentarii*, 52r.

10. Viperano, *De Bello*, 11.

11. Anthoine de Cressy to Grand Prior of France, September 11, 1565, Malta, in Nicolas Camusat, *Mélange Historique, ou recueil de plusieurs actes, traités, lettres missives, et autres mémoires qui peuvent servir en la déduction de l'histoire, depuis l'an 1390 jusques à l'an 1580* (Troyes, FR: N. Moreau, 1619), 52r.

12. Bosio, *Dell'Istoria*, vol. 3, 529. Other chroniclers are silent on whether La Cerda spoke for himself alone or for all those at Fort St. Elmo.

13. Bosio, *Dell'Istoria*, vol. 3, 529.

14. *Colección de libros españoles raros o curiosos, Tomo Decimoquinto*, 98.

15. Bosio, *Dell'Istoria*, vol. 3, 529.

16. Cirni says 150 men. Cirni, *Commentarii*, 52v.

17. Bosio, *Dell'Istoria*, vol. 3, 529.

18. Ibid. Balbi has Valette extending to all Christian prisoners (but not slaves) unspecified benefits for those who "fought like good and brave Christians." Balbi, *Verdadera*, 37r; Bradford, *Siege of Malta*, 54. Truth may lie in the middle; Valette needed to extract the civilians at St. Elmo quickly, and this was a good way to inspire trained oarsmen.

19. Bosio, *Dell'Istoria*, vol. 3, 530. Bosio quotes a letter to Don Garcia written the day after, in which Valette refers to Medrano by his given rank *alfiero* (lieutenant), which raises the question of whether he had formalized the promotion to captain. Valette also expresses his great confidence in Medrano, and interestingly, in La Cerda.

20. Vertot, *Histoire*, vol. 3, 452.

21. Don Garcia to Philip, May 23, CODOIN, vol. 29, 205.

22. CODOIN, vol. 29, 266 .

11. A FATAL OVERSIGHT

Epigraph: Vella Bonavita, "Parere di Gian Giacomo Leonardi," 9. Leonardi, a talented architect, was commissioned in 1557 to consider improving the defenses of Malta.

1. Bosio, *Dell'Istoria*, vol. 3, 532.

2. Çelebi, *History of the Maritime Wars*, 159. Eugenio Alberi, *Relazioni*, vol. 9, ser. 3, 291–95, in Niccolò Capponi, *Victory of the West: The Story of the Battle of Lepanto* (New York: Da Capo, 2007), 35.

3. Cressy, in Camusat, *Mélange Historique*, 53r.

4. Cassola, *Great Siege of Malta*, 17.

5. Peçevi, quoted in Rossi, "L'Assedio di Malta," 150.

6. Rossi, "L'Assedio di Malta," 150. Bosio writes that he would have preferred to attack La Goletta, as "he had proposed to Suleiman." Bosio, *Dell'Istoria*, 532.

7. Cirni, *Commentarii*, 53v.

8. Bosio, *Dell'Istoria*, vol. 3, 539; Quentin Hughes, "How Fort St. Elmo Survived the Siege for So Long," *Treasures of Malta* 8, no. 1 (2002): 109–15.

9. Bosio, *Dell'Istoria*, vol. 3, 539. In 1567 Girolamo Cataneo published *Opera Nuova di fortificare, offendere, et difendere* (Brescia, IT: Gio. Battista Bozola, 1567), in which he states that a thirty-pound half-cannon could use up 2,200 pounds of gunpowder to deliver 110 shots daily. Larger guns required more powder and more time between firings, but with twenty cannons ringing Fort St. Elmo, it is clear that the Muslims were taking their time.

10. Cressy, in Camusat, *Mélange Historique*, 52r.

11. Bosio, *Dell'Istoria*, vol. 3, 540.

12. Ibid. Bosio says Mustapha was consulted; Cirni suggests they acted on their own. Cirni, *Commentarii*, 54v.

13. Curionis, *Caelius Secundus Curione*, 45.

14. Balbi, *Verdadera*, 41r.; Bradford, *Siege of Malta*, 65.

15. For more on this, see James Riddick Partington and Bert S. Hall, *A History of Greek Fire and Gunpowder* (Baltimore: Johns Hopkins University Press, 1999).

16. Bosio, *Dell'Istoria*, vol. 3, 540.

17. Balbi, *Verdadera*, 41r; Bradford, *Siege of Malta*, 65–66.

18. Rossi, *Documenti turchi inediti*, 318.

19. Cirni, *Commentarii*, 54v.

12. THRUST AND PARRY

Epigraph: Vendôme, *Della Historia di Malta*, 28.

1. Bosio refers to him as Giovanni (Juan), Balbi as Andres. Viperano, Cirni, and Curionis skirt the issue by dropping his Christian name altogether.

2. Bosio, *Dell'Istoria*, vol. 3, 543.

3. Balbi, *Verdadera*, 43v.; Bradford, *Siege of Malta*, 68.

4. CSPFS, *Elizabeth*, vol. 17: *January–June 1583 and addenda* (1913), 705.

5. Curionis, *Warr*, 53.

6. Bosio, *Dell'Istoria*, vol. 3, 545.

7. Balbi, *Verdadera*, 45v–46r; Bradford, *Siege of Malta*, 73. Of course, La Cerda had to have been aware that his lieutenant was still in chains for having shown up wounded in Birgu. Cirni, however, says that he was ferried back to Birgu at this time (Cirni, 57v).

8. Balbi, *Verdadera*, 46r; Bradford, *Siege of Malta*, 73.

9. Balbi, *Verdadera*, 46r. Bradford, *Siege of Malta*, 73.

13. FRESH RESOLVE

Epigraph: Balbi, *Verdadera*, 48r., 48v.; Bradford, *Siege of Malta*, 78.

1. Bosio, *Dell'Istoria*, vol. 3, 550. Cirni writes that he was sent back to Birgu on June 8 to recover from his wounds (Cirni, *Commentarii*, 57v.).

2. Bosio, *Dell'Istoria*, 550.

3. Balbi, *Verdadera*, 45r; Bradford, *Siege of Malta*, 72.

4. Marco Amarelli, "Costantino e la casa Castriota, Nuovi contributi sulla biagrafia e gli scritti di 'Filionico Alicarnasseo,'" *Critica Letteraria* 40, no. 1 (154): 128.

5. "Castriota," in *Dizionario biografico degli Italiani*, vol. 22 (1979).

6. Balbi, *Verdadera*, 47r; Bradford, *Siege of Malta*, 72; cf. Bosio, *Dell'Istoria*, vol. 3, 551; Cirni, *Commentarii*, 58v.

7. Bosio, *Dell'Istoria*, vol. 3, 521.

8. Ibid., 553. His rhetoric had moved two newly converted Jews to come as well (ibid.). After inspiring the men on St. Elmo, the Friar accompanied Broglio back to Birgu (Balbi, *Verdadera*, 48r; Bradford *Siege of Malta*, 76). For more on this remarkable man, see Francis Azzopardi, "The Activities of the First Known Capuchin in Malta: Robert of Eboli," *Melita Historica: Journal of the Malta Historical Society* 4, no. 2 (1965): 96–110.

9. Spiteri, *The Great Siege*, 195.

10. Balbi, *Verdadera*, 48r.; Bradford, *Siege of Malta*, 76.

11. Balbi, *Verdadera*, 48r.; Bradford, *Siege of Malta*, 76.

12. Balbi, *Verdadera*, 48v.; Bradford, *Siege of Malta*, 78.

13. Balbi, *Verdadera*, 48v. Bradford, *Siege of Malta*, 78.

14. BULLETS WRAPPED IN SMOKE AND FIRE

Epigraph: Valette to Don Garcia, in Vendôme, *Della Historia di Malta*, 25.

1. Cirni, *Commentarii*, 65r.

2. Viperano, *De Bello*, 11–12.

3. Ibid.

4. Ibid.

5. Bosio, *Dell'Istoria*, vol. 3, 562. Tattoos are forbidden under Islamic law.

6. Ibid.

7. Ibid., 560.

8. Viperano, *De Bello*, 14.

9. Rossi, *Documenti turchi*, 318.

10. Balbi, *Verdadera*, 51r; Bradford translation, 82.

11. Bosio, *Dell'Istoria*, vol. 3, 564. Medrano was buried among the Knights of the Grand Cross, than which Valette could think of no greater honor.

12. Ibid.

13. Curionis, *De Bello Melitensi*, 57.

14. Ibid., 60.

15. Balbi, *Verdadera*, 52r; Bradford, *Siege of Malta*, 83.

16. Bosio tells a simpler story of gunners firing from Fort St. Angelo and getting lucky. Bregante (ASG I.2169), however, who was in the Ottoman camp, affirms Balbi's version. Bosio, *Dell'Istoria*, vol. 3, 566.

15. A PLEA TO GOD

Epigraph: *Liturgies and Occasional Forms of Prayer Set Forth in the Reign of Queen Elizabeth*, ed. William K. Clay (Cambridge: Cambridge University Press, 1847), 519. The siege of Malta was one thing on which both Catholics and Anglicans could agree. Prayers for the safety of the island came even from the sternly anti-Catholic Bishop Jewel of Salisbury.

1. Bosio, *Dell'Istoria*, vol. 3, 566. Balbi (p. 52) claims that he was killed in the same strike that wounded Turgut. He refers to him as *maestro de campo general*.

2. Bosio, *Dell'Istoria*, vol. 3, 566.

3. Ibid.

4. Balbi, *Verdadera*, 52v.; Bradford, *Siege of Malta*, 85. Cf. also Gábor Ágoston, *Guns for the Sultan: Military Power and the Weapons Industry in the Ottoman Empire* (Cambridge: Cambridge University Press, 2004), 108. The weight ascribed to a kantar varied according to the place or commodity weighed.

5. The charge was pending for the duration. Bonello, *Histories of Malta*, 23.

6. Bosio, *Dell'Istoria*, vol. 3, 568.

7. Ibid., 569.

8. Balbi, *Verdadera*, 53r.; Bradford, *Siege of Malta*, 87.

9. Bosio, *Dell'Istoria*, vol. 3, 569.

10. Ibid., 570.

11. Bosio, *Dell'Istoria*, vol. 3, 571.

12. Balbi, *Verdadera*, 54r.; Bradford, *Siege of Malta*, 88.

13. Balbi, *Verdadera*, 54r.; Bradford, *Siege of Malta*, 88. Bosio writes that Miranda held on until the twenty-third (Bosio, *Dell'Istoria*, 572).

14. Bosio, *Dell'Istoria*, vol. 3, 571.

15. Ibid.

16. Cirni, *Commentarii*, 69v.

17. Bosio, *Dell'Istoria*, vol. 3, 573.

18. Ibid., 571.

19. Ibid., 572.

16. THE END OF THE BATTLE

Epigraph: Phayre to Cecil, July 31, 1565, in *CSPFS, Elizabeth*, vol. 7: 1564–1565, 418.

1. Bosio writes that Medrano (not the same Medrano killed earlier) tried to call for a parley,

which attempt failed and led to the inrush of overeager Turks. The Turks, duplicitous as ever, took the opportunity to call out from the tower to the spur that there was no one left to defend the structure. All the soldiers then ran (he writes) to the church to join the nine wounded men. The Turks were then observed executing those who surrendered, which encouraged the survivors to fight to the death. It sounds unlikely. Besieged forts and cities might be surrendered at any time before the actual breaching of the walls, and terms arranged—but this was generally done before the assault was launched, not in the middle of a fight. Besides, the Turks were by now perfectly well able to take the fort without this kind of cheat. Bosio, *Dell'Istoria*, vol. 3, 572. See also Balbi, *Verdadera*, 54v.–55r. Bradford, *Siege of Malta*, 91.

2. Rossi, *Documenti turchi inediti*, 319.

3. Bosio, *Dell'Istoria*, vol. 3, 573.

4. Balbi, *Verdadera*, 55r; Bradford, *Siege of Malta*, 90.

5. Bosio, *Dell'Istoria*, vol. 3, 573.

6. Cassola, *Great Siege of Malta*, 64.

7. Bosio, *Dell'Istoria*, vol. 3, 573.

8. Balbi, *Verdadera*, 55r; Bradford, *Siege of Malta*, 90.

9. Five, according to Cressy (Camusat, *Mélange Historique*, 52r).

10. Rossi, "L'Assedio di Malta," 148.

11. Rossi, *Documenti turchi inediti*, 319.

12. Bosio, *Dell'Istoria*, vol. 3, 576. Ottoman historian Peçevi claims that, "During the conquest of Saint Elmo the greater part of weaponry and powder was consumed." Rossi, "L'Assedio di Malta," 151.

13. Cirni, *Commentarii*, 70r.

14. Rossi, *Documenti turchi inediti*, 318–19.

15. Bregante, ASG, busta I.2169.

16. Cirni, *Commentarii*, 70v. See also Bonello, "The Two Lanfreducci Knights of Malta," in *Histories of Malta*, vol. 1, 23; and Bonello, "Gambling in Malta under the Order," in *Histories of Malta*, vol. 6, 44–45.

17. Natale Conti, *Commentarii Hieronymi Comitis Alexandrini* (Venice: Stellae Iordani Ziletti, 1566), 27. Melchior Robles, a veteran of the siege, claimed that the Ottomans "chewed on living hearts with their teeth" (*et corda palpitantia dentibus admorden*). "Melita a Turcis obsessa et Roblesiorum virtute liberate," in H. A. R. Balbi, "Some Unpublished Records," 26).

18. Çelebi, *History of the Maritime Wars*, 148.

19. Cassola, *Malta Campaign Register*, 339.

20. Cirni, *Commentarii*, 71v.

21. Phayre to Cecil, July 31, 1565, Madrid, in *CSPFS, Elizabeth*, vol. 7: 1564–1565 (1870), 401–19. Two cannonballs reputed to be those which chipped the rock that killed Turgut were later recovered and taken to Sicily, where they were offered to our Lady of Valverde. They can still be seen there, mounted on the walls. (See Bonello, "Great Siege, Small Morsels," 27.)

22. Petremol to M. du Ferrier, July 15 and 23, 1565, Constantinople, in Charrière, *Négociations*, vol. 2, 797.

23. Cassola, *Great Siege of Malta*, 29.

24. Bosio, *Dell'Istoria*, vol. 3, 579. The Ottomans periodically shot off powder for no other purpose than to demonstrate how much of the stuff they actually had.

25. Viperano, *De Bello*, 15ff. He follows this observation with a long speech by Valette.

26. Balbi, *Verdadera*, 58v.; Bradford, *Siege of Malta*, 92. Mustapha effectively said that he was only following orders.

27. Vertot, *Histoire*, vol. 3, 492: "par le moyen du canon, et en place des boulets, il en fit jetter les têtes toutes sanglantes jusque dans leur camp."

28. Laurentius Sirius, *Commentarivs Brevis Rervm in Orbe Gestarvm, ab anno Salutis millesimo quingentesimo, vsq; ad annum LXVI* (Cologne: Calenius and Quentel, 1566), 795.

29. Porter, *Knights of Malta*, 449. Porter (1827–1892) was a major general in the British army, with service in the Crimean War.

17. PICCOLO SOCCORSO

Epigraph: Balbi, *Verdadera*, 54v.; Bradford, *Siege of Malta*, 88. "Buena mano han dado los de sant Ermo a los Turcos."

1. CODOIN, vol. 29, 417. "La poca guardia che fanno i nemici." Two weeks earlier, Turgut had made sure a fleet of sixty ships heading north was visible from Fort St. Angelo. Balbi suggests that this was a feint to unnerve Valette; if so, it didn't work. Balbi, *Verdadera*, 49r.; Bradford, *Siege of Malta*, 79.

2. Phayre to Cecil, July 31, 1565, Madrid, in *CSPFS, Elizabeth*, vol. 7: 1564–1565 (1870), 418.

3. Ibid. Possibly this is what Viperano is referring to when he mentions that Uludj Ali took a few extra days getting back from Algiers: "missus ad componendos Afrorum tumultus" (Viperano, *De Bello*, 24v.).

4. "The King is very poor and has taken up 200,000 ducats of Nicolo Grimaldi"; Robert Hogan to the Earl of Leicester, in "Elizabeth: June 16–30, 1565," *CSPFS, Elizabeth*, vol. 7: 1564–1565 (1870), 399. Don Garcia was also having trouble raising money for some troops and was forced to turn to the local clergy. Cirni, 66r.

5. "Instrucciones de Carlos Quinto a Don Felipe su hijo," in Charles Weiss, *Papiers d'Etat du Cardinal de Grenvelle*, vol. 3 (Paris: Imprimerie Royale, 1842), 292.

6. Philip to Don Garcia de Toledo, July 27, 1565, in CODOIN, vol. 29, 312.

7. Giovanni Battista Adriani, *Istoria de' suoi tempi di Giovambatista Adriani* (Florence: Nella Stamperia de i Giunti, 1583), 734.

8. Don Garcia de Toledo to Philip II, June 2, 1565, in CODOIN, vol. 29, 174, 203.

9. CODOIN, vol. 29, 199.

10. Don Garcia de Toledo to Philip II, June 12, 1565, in CODOIN, vol. 29, 204.

11. Philip II to Don Garcia de Toledo, March 31, 1565, in CODOIN, vol. 29, 79.

12. Don Garcia de Toledo to Philip II, April 11, 1565, in CODOIN, vol. 29, 88.

13. Don Garcia to Philip, June 7, 1565, in CODOIN, vol. 29, 180.

14. CODOIN, vol. 29, 247–54.

15. Cosimo de' Medici to Philip, June 2, 1565, Florence, in CODOIN, vol. 29, 235. See also Roger Vella Bonavita, "From Conception to Birth: The 'Valletta' Project, 1524–1566," in *Valletta: Città, architettura e costruzione sotto il segno della fede e della guerra*, ed. Nicoletta Marconi (Rome: Istituto Poligrafico e Zecca dello Stato, 2011), 17–33

16. Viperano, *De Bello*, 18. The number of those in the Small Relief is variously reported. Don Garcia, closest to the action and presumably more punctilious than later writers, says six hundred (De Toledo to Philip, July 5, 1565, in CODOIN, vol. 29, 253) "not enough to defend the Burgo and St. Michael." The breakdown of those on board is some forty-two knights

of St. John, who had arrived at Messina only after the Turkish invasion at Malta. (Also on board were twenty Italian volunteers, three German, two English, fifty-six gunners, and six hundred imperial foot under the command of Chevalier de Robles.) Balbi (*Verdadera*, 62r.; Bradford, *Siege of Malta*, 101) says seven hundred, among them forty knights and twenty artillerymen. Don Garcia's condition for landing appears in Bosio, *Dell'Istoria*, vol. 3, 560.

17. Diego de la Mota, *Principio de la orden de la cavalleria de Sant Tiago del Espada* (Valencia: Álvaro Franco, 1599), 293.

18. Bosio, *Dell'Istoria*, vol. 3, 585.

19. Ibid.

20. Ibid., 586.

21. CODOIN, vol. 29, 253.

22. Bosio, *Dell'Istoria*, vol. 3, 578.

23. Balbi, *Verdadera*, 58v.; Bradford, *Siege of Malta*, 94.

24. Cassolla, *Great Siege of Malta*, 29.

25. Bosio, *Dell'Istoria*, vol. 3, 582.

26. Balbi, *Verdadera*, 60v.–61r.; Bradford, *Siege of Malta*, 98.

27. Viperano, *De Bello*, 17. The following year, when a second invasion threatened, Valette decreed that the useless mouths of Mdina could leave before the anticipated return of the Ottomans, but that only one hale male family member could accompany them. All others were to remain to help in the fight against invasion. The specific nature of the ukase suggests that this had been a problem in 1565. For more, see Bonello, "Great Siege, Small Morsels," 24.

18. RELIEF INTO BIRGU

Epigraph: Alberti, *De Re Aedificatoria*, bk. 5, chap. 4, 143.

1. Balbi, *Verdadera*, 62r.; Bradford, *Siege of Malta*, 101.

2. Bosio, *Dell'Istoria*, vol. 3, 587. An account said to be by Melchior Robles (H. R. Balbi, "Unpublished Records on the Siege of Malta, 1565," 26) refers to Lascaris as Mustapha's amanuensis (it also says he was transported at night). Ottoman records, however, note only that a certain Mehmed ben Davud crossed over to the Christians on this date and suggest that his timar should be given to another, but otherwise attach no particular importance to the man. Casolla, *Great Siege of Malta*, 70–72.

3. Balbi, *Verdadera*, 62r.; Bradford, *Siege of Malta*, 101.

4. CODOIN, vol. 29, 276.

5. Balbi, *Verdadera*, 62v.–63r.; Bradford, *Siege of Malta*, 101.

6. Bosio, *Dell'Istoria*, vol. 3, 590. Bosio does not explain the discrepancy in numbers.

7. Bosio refers to him in an earlier citation as serving under Coppier, commander of cavalry at Mdina. Bosio, *Dell'Istoria*, vol. 3, 498, 589.

8. Balbi, *Verdadera*, 66r. (not in the Bradford translation).

9. Ibid., 66v.; Bradford, *Siege of Malta*, 105.

10. CODOIN, vol. 29, 277.

11. Adriani, *Istoria*, 734.

12. Cassola, *Malta Campaign Register*, 337. He sent even stronger messages to Tripoli twelve days later.

13. Cassola, *Great Siege of Malta*, 62.

Epigraph: Bosio, *Dell'Istoria*, vol. 3, 606.

1. Ibid., 600. Cf. Vendôme, *Della Historia di Malta*, 71, who says they wished to prove there just what kind of spirit they had (*qual fosse l'animo de' suoi*). Candelissa is yet another corsair whose identity gets confused from source to source. He is variously identified as Ali Fartax, Kara Khodja, Kara Hodja, Caracossa, etc., and is credited as being a native of Chioggia, Fano, or Calabria, possibly a failed Dominican friar. He is also confirmed as being present at Prevesa, being killed on Malta, and being present with Uludj Ali (and being killed) at Lepanto. At times he is also confused *with* Uludj Ali. Bosio claims that he was killed on Malta (Bosio, *Dell'Istoria*, 629). Absent other evidence, it seems likely that Bosio is in this instance mistaken.

2. Vendôme, *Della Historia di Malta*, 71.

3. Balbi, *Verdadera*, 69r.; Bradford, *Siege of Malta*, 109.

4. Balbi, *Verdadera*, 69r.; Bradford, *Siege of Malta*, 109.

5. Balbi, *Verdadera*, 70r.; Bradford, *Siege of Malta*, 111. Bosio dismisses them as being "dressed as women." Bosio, *Dell'Istoria*, vol. 3, 597.

6. Ibid., 603.

7. Balbi, *Verdadera*, 71v.; Bradford, *Siege of Malta*, 111.

8. Balbi, *Verdadera*, 71v; Bradford, *Siege of Malta*, 112.

9. Balbi, *Verdadera*, 71v.; Bradford, *Siege of Malta*, 112.

10. Bosio, *Dell'Istoria*, vol. 3, 601.

11. Ibid., Balbi, *Verdadera*, 73r.; Bradford, *Siege of Malta*, 116.

12. Bosio, *Dell'Istoria*, vol. 3, 605.

13. Balbi, *Verdadera*, 72v.; Bradford, *Siege of Malta*, 115.

14. Balbi, *Verdadera*, p. 73v.–73r.; Bradford, *Siege of Malta*, 115–16.

15. Balbi, *Verdadera*, 72v.; Bradford, *Siege of Malta*, 115. Viperano, *De Bello*, 22, writes, "Around seven boats were sunk, and many damaged." *Septem circiter cymbae depressae, labefactatae plures. Cymbae* are skiffs.

16. Balbi, *Verdadera*, 73r. Bradford's translation (116) makes no mention of Uludj Ali. Giovanni Bonello, "An Overlooked Eyewitness Account of the Great Siege," in *Histories of Malta*, vol. 3, *Versions and Diversions* (Malta: Fondazzjoni Patrimonju Malti, 2002), 129.

17. CODOIN, vol. 29, pp. 380–82. D'Eguaras to Gil de Andrada, May 26.

18. Bosio, *Dell'Istoria*, vol. 3, 600; Balbi, *Verdadera*, 73r.; Bradford, *Siege of Malta*, 116.

19. Bosio, *Dell'Istoria*, vol. 3, 605.

20. Ibid.

21. Ibid.

22. Ibid, 597.

23. Pedro de Salazar, *Hispania victrix* (Madrid: Vincente de Millis, 1570), 214r.

24. Balbi, *Verdadera*, 73r.–73v.; Bradford, *Siege of Malta*, 116.

20 · ENDURANCE

Epigraph: Phayre to Cecil, August 6, 1565, in *CSPFS, Elizabeth*, vol. 7, 1564–1565, 422.

1. Cassola, *1565 Ottoman Malta Campaign Register*, 337.

2. Bosio, *Dell'Istoria*, vol. 3, 612.

3. Vendôme, *Siège de Malte*, 42.

4. Bosio, *Dell'Istoria*, vol. 3, 610.

5. Biblioteca Angelica, Rome, Ms 1837 139v.

6. Bosio, *Dell'Istoria*, vol. 3, 613.

7. Balbi, *Verdadera*, 127v. Bradford, *Siege of Malta*, 189 (pagination in Balbi is missing p. 128).

8. Thomas Freller, *Spies and Renegades in Hospitaller Malta* (Malta: Pietà, 2004), 61ff.

9. Bosio, *Dell'Istoria*, vol. 3, 612.

10. Ibid., 613.

11. Viperano, *De Bello*, 24.

12. Sebastiano Pauli, *Codice Diplomatico* (Lucca: Marescandoli, 1737), 217.

13. Cirni, *Commentarii*, 85r. What sort of gun a *morlacca* might be is obscure, but it cannot have been insignificant. The word turns up in Bosio as well.

14. Balbi, *Verdadera*, 79v.; Bradford, *Siege of Malta*, 127.

15. Balbi, *Verdadera*, 84r.; Bradford, *Siege of Malta*, 134.

16. Balbi, *Verdadera*, 85r.; Bradford, *Siege of Malta*, 135.

17. Balbi, *Verdadera*, 86r.; Bradford, *Siege of Malta*, 136.

18. Ibid.

19. Balbi, *Verdadera*, 88v.; Bradford, *Siege of Malta*, 140.

20. Balbi, *Verdadera*, 88v.; Bradford, *Siege of Malta*, 141.

21. Bosio, *Dell'Istoria*, vol. 3, 626.

22. Balbi, *Verdadera*, 89r.; Bradford, *Siege of Malta*, 140.

21. ONSLAUGHT OF THE OTTOMANS

Epigraph: Balbi, *Verdadera*, 90r.; Bradford, *Siege of Malta*, 143.

1. BA, Ms 1837, 141v.

2. Bosio, *Dell'Istoria*, vol. 3, 629.

3. Ibid., 628.

4. Balbi, *Verdadera*, 90v.; Bradford, *Siege of Malta*, 143.

5. Balbi, *Verdadera*, 90v.; Bradford, *Siege of Malta*, 144.

6. Balbi, *Verdadera*, 90v.; Bradford, *Siege of Malta*, 144.

7. Cirni, *Commentarii*, 97r.

8. Salazar, *Hispania*, 232.

9. Cirni, *Commentarii*, 97r.

10. AOM 91 f 58v., cited in Giovanni Bonello, "The Murder of El Greco's Knight," in *Histories of Malta*, vol. 3, *Versions and Diversions* (Malta: Fondazzjoni Patrimonju Malti, 2002), 120; cf. Pellini, *Della historia di Perugia*, 1059. Reprint (Perugia: Fonti per la storia dell'Umbria, 1970).

11. Balbi states that this cry was a deliberate subterfuge ordered by Lugny. Balbi, *Verdadera*, 91v.; Bradford, *Siege of Malta*, 145.

12. Bosio, *Dell'Istoria*, vol. 3, 629.

13. Balbi, *Verdadera*, 92v.; Bradford, *Siege of Malta*, 146–73.

14. Here, as in too many other places, details vary according to our sources. The most significant breakdown is between those who give Anastagi sole credit (Viperano, *De Bello*,

26; Pompeo Pellini, *Della historia di Perugia*, 1060) and those who say that Lugny (with possibly Boisbreton) was involved either from the outset or as a latecomer to the fight (Balbi, *Verdadera*, 92v; Bradford, *Siege of Malta*, 145; Bosio, *Dell'Istoria*, vol. 3, 629; Cirni, *Commentarii*, 97v.).

15. Balbi, *Verdadera*, 95v.; Bradford, *Siege of Malta*, 151. By the end of the siege only forty-five horses would remain alive.

22. TWO GENTLEMEN OF PERUGIA

Epigraph: Busbecq, *Legationis Turcicae*, 237–38; Forster, *Turkish Letters*, 112.

1. For a full discussion of the Capuchin's vision and how it was recorded, see Azzopado, "The Activities of the First Known Capuchin in Malta, Robert of Eboli."

2. Viperano, *De Bello*, 29.

3. Bosio, *Dell'Istoria*, vol. 3, 635. Cf. Cirni, *Commentarii*, 114.

4. Biblioteca Angelica, Rome, Ms 1837, 143r.

5. Balbi, *Verdadera*, 96v.; Bradford, *Siege of Malta*, 154.

6. Cirni, *Commentarii*, 101r.

7. Setton, *Papacy and the Levant*, 838

8. Viperano, *De bello*, 24.

9. Bosio, *Dell'Istoria*, vol. 3, 616.

10. Ettore Calzolare, "Ascanio della Corgna, i combattenti umbri e il "gran soccorso" di Malta nella canzone di un anonimo coevo," *Bollettino della Deputazione di Storia, Patria per l'Umbria*, vol. 94 (Perugia, 1997), 173.

11. Bosio, *Dell'Istoria*, vol. 3, 616. Samuel Steinherz, *Nuntiaturberichte aus Deutschland, 1560–1572*, pt. 2, vol. 4, no. 74 (Vienna, 1914), 277. Murder (*homocidii*), not rape, by this account. Pope Pius IV had named him Marquis of Castiglione e del Chiugi in 1563. Not content, Della Corgna attempted to extend the boundary markings into papal area, a move that did not boost his stock in the papacy. Giving back the land a partial condition of his release.

12. Phayre to Cecil, "Ascanio De la Cornea has been released, but has given to the Pope 25,000 ducats and two towns in the Romagna," August 6, 1565, in *CSPFS, Elizabeth*, vol. 7, *1564–1565*, 419. See, however, Ludovicus Bondonus de Branchis, *Regis Catholici Diarium*, cited in Ludwig von Pastor, *History of the Popes from the Close of the Middle Ages*, vol. 16 (London: Routledge and Keegan Paul, 1951), 367. *Die 3 iulii ill.mus dominus Ascanius de Cornea fuit a carceribus liberatus et de arce S. Angeli. Et die 12 dicti mensis discessit ab Urbe Melitam versus ad instantiam.*

13. CODOIN, vol. 29, 454.

14. The Bibliothèque Nationale de France has a small collection of these, most available online.

15. Guzman to King Philip, London, July 13, 1565, "Simancas: July 1565," *Calendar of State Papers, Spain* (henceforth *CSP, Spain*) (Simancas), vol. 1: *1558–1567* (1892), 442–58.

16. Guzman to King Philip, London, July 23, 1565, "Simancas: July 1565," *CSP, Spain* (Simancas), vol. 1: *1558–1567* (1892), 442–58. For more on English perspectives on the siege, see Helen Vella-Bonavita, "Key to Christendom: The 1565 Siege of Malta, Its Histories, and Their Use in Reformation Polemic," *Sixteenth Century Journal* 33, no. 4 (2002): 1021–43.

17. Cassola, *Great Siege of Malta*, 25–26.

18. For Venice and Fort St. Elmo, see Garci Hernandez to Philip II, July 26, 1565, Simancas Eo 1325, in Braudel, *Mediterranean*, 1022.

19. Bosio, *Dell'Istoria*, vol. 3, 651. This was on top of the pressure Toledo was getting from Malta itself, both firsthand from letters from Valette, and secondhand from letters from the likes of Mesquita to knights still at Messina, asking them to nudge the viceroy along. Ulloa cites a letter from Mesquita to Baigli, a knight at Messina, telling of the fall of St. Elmo and urging that Baigli press the need for more help with Don Garcia (Pauli, *Codice Diplomatico*, 219).

20. Bosio, *Dell'Istoria*, vol. 3, 657.

21. Ibid., 658.

22. F. X. Cassar, "Documents of the Ottoman Maghreb during the Siege of Malta, 1565," *Malta Independent*, June 12, 1994.

23. Viperano, *De Bello*, 30. Quoted is too strong a word. Historians at the time believed in poetic license when reporting speeches. Cf. Viperano, *De Scribenda Historia*, in Viperanus, *Operum pars prima, continens res oratorias, historicas, et poeticas* (Naples: Carlini, 1606), 177.

24. Cirni refers to a letter written from Anastagi to Della Corgna (Cirni, *Commentarii*, 101r.); Bosio (634, 654) refers to this report, but does not name the addressee. The text can be found in Pompeo Pellini's 1664 volume *Della Historia di Perugia*. See Giovanni Bonello, *Histories of Malta*, vol. 3, *Versions and Diversions* (Malta: Fondazzjoni Patrimonju Malti, 2003). A Vatican document claims that Della Corgna had himself gone to Malta for reconnaissance, which accords nicely with Anastagi's document: *Ascanio della Cornia, qual era stato a riconoscer Malta et l'armata nemica et ritornato* (Vatican Apostolic Library, Cod. Urb. Lat. 10450 fol. 70–71r., 73, 78ff in Setton, *Papacy and the Levant*, vol. 4). It is possible that Don Garcia, seeking to boost his friend's standing in the wider world, either implicitly or explicitly gave this impression to others and let the rumor fly.

25. Pellini, *Della Historia di Perugia*, 1068. Cf. Bonello, 129. Anastagi also makes a slight swipe at Don Garcia on the subject of a naval battle: "Had battle been fought at sea the result would have been certain, considering the weakness of the Turkish armada, which in my roles as your servant, I tell you truly, is only an collection of unarmed vessels, and this is the case, although I have heard from the said Captain (Salazar) that the Viceroy will not even consider fighting the enemy at sea." Bonello, 128; Pellini, *Della Historia*, 1066. It is easier to criticize a viceroy than a king . . .

26. CODOIN, vol. 29, 174.

27. Bosio, *Dell'Istoria*, vol. 3, 636.

28. Balbi, *Verdadera*, 98v.–98r.; Bradford, *Siege of Malta*, 154.

29. Bosio, *Dell'Istoria*, vol. 3, 638.

30. Cirni, *Commentarii*, 102v.

31. Bosio, *Dell'Istoria*, vol. 3, 638.

32. Ibid.

33. Ibid., 646.

34. Balbi, *Verdadera*, 99v.; Bradford, *Siege of Malta*, 158. Most serious battles, according to Balbi, lasted five hours.

35. Balbi, *Verdadera*, 99v.; Bradford, *Siege of Malta*, 157.

Epigraphs: Cassola, *Great Siege of Malta*, 32. "A copie of the last aduertisement that came from Malta of the miraculous deliuerie of the isle from the longe sieg[e] of the Turke, both by sea and land . . . Translated out of ye Italian tongue, into English Date: 1565."

1. August 5, 1565, AGS Estado, legado 1054, fol. 173.

2. Viperano, *De Bello*, 31.

3. Balbi, *Verdadera*, 101r.; Bradford, *Siege of Malta*, 160.

4. Bosio, *Dell'Istoria*, vol. 3, 673.

5. Cirni, *Commentarii*, 93v. Cf. Bosio, *Dell'Istoria*, vol. 3, 647. "In person against the post of Castile, Mustapha now shared his lessening expectations with a small number of his chosen confidants." He got over it. "For the next assault he was challenged to lead from the front, and laughing, the Pasha showed that he felt great contentment, which shamed the remaining sphahis and Janissaries to follow him."

6. Bosio, *Dell'Istoria*, vol. 3, 674. Given the effort that the little people were putting into the fight at this last desperate time, his loyalty is absolutely correct. Moreover, staying with them was a good way to make sure they didn't take any calls for surrender, as had happened in Rhodes.

7. Ibid., 681.

8. Ibid., 658.

9. Balbi, *Verdadera*, 106v.; Bradford, *Siege of Malta*, 170.

10. In a letter to the pope (1567?), the volunteer Rangone claims that Don Garcia seized the ship and its cargo for his personal use "to general annoyance" (*gran mala soddisfattione*). It's an unsubstantiated story, but one that shows in what direction Don Garcia's reputation was going. Scicluna, "L'Assedio di Malta," 39. See also Bonello, "Pallavicino Rangone," in *Histories of Malta*, vol. 9, 68.

11. Balbi, *Verdadera*, 112v.; Bradford, *Siege of Malta*, 172.

12. Balbi, *Verdadera*, 113v.; Bradford, *Siege of Malta*, 174.

13. Balbi, *Verdadera*, 112v.; Bradford, *Siege of Malta*, 172. CODOIN, vol. 29, 500, makes no mention of any Doria wounding, but that could be modesty. CODOIN, vol. 29, 503, also says one vessel. See also Doria's accounts in CODOIN, vol. 29, 479, dated September 1, and CODOIN, vol. 29, 495.

14. Salazar, *Hispania*, 249.

15. Don Garcia to Francisco de Eraso, September 7: *desembarco en Malta de 9600 soldadoes*; CODOIN, vol. 29, 482. Animals noted in Cirni, *Commentarii*, 120v.

16. Balbi, *Verdadera*, 114v.–115r., Bradford, *Siege of Malta*, 177.

17. Balbi, *Verdadera*, 112v.; Bradford, *Siege of Malta*, 173.

18. CODOIN, vol. 29, 444–45. Though he seems unable to bring a whole lot of enthusiasm to the choice: " . . . no puedo quitarle el cargo que el rey le ha dado"; CODOIN, vol. 29, 444–45.

19. Busbecq, *Legationis Turcicae*, 226 (Foster, *Turkish Letters*, 171).

20. August 16, 1565, CODOIN, vol. 29, 444–45. Cirni confirms that Don Garcia wanted to keep Sande from total control (Cirni, Commentarii, 105r.).

21. Busbecq, *Legationis Turcicae*, 274 (Foster, *Turkish Letters*, 218).

22. CODOIN, vol. 29, 445. Bosio makes it sound as if Chiappino was a happy-go-lucky fellow ready to give in to the greater good: "Chiappino Vitelli was content to travel in that

company as a simple adventurer rather than undermine (Sande's) claims." Bosio, *Dell'Istoria*, vol. 3, 688.

23. "Because in these circumstances it is also desirable that there is a Field Master whose office has overall charge of the aforementioned people . . . we name Ascanio della Corgna." Curiously, Don Garcia also decreed that, should Don Álvaro be killed, Don Sancho de Londoño should take over. A. G. S. Estado, Sicilia, leg. 1, 129 folio 118. Don Garcia de Toledo to Philip, August 24, 1565, in *Don Álvaro de Sande y la Orden de Malta*, 62.

24. Viperano, *De Bello*, 32.

25. Vendôme, for example, describes Della Corgna as *Maestro di campo general* and Sande as in charge of Spanish foot (*Generale della fanteria spagnuola*) (Vendôme, *Siège de Malte*, 107). Conti refers to *Ascanius Cornis Magister exercitus, Alvarus Sandes, Hispanis cohortibus praefectus* (Natale Conti, *Commentarii Hieronymi Comitis Alexandrini de acerrimo, ac omnium difficillimo Turcarum bello, in insulam Melitam gesto, anno MDLXV* [Venice: Zileti, 1566], 58), as does Viperano, at least as far as limiting Sande to Spanish troops only (*Alvarum Sandeum clarum inter hispanos ducem, atque Ascanium Corneum castrorum magistrum*, Viperano, *De Bello*, 32). See also Cirni, *Commentarii*, 115r. For a contemporary discussion of rank order at that time, see Francesco Feretti, *Della Osservanza Militare del Capitan Francesco Ferretti D'Ancona* (Venice: Borgomineri, 1576).

26. "We order the said Don Álvaro that, if a difference of opinion should arise among the above-cited in the resolutions, then what appears to be the consensus of the above-named should always be executed." A. G. S Estado Sicilia leg. 1.129 fol. 118. Don García de Toledo to Felipe II, August 24, Syracuse, Italy, in Aguareles, "Don Álvaro de Sande y la Orden de Malta," 62. Don Garcia tried to put the best possible spin on it—"As to decision making, I have thought to give [Don Álvaro] a companion because it seemed to me that such important matters should not rest entirely in one single head." Ibid.

27. Viperano, *De Bello*, 32. Cirni puts it at one Janissary (Cirni, *Commentarii*, 114r.).

28. Balbi, *Verdadera*, 103v.; Bradford, *Siege of Malta*, 166; Cirni, *Commentarii*, 104r. This was something of a turnaround; earlier there had been enough grain in Birgu that it was sold freely. Adriani, *Istoria*, 741. For an English translation of relevant passages, see Giovanni Bonello, "Giovanni Battista Adriani's Great Siege of Malta, 1565," in *Histories of Malta*, vol. 9, *Confessions and Transgressions* (Malta: Fondazzjoni Patrimonju Malti, 2008), 39–57.

29. Balbi, *Verdadera*, 102v.; Bradford, *Siege of Malta*, 164.

24. MUSTAPHA'S LAST HAZARD

Epigraph: Francesco Laparelli, "Codex of Francisco Laparelli of Cortona," in Quentin Hughes, "How Fort St. Elmo Survived the Siege for So Long" (forthcoming).

1. Balbi, *Verdadera*, 103v.; Bradford, *Siege of Malta*, 166.

2. Bosio, *Dell'Istoria*, vol. 3, 647.

3. Balbi, *Verdadera*, 104r.; Bradford, *Siege of Malta*, 167.

4. Grain from Ragusa en route to Djerba to be baked into biscuit was seized by the *Gran Soccorso*, and Mustapha had asked for more. Adriani, *Istoria*, 743; Charrière, *Négotiations*, vol. 2, 802.

5. Cirni, *Commentarii*, 119v.

6. Balbi, *Verdadera*, 104v; Bradford, *Siege of Malta*, 168.

7. Balbi, *Verdadera*, 117r.; Bradford, *Siege of Malta*, 181. Armchair generals may make judgments without knowledge of "orders generals may have had from their princes, nor their plans, which they are not obliged to make public."

8. The source is a contemporary volunteer, Pallavicino Rangone, who for reasons best known to himself later wrote a poisonous account of the siege for Pope Pius V. He was at least bipartisan in his views, ripping into both Don Garcia, whose bad planning and pusillanimity nearly ruined the *Grand Soccorso*, and Valette, whose greed and foolishness brought the siege about in the first place. For his unusual account, see Lib. Ms. 1184 Archivum Melitense, vol. 8, no. 1 (April 1929): 35–42; Bonello, "Pallavicino Rangone," in *Histories of Malta*, vol. 9, 58–66.

9. Adriani, *Istoria*, 743.

10. CODOIN, vol. 29, 520.

11. Balbi, *Verdadera*, 118v.; Bradford, *Siege of Malta*, 183.

12. Bosio, *Dell'Istoria*, vol. 3, 699. Figures, alas, are notoriously unreliable in contemporary historians.

13. Balbi, *Verdadera*, 117v.; Bradford, *Siege of Malta*,182.

25. THE GRAN SOCCORSO AT WAR

Epigraph: Bosio, *Dell'Istoria*, vol. 3, 701.

1. Valette to Don Garcia, September 11, 1565, in CODOIN, vol. 29, 513.

2. Bosio, *Dell'Istoria*, vol. 3, 697. Della Corgna had an uphill climb on this request. Unlike Don Álvaro, he had not met the grand master, nor fought on his behalf, nor even fought the Ottomans. Worse, until recently he had been imprisoned by the pope, Valette's direct superior. Even absent the written commission, there was no incentive for the grand master to change the order of command. Viperano notes delicately that the two men, Ascanio and Sande, were "not of the same mind" (Viperano, *De Bello*, 38).

3. CODOIN, vol. 29, 514. Cf. Balbi, *Verdadera*, 118v.; Bradford, *Siege of Malta*, 183 (Bradford's translation is missing a line). Bradford writes that they should do as appeared best to them to secure victory "if they should come to blows with the Turks." Rangone put the number of Ottoman troops at eighteen thousand (Bonello, "Pallavicino Ragone," in *Histories of Malta*, vol. 9, 65).

4. Viperano, *De Bello*, 38; cf. Bosio, *Dell'Istoria*, vol. 3, 698.

5. Bosio, *Dell'Istoria*, vol. 3, 698; Viperano says that he "leapt out of his tent and gathered 300 Spanish fusiliers, seeking to take a dominating hill. Della Corgna protested that he had not been consulted." Viperano, *De Bello*, 38.

6. Viperano, *De Bello*, 38.

7. Cirni, *Commentarii*, 121v.

8. Ibid., 123v.; cf. Bosio, *Dell'Istoria*, vol. 3, 699.

9. Balbi, *Verdadera*, 119v.; Bradford, *Siege of Malta*, 184; Cirni, *Commentarii*, 123v.

10. CODOIN, vol. 29, 514.

11. Ibid., 521.

12. Cirni, *Commentarii*, 123r.

13. Selaniki, in Rossi, "L'Assedio di Malta," 149.

14. Bosio, *Dell'Istoria*, vol. 3, 701.

15. Ibid.

16. Valette to George von Hohenheim, prior of the German order, October 9, 1565, Malta, in Sebastiano Pauli, *Codice Diplomatico del Sacro Militare Ordine Gerosolimitano oggi di Malta* (Lucca, IT: Marescandoli, 1737), 220–21; and Curionis, *De Bello Melitae*, 503.

17. Bosio, *Dell'Istoria*, vol. 3, 701; cf. Cirni, *Commentarii*, 122v.

18. "Más vale aquí, señor Ascanio, que en la cara." Aguareles, "Don Álvaro de Sande y la Orden de Malta," 71.

19. Balbi, *Verdadera*, 120v.; Bradford, *Siege of Malta*, 185. In his report to Philip, Sande puts the number at "more than a thousand barrels" (CODOIN, vol. 29, 524). Valette seems to have thought that the barrels were the only reason for the overland trip to St. Paul's Bay ("para acabar de hacer la aguada," CODOIN, vol. 29, 513), since they had been unable to get water at the Marsa.

20. Cirni, *Commentarii*, 123v.

21. "[A] Mostafa Bajá herido de dos arcabuzazos le salvaron con gran trabajo Avisos de Constantinopla para el Duque de Alcalá." October 13 and 19, 1565, Constantinople, AGS Estado, legajo 1054, doc. 215, in Sola, *Despertar al que dormía*, 77.

22. Selaniki, in Rossi, "L'Assedio di Malta," 149.

23. Cirni, *Commentarii*, 123v.

24. Selaniki, in Rossi, "L'Assedio di Malta," 149.

25. Cirni, *Commentarii*, 124r.

26. Ibid., 124v.

27. CODOIN, vol. 29, 524. Cirni claims that Mustapha bemoaned a loss of two thousand (Cirni, *Commentarii*, 124v.).

28. Adriano, *Istoria*, 193. See also Bonello, *An Overlooked History*, 54.

29. Cirni, *Commentarii*, 124r.

26. FROM THE ASHES

Epigraph: Schermerhorn, *Malta of the Knights*, 50. Her quote, though compelling, comes through something like a game of telephone. She is quoting from Jurien de La Gravière (*Les Chevaliers de Malte et la Marine de Philippe II*), who is in turn quoting from Brantôme (*Œuvres complètes*), who loved nothing better than a good story. Made up was close enough for the sixteenth-century historians, so long as the basic intent was in keeping with the truth. See Viperano, *De Historia Scribendi*, 39.

1. Anthoine de Cressy to Grand Prior of France, September 11, 1565, Malta, in Camusat, *Mélange Historique*, 52v., 53r.

2. Cirni, *Commentarii*, 124r.

3. Balbi, *Verdadera*, 121r; Bradford, *Siege of Malta*, 184.

4. Cirni, *Commentarii*, 124v. In his initial report, Sande puts the figure at closer to fifteen hundred—one can hardly expect Mustapha to have been precise at just that moment. (CODOIN, vol. 29, 524).

5. Cirni, *Commentarii*, 121v.

6. Valette appears to have had a genuine affection for the Dorias. There is a dual portrait of him and the old admiral.

7. The value assumes one ounce of gold is US$1,200; a gold ducat contains 3.5 grams of

gold. Silver reals varied considerably in value even then. This kind of black marketeering was investigated after the siege. Bonello, "Great Siege, Small Morsels," in *Histories of Malta*, vol. 9, 23.

8. Cassola, *1565 Ottoman Malta Campaign Register*, 349.

9. Braudel, *Mediterranean*, 1019; cf. Charrière, *Négotiations*, vol. 2, 801–7.

10. Raimond de Beccarie de Pavie Baron de Fourquevaux, *Dépêches de M. de Fourquevaux* (Paris: Plon-Nourrit, 1896), 8.

11. Bartolomeo Foresti to Cosimo de' Medici, December 15, 1565, Medici Archives, Florence, MdP 518, Doc ID22229, Folio Start 767. (Three days later, he was reportedly seeking diggers from Sicily. Giuseppe Cambiano to Cosimo de' Medici, Medici Archives, Florence, MdP 518, Doc ID22255, Folio Start 784.)

12. Toledo to Philip, November 26, 1565, Messina, in CODOIN, vol. 30, 13.

13. Braudel, *Mediterranean*, 1022. Philip was, however, more concerned with Goletta in 1566. Rafael Vargas-Hidalgo, *Guerra y diplomacia en el Mediterráneo: Correspondencie inédita de Felippe II con Andrea Doria y Juan Andrea Doria* (Madrid: Ediciones Polifemo, 2002), 464.

14. Charrière, *Négociations*, vol. 2, 806. A Spanish report goes further, noting that locals mourning their husbands, sons, and brothers threw stones through the windows of Christian houses. Garci Hernandez to the King, November 13, 1565, Venice, AGS Estado, legajo 1325, doc. 123, in Sola, *Despertar al que dormía*, 82–83.

15. Charrière, *Négociations*, vol. 2, 805.

16. Notices from Constantinople for the Duke of Alcalá, October 13 and 19, 1565, Constantinople, AGS Estado, legado 1054, doc. 215, in Sola, *Despertar al que dormía*, 76–80.

17. H. A. R. Balbi, "Some Unpublished Records on the Siege of Malta, 1565," 5–6.

18. Imber, *Navy of Suleiman the Magnificent*, 259.

19. Çelebi, *History of the Maritime Wars*, 120.

20. DiGiorgio, in Spiteri, *Fortresses of the Knights*, 264.

21. Paula S. Fichtner, *Emperor Maximilian II* (New Haven, CT: Yale University Press, 2001), 121ff.

22. Christine Isom-Verhaaren, "Suleyman and Mihrimah: The Favorite Daughter," *Journal of Persianate Studies* 4 (2011): 74.

23. William Stirling Maxwell, *Don John of Austria*, vol. 1, 469; von Hammer, vol. 6, 434.

24. Alberi, *Relazioni*, ser. 3, 1863–1893, vol. 1, 67, 18–19; vol. 3, 151–52, 153, 191.

25. Andrew C. Hess, "The Battle of Lepanto and Its Place in Mediterranean History," *Past and Present* 57, no. 1 (1972): 65.

26. Michel Fontenay, "Corsaires de la foi ou rentiers du sol? Les Chevaliers de Malte dans le 'corso' méditerranéen au XVII siecle," *Revue d'Histoire Moderne et Contemporaine* (1988): 361–84.

27. For more on this topic, see Thomas Freller, *The Cavaliers' Tour and Malta in 1663: One Journey and Two Accounts* (Malta: Pietà, 1998).

28. Fontenay, "Il mercato maltese degli schiavi al tempo dei Cavalieri di San Giovanni (1530–1798)," *Scheda Rivista*, no. 2 (August 2001): 394.

29. Emir Mehmet ibn-Emir es-Su'udi, 1580, quoted in W. E. D. Allen, *Problems of Turkish Power in the Sixteenth Century* (London: Central Asian Research Centre, 1963), 30.

27. VERDICT

Epigraph: Voltaire, *Annales de l'Empire depuis Charlemagne*, vol. 13 of *Œuvres Complètes de Voltaire* (Paris: Garnier Frères, 1878), 536. The same phrase was used by Viperano in his *De Scribendi Historia*: "Hoc bellum, quo nullum acrius neque nostra neque maiorum nostrorum memoria gestum fuisse uidebatur," 4.

1. Raimond de Beccarie de Pavie Fourquevaux, *Dépêches de m. de Fourquevaux, ambassadeur du roi Charles IX en Espagne, 1565–1572*, vol. 1 (Paris: E. Leroux, 1896–1904), 7–8. This belief may have precipitated Philip's decree against all things Moorish in 1567, which indeed precipitated revolt—but absent outside aid, a failed revolt.

2. "A Form to be used in common prayer every Wednesday and Friday within the city and Diocese of Sarum: to excite all godly people to pray unto God for the delivery of those Christians that are now invaded by the Turk." In *Liturgies and Communal Forms of Prayer Set Forth in the Reign of Queen Elizabeth*, ed. William Keatinge Clay (Cambridge: Cambridge University Press, 1847), 519.

3. Fourquevaux, *Dépêches*, vol. 1, 6.

4. Hess, "The Battle of Lepanto," 70–71.

5. Battista Mantovano, *De Calamitatibus Temporum*, bk. 5, fol. 25 (Paris: Georg Wolff and Johann Philippi, 1494–1495).

6. Hess, "The Battle of Lepanto," 70–71.

28. THE SURVIVORS

Epigraphs: Adriani, *Istoria de' suoi tempi di Giovambatista Adriani*, 744–45. Selaniki, in Rossi, "L'Assedio di Malta," 148.

1. Bosio, *Dell'Istoria*, vol. 3, 936.

2. Giovanni Bonello, "Grand Masters in the Cinquecento: Their Persona and Death," *Malta Medical Journal* 15, no. 2 (November 2003): 47.

3. Scicluna, *L'Assedio di Malta*, 35–42. See also Giovanni Bonello, "Pallavicino Rangone: Intemperate Critic of Valette," *Histories of Malta*, vol. 9, *Confessions and Transgressions* (Malta: Fondazzjoni Patrimonju Malti, 2008), 58–67.

4. Malia-Milanes, "Frà Jean de la Valette, 1495–1568: A Reappraisal," 125.

5. Bonello, "Grand Masters in the Cinquecento," 47.

6. Ibid., 48.

7. Peçevi, in Rossi, "L'Assedio di Malta," 151. Petremol's last letter from Constantinople ends on the subject of Mustapha and Piali: Petremol to du Ferrier, October 15–25, 1565, Charrière, *Négociations*, vol. 2, 806.

8. Richard Blackburn, *Journey to the Sublime*, 171. He should not be confused—though he all too often is—with Lala Kara Mustapha Pasha (1500–1580), who figured prominently in the battle for Cyprus, 1570.

9. "Instrucciones de Carlos Quinto a Don Felipe," in *Papiers d'Etat du Cardinal de Grenvelle*, 292.

10. CODOIN, vol. 29, 559.

11. Charrière, *Négociations*, vol. 2, 808.

12. Cesare Caporali, "Sopra la liberazione di Malta dall'Assedio de' Turchi del 1565 al Si-

gnor Ascanio della Corgna," in *Poesia di Cesare Caporali* (Perugia, IT: Reginaldi, 1770), 447. *Se'l duro Scita, che i due chiari segni / D'Ercole scorse, e quasi vincitore / Coperse i nostri mare con tanti legni, / Che'l mondo empì di fama e di terrore, / Non avea contra i suoi fieri disegni, / Signor, la vostra mano pronta e'l valore, / Avria sin oggidi, ch'ognun v'esalta, / Piantato in Traci il gran Trofeo di Malta.*

Scythia was close enough for poetry to refer to Ottoman Turks, or specifically Suleiman. Coincidentally, Hercules is said to have fathered two children with the Scythian princess Echidnea, which might lead other Scythians to imagine a proprietary interest in their ancestors' twin pillars.

13. Joseph Galea, "Vincenzo Anastasi [*sic*] Knight of Malta: Biographical Notes on His Career in the Order of St. John of Jerusalem," *Annales de l'Ordre Souverain Militaire de Malte* 18, no. 2 (April–June 1960): 26–31.

14. Giovanni Bonello, "The Murder of El Greco's Knight of Malta," in *Histories of Malta*, vol. 2, *Versions and Diversions* (Malta: Fondazzjoni Patrimonju Malti, 2002), 115–23.

15. Brantôme, *Œuvres complètes*, vol. 6 (Paris, 1878), 245.

16. "Avignon M. de Sevre prayed him in behalf of Oliver Sterley [*sic*] Knight of Rhodes, who is in Malta. He is desirous to return into England, and be a faithful subject to her. He is in credit amongst them of the Council of Malta, and has the watch of the isle. He is chief of the English there." *CSPFS, Elizabeth*, October 4, 1564, 218.

17. Bonello, "Sir Oliver Starkey, Paragon and Victim," in *Histories of Malta*, vol. 2, *Versions and Diversions*, 42–53.

18. Vendôme, *Le Siège de Malte*, 50.

19. Balbi, *Verdadura*, 62r.; Bradford, *Siege of Malta*, 100.

20. *CSPFS, Elizabeth*, 1565, 520.

21. Ibid., 518–19.

22. Ibid., 533.

23. Bonello, "Pallavicino Rangone," in *Histories of Malta*, vol. 2, *Confessions and Transgressions* 58–66.

24. Brantôme, *Œuvres complètes*, vol. 2, *Grands capitaines estrangers* (1866), 45ff.

25. Gravière, *Les Chevaliers de Malte*, passim.

26. Guilmartin, *Gunpowder and Galleys*, 137–47. Bosio, *Dell'Istoria*, vol. 3, 554.

Bibliography

Abun-Nasr, Jamil M. *A History of the Magrib*. New York: Cambridge University Press, 1971.

Adriani, Giovanni Battista. *Istoria de' suoi tempi di Giovambatista Adriani*. Florence: Nella Stamperia de i Giunti, 1583.

Ágoston, Gábor. *Guns for the Sultan: Military Power and the Weapons Industry in the Ottoman Empire*. Cambridge: Cambridge University Press, 2005.

Aguareles, Eugenio Serrablo. "Don Alvaro de Sande y la Orden de Malta." *Revista de Archivos, Bibliotecas y Museos* 61 (1955): 53–79.

Alberi, Eugenio. *Relazioni degli ambasciatori veneti al senato*, ser. 3 vol. 9. Florence: Clio, 1863–1893.

Alberti, Leon Battista. *Libri de Re Aedificatoria Decem*. Paris: Berthold Rembolt, 1512.

Allen, Bruce Ware. "The Siege That Made Suleiman Magnificent." *MHQ: Quarterly Journal of Military History* 19 (autumn 2006): 6–16.

——— . "Captain Juan de la Cerda and the Great Siege of Malta—A Confused Story." *Treasures of Malta* 19, no. 1 (2012): 38–45.

Allen, W. E. D. *Problems of Turkish Power in the Sixteenth Century*. London: Central Asian Research Centre, 1963.

Amarelli, Marco. "Costantino e la casa Castriota, nuovi contributi sulla biagrafia e gli scritti di 'Filionico Alicarnasseo.'" *Critica Letteraria* 40, no. 1 (154): 109–31.

Anderson, R. C. *Naval Wars in the Levant, 1559–1853*. Princeton, NJ: Princeton University Press, 1952.

——— . *Oared Fighting Ships: From Classical Times to the Coming of Steam*. London: Percival Marshall, 1962.

Argenti, Philip. *Chius Vincta, or, The Occupation of Chios by the Turks (1566): And Their Administration of the Island (1566–1912)*. Cambridge: Cambridge University Press, 1941.

——— . *Occupation of Chios by the Genoese and Their Administration of the Island 1346–1566*. Cambridge: Cambridge University Press, 1958.

Ascham, Roger, *The English Works of Roger Ascham, Preceptor to Queen Elizabeth*. London: White, Cochran, 1815.

Azzopardi, Francis. "The Activities of the First Known Capuchin in Malta: Robert of Eboli." *Melita Historica: Journal of the Malta Historical Society* 4, no. 2 (1965): 96–110.

Balbi, H. A. R. "Some Unpublished Records on the Siege of Malta, 1565." *Institute of Historical Research, Malta*, no. 6 (1937): 5–36. Bulletin.

Balbi da Correggio, Francesco. *La Verdadera Relación de todo lo que el año de MDLXV ha succedido en la isla de Malta*. Barcelona: Pedro Reigner, 1568.

——— . *The Siege of Malta, 1565*. Trans. Ernle Bradford. London: Folio Society, 1965.

——— . *The Siege of Malta, 1565*. Trans. Henry Alexander Balbi. Copenhagen: O. F. Gollcher and O. Rostock, 1961.

Baray, Bernard. *De Rhodes à Malte: Le grand Maître Philippe de Villiers de L'Isle-Adam (1460–1534) et l'ordre de Malte*. Paris: Somogy Editions d'Art, 2004.

Basset, René. *Documents musulmans sur le Siège d'Algier en 1541, publiés, traduits et annotés par René Basset*. Paris: Ernest Leroux, 1890.

Berbrugger, Adrien, *Le Pégnon d'Alger ou Les origines du gouvernement turc en Algérie*. Algiers: Bastide, 1860.

——— . "Négociations entre Hassan Aga et le Comte d'Alcaudete, Gouverneur d'Oran, 1541–1542." *Revue Africaine* 9 (1865): 379–85.

——— . "L'Expédition Espagnole de 1541 contre Alger." *Revue Afrique* 35 (1891): 177–206.

Berenger, Jean. "La collaboration militaire franco-ottomane à l'époque de la Renaissance." *Revue Internationale d'Histoire Militaire* 68 (1987): 51–66.

Bertrand, Louis. *The History of Spain*. London: Eyre and Spottiswood, 1956.

Blackburn, Richard. *Journey to the Sublime Porte: The Arabic Memoir of a Sharifian Agent's Diplomatic Mission to the Ottoman Imperial Court in the Era of Suleyman the Magnificent*. Beirut: Orient-Institut, 2005.

Bombaci, Alessio. "Le Fonti turche della Battaglia delle Gerbe." *Rivista degli studi orientali* 19, no. 1 (1941): 193–248.

——— . "Un rapporto del Grande Ammiraglio Piyale Pascià a Solimano sull'Assedio delle Gerbe (1560)." In *Festschrift Friedrich Giese aus Anlass des siebenzigsten Geburtstags überreicht von Freunden und Schülern*, ed. Gotthard Jäschke (Leipzig: Deutsche Gesellschaft für Islamkunde, 1941), 80. Also in *Die Welt des Islams* 23 (1941): 75–83.

Bonello, Giovanni. "The Two Lanfreducci Knights of Malta." In *Histories of Malta*. Vol. 1, *Deceptions and Perceptions*, 23–32. Malta: Fondazzjoni Patrimonju Malti, 2000.

——— . "The Murder of El Greco's Knight of Malta." In *Histories of Malta*. Vol. 3, *Versions and Diversions*, 115–122. Malta: Fondazzjoni Patrimonju Malti, 2002.

——— . "An Overlooked Eyewitness Account of the Great Siege." In *Histories of Malta*. Vol. 3, *Versions and Diversions*, 123–134. Malta: Fondazzjoni Patrimonju Malti, 2002.

——— . "Sir Oliver Starkey: Paragon and Victim." In *Histories of Malta*. Vol. 3, *Versions and Diversions*, 42–53. Malta: Fondazzjoni Patrimonju Malti, 2002.

——— . "Grand Masters in the Cinquecento: Their Persona and Death." *Malta Medical Journal* 15, no. 2 (November 2003): 44–49.

——— . "Persona and Deaths of Six 16th Century Grand Masters of the Order of St John." *Malta Medical Journal* 16, no. 2 (July 2004): 47–50.

——— . "Unpublished Documents from Ragusa about the Great Siege, 1565." In *Histories of Malta*. Vol. 8, *Mysteries and Myths*, 27–53. Malta: Fondazzjoni Patrimonju Malti, 2007.

——— . "Giovanni Battista Adriani's Unknown History of the Great Siege." In *Histories of Malta*. Vol. 9, *Confessions and Transgressions*, 34–57. Malta: Fondazzjoni Patrimonju Malti, 2008.

———. "Great Siege, Small Morsels." In *Histories of Malta*. Vol. 9, *Confessions and Transgressions*, 18–33. Malta: Fondazzjoni Patrimonju Malti, 2008.

———. "Pallavicino Ragone: Intemperate Critic of La Valette." In *Histories of Malta*. Vol. 9, *Confessions and Transgressions*, 58–66. Malta: Fondazzjoni Patrimonju Malti, 2008.

Bonello, Vincenzo. *Il Ninfeo del Giardino di d'Omedes*. Estratto dal "Malta" del 1 Luglio, 1939.

Bonfadio, Jacopo. *Le lettere e una scrittura burlesca*. Rome: Bonacci, 1978. Borghesi, Vilma. *Vita del Principe Giovanni Andrea Doria scritta da lui medesimo incompleta*. Genoa: Compagnia dei Librai, 1997.

Bosio, Iacomo. *Dell'Istoria della Sacra Religione et Illma: Militia di San Giovanni Gierosolimitano*. Rome: Stamperia Apost. Vaticana, 1594–1602.

Bourbon, Jacques de. *La Grand et Merveilleuse et très cruelle oppugnation de la noble cité de Rhodes prinse naguères par Sultan Seliman à présent Grand Turcq, ennemy de la très sainte foy catholique rédigée par escript par excellent et noble cheualier Frère Jacques Bastard de Bourbon, Commandent de Sanct Maulviz, Doysemon, et Fonteyne au prieuré de France*. Paris: Pierre Vidoue, 1526.

Bowerman, H. G. *The History of Fort St. Angelo*. Malta: Progress Press, 1947.

Bradford, Ernle. *The Great Siege: Malta 1565*. London: Hodder and Stoughton, 1961.

Bracco, P. Raffaele. *Il Principe Giannandrea Doria: Patriae Libertatis Conservator*. Genoa: Scuola Grafica Opera SS. Vergine di Ponpei, 1960.

Brandi, Karl. *The Emperor Charles V*. London: J. Cape, 1939.

Brantôme, Pierre de Bordeille, Seigneur de Abbé de Brantôme. *Œuvres complètes de Pierre de Bourdeilles, Abbé et Seigneur de Brantôme*. Paris: Plon, 1858–1895.

Braudel, Fernand. *The Mediterranean and the Mediterranean World in the Age of Philip II*. Trans. Siân Reynolds. New York: Harper and Row, 1973.

———. "Les Espagnols et l'Afrique du Nord de 1492 à 1577." *Revue Africaine*, nos. 2 and 3 (1928): 184–233, 351–428.

Bregante, Gregorio. "Lettere Ministri Constantinopli." Archivio Segreto Genoa, envelope 1–2169.

Brennan, Michael G. "Christopher Marlowe's *The Jew of Malta* and Two Newsletter Accounts of the Siege of Malta 1565." *Notes and Queries* 238, no. 1 (1993): 157–60.

Bridge, Antony. *Suleiman the Magnificent: Scourge of Heaven*. London: Granada Publishing, 1983.

Brockman, Eric. *The Two Sieges of Rhodes: The Knights of St. John at War 1480–1522*. London: J. Murray, 1969.

———. "D'Amaral: Martyr or Traitor?" Annales de l'Ordre Souverain Militaire de Malte 24, no. 1 (1966): 18–25.

Brummett, Palmira. *Ottoman Seapower and Levantine Diplomacy in the Age of Discovery*. Albany: State University of New York Press, 1994.

———. "Foreign Policy, Naval Strategy, and the Defence of the Ottoman Empire in the Early Sixteenth Century." *International History Review* 11, no. 4 (November 1989): 613–27.

———. "The Ottomans as a World Power: What We Don't Know about Ottoman Seapower." *Orient Moderno* 20, no. 81 (2001): 1–21.

Busbecq, Ogier Ghislain de. *Legationis Turcicae Epistolae Quatuor*. Frankfurt: Andrea Wecheli, 1595.

———. *The Turkish Letters of Ogier Ghiselin de Busbecq*. Trans. E. S. Forster. Oxford: Oxford University Press, 1927.

Busuttil, Joseph. "Pirates in Malta." *Melita Historica* 5 (1971): 308–10.

Calabritto, Giovanni. "Un Poemetto Popolare sul Grande Assedio di Malta." *Archivum Melitense* 8, no. 3 (July 1931): 112–77.

Calendar of State Papers, Foreign Series, of the Reign of Edward the VI, 1547–1553. London: State Paper Department, Her Majesty's Public Record Office, 1861.

Calendar of State Papers, Foreign Series, of the Reign of Mary, 1553–1558. London: State Paper Department, Her Majesty's Public Record Office, 1861.

Calendar of State Papers, Foreign Series, of the Reign of Elizabeth, 1558–1559. London: State Paper Department, Her Majesty's Public Record Office, 1863.

Calendar of State Papers, Foreign Series, of the Reign of Elizabeth, 1559–1560. London: State Paper Department, Her Majesty's Public Record Office, 1864.

Calendar of State Papers, Foreign Series, of the Reign of Elizabeth, 1560–1561. London: State Paper Department, Her Majesty's Public Record Office, 1865.

Calendar of State Papers, Foreign Series,, of the Reign of Elizabeth, 1561–1562. London: State Paper Department, Her Majesty's Public Record Office, 1866.

Calendar of State Papers, Foreign Series, of the Reign of Elizabeth, 1562. State Paper Department, Her Majesty's Public Record Office. Ed. Joseph Stevenson. London: Longman, Green, 1867.

Calendar of State Papers, Foreign Series, of the Reign of Elizabeth, 1563. State Paper Department, Her Majesty's Public Record Office. Ed. Joseph Stevenson. London: Longman, Green, 1868.

Calendar of State Papers, Foreign Series, of the Reign of Elizabeth, 1564–1565. London: State Paper Department, Her Majesty's Public Record Office, 1870.

Calendar of Letters, Despatches, and State Papers Relating to the Negotiations between England and Spain in the Archives of Simancas and Elsewhere. Vol. 4, pt. 2: 1531–1533. London: State Paper Department, Her Majesty's Public Record Office, 1882.

Calzolare, Ettore. "Ascanio della Corgna: I combattenti umbri e il 'gran soccorso' di Malta nella canzone di un anonimo coevo." *Bollettino della Deputazione di Storia: Patria per l'Umbria* 94 (Perugia, 1997): 161–86.

Camusat, Nicolas. *Mélange Historique, ou recueil de plusieurs actes, traités, lettres missives, et autres mémoires qui peuvent servir en la déduction de l'histoire, depuis l'an 1390 jusques à l'an 1580.* Troyes: N. Moreau, 1619.

Capasso, Carlo. "Barbarossa e Carlo V." *Rivista Storica Italiana* (1931): 328–34.

Caporali, Cesare, *Poesia di Cesare Caporali.* Perugia: Reginaldi, 1770.

Capponi, Niccolò. *Victory of the West: The Story of the Battle of Lepanto.* New York: Da Capo, 2007.

Cassar, Carmel. "O Melita Infelix: A Poem on the Great Siege Written in 1565." *Melita Historica* 8 (1981): 149–55.

Cassar, F. X. "Documents of the Ottoman Maghreb during the Siege of Malta, 1565." *Malta Independent*, June 12, 1994.

Cassar, George, ed. *The Great Siege 1565: Separating Fact from Fiction.* Malta: Sacra Militia Foundation, 2005.

Cassar, Paul. "Psychological and Medical Aspects of the Siege of 1565." *Journal of the Malta Historical Society* 1, no. 3 (1954): 129–40.

———. "Psychological and Medical Aspects of the Siege of 1565." Pt. 2. *Journal of the Malta Historical Society* 1 (1955): 193–226.

Cassola, Arnold. *Great Siege of Malta and the Istanbul State Archives.* Malta: Said International, 1995.

———. *The 1565 Ottoman Malta Campaign Register.* With Idris Bostan and Thomas Scheben. Malta: Publishers Enterprises Group, 1998.

Cataneo, Girolamo. *Di fortificare, offendere, et difendere.* Brescia: Gio. Battista Bozola, 1567.

Çelebi, Kâtip. *History of the Maritime Wars of the Turks.* Trans. James Mitchell. London, 1831. Edited with a new introduction, commentary, and additional newly translated documents by Svat Soucek. Princeton, NJ: Markus Wiener, 2011.

Çelebi, Seyyid Murad aka Murādī. *La Vida, y Historia de Hayradin, Llamado Barbarroja.* Spanish trans. of *Gazavat-I Hayreddin Pasa.* Madrid, 1578. Ed. Miguel A. de Bunes y Emilio Sola. Granada, 1997.

———. *La Vita e la Storia di Ariadeno Barbarossa.* Ed. Giuseppe Bonaffini. Palermo: Sellerio, 1993.

Champollion-Figeac, J. J., ed. *Documents historiques inédits des collections manuscrites de la Bibliothèque royale.* 4 vols. Paris, 1847.

Charrière, E. *Négociations de la France dans le Levant.* Paris: Imprimerie Impériale, 1848–1860.

Chesneau, Jean. *Le Voyage de Monsieur d'Aramon: Ambassadeur pour le Roy en Levant.* Ed. Charles Shefer. Recueil des Voyages et de Documents pour Servir à l'Histoire de la Géographie. Vol. 8. Paris, 1887.

Cirni Corso, Antonfrancesco. *Svccessi dell'armata della Maestà Cattolica destinata all'impresa di Tripoli di Barbaria, della presa delle Gerbe e progressi del' armata turchesca.* Florence: Lorenzo Torrenti, 1560.

———. *Commentarii d'Antonfrancesco Cirni Corso.* Rome: Giulio Accolto, 1567.

Clay, William K., ed. *Liturgies and Occasional Forms of Prayer Set Forth in the Reign of Queen Elizabeth.* Cambridge: Cambridge University Press, 1847.

Clot, André. *Suleiman the Magnificent: The Man, His Life, His Epoch.* Trans. Matthew J. Reisz. New York: Saqi Books, 1992.

———. *Memorial histórico español: Colección de documentos, opusculos y antiguedades, que publica la Real Academia de la Historia.* Madrid: Imprenta de la Real Academia de la Historia, 1853.

Colin, Edme René. *Alger avant la conquête: Eudj'ali, corsaire barbaresque, beglier-bey d'Afrique et grandamiral.* Paris: Defontin-Maxange, 1930.

Conti, Natale. *Commentarii Hieronymi Comitis Alexandrini de acerrimo, ac omnium difficillimo Turcarum bello, in insulam Melitam gesto, anno MDLXV.* Venice: Stellae Iordani Ziletti, 1566.

Correas, Gonzalo. *Vocabulario de Refranes y Frases Proverbiales.* 1627. Reprint, Madrid: Jaime Ratés, 1906.

Cousin, R. J. D. *A Diary of the Siege of St. Elmo, Malta.* Malta, 1965.

Curionis, Caelo Secondo. *De Bello Melitensi.* Basel: Johannes Operinus, 1567.

———. *Caelius Secundus Curione: His Historie of the Warr of Malta.* Trans. Thomas Mainwaring, ed. Helen Vella Bonavita. Tempe: Arizona Center for Medieval and Renaissance Studies, 2007.

Currey, E. Hamilton. *Sea-Wolves of the Mediterranean: The Grand Period of the Moslem Corsairs.* London: John Murray, 1910.

D'Autun, Jean Quintin. *Insulae Melitae Descriptio ex Commentariis Rerum Quotidianarum.* Lyons, 1536.

———. *The Earliest Description of Malta (Lyons 1536).* Trans. and notes Horatio C. R. Vella. Malta: Progress Press,, 1980.

Davis, Robert. *Christian Slaves, Muslim Masters: White Slavery in the Mediterranean, the Barbary Coast, and Italy, 1500–1800.* New York: Palgrave Macmillan, 2003.

de Bunes, Miguel Angel. *Los Barbarroja: Corsarios del Mediterraneo.* Madrid: Aldebarán, 2004.

De Castillo, Diego. *Historia de la presa de los Gelves.* In *Colección de libros españolos raros ó curiosos.* Vol. 9, 1–248. Madrid: M. Ginestra, 1890.

de la Mota, Diego. *Principio de la orden de la cavalleria de Sant Tiago del Espada.* 1599.

De La Primaudaie, F. Elie. "Documents inédits sur l'histoire de l'occupation espagnole en Afrique, 1506–1574." *Revue Africaine* 20 (Algiers, 1876): 129–32.

Deny, Jean, and Laroche, Jane. "L'Expédition en Provence de l'armée de mer du Sultan Suleyman sous le commandement de l'amiral Hayreddin Pacha, dit Barberouse (1543–1544)." *Turcica* 1 (Paris, 1969): 161–211.

"Diary July 5–September 16." Ms. 1837, cc138r.–152v. Biblioteca Angelica, Rome.

Donati-Guerrieri, M. Gabriella. *Lo stato di Castiglione del Lago e i della Corgna.* Perugia: Edizioni Grafica, 1972.

Efendí, Evliyá. *Narrative of Travels in Europe, Asia, and Africa.* Trans. Joseph von Hammer. London: Oriental Translation Fund of Great Britain and Ireland, 1844.

Ehrlichman, Howard J. *Conquest, Tribute and Trade: The Quest for Precious Metals and the Birth of Globalization.* Amherst, NY: Prometheus Books, 2010.

Encyclopaedia of Islam. 2nd ed. 12 vols. Leiden, NL: E. J. Brill, 1966–2005.

Expédition de Charles Quint à Alger en 1541 par un anonyme. Collections des voyages des souverains des Pays-Bas, vol. 3. Brussels: F. Hayez, 1874.

Feretti, Francesco. *Della Osservanza Militari del Capitan Francesco Ferretti.* Venice: Borgomineri, 1576.

Fernández Duro, Cesáreo. *El desastre de los Gelves (1560–1561).* Vol. 88 of *Estudios históricos del reinado de Felipe II.* Madrid: M. Tello, 1890.

——— . *Armada española desde la union de los reinos de Castilla y de Aragon.* Madrid: Sucesores de Rivadeneyra, 1896.

Fernández de Navarrete, Martin. *Colección de documentos y manuscritos compilados por Fernández de Navarrete.* Ed. Museo Naval. 32 vols. Madrid: Impr. de la Viuda de Calero, 1842–1895. Reprint, Nendeln, LI: Kraus-Thomson, 1971.

Fichtner, Paula S. *Emperor Maximilian II.* New Haven, CT.: Yale University Press, 2001.

Finkel, Caroline. *Osman's Dream: The History of the Ottoman Empire.* New York: Basic Books, 2005.

Fiorini, Stanley. "Mattew alias Josep Callus: Patriot or Opportunist?" *Treasures of Malta* 12, no. 3 (2006).

Fisher, Godfrey. *Barbary Legend: War Trade and Piracy in North Africa 1415–1830.* Oxford: Clarendon Press, 1957.

Fisher, Sydney Nettleton. *Foreign Relations of Turkey, 1481–1512.* Urbana: University of Illinois Press, 1948.

Foglietta, Huberto. *Vida de Don Alvaro de Sande.* Annot. Miguel Angel Orti Belmonte. Madrid: Juan Bravo, 1962.

——— . *Istoria di Mons. Vberto Foglietta nobile genovese della Sacra lega contra Selim, e d'alcune altre imprese di suoi tempi, cioè: Dell'impresa del Gerbi, soccorso d'Oram, impresa del Pignon, di Tunigi, and assedio di Malta, fatta volgare per Givlio Gvastavini.* Genoa: Pavoni, 1598.

Fontano, Iacobo. *De Bello Rhodio Libri Tres.* Rome: Francesco Minizio Calvo, 1524.

Fontenay, Michel. "Il mercato maltese degli schiavi al tempo dei Cavalieri di San Giovanni (1530–1798)." *Quaderni Storici*, no. 2 (August 2001): 391–414.

"*Malte au temps de Charles Quint et Philippe II: Un enjeu de la politique espagnole en Méditerranée.*" In Ernest Belenguer Cebrià, *Actas del Congreso Internacional Felipe II y el Mediterráneo*. Barcelona, 1998. Reprint, Madrid: Sociedad Estatal para la Conmemoración de los Centenarios de Felipe II y Carlos V, 1999, 271–99.

Forey, Alan J. "The Militarization of the Hospital of St. John." *Studia Monastica* 26 (1984): 75–89.

Forrer, Ludwig. *Die Osmanische Chronik des Rüstem Pascha.* Leipzig: Mayer and Muller, 1923.

Fourquevaux, Raymond, Baron de. *Dépêches de M. de Fourquevaux, Ambassadeur du Roi Charles IX en Espagne, 1565–1572.* Paris: Plon–Nourrit, 1896.

Freller, Thomas. *Spies and Renegades in Hospitaller Malta.* Pietà, Malta: PIN, 2004.

——. *The Cavaliers' Tour and Malta in 1663: One Journey and Two Accounts.* Pietá, Malta: PIN, 1998.

Fuentes, Diego de. *Conquista de Africa.* Antwerp: Ph. Nuto, 1570.

Gachet, Emile. *Documents inédits relatifs à la conquête de Tunis, par l'Empereur Charles-Quint, en 1535.* Brussels: F. Hayez, 1844.

Galea, Joseph. "The Great Siege of Malta from a Turkish Point of View." *Melita Historica* 4, no. 2 (1965): 111–16.

——. "Vincenzo Anastagi Knight of Malta—Marginal Notes in His Biography." *Malta Year Book* (1967): 336–44.

——. "Vincenzo Anastasi [sic] Knight of Malta: Biographical Notes on His Career in the Order of St. John of Jerusalem." *Annales de l'Ordre Souverain Militaire de Malte* 18, no. 2 (April–June 1960).

Galotta, A. "Il Gazavat-I Hayreddin Pasa Pars Secunda e la spedizione in Francia di Hayreddin Barbarossa (1543–1544)." In *Studies in Ottoman History in Honour of Professor V.C. Ménage*, 77–89. Istanbul: ISIS Press, 1994.

Garnier, Edith. *L'Alliance impie.* Paris: Editions du Félin, 2008.

Giovio, Paolo. *Commentario de le cose de' Turchi.* Rome, 1541.

——. *Elogi degli uomini illustri.* Turin: Giulio Einaudi, 2006.

Glete, Jan. *Warfare at Sea, 1500–1650: Maritime Conflicts and the Transformation of Europe.* London: Routledge, 2000.

Gould, Harry D. "Cicero's Ghost: Rethinking the Social Construction of Piracy." In *Maritime Piracy and the Construction of Global Governance.* Ed. M. Struett. New York: Routledge, 2013.

De Grammont, H. D. "L'Expédition espagnole de 1541 contre Alger." *Revue Africaine* 35 (1891): 177–204.

Granvelle, Antoine Perrenot de. *Papiers d'état du Cardinal de Granvelle d'après les manuscrits de la bibliothèque de Besançon publiés sous la direction de M. Ch. Weiss.* Paris: Imprimerie Royale, 1842–1850.

Gregorovius, Ferdinand. *Geschichte der Stadt Rom im Mittelalter.* Stuttgart: J. Cotta, 1872.

Guilmartin, John F. *Gunpowder and Galleys.* 2nd ed. Annapolis, MD: Naval Institute Press, 2003.

——. "The Siege of Malta 1565." In *Amphibious Warfare 1000–1700.* Ed. D. J. B. Trim and Mark Charles Fissel, 148–180. Leiden, NL: Brill, 2006.

——. "The Tactics of the Battle of Lepanto Clarified: The Impact of Social, Economic, and Political Factors on Sixteenth Century Galley Warfare." In *New Aspects of Naval History: Selected Papers Presented at the Fourth Naval History Symposium, United States Naval Academy 25–26 October 1979*. Edited by Craig L. Symonds, 41–65. Annapolis, MD: United States Naval Institute, 1981. http://www.angelfire.com/ga4/guilmartin.com/Lepanto.html.

———. "Lepanto: The Battle That Saved Christendom?" Paper delivered at conference on "Autour de Lépante: Guerre et géostratégie en Méditerranée au tournant des XVIe et XVIIe siècles," October 22–24, 2001, Centre d'Études d'Histoire de la Défense, Paris. http://www.angelfire.com/ga4/guilmartin.com/CEHD.html.

———. "The Logistics of Sixteenth Century Warfare at Sea: The Spanish Perspective." In *Feeding Mars: Logistics in Western Warfare from the Middle Ages to the Present*, ed. John Lynn, 109–36. Boulder, CO: Westview Press, 1993.

Gürkan, Emrah Safa. "The Center and the Frontier: Ottoman Cooperation with the North African Corsairs in the Sixteenth Century." *Turkish Historical Review* 1 (2010): 125–28, 133–156.

———. "Espionage in the 16th Century Mediterranean: Secret Diplomacy, Mediterranean Go-Betweens, and the Ottoman Habsburg Rivalry." PhD diss., Georgetown University, Washington, DC, 2012.

Haëdo, Fray Diégo de. *Topographia e Historia General de Argel*. Valladolid: Diego Fernandez de Cordova y Oviedo, 1612.

———. *Histoire des rois d'Alger (Epitome de los Rayes de Argel Valladolid, 1612)*. Trans. H. D. de Grammont. Algiers: Adolph Jourdan, 1881.

Hallam, Elizabeth. *Chronicles of the Crusades: Eyewitness Accounts of the Wars between Christianity and Islam*. London: Weidenfeld and Nicolson, 1989.

Har-El, Shai. *Struggle for Domination in the Middle East: The Ottoman-Mamluk War, 1485–91*. Leiden, NL: E. J. Brill, 1995.

Helgerson, Richard. *A Sonnet from Carthage: Garcilaso de la Vega and the New Poetry of Sixteenth Europe*. Philadelphia: University of Pennsylvania Press, 2007.

Henry, M. *Documents relatifs au séjour de la flotte turque de Barberousse à Toulon pendant l'hiver de 1543–1544*. Vol. 3 of *Documents historiques inédits tirés des collections manuscrites de la Bibliothèque royale*, ed. J. J. Champollion-Figeac, 518–66. Paris: Didot Frères, 1847.

Hess, Andrew C. "The Battle of Lepanto and Its Place in Mediterranean History." *Past and Present* 52 (1972): 543–73.

———. *The Forgotten Frontier: A History of the Sixteenth-Century Ibero-African Frontier*. Chicago: University of Chicago Press, 1978.

Heywood, C., and C. Imber. *Studies in Ottoman History in Honour of Professor V. C. Ménage*. Istanbul: Isis Press, 1994.

Hook, Christine. *Siege of Rome*. London: Methuen, 1973.

Hoppen, Alison. *The Fortification of Malta by the Order of St. John, 1530–1798*. Edinburgh: Scottish Academic Press, 1979.

"The Finances of the Order of St John of Jerusalem in the Sixteenth and Seventeenth Centuries." *European Studies Review* 3, no. 2 (1973): 103–19.

Hughes, Quentin. "How Fort St. Elmo Survived the Siege for So Long." *Treasures of Malta* 8, no. 1 (2002): 109–15.

———. *Fortress: Architecture and Military History in Malta*. London: Humphreys, 1969.

Imber, C. H. "The Navy of Suleiman the Magnificent." *Archivum Ottomanicum* 6 (1980): 210–81.

———. *The Ottoman Empire, 1300–1650: The Structure of Power.* London, 2003.

Isom-Verhaaren, Christine. *Allies with the Infidel: The Ottoman and French Alliance in the Sixteenth Century.* London: Tauris, 2011.

———. "'Barbarossa and His Army Who Came to Succor All of Us': Ottoman and French Views of Their Joint Campaign of 1543–1544." *French Historical Studies* 30, no. 3 (summer 2007), 395–426.

———. "Süleyman and Mihrimah: The Favorite's Daughter." *Journal of Persianate Studies* 4 (2011): 64–85.

Jenkins, Hester Donaldson. *Ibrahim Pasha: Grand Vizir of Suleiman the Magnificent.* New York, 1911.

Jurien de la Gravière, Edmond. *Doria et Barberousse.* Paris: Plon, 1886.

———. *Les Chevaliers de Malte et la marine de Philippe II.* Paris: Plon, 1887.

———. *Les corsaires barbaresques et la marine de Soliman le Grand.* Paris: Plon, 1887.

Kinross, Patrick Balfour, Lord. *The Ottoman Centuries: The Rise and Fall of the Turkish Empire.* New York: W. Morrow, 1977.

Knolles, Richard. *The Generall Historie of the Turkes.* 2nd ed. Oxford: Adam Islip, 1610.

Koloğu, Orhan. "Renegades and the Case [*sic*] Uluç/Kiliç Ali." In *Mediterraneo in Armi.* Vol. 2, *Quaderni Mediterranea: Ricerche storiche Palermo,* no. 4, sec. 15–18. Ed. Rossella Cancila. Palermo: Associazione Mediterranea, 2007.

Krey, August Charles. *The First Crusade: The Accounts of Eye-Witnesses and Participants.* Princeton, NJ: Princeton University Press, 1921.

La Primaudaie, F. Elie De. *Documents inédits sur l'histoire de l'occupation espagnole en Afrique, 1504–1574.* Algiers: Jourdan, 1876.

Lana, Guido. *Ascanio della Corgna ed il suo tempo.* Castiglione del Lago: Nuova Stampa, 1999.

Lanz, Karl. *Correspondenz des Kaisers Karl V.* 3 vols. Leipzig: Brockhaus, 1844–1846.

Leib, Kiliani. "Kiliani Leib, Prioris Rebdorfensis Canon Reg. S. Aug. Historiarum sui temporis ab anno 1524 usque ad annum 1548." In Johann Joseph Ignaz von Dollinger, *Beiträge zur politischen, kirchlichen und Cultur-Geschichte der sechs letzten Jahrhunderts,* 445–611. Regensburg, DE: George Joseph Manz, 1863.

Letters and Papers, Foreign and Domestic, Henry VIII. Vol. 5: 1531–1532. London: Her Majesty's Stationery Office, 1880.

López de Gómara, Francisco. *Annals of the Emperor Charles V.* Trans Roger Bigelow Merriman. Oxford: Clarendon Press, 1912.

———. "Cronica de los muy nombrados Omiches y Haradin Barbarrojas." In *Memorial Histórico Español: Colección de documentos, opúscolos, y antiguedades,* vol. 6. Madrid: Real Academia de la Historia, 1853.

Lütfi Paşa. *Das Asafname, nach den Handschriften zu Wien, Dresden und Konstantinopel zum ersten Male.* Tran. Rudolf Tschudi. Berlin, 1910.

Luttrell, Anthony. "The Hospitallers of Rhodes Confront the Turks, 1306–1421." In *Christians, Jews, and Other Worlds: Patterns of Conflict and Accommodation: The Avery Lectures in History,* ed. P. F. Gallagher (Lanham, Md.: University Press of America, 1988), 80–116.

Mallia–Milanes, Victor. "Charles V's Donation of Malta to the Order of St. John." In *Peregrinationes: Acta et Documenta: Carlo V e Mercurino di Gattinara suo Gran Cancelliere.* Vol. 2, pt. 2. Fort St. Angelo, MT: Accademia Internazionale Melitense, 2001.

———. "Frà Jean de la Valette, 1495–1568: A Reappraisal." In *The Maltese Cross,* ed. T. Cortis, 117–29. Msida, MT: University Publications, 1995.

———. *Venice and Hospitaller Malta, 1530–1798*. Malta: Publishers Enterprises Group, 1992.

Manfredi, Francesco Baronio. *De Panormitana Majestate Libri IV*. Leiden: Peter Vander Aa, 1725.

Mantalto, John. *The Nobles of Malta, 1530–1800*. Valletta, MT: Midsea Books, 1979.

Mantovano, Battista. *De Calamitatibus Temporum*. Paris: Georg Wolff and Johann Philippi, 1494–1495.

Massarelli, Angelo. *Diarium Septimum*. In *Concilium Tridentinum*. Ed. Sebastien Merkle. 4 vols. Freiburg: Herder, 1901.

Maurand, Jérome. *Itinéraire de J Maurand d'Antibes à Constantinople (1544)*. Paris: Ernst Leroux, 1901.

Maxwell, Sir William Stirling. *Don John of Austria*. London: Longmans, Green, 1883.

McManamon, John M. "Maltese Seafaring in Mediaeval and Post-Mediaeval Times." *Mediterranean Historical Review* 18, no. 1 (June 2003): 32–58.

Melis, Nicola. "Malta nei Mühimme Defterleri ('Registri degli Affari Importanti') del 1565," nn. 5–6. In *Contra Moros y Turcos: Politiche e sistemi di difesa degli Stati mediterranei della Corona di Spagna in Età Moderna*. Proceedings of the International Research Conference, September 20–24, 2005, Consiglio Nazionale delle Ricerche, Cagliari, Sardinia, Italy, 2008.

Merriman, Roger Bigelow. *Suleiman the Magnificent, 1520–1566*. Cambridge: Harvard University Press, 1944.

———. *The Rise of the Spanish Empire in the Old World and the New*. New York: Cooper Square Publishers, 1962.

Monchicourt, Charles. "Dragut, Amiral turc." *Revue Tunisienne* (1930): 106–18.

———. "Episodes de la carrière tunisienne de Dragut (1550–1551)." *Revue Tunisienne* (1917): 317–24.

———. "L'insécurité en Méditerranée durant l'été 1550." *Revue Tunisienne* (1918): 263–73.

———. *L'Expédition espagnole de 1560 contre l'ile de Djerba*. Paris: Ernst Leroux,, 1913.

Montluc, Blaise de. *Commentaires de messire Blaise de Montluc: Maréchal de France*. Paris: Gallimard, 1594.

Montoiche, Guillame de. *Voyage et expédition de Charles-Quint au pays de Tunis (de 1535)*. In vol. 3 of *Collections des voyages des souverains des Pays-Bas*. Edited by Louis Prosper Gachard and C. Piot. Brussels: Hayez, 1881.

Morgan, Joseph. *Complete History of Algiers*. London: Bettenham, 1731.

Mota, Diego de la. *Principio de la orden de la cavalleria de Sant Tiago del Espada*. Valencia: Alvaro Franco, 1599.

Muḥammad ibn Mūsá Damīrī. *Ad-Damîrî's Ḥayāt al-ḥaayawan: A Zoological Lexicon*. Ed. and trans. A. S. G. Jayakar. London: Luzac, 1906–1908.

Mula, Joseph. *The Princes of Malta: The Grand Masters of the Order of St. John in Malta, 1530–1798*. San Gwann, MT: Publishers Enterprises Group, 2000.

Muñoz de San Pedro, Miguel. "Don Alvaro de Sande: Cronista del desastre de los Gelves." *Revista de Estudios Extremeños* 10 (Badajoz, 1954): 467–509.

Murphey, Rhoads. "Seyyid Muradi's Prose Biography of Hizir Ibn Yakub, Alias Hayreddin Barbarossa: Ottoman Folk Narrative as an Underexploited Source for Historical Reconstruction." *Acta Orientalia Academiae Scientiarum Hungarium* 54 (2001): 519–32.

Nicolay, Nicolas de. *Dans l'empire de Soliman le Magnifique*. Introduction and annotations. Marie-Christine Gomez-Géraud and Stéphane Yérasimos. Paris: Presses de CNRS, 1989.

———."Navigations, Peregrinations and Voyages Made into Turky." Trans. T. Washington the Younger. In *A Collection of Voyages and Travel*. London: Thomas Osborne, 1745.

Olivier, Bridget Cassar Borg. *The Shield of Europe: The Life and Times of La Valette*. Valletta, MT: Progress Press, 1977.

O'Malley, Gregory. *The Knights Hospitaller of the English Langue, 1460–1565*. Oxford: Oxford University Press, 2005.

Önalp, Ertuğrul. "La expedición espanola contra la Isla de Gerves en 1560." *OTAM Ankara Universitesi Osmanli Tarihi Arastirma ve Uygulama Merkezi dergisi* 7 (1996): 135–60.

Pacini, Arturo. *La Genova di Andrea Doria nell'Impero di Carlo V*. Florence: Leo S. Olschki, 1999.

Partington, James Riddick, and Bert S. Hall. *A History of Greek Fire and Gunpowder*. Baltimore, MD: Johns Hopkins University Press, 1999.

Pastor, Ludwig von. *History of the Popes from the Close of the Middle Ages*. Vol. 16. London: Routledge and Keegan Paul, 1951.

Pauli, Sebastiano. *Codice Diplomatico del Sacro Militare Ordine Gerosolimitano oggi di Malta*. Lucca: Marescandoli, 1737.

Pellini, Pompeo. *Della historia di Perugia*. Pt. 3, with an intro. by Luciano Faina. Perugia: Fonti per la storia dell'Umbria, 1970.

Perria, Antonio. *Il Corsaro Andrea Doria*. Milan: Odoya, 1972.

Petiet, Claude. *Des Chevaliers de Rhodes aux Chevaliers de Malte: Villiers de L'Isle-Adam*. Paris: France-Empire, 1994.

———. *L'Ordre de Malte face aux Turcs: Politique et stratégie en Méditerranée au XVIe siècle*. Paris: Éditions Hérault, 1997.

Petit, Edouard. *André Doria: Un Amiral Condottiere au XVIe siècle (1466–1560)*. Paris: Maison Quantin, 1887.

Porter, Whitworth. *The Knights of Malta or the Order of St John of Jerusalem*. London: Longmans, Green, 1883.

Prescott, William H. *The History of the Reign of Ferdinand and Isabella*. Boston: American Stationers' Company, 1838.

———. *History of the Reign of Phillip II*. London: R. Bentley, 1855–1859.

Pryor, John H. *Geography, Technology, and War: Studies in the Maritime History of the Mediterranean*. Cambridge: Cambridge University Press, 1988.

Quintin d'Autun, Jean. *The Earliest Description of Malta (Lyons 1536)*. Trans. and annot. Horatio C. R. Vella. Sliema, MT: De Bono Enterprises, 1980.

Quintanilla, Condesa de. "La defensa de Malta en 1565, relatada por Don Alvaro de Sande." *Revista de Estudios Extreños* 12 (1956): 251–62.

Rhoads, Murphey. *Ottoman Warfare, 1500–1700*. New Brunswick, NJ: Rutgers University Press, 1999.

Roncetti, Mario. "Ascanio della Corgna e il *Gran Soccorso*." *Bollettino della Deputazione di storia patria per l'Umbria* 95 (1998): 157–63.

Roncière, Charles de la. "François Ier et la défense de Rhodes." In *Bibliothèque de l'Ecole des Chartres Yearbook*, vol. 62 (1901), 223–40.

Rose, Susan. "Islam versus Christendom: The Naval Dimension, 1000–1600." *Journal of Military History* 63, no. 3 (1999): 561–78.

Rossi, Ettore. "L'Assedio di Malta nel 1565 secondo gli storici ottomani." *Malta Letteraria* 1, no. 5 (1926): 143–52.

———. *Storia della marina dell'Ordine di S. Giovanni di Gerusalemme di Rodi e di Malta.* Rome: Seai, 1926.

———. *Assedio e conquista di Rodi nel 1522 secondo le relazioni edite ed inedite dei Turchi.* Rome: Libreria di Scienze e Lettere, 1927.

———. "Documenti turchi inediti dell'Ambrosiana sull'assedio di Malta nel 1565." In *Miscellanea Giovanni Galbiati*, vol. 3. Milan: Hoepli, 1951.

———. *Storia di Tripoli e della Tripolitania.* Rome: Instituto per l'Oriente, 1968.

———. *Il dominio degli Spagnoli e dei Cavalieri di Malta a Tripoli (1510–1551): Con appendice di documenti dell'Archivio dell'Ordine a Malta.* Rome: Airoldi, 1937.

Ryan, Francis Rita, and H. S. Fink. *Fulcher of Chartres: A History of the Expedition to Jerusalem, 1095–1127.* Nashville: University of Tennessee Press, 1969.

Salazar, Pedro de. *Hispania victrix: Historia en la qual se cuenta[n] muchas guerras succedidas entre Christianos i infieles.* Medina del Campo, ES: Vincente de Millis, 1570.

Sandoval, Fray Prudencio de. *Historia de la vida y hechos del Emperador Carlos V.* Madrid: Atlas, 1956.

Sanuto, Marino. *I Diarii Marino Sanuto.* Vol. 57. Venice: F. Visentini, 1879–1903.

Sassetti, Filippo. *Vita di Francesco Ferrucci: Scritta da Filippo Sassetti coll'aggiunta della lettera di Donato Giannotti a Benedetto Varchi sulla vita e sulle azioni di esso Ferrucci e con un saggio delle sur lettere ai Dieci della guerra.* Milan: G. Daelli, 1863.

Schermerhorn, Elizabeth W. *Malta of the Knights.* London: Heinemann, 1929.

Scicluna, H. P. "L'Assedio di Malta: Informatione di Malta del 'Rangone.'" *Archivum Melitense* 8, no. 1 (April 1929): 35.

Setton, Kenneth. *Papacy and the Levant (1204–1571).* 4 vols. Philadelphia: American Philosophical Society, 1984.

Sirius, Laurentius. *Commentarivs Brevis Rervm in Orbe Gestarvm, ab anno Salutis millesimo quingentesimo, vsq; ad annum LXVI.* Cologne: Calenius and Quentel, 1566.

———. "The Siege of Malta from the 'Commentary' of Sirius the Carthusian." Trans. A. Agius. *Archivum Melitense* 6, no. 4 (August 1925): 165–77.

Sola, Emilio. *Uchalí, el Calabrés Tiñoso, o el mito del corsario muladí en la frontera.* Barcelona: Edicions Bellaterra, 2010.

———. "Despertar al que dormía: Los últimos años de Solimán en la literatura de avisos del Siglo de Oro Español." *Clásicos Mínimos—Mediterráneo.* Accessed March 14, 2015. http://www.archivodelafrontera.com/wp-content/uploads/2011/07/CLASICOS036.pdf.

Soucek, Svatopluk. "The Rise of the Barbarossas in North Africa." *Archivum Ottomanicum* 3 (1971): 240–51.

———. "Naval Aspects of the Ottoman Conquest of Rhodes, Cyprus and Crete." *Studia Islamica* 98/99 (2004): 219–61.

Spencer, William. *Algiers in the Age of Corsairs.* Norman: University of Oklahoma Press, 1976.

Spiteri, Stephen. *Fortresses of the Knights.* Malta: Book Distributors, 2001.

———. *The Great Siege: Knights versus Turks MDLXV: Anatomy of a Hospitaller Victory.* Malta: Gutenberg Press, 2005.

Steinherz, S. *Nuntiaturberichte aus Deutschland, 1560–1572,* pt. 2, vol. 4, no. 74. Vienna: A. Hölder, 1914.

Testa, Carmella. *Romegas.* Malta: Midsea Books, 2002.

Testa, Ignaz de. *Recueil des traités de la Porte Ottomane avec les puissances étrangères depuis le premier traité conclu en 1536 entre Sulayman I et François I jusqu'à nos jours.* 8 vols. Paris: Amyot, 1864–1901.

Tracy, James D. *Emperor Charles V, Impresario of War: Campaign Strategy International Finance, and Domestic Politics.* Cambridge: Cambridge University Press, 2002.

———. "Emperor Charles V's Crusades against Tunis and Algiers: Appearance and Reality." James Ford Bell Lectures, no. 38. Minneapolis: Associates of the James Ford Bell Library, 2001.

"Treccani." In *Dizionario biografico degli Italiani,* vol. 22 (Rome: Istituto dell'Enciclopedia Italiana, 1979). http://en.wikipedia.org/wiki/Istituto_dell%27Enciclopedia_Italiana.

Tyler, Royall. *The Emperor Charles the Fifth.* New Jersey: Essential Books, 1956.

Ursu, J. *La politique orientale de François Ier, 1515–1547.* Paris: Honoré Champion, 1908.

Valente, Gustavo. *Vita di Occhiali.* Milan: Ceschina, 1960.

Vandenesse, Jean de. *Itinéraire de Charles-Quint de 1506 à 1531: Journal des voyages de Charles-Quint, de 1514 à 1551.* In *Collections des voyages des souverains des Pays-Bas,* vol. 2. Brussels: F. Hayes, 1874.

Vargas-Hidalgo, Rafael. *Guerra y diplomacia en el Mediterráneo: Correspondencie inédita de Felippe II con Andrea Doria y Juan Andrea Doria.* Madrid: Ediciones Polifemo, 2002.

Vatin, Nicolas. *L'ordre de Saint-Jean de Jérusalem, l'Empire ottoman et la Méditerranée orientale entre les deux sièges de Rhodes (1480–1522).* Paris: Editions Peeters, 1994.

Vaughan, Dorothy M. *Europe and the Turk: A Pattern of Alliances 1350–1700.* Liverpool: Liverpool University Press, 1954.

Veinstein, Giles. "Les campagnes navales franco-ottomanes en Méditerranée au XVIe siècle." In *La France et la Méditerranée: Vingt-sept siècles d'interdépendance,* 311–34. Leiden: E. J. Brill, 1990.

Vella, Andrew P. "The Order of Malta and the Defence of Tripoli 1530–1551." *Melita Historica: Journal of the Malta Historical Society* 6, no. 4 (1975): 362–81.

Vella, Horatio C. R. "The Report of the Knights of St John's 1524 Commission to Malta and Quintinus' Insulae Melitae Descriptio." *Melita Historica: Journal of the Malta Historical Society* 8, no. 4 (1983): 319–24.

Vella Bonavita, Helen. "Key to Christendom: The 1565 Siege of Malta, Its Histories, and Their Use in Reformation Polemic." *Sixteenth Century Journal* 33, no. 4 (2002): 1021–43.

Vella Bonavita, Roger. "Parere di Gian Giacomo Leonardi, Conte di Montelabbate, sulla Fortezza Gerosolimitana di Malta, 31 ottobre 1557." *Melita Historica: Journal of the Malta Historical Society* 14, no. 1 (2004): 1–27.

———. "The Opinion of Gian Giacomo Leonardi Counte of Montelabbate on the Design of the Fortress That the Knights of St. John of Jerusalem to Build in Malta 31 October 1557." *Fort, Fortress Study Group,* no. 34 (2006).

———. "Francesco Laparelli, Military Architect at Malta." In *Francesco Laparelli, architetto cortonese a Malta,* ed. E. Mirri, 47. Cortona: Tiphys, 2009.

———. "From Conception to Birth: The 'Valletta' Project, 1524–1566." In *Valletta: Città, architettura e costruzione sotto il segno della fede e della guerra,* ed. Nicoletta Marconi, 17–33. Rome: Istituto Poligrafico e Zecca dello Stato, 2011.

Vendôme, Pierre Gentil de. *Della Historia di Malta et Successo della Guerra seguita tra quiei Religiosissimi Cavalieri e il potentissimo gran turcho Sulthan Solimano l'anno MDLXV.* Rome: G. Rossi, 1565.

———. *Le Siège de Malte par les Turcs en 1565, publié en français et en grec d'après les éditions de 1567 et de 1571.* Paris: Hubert Pernot, 1910.

Vertot, L'Abbe René-Aubert de. *Histoire des chevaliers hospitaliers de S. Jean de Jerusalem: Appellez depuis chevaliers de Rhodes, et aujourd'hui chevaliers de Malthe.* Paris: Rolin, 1726.

Villegaignon, Nicolas Durand de. *Caroli V Imperatoris Expeditio in Africam ad Argieram.* Antwerp: Ioannes Steelsius, 1542.

———. *De Bello Melitensi ad Carolum Caesarem Nicolai Villagagnonis equitis Melitensis commentarius.* Paris: Carolus Stephanus, 1553.

———. *Relation de l'expédition de Charles Quint contre Alger par Nicolas Durand de Ville-gaignon suivie de la traduction du texte latin par Pierre Tolet.* Paris: A. Aubry, 1874.

Viperanus, J. A. *De Bello Melitensi Historia.* Perugia, 1567.

———. *De Scribendi Historia.* Antwerp, 1569.

———. *Operum pars prima, continens res oratorias, historicas, et poeticas.* Naples: Carlini, 1606.

von Gévay, Anton. *Urkunden und Actenstücke zur Geschichte der Verhältnisse zwischen Öster-reich, Ungarn und der Pforte im XVI. und XVII. Jahrhunderte.* Vienna: Strauss 1838–1842.

Voltaire. *Oeuvres complètes de Voltaire.* Ed. Louis Moland. Paris: Garnie, 1877–1885.

Von Hammer, J. *Histoire de l'Empire ottoman depuis son origine jusqà nos jours.* Trans. J. J. Hellert. Paris: Dochet, 1841.

Watbled, E., and Dr. Monnereau. "Négociations entre Charles V et Kheir ed-Din." *Revue Africaine* (Paris 1871): 138–48.

Weber, Bernard Clarke. "An Unpublished Letter of Jean de la Valette." *Melita Historica: Journal of the Malta Historical Society* 3, no. 1 (1960): 71–73.

Wettinger, Godfrey. "Early Maltese Popular Attitudes to Government of St. John." *Melita Historica: Journal of the Malta Historical Society* 6, no. 3 (1974): 255–78.

———. *Slavery in the Islands of Malta and Gozo ca.1000–1812.* Malta: Publishers Enterprises Group, 2002.

Wolf, James B. *The Barbary Coast: Algeria under the Turks.* New York: Norton, 1979.

Wright, Stephen. "Sir Oliver Starkey, Knight of St John." In *St. John Historical Society Proceedings*, vol. 9, 1997.

Zachariadou, Elizabeth, ed. *The Kapudan Pasha: His Office and His Domain.* Rethymno, Crete: Institute for Mediterranean Studies, Crete University Press, 2002.

Zarb, Seraphim M. "A Contemporary Letter Describing the Occupation of Jerba in 1560 by the Christians." *Scientia* 21, no. 2 (April–June 1955): 54–70.

Index

Page numbers in *italics* refer
to the illustrations following page 166.

Giou (knight), 51, 73–74, 76–77, 93, 100, 110

Gonzaga, Giulia, 36

Gonzaga, Vincenzo, 211

Gozo: defenses, 53; *Gran Soccorso*, 227, 228, 229; map, *166*; in Ottoman strategy, 113, 125; raids on, 52, 54, 63; resources, 68, 108, 194, 231, 284n6

Grand Harbor, Malta: defenses, 94, 95; map, *166*; Ottoman forces, 113–15, 117, 150, 182–83, 185, 204, 234, 235; storm, 74–75

Gran Soccorso, 226–28, 235–38, 241–42, 250, 297n4

Gravina, Girolamo di, 181, 291n7

Grugno (knight), 152, 288n1

Guevara, Francesco di, 127, 128, 129

Guilmartin, John, 70, 264

Guimeran (knight), 51, 73–74

Guiral, Francisco de, 189–90

Guzman, Diego de, 230

Hadrian VI, Pope, 12, 21

Hassan Agha, 41, 78

Hassan ben Khairedihn, 78, 83, 185–86, 188, 246–47, 280n57

Hassan Rais Esse, 275n28

Henry VIII, King (England), 2, 26, 93

Hess, Andrew, 5, 258

Hook, Judith, 271n26

Hughes, Quentin, 126

Hungary, invasions of, 31, 253, 257

Hurrem (sultana), 72, 73, 74, 253

Ibrahim Pasha, 27, 35

Isabella II, Queen (Spain), 33

Italy, wars and invasions, 24, 42–43, 57–58

John of Austria, 254, 264

Julius III, Pope, 56

Kapudan Pasha, 261

Khairedihn. *See* Barbarossa, Khairedihn

Knights of St. John: Algiers, 41; current status, 255; dissolution fears, 28–29; Djerba, 61–63; galley, *166*; loss of relevance, 254–55; Mahdia, 50–51; Mediterranean holdings, 2–3, 4, 32, 259; membership, 2, 93, 282n36; Modon, 30–31, 272n3; origins, 2; permanent home, 21–22, 25, 29, 39, 48, 56; as pirates, 4, 5–6, 73–78; Rhodes, 10–19; Tripoli, 36, 45, 47–49, 54–56, 60; Tunis, 37–39

Knights of St. John, siege of Malta: aftermath, 251, 259; casualties, 103, 112, 129, 145, 149, 192, 247; command conflicts, 142, 243; command structure, 93, 230, 242; defenses, 93–95, 104, 106, 109, 112, 241–42, 283n20; deserters, 199–200; food supply, 231; medical care, 193–94; morale, 106, 138–41, 161, 196, 198; motivation, 256–57; prayers for, 152, 288n; preparations, 91–92; prisoners, 120, 160, 164–65, 195, 249–50, 285n18; reinforcements, 99, 196–97, 206, 215, 230 (See also *Gran Soccorso; Piccolo Soccorso*); retreat proposal, 225–26; troops, 100, 104, 107, 283n6; weapons, 111, 187, 224–25. *See also specific battles*

Knolles, Richard, 273n4

Kurtoğlu Muslihiddin Reis, 11, 12, 15–16

Kust Ali Abdul Rahman, 46, 274n16

La Cassière (grand master), 263

La Cerda, Gaston, 65, 276n24, 285n19

La Cerda, Juan de (captain): death, 220; Fort St. Elmo, 107–8, 117, 119–21, 129–30, 132, 137–38, 150, 285n12, 287n7; post of Maestro di Campo, 220; strategy, 140; wounds, 150, 287n1

La Cerda, Juan de (viceroy), 60–66, 68

La Goletta: Charles V's control, 37, 39; Christian defenses, 170–71, 300n13; Ottoman strategy, 36, 90, 92, 96, 124, 286n6; Selim's siege, 254; twin forts, 34, 37

La Gravière, Jurien de, 264, 299n

La Motte, Gaspard de, 73–75, 100, 110, 120

Lanci, Baldassare, 92

Lanfreducci, Francesco, 128

Lanfreducci, Frederico, 160, 161

Laparelli, Francesco, 108, 232, 252

La Rivière, Adrien de, 101–5, 107, 112, 283nn12–13, 283n21, 284nn17–18

la Roche, Antoine de, 131, 140–42, 249

Lascaris, Philip, 179–82, 263–64, 291n2

Lastic, Louis de, 215

League of Cognac, 27–28

Leonardi, Gian Giacomo, 123, 128, 286n

Lepanto, battle of, 253, 258, 261–63

Lescout, Mathurin d'Aux de. *See* Romegas (Mathurin d'Aux de Lescout)

Leynì, Andrea Provana di, 197

Leyva, Sancho de, 61, 86, 227, 229–30, 238

L'Isle-Adam, Philippe de Villiers de, *166*; Crete, 20; as grand master, 10–11, 25, 28–29, 271n12; Malta, 21–23; Rhodes, 11–19, 25, 26, 269n11

Loaysa, Geofrè de, 182, 196

Londoño, Sancho de, 297n23

Louis, King (Hungary), 4–5

Lugny (knight), 207, 293n11, 294n14

Magro, Orlando, 213

Mahdia, 39, 50–52, 86, 275n28, 275n32

Malta: agriculture, 22, 270n5; citizens, 22, 59, 100; defenses, 53, 57, 74; invasion rumors, 71; map, *166*; as Order's home, 21–22, 25, 29, 48, 59, 271n12; Sinan Pasha's attack, 52–54; strategic location, 22, 135–36, 252

Malta, siege of: aftermath, 249–52, 258, 299n7; alternate scenarios, 257–58; civilians, 99, 116–17, 183–84, 195, 207–8; final battle, 244–48; horses, 207, 208, 294n15; initial battle, 109–12; livestock, 107; medical care, 193–94; motivation for, 78–79, 256–57; popular accounts, 212–13, 265, 294n14; siege of Rhodes comparisons, 249; threatening Europe, 79, 87; water resources, 107–8, 112, 196, 198, 284nn5–6, 299n19; weapons, 110–11, 125–26, 144–45. *See also* Knights of St. John, siege of Malta; Ottoman Empire,

siege of Malta; *specific battles*

Mantovano, Battista, 258

maps, *166*

Marsa, Malta, 107–8, 112, 205–7, 234, 293n11, 299n19

Marsamxett, Malta, 235, 237

Marsaxlokk bay, Malta, 101, 103–4, 107, 113, 150

Marseilles, 42–43

Marsile (knight), 47–48

Martinengo, Gabriele Tadini de, 9–10, 15, 19, 269n3, 269n11

Mary, Queen (England), 282n37

Mas, Colonel (Pierre de Massuez-Vercoirin): Fort St. Elmo, 114, 117, 121–22, 127, 134, 140–42, 149, 155, 156, 160; initial Malta battle, 110; Ottoman arrival in Malta, 100

Maximilian II, Holy Roman emperor, 212, 253

Mdina, Malta: Christian defenses, 93–94, 100, 104, 116–17, 241–42, 291n7, 291n27; Christian reinforcements, 172–73, 180–81, 236–38; Christian supplies and messages, 136, 153, 204; civilians, 116, 177, 285n4, 291n27; Ottoman forces, 113, 164, 177, 207, 226; Sinan Pasha's attack, 54

Méaulle, Fortuné Louis, *166*

Medici, Cosimo I de', 58, 88, 92, 171

Medina, Francisco Ruys de, 140–42

Medrano (soldier), 288n1

Medrano, Captain, 100, 110, 121–22, 127, 131–32, 135–36, 150, 285n19, 288n11

Mehmed ben Mehmed, 102

Mehmed ben Mustafa, 103, 160

Mehmed II, Sultan, 4, 279n32

Mendosa, Pietro de, 219

Mesquita, Dom, 93, 116, 146, 173, 208, 229, 295n19

Mesquita, Vendo de, 102–3

Mihrimah (Suleiman's daughter), 52, 72, 75–76, 78

Minorca, 39–40

Miraglia, Pietro, 155

Miranda, Juan de: death, 159, 213, 288n13;

Fort St. Elmo, 131–33, 135, 143, 147, 150, 153, 156, 159, 161, 288n13; name, 286n1
Modo, Marietta de, 195
Modon, Greece, 30–32, 100, 182, 193, 251, 272n3
Mohammad Pasha, 80
Mohammed Bey, 115
Moncada, Hugo de, 62
Monserrat, Melchior de, 147, 149, 153, 155–56
Monsuar, Nostre de, 216
Montluc, Blaise de, 74, 281n3
Morgut, Jean Antoine de, 107
Moriscos, 257, 258, 301n1
Muhammad Ibn-Mūsā ad-Damīrī, 278n10
Mulazzo, Vespasiano Malaspina dei Marchesi di, 235
Muley Hassan, 36, 39, 272n13
Muñatones, Andres de, 198
Murad, Hajji, 211
Mustafa Pasha, Lala Kara, 279n38, 301n8
Mustapha (Suleiman's son), 72–73
Mustapha Pasha: abuse of Christian corpses, 160, 164–65, 290n26; Birgu, 106; chain of command, 80, 89–90, 109, 124, 233, 280n56, 284n19, 291n2; command conflicts, 89–90, 103, 125, 162–63, 238–39, 260–61, 282n17, 301n7; correspondence with Suleiman, 112, 114, 149, 158–59, 161, 175, 213–14, 223, 233; failures at Malta, 234, 239–40; faith, 231; final Malta battle, 241, 244–46, 248, 250, 299n4, 299n27; Fort St. Elmo, 117–19, 126–27, 129–30, 144–51, 156, 158–61; Fort St. Michael, 175–76, 186, 188, 197, 201–3, 205–6, 210, 217–18; Grand Harbor, 182–83; identity, 301n8; Marsa, 206–7; military intelligence, 146, 200; Naxxar, 242–44; peace terms, 175–78; poetry, 160–61; post-siege, 233, 260–61; prisoners, 104–5, 112, 146, 181; state of war, 214, 216–17, 226; strategy, 113–14, 117–18, 124–25, 163, 180, 225, 239–40; supplies, 182, 193, 217, 291n12; in vanguard of attack, 214, 218,

220, 296n5; weapons, 224
Mustapha Reis, 83–84

Napoleon, 255
Napolitano, Girolamo Pepe, 126
Navarro, Pedro de, 62
Naxxar, Malta, 242–44
Nice, 43, 273n4
Nicolay, Nicholas de, 55, 72

Oliventia, Martinez de, 226–28
Oran, 64, 169, 262
Order of the Knights of St. John. See Knights of St. John, siege of Malta
Ottoman Empire: alliance against, 40; decline, 255; Djerba, 63–68; extent of empire, 3–4; foreign relations, 10, 12, 20, 79, 254; invasion of Italy, 42–43; Mediterranean theater, 5–6, 79, 258; Rhodes, 4, 11–19, 26, 269n6
Ottoman Empire, siege of Malta: aftermath, 251–53; battle formations, 110; casualties, 112, 129, 145, 149, 192, 247, 250, 299n4, 299n27; chain of command, 112–13, 124, 284n19; command conflicts, 103, 145, 195, 238–39; costs, 161; defectors, 179–81; illnesses, 193; military intelligence, 104–5, 146; morale, 225, 233; motivation, 78–79; navy, 88–89, 100–101, 169, 281n14, 283n8; omens, 89, 90, 91, 282n27; preparations, 80–83; prisoners, 102–5, 146; reinforcements, 185–86; strategy, 94–95, 113–14, 180; supplies, 103, 108–9, 227, 289n24, 297n4; tent village, 108–9; troops, 88–89, 91, 103–4, 123–24, 298n3; water resources, 107–8, 198, 284nn5–6; weapons, 110–11, 118, 125–26, 224–25, 293n13

Pantoja de la Cruz, Juan, 166
Parisot, Henri, 194–95
Peçevi (historian), 260–61, 266, 284n19, 289n12
Pegullo, Ambrogio, 154
Peloponnese, 31–33

Peñon de Velez de la Gomera, 78, 86, 170
Persia, 58, 73
Petit, Edouard, 272n4
Petremol, Antoine, 78, 82, 89–90, 99, 234,
    251, 280n41, 282n24, 301n7
Phayre, 158, 193, 264
Philip II, King (Spain), *166*; as armchair
    general, 60; ascension to throne, 59;
    correspondence with Sande, 237, 244,
    299n19; correspondence with Toledo,
    92, 116, 121, 170–71, 173, 211, 251, 282n33;
    correspondence with Valette, 117, 217,
    250; Djerba, 60–61, 66; La Goletta, 92,
    170–71, 254, 300n13; Malta preparations,
    87–88, 92, 100, 238, 281n7; Moorish
    decree, 301n1; navy, 70–71, 170, 230, 262;
    Ottoman relations, 79, 254; post-siege,
    251
Piali Pasha: abuse of Christian corpses,
    164, 165; background, 58, 64, 276n17;
    Birgu, 218; chain of command, 89–90,
    124, 282n17, 284n19; Chios, 252; com-
    mand conflicts, 103, 125, 195, 238–39,
    260–61, 301n7; command of navy, 59,
    60, 80, 81, 115, 233, 239–40, 280n56,
    283n7; Djerba, 63–68, 276n29; failures
    at Malta, 124, 234; final Malta battle,
    246–48; Fort St. Elmo, 119, 148, 157,
    158; Fort St. Michael, 188; Malta strat-
    egy, 113–14, 163; in poetry, 161; Post
    of Castile, 202, 206; post-siege, 233,
    260–61; revenge for Marsa raid,
    207–8
Piccolo Soccorso, 171–73, 180–82, 250,
    290n16
Pius IV, Pope, 87–88, 197, 212, 250,
    294nn11–12
Pius V, Pope, 259–60
plague, 21, 70, 71
Pliny, 278n10
Ponte, Piero del, 36
Porter, Whitworth, 165, 290n29
Puglia, 71, 278n5

Quincy (knight), 172

Rabelais, François, 43
Rangone, Pallavicino, 78, 259, 264, 279n26,
    296n10, 298n3, 298n8
Rhodes, 2–3, 4, 12, 13, 26
Rhodes, siege of, 9–20, 249, 271n19
Ribera, Matias de, 224
Robert of Eboli, 143–44, 148, 209, 287n8
Roberts, Nicholas, 17
Robles, Melchior de, 171–73, 181, 188, 195,
    198–99, 202, 210, 289n17, 291n2
Rome, sack of, 28
Romegas (Mathurin d'Aux de Lescout): as
    corsair, 73–78; Djerba, 62; Lepanto, 253;
    Mont-de-Marsan, 281n3; post-siege, 263;
    siege of Malta, 93, 110, 157, 199, 202, 241
Rosso, Camillo, 108
Rüstem Pasha, 52, 58, 70, 72

Salazar, Captain, 216, 295n25
Salazar, Pedro de, 192
Salih ben Mahmud, 184
Salvago (knight), 131–32
Sanchez Coello, Alonso, *166*
Sande, Álvaro de: Algiers, 41; command
    structure, 230, 231, 242, 243, 296n18,
    296n20, 297nn22–23, 297nn25–26,
    298n2; Djerba, 61, 62, 65–68, 227; final
    Malta battle, 245, 246, 247, 299n4;
    Malta strategy, 238, 241; Mdina, 242,
    298n5; Naxxar, 243–44; post-siege,
    262; as prisoner, 69, 277n40; reports to
    Philip II, 237, 244, 299n19; Siena, 86
Sangiorgio, Federico, 191
Sanoguera, Jaime de, 179, 187, 190
Sanoguera, Juan de, 196
Santa Anna (carrack), 39, 273n21
Sciberras, Malta, 94–95, 114, 125, 145, 151,
    158, 179, 180, 237, 254
Scythia, 262, 302n12
Selaniki (historian), 80, 84, 85, 90, 160, 259,
    266
Selim (Suleiman's son), 73, 253–54, 261
Selim I, Sultan, 1–2, 4, 34–35, 49, 71
Semiz Ali Pasha, 90
Sengle, Claude de la, 59

Senglea, Malta: Christian defenses, 93–96,
100, 104, 106, 136, 178, 183–84, 186–88,
250; name, 59; Ottoman assault, 178,
180, 190–92, 207, 218, 220, 235, 244, 250,
252. See also Fort St. Michael

Sésé (knight), 111

Sesse, Galatian de, 54

siege of Malta. See Knights of St. John,
siege of Malta; Malta, siege of; Ottoman
Empire, siege of Malta

Siena, 58, 59, 86, 212

Simeoni, Paolo, 38–39

Sinan Pasha, 52–56, 58, *166*

Skanderbeg, 3–4

slaves, 74, 174, 182, 274n16

Sokollu Mehmed Pasha, 253, 261

Spain: foreign relations, 5–6, 23–25, 28,
42, 59, 254; Moriscos, 257, 258, 301n1;
reconquista, 33

Spiteri, Stephen C., *166*, 266

Starkey, Oliver, 93, 153, 260, 263, 282nn36–
37, 288n5, 302n16

St. Aubin, Pierre Antoine de Roquelaure
de, 114–15

St. Paul's Bay, Malta, 246–47, 299n19

Strozzi, Leone, 57

Suleiman I, Sultan, *166*; allies, 83–84;
alternate Malta scenarios, 257–58;
Belgrade, 4–5, 269n7; character, 4, 16,
78, 161; correspondence with Mustapha,
112, 114, 149, 158–59, 161, 163, 175, 213–14,
223, 233; death, 253, 257; Djerba, 63,
68; and Francis I, 27, 79; Hungary
campaigns, 31, 32, 42, 253, 257; Italy
campaign, 42–43; local problems,
71; Mahdia, 51, 52; Malta aftermath,
251–53, 256; Malta commanders, 80–81,
89–90, 112–13, 124, 185, 280n56, 282n17,
284n19; Malta motivation, 78–79;
Malta preparations, 80–83, 91; Malta
strategy, 176, 177, 234, 239–40, 286n6;
Mediterranean theater, 5–6, 32–33,
79; navy, 6, 33, 35–36, 51; Persian war,
58; plots against, 25–26, 71, 278n8; in
poetry, 161; Rhodes, 10, 11–19, 269n6;

and Sande, 69; successor, 71–73, 253;
and Turgut, 50, 52, 58–59, 163; and
Venice, 4, 5, 20, 58–59, 269n6

Sultana (galleon), 76–78, 232–33

Taddei, Giannetto, 211–12

Tagiura, 47–48

Taylor, T., *166*

Temple, Grenville T., *166*

tercio (military formation), 37–38

Tessières, Carlo Urre de, 60, 61, 62, 63

Tigné, Point, Malta, 145, 150–51

Toledo, Don Garcia de, *166*; Algiers, 41;
career, 68, 85–86, 106; correspondence
with Philip II, 92, 116, 173, 211, 251,
282n33; correspondence with Valette,
108, 117, 120–21, 132, 178, 204, 213,
243–44, 285n19, 295n19; criticism
of, 215, 264, 295n25, 296n10, 298n8;
Djerba, 66; Fort St. Elmo, 127, 130; *Gran
Soccorso*, 226–30; health, 86, 281n6;
Mahdia, 50–51, 274n28, 275n28; Malta
command structure, 230, 242, 281nn7–8,
296n18, 296n20, 297n23, 297n26; Malta
defenses, 84, 93–96; Malta preparations,
86–88, 100, 281nn7–8, 281n12, 295n24;
Malta reinforcements, 99, 132, 136, 150,
169–72, 195–97, 211–12, 215–17, 290n4;
Malta strategy, 95–96, 171–73; Malta
troops, 91–93; Malta water resources,
284n6; Peñon de Velez, 78, 170; *Piccolo
Soccorso*, 171–72, 182, 290n16; post-siege,
250–51, 262, 264; Siena, 58; Tunis, 37

Toledo, Faderigo de, 93, 112, 117, 153–54, 190

Toledo, Fernando Alvarez de, 211

Toledo, Pedro de, 36, 141

Toulon, 43–44

Tripoli, 21–23, 29, 36, 45, 47–49, 53–56,
60–61, 74, *166*, 195

Tunis, 33–34, 36–40, 51, 83, 86, 254, 261

Turgut Reis: chain of command, 80, 89–
90, 112–13, 124, 280n56, 284nn19–20; as
corsair, 44, 49, 71, 74, 278n5; death, 124,
162, 163, *166*, 173–74, 289n21; Djerba,
51–52, 62, 65–66; Fort St. Elmo, 126–27,